THE UN SECURITY COUNCIL AND THE MAINTENANCE
OF PEACE IN A CHANGING WORLD

How can the UN Security Council contribute to the maintenance of international peace and security in times of heightened tensions, global polarisation, and contestation about the principles underlying the international legal and political order? In this Trialogue, experts with diverse geographic, socio-legal, and ideational backgrounds present their perspectives on the Security Council's historic development, its present functions and deficits, and its defining tensions and future trajectories. Three approaches engage with each other: a power-focused approach emphasising the role of China as an emerging actor; an institutionalist perspective exploring how less powerful states – particularly the elected members of the Security Council – exert influence and may strengthen rule-of-law standards; and a regionalist perspective investigating how the Security Council, as the central actor, can cooperate with regional organisations towards maintaining international peace and security. This title is also available as Open Access on Cambridge Core.

Congyan Cai is a professor of international law at Fudan University, China. He engages with international legal theory, foreign relations law, and Chinese international legal policies and practice. Professor Cai's recent books include *The Rise of China and International Law* (2019) and *The Cambridge Handbook of China and International Law* (Cambridge, 2024, co-editor).

Larissa van den Herik is a full professor at the Grotius Centre for International Legal Studies of Leiden University. She served as vice dean of Leiden Law School and previously chaired the ILA Study Group on UN Sanctions and International Law. Professor Van den Herik is general editor of the *Cambridge Studies in International and Comparative Law* and of the *Leiden Journal of International Law*. She is a member of the Permanent Court of Arbitration and the Netherlands National Group.

Tiyanjana Maluwa is the H. Laddie Montague Chair in Law and a professor of law and international affairs at Pennsylvania State University School of Law, as well as a member of the Institut de Droit International. Professor Maluwa's recent publications include *The Pursuit of a Brave New World in International Law: Essays in Honour of John Dugard* (2017, co-editor), and *Dugard's International Law: A South African Perspective* (5th edn, 2018).

Anne Peters is a director at the Max Planck Institute for Comparative Public Law and International Law in Heidelberg, a professor at Heidelberg, FU Berlin, and

Basel, and L. Bates Lea Global Law Professor at the University of Michigan. She is a member of the Permanent Court of Arbitration and an associate member of the Institut de Droit International.

Christian Marxsen is a professor of international law at Humboldt-University of Berlin and a research group leader at the Max Planck Institute for Comparative Public Law and International Law, Heidelberg.

MAX PLANCK TRIALOGUES ON THE LAW OF PEACE AND WAR

In a *Max Planck Trialogue*, three authors discuss one topic within the international law surrounding armed conflict. Each trio is composed so as to engage different modes of legal thinking, intellectual paradigms, regional backgrounds, and professional specialisation. By bringing the pluralism of premises and methods to the fore, the *Trialogues* facilitate the emergence and global refinement of common legal understandings.

Series Editors

Professor Anne Peters
Max Planck Institute for Comparative Public Law and International Law

Professor Christian Marxsen
Humboldt-University of Berlin

A list of books in the series can be found at the end of this volume.

The UN Security Council and the Maintenance of Peace in a Changing World

CONGYAN CAI

Fudan University, Shanghai

LARISSA VAN DEN HERIK

Universiteit Leiden

TIYANJANA MALUWA

Pennsylvania State University

Series Editors

Anne Peters

Max Planck Institute for Comparative Public Law and Public International Law

Christian Marxsen

Humboldt-University of Berlin

CAMBRIDGE
UNIVERSITY PRESS

Shaftesbury Road, Cambridge CB2 8EA, United Kingdom

One Liberty Plaza, 20th Floor, New York, NY 10006, USA

477 Williamstown Road, Port Melbourne, VIC 3207, Australia

314–321, 3rd Floor, Plot 3, Splendor Forum, Jasola District Centre,
New Delhi – 110025, India

103 Penang Road, #05–06/07, Visioncrest Commercial, Singapore 238467

Cambridge University Press is part of Cambridge University Press & Assessment,
a department of the University of Cambridge.

We share the University's mission to contribute to society through the pursuit of
education, learning and research at the highest international levels of excellence.

www.cambridge.org
Information on this title: www.cambridge.org/9781009423472

DOI: 10.1017/9781009423458

First published 2024

A catalogue record for this publication is available from the British Library

A Cataloging-in-Publication data record for this book is available from the Library of
Congress

ISBN 978-1-009-42347-2 Hardback
ISBN 978-1-009-42344-1 Paperback

Contents

Introduction

The UN Security Council's Four Defining Fields of Tension

Christian Marxsen

How can the United Nations (UN) Security Council contribute to the main-tenance of international peace and security in times of heightened tensions, global polarisation, and contestation about the principles underlying the international legal and political order? In this Trialogue, three experts rooted in diverse geographic, socio-legal, and ideational backgrounds present their perspectives on the Security Council's historic development, its present func-tions and deficits, and its defining tensions and future trajectories.

This introduction sets the scene for the authors' engagement by briefly reflecting on the Security Council's functions in the international peace and security architecture (section I). It then discusses the changing political environment (section II), and how states and other actors have responded to the Security Council's dysfunction in the past (section III). Based on this, four tensions are identified, in this introduction, that define the current role and work of the Security Council (section IV). Lastly, it introduces the authors of the Trialogue (section V).

I. THE UN SECURITY COUNCIL'S FUNCTIONS IN THE PEACE AND SECURITY ARCHITECTURE

The UN Security Council is the most crucial actor in terms of international peace and security. According to Article 24(1) UN Charter, UN members have conferred upon the Security Council the 'primary responsibility for the maintenance of international peace and security, and agree that in carrying out its duties under this responsibility the Security Council acts on their behalf'. The Security Council is the system's most powerful institutional actor. Its decisions are binding for UN members and it has the power, under Chapter VII of the UN Charter, to authorise enforcement actions.

The Council fulfils important functions for the maintenance of international peace and security. Its most general function is as an institutional arena for debate and exchange – especially for conflict and contestation with implications for international peace and security. As conflict studies underline, a forum for contestation is a crucial asset in avoiding radicalisation and escalation into military conflicts.[1] Accordingly, even when the Security Council fails to decide on substantive outcomes, its very existence is a significant factor – keeping opponents in touch with one another, and facilitating and structuring their exchanges – that can prove decisive in reaching substantive agreement in the future.

Beyond this, the Council has more concrete functions for the maintenance of peace. One of its classical functions has been the authorisation of peacekeeping missions. While the UN General Assembly mandated the first comprehensive peacekeeping mission – namely, the UN Emergency Force in the Suez (UNEF I), established after the 1956 Suez crisis – later peacekeeping operations were established by the Security Council. The Council initially relied on Chapter VI of the UN Charter, then later – and especially after the end of the Cold War – it established robust peacekeeping missions under Chapter VII. The binding measures set out in that chapter also provide for other, more generally important functions of the Security Council. Such functions – aimed at the maintenance or restoration of international peace and security – include: issuing directives and recommendations to conflicting parties; authorising economic sanctions; making referrals to the International Criminal Court; and – as a measure of last resort – authorising the use of military force as an enforcement action.

The Council has additionally become an important actor in law-making, although this function remains particularly disputed.[2] The Security Council has significant influence on the development of international law.[3] It has

---

[1] Lisbeth Zimmermann, Nicole Deitelhoff, Max Lesch, Antonio Arcudi, and Anton Peez, *International Norm Disputes: The Link between Contestation and Norm Robustness* (Oxford: Oxford University Press, 2023), sect. 1.6.3.

[2] See Anne Peters, 'Article 24', in Bruno Simma, Daniel-Erasmus Khan, Georg Nolte, and Andreas Paulus (eds), *The Charter of the United Nations: A Commentary* (Oxford: Oxford University Press, 4th edn, 2024 forthcoming), MN 70–84. See also, critically, Michael Wood and Eran Sthoeger, *The UN Security Council and International Law* (Cambridge: Cambridge University Press, 2022), 11–14.

[3] Gregory H. Fox, Kristen Boon, and Isaac Jenkins, 'The Contributions of United Nations Security Council Resolutions to the Law of Non-International Armed Conflict: New Evidence of Customary International Law', *American University Law Review* 67 (2018), 649–732; Gregory H. Fox, 'Invitations to Intervene after the Cold War: Towards a New Collective Model', in Dino Kritsiotis, Olivier Corten, and Gregory H. Fox, *Armed Intervention and Consent*, Max Planck Trialogues on the Law of Peace and War (Anne

issued various far-reaching and general resolutions, such as those on state obligations regarding terrorism, which can produce identifiable legislative effects, including requiring states to create certain domestic legal rules.[4] Moreover, the Security Council offers a forum in which UN members can tackle and respond to new threats, such as COVID-19 or the climate crisis – even though it remains controversial among states whether and to what extent this is, in fact, part of its mandate.[5]

II. THE CHANGING POLITICAL ENVIRONMENT

The Security Council's ability to fulfil these functions has always been strongly affected by world politics. These effects are reflected, among other things, in the number of resolutions passed each year and the number of vetoes issued by the five permanent members (P5).

After an initial period of activity in the 1940s, during which the P5 issued a significant number of vetoes, the Council's activity declined significantly for much of the Cold War.[6] The Council was barely operational at that time, as divisions between the oppositional parties translated into procedural blockages.

The end of the Cold War and the resulting new political constellation saw a period of reactivation. In the 1990s, the Security Council was able to adopt a cooperative approach that was unprecedented in the breadth and depth of its activities.[7] This period was characterised by relative unity among the Security Council members – particularly among the P5 – with low rates of both vetoes

Peters and Christian Marxsen, series eds), vol. 4 (Cambridge: Cambridge University Press, 2023), 179–318 (262–8).

[4] See, e.g., SC Res. 1373 of 28 September 2001, UN Doc. S/RES/1373(2001), on the financing of terrorism; SC Res. 2178 of 24 September 2014, UN Doc. S/RES/2178(2014), on foreign terrorist fighters; SC Res. 2396 of 21 December 2017, UN Doc. S/RES/2396(2017), on anti-terror cooperation – especially on foreign terrorist fighters and information and data-sharing.

[5] Paolo Palchetti, 'Débattre des changements climatiques au Conseil de sécurité: pour quoi faire?', *Questions of International Law, Zoom-Out* 91 (2022), 39–50; Erin Pobjie, 'COVID-19 and the Scope of the UN Security Council's Mandate to Address Non-Traditional Threats to International Peace and Security', *Heidelberg Journal of International Law* 81 (2021), 117–46.

[6] In the 1940s, the Council passed around 20 resolutions each year. Around ten resolutions were vetoed each year, almost exclusively by the Soviet Union – in most cases, blocking states from becoming members of the United Nations. The Cold War led to a stark decline in the Security Council's activity. Only 54 resolutions were passed between 1950 and 1959; during the same time, 36 resolutions were vetoed. From the 1960s on, activity increased, and an average of around 18 resolutions were passed each year between 1960 and 1989.

[7] Peter Wallensteen and Patrik Johansson, 'Security Council Decisions in Perspective', in David M. Malone (ed.), *The UN Security Council: From the Cold War to the 21st Century* (Boulder, CO: Lynne Rienner, 2004), 17–33 (21).

and abstentions.[8] An average of around 64 resolutions were concluded each year in the 1990s and that high level of activity lasted throughout the subsequent two decades.

Nevertheless, underlying tensions had developed and, in the 2010s, the Security Council entered a phase of renewed confrontation. Its members were unable to agree on common courses of action in response to major international crises. A recurring dynamic saw Western states pushing for interventions under Chapter VII of the UN Charter, while China and Russia were reluctant to authorise military action. When Security Council members could not agree on a response to severe human rights violations in Kosovo, Western states alone initiated the 1999 Kosovo War. In 2003, when no unity could be established regarding enforcement of Iraq's disarmament obligations, the United States and its 'coalition of the willing' attacked Iraq without Security Council authorisation or any other basis in international law. Notwithstanding Chinese and Russian opposition to these two interventions, both states ultimately supported – or, at least, neither vetoed – resolutions aiming to settle the post-conflict situations.[9]

The 2011 Libya intervention is a consequential case for the further workings of the Security Council that is analysed thoroughly in the three chapters of this book.[10] This intervention was authorised by the Security Council, but Russia and China later complained that the Council had overstepped the boundaries of Resolution 1973 in doing so.[11] In light of that experience, Russia has since taken a much more uncompromising position during the ongoing civil war that first unfolded in Syria in 2011. Western states aimed to support the opposition against oppression by the Assad government, but Russia vetoed

---

[8] See the figures cited in Joel Wuthnow, *Chinese Diplomacy and the UN Security Council: Beyond the Veto* (London: Routledge, 2013), 19, 21, and 29.

[9] SC Res. 1244 of 10 June 1999, UN Doc. S/RES/1244(1999), established a UN-mandated interim administration in Kosovo. Russia supported the resolution, while China abstained. The political situation after the 2003 US invasion of Iraq was also addressed by the Security Council through several resolutions, which Russia and China supported, including: SC Res. 1483 of 22 May 2003, UN Doc. S/RES/1483(2003); SC Res. 1500 of 14 August 2003, UN Doc. S/RES/1500(2003); SC Res. 1511 of 16 October 2003, UN Doc. S/RES/1511(2003).

[10] Congyan Cai, 'The UN Security Council: Maintaining Peace during a Global Power Shift', Chapter 1 in this volume, section V.B (pp. 79–81); Larissa van den Herik, 'The UN Security Council: A Reflection on Institutional Strength', Chapter 2 in this volume, section IV.A (pp.123–131); Tiyanjana Maluwa, 'The UN Security Council: Between Centralism and Regionalism', Chapter 3 in this volume, section III.B (pp. 203–231).

[11] See the discussion of the Russian reaction and the context in Christian Marxsen, 'International Law in Crisis: Russia's Struggle for Recognition', *German Yearbook of International Law* 58 (2015), 11–48 (32–3). On the Chinese position, see Cai, 'Maintaining Peace during a Global Power Shift', Chapter 1 in this volume, section V.B (p. 80).

many Security Council actions directed against that government – referencing the Libya intervention to argue that it would not accept any further action aimed at regime change.[12]

With the war in Ukraine, the situation has worsened still. It has been described – including by Congyan Cai, in this volume – as a 'new Cold War'.[13] In this context, it is apparent that the Security Council is incapable of fulfilling its mandate: it can neither take action nor make a recommendation in regard to the Russian aggression, because decisions have been and would continue to be vetoed by Russia itself.[14] The Security Council thus remains paralysed with regard to the war in Ukraine.

Secondly, we are witnessing an ideological polarisation: competing visions for international law are developing, and the Western and US-led dominance that emerged during the 1990s is being challenged.[15] Western states compete with Russia and China over the relevance and definition of concepts such as sovereignty, democracy, and the rule of law. Thus they struggle over the normative values underlying and implemented in the international legal system.

Indeed, Russia has openly declared its intention to strive for a 'new world order'.[16] The United Nations – and, in particular, the Security Council – is very much at the centre of this vision. In March 2023, Russia's President Vladimir Putin announced, at a joint press conference with China's President Xi Jinping: 'We [will] jointly work to create a more just and democratic multipolar world order, which should be based on the central

---

[12] See the Russian statement to the UN Security Council at its 6627th meeting of 4 October 2011, UN Doc. S/PV.6627, 3–5 (4): 'The situation in Syria cannot be considered in the Council separately from the Libyan experience. . . . For us, Members of the United Nations, including in terms of a precedent, it is very important to know how the resolution was implemented and how a Security Council resolution turned into its opposite.'

[13] Cai, 'Maintaining Peace during a Global Power Shift', Chapter 1 in this volume, section VII (p. 108).

[14] See Draft SC Res. S/2022/155, vetoed by Russia at the meeting of 25 February 2022, UN Doc. S/PV.8979, 6: voting result, yes – 11, no – 1 (Russia), abstained – 3 (China, India, United Arab Emirates); Draft SC Res. S/2022/720, vetoed by Russia at the meeting of 30 September 2022, UN Doc. S/PV.9143, 4: voting result, yes – 10, no – 1 (Russia), abstained – 4 (Brazil, China, Gabon, and India).

[15] See Tanja A. Börzel and Michael Zürn, 'Contestations of the Liberal International Order: From Liberal Multilateralism to Postnational Liberalism', *International Organization* 75 (2021), 282–305 (283).

[16] On 7 April 2023, at a press conference during a visit to Turkey, Russian Foreign Minister Sergei Lavrov declared that negotiations about the war in Ukraine would need to 'be about the principles on which the new world order will be based': quoted in *The Guardian*, 'Kremlin's Strategic Aim in Ukraine is "New World Order"', 7 April 2023, available at www.theguardian .com/world/live/2023/apr/07/russia-ukraine-war-live-pentagon-investigating-leak-of-us-and-nato-files-report-macron-and-von-der-leyens-last-day-in-china.

role of the UN, its Security Council, international law, and the purposes and principles of the UN Charter.'[17] Russia's domestic authoritarianism and blatant violations of international law indicate that its approach to and use of that framework is cynical. At the same time, Putin's statement clearly indicates the type of ideological confrontation that is likely in the years to come, with effect too on confrontations within the Security Council.

There remain, however, some significant differences between the Security Council now and the Security Council in the Cold War context. It is, first of all, important to take account of the fact that the Security Council remains quite active – obstruction of action in relation to specific conflicts or measures notwithstanding. Even in the context of polarising conflicts such as that in Syria, in relation to which Russia has vetoed a significant number of resolutions, the count of adopted resolutions is still higher than that of resolutions that have been vetoed.[18] The Security Council is far from being generally blocked: it passed 54 resolutions even in 2022 – the year in which Russia waged its war of aggression against Ukraine – which is only slightly below the average of the last 25 years.[19]

The situation also appears different in that the Cold War context was characterised by bipolarity; today's situation and dynamic is significantly more complex, and often labelled an emerging 'multipolar order'.[20] Much uncertainty exists: the main poles of the confrontation are still taking shape

---

[17] Vladimir Putin, Press statements by President of Russia and President of China, 21 March 2023, available at www.en.kremlin.ru/events/president/transcripts/70750.

[18] As of January 2023, Russia has vetoed 17 draft SC resolutions on Syria (S/2011/612, S/2012/77, S/2012/538, S/2014/348, S/2016/846, S/2016/1026, S/2017/172, S/2017/315, S/2017/884, S/2017/962, S/2017/970, S/2018/321, S/2019/756, S/2019/961, S/2020/654, S/2020/667, and S/2022/538) but has consented to 29 such resolutions (S/RES/2042, S/RES/2043, S/RES/2059, S/RES/2118, S/RES/2139, S/RES/2165, S/RES/2170, S/RES/2178, S/RES/2191, S/RES/2199, S/RES/2209, S/RES/2235, S/RES/2249, S/RES/2254, S/RES/2258, S/RES/2268, S/RES/2314, S/RES/2319, S/RES/2328, S/RES/2332, S/RES/2336, S/RES/2393, S/RES/2401, S/RES/2449, S/RES/2504, S/RES/2533, S/RES/2585, S/RES/2642, and S/RES/2672). Those resolutions that were adopted concerned, inter alia, the establishment of observer missions, the destruction of Syria's chemical weapons stockpiles, the use of chemical weapons in Syria, humanitarian access, the prevention of the recruitment of foreign fighters, and the political solution to the crisis in Syria. Russia vetoed, inter alia, resolutions that condemned Syria's use of force against its own population, referred the situation to the International Criminal Court, established, renewed, or extended investigative mechanisms, aimed at providing humanitarian access, and condemned specific uses of chemical weapons on Syrian territory.

[19] On average, the Security Council passed around 64 resolutions a year in the 1990s, 62 in the 2000s, and 60 in the 2010s.

[20] The term has been used for some time in international relations discourse: see, e.g., Barry R. Posen, 'From Unipolarity to Multipolarity: Transition in Sight?', in G. John Ikenberry, Michael Mastanduno, and William C. Wohlforth (eds), *International Relations Theory and the Consequences of Unipolarity* (Cambridge: Cambridge University Press, 2011), 317–41.

and remain volatile. On one side of the equation, Western states – at the time of writing – appear to be in solidarity (particularly in their united reaction to the Russian aggression against Ukraine) and concerns about the 'brain death' of the North Atlantic Treaty Organization (NATO) have been muted.[21] Nevertheless, sudden changes seem possible – especially as a consequence of domestic power shifts within the United States or elsewhere – and these could lead to a radical realignment of international politics.

On the other side of the equation is China. As the main challenger to Western dominance, China is assuming a more assertive position, but its stance towards Russia and the nature of future cooperation between the two states remains unclear. China and Russia have, on the one hand, announced that 'friendship between the two States has no limits' and that 'there are no "forbidden" areas of cooperation'.[22] On the other hand, China does not currently appear ready to be drawn into Russia's war.

In the current situation, much also depends on how developing countries will position themselves. Western states are increasingly recognising their importance as crucial actors for creating majorities, such as in the case of Russia's aggression against Ukraine. As a consequence, developing states have gained political weight because the main rivals are on the lookout for allies.

III. PAST RESPONSES

The Security Council has always had to fulfil its functions under difficult circumstances. During much of its existence, its effective operation was limited – particularly because of the veto power. Thus numerous strategies have been discussed and developed to keep it operational and to mitigate the consequences of any dysfunction.

A. *Formal Reform*

Critiques of the Security Council have always triggered debate about the possibility of formal reforms. Two main points stand out. First, the Security Council has – with its 15 members – a relatively small membership and thus

---

[21] See the statement by French President Emmauel Macron in *The Economist*, 'Emmanuel Macron Warns Europe: NATO is Becoming Brain-Dead', 7 November 2019, available at www .economist.com/europe/2019/11/07/emmanuel-macron-warns-europe-nato-is-becoming-brain-dead.

[22] Joint Statement of the Russian Federation and the People's Republic of China on the International Relations Entering a New Era and the Global Sustainable Development, 4 February 2022, available at www.en.kremlin.ru/supplement/5770.

the scope of its representation is limited. This is particularly problematic because it is supposed to act on behalf of all of its 193 UN members.[23]

Secondly, the Security Council is essentially an institutionalisation of privilege that is at odds with the principle of sovereign equality.[24] The P5 are in a unique position to block Security Council action, even against a majority of other members. Accordingly, the legitimacy of such privileges – particularly the abuse of the veto – has been a focus of criticism for decades, inspiring initiatives for formal reform.

Deliberations about and plans for formal institutional reform of the UN Charter have been broad in scope, but very high hurdles block the path to their realisation. Under Article 108 UN Charter, permanent members have the power to veto any Charter amendments. Reform of the provisions on the Security Council has been successful only once, when the number of elected Council members was increased from six to ten in response to the significant increase in UN membership.[25] Several proposals have suggested that the number of permanent and elected members be increased.[26] However, all such suggestions have failed to garner sufficient support, and hence the 2005 World Summit Outcome included only an abstract expression of support for Security Council reform and no concrete proposals.[27] Since then, those debating formal reform of the Security Council have gone relatively quiet. One reason for this is undoubtedly that efforts at formal reform emerged against a backdrop of relative political unity among UN members. In the 1990s, a reform proposal supported by two-thirds of UN members, plus the P5, seemed possible; in the current context of polarised international affairs, the majority needed for formal reform no longer appears to be a realistic option.

---

[23]   Art. 24(1) UN Charter.
[24]   Nico Krisch, 'The Security Council and the Great Powers', in Vaughan Lowe, Adam Roberts, Jennifer Welsh, and Dominik Zaum (eds), *The United Nations Security Council and War* (Oxford: Oxford University Press, 2008), 133–53 (135).
[25]   GA Res. 1991 of 17 December 1963, UN Doc. A/RES/1991(XVIII).
[26]   Bardo Fassbender, *Key Documents on the Reform of the UN Security Council 1991–2019* (Leiden: Brill Nijhoff, 2020), 15–35. See the proposal of Ismail Razali, suggesting an increase to the Council's membership of five permanent and four non-permanent members: Report of the Open-Ended Working Group on the Question of Equitable Representation on and Increase in the Membership of the Security Council and Other Matters Related to the Security Council, UN Doc. A/51/47, 8 August 1997, Annex II. See also the Italian counter-proposal: *ibid.*, Annex XIII. See also the different proposals and criteria formulated in *A More Secure World: Our Shared Responsibility*, Report of the High-Level Panel on Threats, Challenges and Change, 2 December 2004, UN Doc. A/59/565, 8–99 (paras 249–60). See also the discussion by Maluwa, 'Between Centralism and Regionalism', Chapter 3 in this volume, section V.A (pp. 254–58).
[27]   GA Res. of 16 September 2005 (World Summit Outcome), UN Doc. A/RES/60/1, para. 153.

B. *Empowering Other UN Organs*

During the Cold War and again today, much of the wrangling over the workings of the Security Council and potential amendments to its procedures has been carried out in less formal ways – particularly by interpreting the UN Charter.

In 1950, the Soviet Union stayed away from Security Council meetings to protest the Republic of China holding China's seat in the Security Council rather than the then newly formed People's Republic of China.[28] The Soviet Union held the legal view that its absence would block the Security Council from making any decisions[29] – a view based on Article 27(3) UN Charter, which then stated that Security Council decisions on matters other than procedural questions 'shall be made by an affirmative vote of seven [now nine] members including the concurring votes of the permanent members'. The Soviet Union's interpretation seemed a reasonable approach to the wording of Article 27(3). Nevertheless, the Security Council took action with regard to the war unfolding in Korea, issuing a recommendation that UN members render assistance to the Republic of Korea as necessary to repel North Korea's armed attack.[30] The members of the Security Council thus made it clear that they would not accept the Soviet Union's attempt to bind the Council's hands and it resorted to dynamic interpretation to this end.[31] When the Soviet Union realised that it would not be able to block Council action merely by staying away, it returned to the meetings and participated: it blocked further actions and recommendations with regard to Korea by issuing a veto.[32]

This is the background against which the UN General Assembly adopted the 'Uniting for Peace' Resolution, whereby it declared that:

> [I]f the Security Council, because of lack of unanimity of the permanent members, fails to exercise its primary responsibility for the maintenance of international peace and security in any case where there appears to be a threat to the peace, breach of the peace, or act of aggression, the General Assembly shall consider the matter immediately with a view to making appropriate recommendations to Members for collective measures, including in the case of a breach of the peace or act of aggression the use of armed force when necessary, to maintain or restore international peace and security.[33]

[28] UN Doc. S/PV.461, 13 January 1950, 10.
[29] UN Doc. S/PV.480, 1 August 1950, 20.
[30] SC Res. 83 of 27 June 1950, UN Doc. S/RES/83(1950).
[31] See, in detail on this question, Andreas Zimmermann, 'Article 27', in Simma et al. (eds), *The Charter of the United Nations* (n. 2), MN 184–89.
[32] UN Doc. S/PV.496, 5 September 1950, 18 (vetoing Draft SC Res. S/1653 of 31 July 1950).
[33] GA Res. 377(V) of 3 November 1950, UN Doc. A/RES/377(V), OP 1.

The Resolution was advocated by the United States and was an attempt to change the institutional balance within the UN system, giving more weight to the General Assembly, whose resolutions could not be blocked by the Soviet Union and in which Western states had, at the time, a clear majority.[34] The Resolution was thus meant to overcome the institutional blockade and it aimed to alleviate the overall effects in the Security Council of the far-reaching veto right.

Supporters of the Soviet Union complained that the 'Uniting for Peace' Resolution was meant to 'bypass the veto' and to 'establish within the United Nations the predominance of one group of Powers to the detriment of the rights and interests of other Powers and of the Organization as a whole'.[35] They argued that it was 'illegal'[36] and 'an ill-concealed attempt to alter the Charter'.[37] Nevertheless, the Resolution was supported by an overwhelming majority.[38]

The International Court of Justice has also accepted this interpretation of the General Assembly's competences as consistent with the UN Charter.[39]

The 'Uniting for Peace' Resolution remains of great importance even today – as was evident in the General Assembly's emergency special session convened in response to the war in Ukraine. In this General Assembly debate, Russia echoed its old critique concerning the competences of the UN organs, claiming that the 'attempt to circumvent and disregard the position of the Russian Federation contradicts the very foundation of the Charter of the United Nations'.[40]

Even more recently, the General Assembly has claimed a role in critically assessing the use of the veto.[41] On the initiative of Liechtenstein – co-sponsored by 83 UN member states, including France, the United Kingdom, and the United States – the UN General Assembly has decided

---

[34] See, on the background, Thomas Franck, *Nation against Nation* (Oxford: Oxford University Press, 1985), 39–41.
[35] UN Doc. A/PV.300, 2 November 1950, para. 102 (Belarus).
[36] UN Doc. A/PV.299, 1 November 1950, para. 170 (Poland).
[37] *Ibid.*, para. 190 (Poland). See also UN Doc. A/PV.300, 2 November 1950, para. 51 (Czechoslovakia).
[38] The resolution was adopted with 52 votes for, 5 against and 2 abstentions: *ibid.*, para. 73.
[39] ICJ, *Legal Consequences of the Construction of a Wall in the Occupied Palestinian Territory*, Advisory Opinion, ICJ Reports 2004, 136, paras 27–8.
[40] UN Doc. A/ES-11/PV.1, 28 February 2022, 11.
[41] See, on this point, Van den Herik, 'A Reflection on Institutional Strength', Chapter 2 in this volume, section III (p. 121). See also Raphael Schäfer, 'The Echo of Quiet Voices: Liechtenstein's Veto Initiative and the American Six Principles', *EJIL:Talk!*, 10 October 2022, available at www.ejiltalk.org/the-echo-of-quiet-voices-liechtensteins-veto-initiative-and-the-ame rican-six-principles/.

that it will hold a formal meeting each time a veto is cast by a permanent member of the Security Council.[42] The General Assembly has also invited the Security Council to submit a special report each time a veto is cast. Thus the General Assembly has assumed a sort of oversight role in relation to the veto – even though it has no formal authority to hold the Security Council to account, other than by stirring public scrutiny and debate. The 2022 Resolution was adopted without recorded vote and despite opposition by Russia, which rejected it as 'an attempt to create an instrument that exerts pressure on the permanent members of the Security Council'.[43]

The blockade of the Security Council has thus been, and is likely to continue being, a potential trigger for power shifts within the UN system. When the Security Council is blocked, other UN bodies – particularly the UN General Assembly – will step in and claim (limited) institutional roles in matters of peace and security.

C. *Informal Mechanisms*

In addition, UN member states have established working mechanisms and proposals aimed at increasing the inclusiveness, transparency, and legitimacy of decision-making within the UN Security Council. 'Arria formula' meetings have been established as flexible consultations, allowing Security Council members to informally exchange their views and engage with representatives of states who are not members of the Security Council, with representatives of international organisations, and with non-governmental organisations. Arria formula meetings can also be used to initiate exchange when an agreement to hold formal Security Council meetings cannot be reached.[44] Groups of states have advocated for voluntary restraint in the use of the veto by calling for its suspension in cases of mass atrocities.[45] The Accountability, Coherence and Transparency (ACT) Group has, moreover, presented a code of conduct, whereby signatory states pledge not to vote against credible Security Council resolutions that aim to take action against the commission of genocide, crimes

---

[42] GA Res. 76/262 of 26 April 2022, UN Doc. A/RES/76/262.

[43] UN Doc. A/76/PV.69, 15. Other states (Indonesia, India, Brazil) complained about the lack of debate and the lack of inclusiveness in drafting Resolution 76/262: see *ibid.*, 6 and 10.

[44] See Van den Herik, 'A Reflection on Institutional Strength', Chapter 2 in this volume, section III (p. 122).

[45] See the initiative led by France and Mexico: Global Centre for the Responsibility to Protect, 'Political Declaration on Suspension of Veto Powers in Cases of Mass Atrocities', 1 August 2015, available at www.globalr2p.org/resources/political-declaration-on-suspension-of-veto-powers-in-cases-of-mass-atrocities/.

against humanity or war crimes, or to prevent such crimes.[46] Larissa van den Herik analyses these mechanisms in detail in this volume.[47]

D. *Authority of External Actors*

The lack of Security Council action in response to certain crises has also triggered actors – states, groups of states, and international organisations – to take actions outside of the UN framework. The centrality of the UN Security Council in peace and security matters has thus been called into question. This includes the question of whether regional organisations or individual states may initiate military interventions to prevent severe violations of human rights – a debate that raged after the 1999 Kosovo intervention in which NATO member states intervened without Security Council authorisation when the Council could not establish a consensus. It also includes the question of whether regional organisations can authorise military interventions to prevent such crimes, as foreseen in Article 4(h) of the Constitutive Act of the African Union (AU), and if so, under which conditions.[48]

The AU provision acknowledges 'the right of the Union to intervene in a Member State pursuant to a decision of the Assembly in respect of grave circumstances, namely: war crimes, genocide and crimes against humanity'.[49] Whether, and to what extent, this right may conflict with the central role of the UN Security Council is subject to dispute and Tiyanjana Maluwa discusses the question thoroughly in this volume.[50] It has recently been argued that it may be described as a form of 'dormant contestation'[51] – that is, a conflict about institutional competences that remains latent and has not become acute, which may nevertheless lead to conflicts in the future – but Maluwa argues that such conflicts are unlikely ever to happen.[52]

---

[46]   Letter dated 14 December 2015 from the Permanent Representative of Liechtenstein to the United Nations addressed to the Secretary General, UN Doc. A/70/621–S/2015/978.

[47]   See Van den Herik, 'A Reflection on Institutional Strength', Chapter 2 in this volume, section III (pp. 118–19).

[48]   Maluwa, 'Between Centralism and Regionalism', Chapter 3 in this volume, section III.A (pp. 197–203).

[49]   Article 4(h) AU Constitutive Act.

[50]   Maluwa, 'Between Centralism and Regionalism', Chapter 3 in this volume, section III.A (pp. 197–203).

[51]   See John-Mark Iyi, 'Of Norms and Ambiguity: The Contested Authority of UN Security and African Union in the Use of Force in Africa', *Heidelberg Journal of International Law* 83 (2023), 91–118 (114).

[52]   See Maluwa, 'The UN Security Council between Centralism and Regionalism', Chapter 3 in this volume, section III.A (p. 200).

Another field in which states have resorted to actions outside of the Security Council is that of unilateral sanctions. It remains contested whether such unilateral sanctions are a challenge to the Security Council's responsibilities for maintaining peace and security or, alternatively, a necessary correction in constellations in which the Security Council remains inactive and dysfunctional.[53]

Legally speaking, all this shows that the P5 dominate the Security Council and have the power to both steer and block its workings. Such barriers are a double-edged sword: other members, as well as outside actors, will not accept their action being blocked and will develop workarounds – be they progressive interpretations of the UN Charter or action outside of the Security Council framework – thereby creating precedents and new institutional procedures.

IV. TRAJECTORIES OF AND TENSIONS IN THE SECURITY COUNCIL'S OPERATION

This brief overview of its past dynamics illustrates a number of competing and overlapping trajectories in the Security Council's development that are thoroughly investigated throughout this volume.

The Security Council is currently defined by four fields of tension. First, the Security Council operates in tension between *law and power* as competing mechanisms. The UN Charter has legalised the privileges of a few powerful states so that the Council's operation is inherently tied to continuity in the (political) support of those states – namely, the P5. At the same time, however, the Council does not operate in a legal vacuum; legal limitations of the Security Council and its members can be established by interpreting the UN Charter.[54] Moreover, as elaborated earlier in this introduction, the political power of the P5 can be constrained and at least soft accountability mechanisms established through the Council's institutional embeddedness and the activities of its elected members. Advocating such limits and mechanisms may ultimately contribute to the taming of the Security Council's permanent members; alternatively, it may undermine the Council's position as political support for its legal framework diminishes. The authors of this Trialogue will engage deeply with this disputed question.

Secondly, the Security Council and visions for its future operation oscillate between *centralisation and institutional diversification*. The centralist

---

[53] The latter view is taken by Van den Herik, 'A Reflection on Institutional Strength', Chapter 2 in this volume, section V.A (p. 159).

[54] Jennifer Trahan, *Existing Legal Limits to Security Council Veto Power in the Face of Atrocity Crimes* (Cambridge: Cambridge University Press, 2020); Anne Peters, 'Article 25', in Simma et al. (eds), *The Charter of the United Nations* (n. 2), MN 63–146.

approach highlights the importance of having a single unified actor in peace and security matters, as envisioned in the UN Charter. According to this perspective, a lack of unity indicates that necessary majorities for the adoption of (legal) measures have not (yet) been established and such a lack of unity among powerful states must therefore not be circumvented. The counter-position emphasises that other actors may fulfil important roles in overcoming an institutional blockade of the Security Council. The empowerment of other actors – particularly within the United Nations, as discussed with regard to the General Assembly earlier in this introduction – is then meant to overcome (or at least alleviate) the difficulties in Security Council decision-making, espe-cially in view of the veto.

This ties in with a third contested field: the tension between *universality and regionalism*. The balance between universal and regional aspects of the inter-national peace and security architecture was controversial during the drafting process of the UN Charter, as Maluwa explains in this volume.[55] It continues to be an issue in debates about the authority of regional organisations, for example in regard to the African Union, but also with a view to NATO and other regional organisations who might claim the authority to act when the Security Council is not able to operate effectively.

Lastly, the Security Council, as well as plans for its future operations, oscillate between *formalisation and informalisation*. On the one hand, the UN Charter's formal regulations about UN organs and their competences establish the relevant normative framework and (some) actors insist that any change must be made through formal amendment procedures. On the other hand, shifts in powers and competences are being introduced through infor-mal mechanisms, as explored earlier in this introduction.

How can, and should, the Security Council go forward in a time of global polarisation and an apparent shrinking of the lowest common denominator in international peace and security matters? How can, and should, it navigate between the four defining tensions? This Trialogue provides a survey of past and present problems, explores these trajectories, and offers possible lines of development.

V. THREE VOICES IN A TRIALOGUE

The Max Planck Trialogues on the Law of Peace and War aim to generate a better and deeper understanding of questions of international law by

---

[55] Maluwa, 'Between Centralism and Regionalism', Chapter 3 in this volume, section II.A (pp. 191–92).

juxtaposing diverging perspectives. They productively employ what we call 'multiperspectivism',[56] to better understand where, on the one hand, international law is truly international[57] – that is, where rules and foundational principles are carried by a substantive international consensus – and where, on the other hand, such law is essentially contested and significantly depends on diverging preconceptions (*Vorverständnisse*), geographical origins, and political interests.

This Trialogue's authors are:

- Congyan Cai, a professor at Fudan University School of Law, based in Shanghai, China;
- Larissa van den Herik, a professor at the Grotius Centre for International Legal Studies at Leiden University, The Netherlands; and
- Tiyanjana Maluwa, a professor at the School of Law at Pennsylvania State University, United States, who has previously served as legal counsel to the Organisation of African Unity (now the African Union) and then as legal adviser to the Office of the UN High Commissioner for Human Rights.

All three of these contributors approach the question of the Security Council's role in the maintenance of peace from distinctive positions of various geographical and ideational rootedness and with related normative visions.

- Cai focuses on the role of power and law, and emphasises the role of China as an emerging actor aiming to shape the future international legal order and the working of the Security Council.
- Van den Herik takes the perspective of the less powerful states – particularly of the elected members of the Security Council – and explores their role in influencing international peace and security matters vis-à-vis its permanent members.
- Maluwa investigates the past, present, and future relationships between regional organisations and the Security Council and – using the example of the African Union – explores how the Security Council, as

---

[56] Anne Peters, 'Introduction', in Mary-Ellen O'Connell, Christian Tams, and Dire Tladi, *Self-Defence against Non-State Actors*, Max Planck Trialogues on the Law of Peace and War (Anne Peters and Christian Marxsen, series eds), vol. 1 (Cambridge: Cambridge University Press, 2019), xi–xxv.

[57] This approach has significant overlap with the research agenda of comparative international law: see Anthea Roberts, *Is International Law International?* (Oxford: Oxford University Press, 2017); Mireille Delmas-Marty, 'Comparative Law and International Law: Methods for Ordering Pluralism', *University of Tokyo Journal of Law and Politics* 3 (2006), 43–59; Martti Koskenniemi, 'The Case for Comparative International Law', *Finnish Yearbook of International Law* 20 (2009), 1–8; Boris N. Mamlyuk and Ugo Mattei, 'Comparative International Law', *Brooklyn Journal of International Law* 36 (2011), 385–452.

the central actor, can cooperate with regional organisations towards maintaining international peace and security.

Congyan Cai's starting point is an observation that the Security Council is 'deeply embedded in power politics [. . .], whether we like it or not'.[58] The great powers – the P5 – are crucial in giving the Security Council the political weight necessary to act effectively in peace and security matters. Any legal reform proposals, so Cai argues, need to take account of the political environment and political dynamics – particularly since politics usually prevail over legal constraints.[59] In his diagnosis, tensions have developed into what he describes as a 'new Cold War': lacking unity among the P5, the Security Council is at risk of being marginalised, as it was during the original Cold War.[60] A crucial factor for the Security Council's future operation, says Cai, will be the role of China, which is developing a much more 'aggressive' international agenda with the aim of shaping and setting international norms.[61] China thus aims to reshape the established global power relations and – Cai's crucial point – will counter Western dominance by introducing and developing legal principles.

Larissa van den Herik's account of the Security Council places less emphasis on the powers and actions of individual states and focuses instead on the institutional embeddedness of all actors. From this perspective, she investigates how the less powerful states can develop mechanisms to effectively constrain the Security Council, including the P5, shifting the relationship between law and power in favour of the rule of law and institutional procedures. Van den Herik shows both how checks and balances can be established and that some are already operational at the Security Council. She espouses an 'institutionalist perspective' that is 'premised on the idea that, even in the setting of intense power politics in which the Security Council operates, the Council is not entirely unbounded; rather, it is governed by its own institutional and procedural framework.'[62] Moreover, she argues that a 'new balance' is needed between the Security Council and other actors, such as the General Assembly, as well as international and regional organisations.[63] Where the Security Council is blocked, other actors will step in, and hence it is important, Van den Herik argues, to establish institutional procedures for these arrangements.

---

[58]   Cai, 'Maintaining Peace during a Global Power Shift', Chapter 1 in this volume, section I (p. 22).

[59]   *Ibid.*, section II.D (p. 33).

[60]   *Ibid.*, section VII (p. 108).

[61]   *Ibid.*, section V.B (p. 81).

[62]   Van den Herik, 'A Reflection on Institutional Strength', Chapter 2 in this volume, section I (p. 112).

[63]   *Ibid.*, section VIII (p. 184–85).

Tiyanjana Maluwa explores the role of regional actors by focusing on relationships and cooperation between the Security Council and the African Union. He diagnoses a 'reconfiguration of regionalism' – that is, the regional approach that was once contemplated during the United Nations' formative phase and which has again come to the fore since the end of the Cold War, through partnership peacekeeping whereby regional organisations such as the African Union act as UN partners in safeguarding or enforcing peace and security. This reconfiguration has not, Maluwa argues, led to a challenge to the Security Council's centrality in peace and security matters but rather focused a cooperative approach. Regional organisations do not aim to challenge the Security Council but to complement it by providing regional expertise and legitimacy.

The authors' exchange highlights the political stakes and shows how situatedness affects positions on law and policy. While no author directly represents a certain state or region, each nevertheless develops accounts and explanations that are, in effect, in favour of specific regional interests – interests that will be crucial to the future working of the Security Council. Cai's approach aims to emphasise more clearly the role of political power within the legal discourse and in the centrality of the Security Council, with the de facto effect that Chinese interests have an unhampered influence on the Security Council. Van den Herik investigates the role of smaller states and how legal mechanisms and institutions can be used to counter the hegemony of the great powers. Maluwa is interested in understanding and establishing how the workings of the African Union and the Security Council can be conceptualised as synergistic and harmonious.

The authors partly converge and partly disagree on the working methods and procedures of the Security Council, Security Council competences in regard to new threats, Security Council reform, and past conflicts such as that surrounding the 2011 intervention in Libya. In doing so, they provide a nuanced assessment that is acutely relevant to the challenges that lie ahead. These conversations can be traced through numerous cross-references that highlight the intensive exchanges that have engaged the authors.

Anne Peters concludes the book by drawing these threads of the debate together and reflecting in particular on its effects on the war unfolding in Ukraine.

1

The UN Security Council: Maintaining Peace during a Global Power Shift

Congyan Cai

I. INTRODUCTION

Since international and domestic society are distinct in terms of their structure and governance,[1] any significant realignment of international power is more likely to influentially impact the legal order in international society than in domestic society. Such realignment of international power refers, in particular, to the cyclical rise and fall of great power,[2] which Georg Schwarzenberger has labelled the change of 'international oligarchy'.[3] In fact, the rise and fall of great powers is the very thread Wilhelm G. Grewe used to examine the evolution of the international legal order from the 16th century to the second half of the 20th century.[4]

World peace is especially threatened at the moment when great powers rise and fall. In the 16th century, a handful of Western powers with a shared background of Christian civilisation and then, in the 20th century, a shared liberal ideology became the prominent players in international relations, encountering few meaningful challenges. However, that dominance was interrupted in the early 20th century by the rise of the Union of Soviet Socialist Republics (USSR), which – with its Marxist ideology – was considered a non-Western country. The established world order began to split as a result.

---

[1] See below, section II.A.
[2] Paul Kennedy, *The Rise and Fall of the Great Powers* (New York: Random House, 1987).
[3] Georg Schwarzenberger, *Power Politics: A Study of World Society* (London: Stevens & Sons, 1964), 110–20.
[4] Wilhelm G. Grewe, *The Epochs of International Law* (Berlin: Walter de Gruyter, 2000, transl. and rev'd Michael Byers).

Beginning in the late 1940s, the Cold War lasted four decades.[5] As a result, some Western observers began to question the imagined universality of international law.[6] This was especially true of the United Nations' Security Council, which, in accordance with Article 24 UN Charter, was entrusted with the 'primary responsibility for the maintenance of international peace and security'. The Security Council was largely paralysed by the struggles between the United States and the USSR.[7] In the early 21st century, a similar concern looms in the context of the rise of China – another socialist country with a Sinic civilisation.[8] China may have even more potential than did the since-dissolved USSR to shape the contours of international relations and the international legal order.

Given the history of the rise and fall of great powers and the more recent experience of the Cold War, a concern has emerged that China may become a new major threat to world peace,[9] the future of the West,[10] and the established international legal order.[11] It is feared that a more powerful China, with permanent membership of the Security Council, could manoeuvre this UN body into a struggle with the Western powers.[12] Indeed, China has irritated some Western powers in recent years: it has begun to exercise the veto power more often – or, at least, has threatened to do so – which has prevented or delayed the UN enforcement measures the Western powers have sought. Thus, they have argued, China – together with Russia – should be blamed for the Security Council's failure, again and again, to address threats to peace in a timely and effective manner.[13] Relations between China and the United States have deteriorated in recent years – especially since Russia initiated its

---

5   Antonio Cassese, *International Law in A Divided World* (Oxford: Oxford University Press, 2nd edn, 2005), 57–8.

6   Kurt Wilk, 'International Law and Global Ideological Conflict: Reflections on the Universality of International Law', *American Journal of International Law* 45 (1951), 648–70.

7   See below, sections III.A, III.B, and III.C.

8   Congyan Cai, *The Rise of China and International Law* (Oxford: Oxford University Press, 2019).

9   Barry Buzan, 'China in International Society: Is "Peaceful Rise" Possible?', *Chinese Journal of International Politics* 3 (2010), 5–36; John J. Mearsheimer, *The Tragedy of Great Power Politics* (New York: W.W. Norton & Co., 2001).

10 G. John Ikenberry, 'The Rise of China and the Future of the West', *Foreign Affairs* 87 (2008), 23–37.

11 Tom Ginsburg, 'Authoritarian International Law', *American Journal of International Law* 114 (2020), 221–60; James V. Feinerman, 'Chinese Participation in the International Legal Order: Rogue Elephant or Team Player?', *The China Quarterly* 141 (1995), 186–210.

12 Matthieu Burnay, *Chinese Perspectives on the International Rule of Law* (Cheltenham: Edward Elgar, 2018), 175–214; Lisa MacLeod, 'China's Security Council Engagement: The Impact of Normative and Causal Beliefs', *Global Governance* 23 (2017), 383–401.

13 See below, section III.C.

so-called special military operation (SMO) against Ukraine in February 2022, which has brought the relationship between Russia and the West into freefall. A new Cold War seems imminent.[14] This intensifies concerns about whether China would be willing to have recourse to the Security Council in a struggle with the United States and its allies.

Because of the broad authority entrusted to the Security Council, together with the legal privileges granted to the great powers, it is inevitably a major forum for power politics. International lawyers are generally used to conducting textual analysis, examining case studies, and exercising their legal imagination in connection with the Security Council.[15] Some commentators engage in a more general evaluation of the workings of the Security Council from the perspective of law and politics. For example, after making a brief survey of the privileges enjoyed by the great powers in the Security Council, Nico Krisch examines the existing limits of those privileges.[16] In his view, these limits can be external, such as growing pressure for more transparency from other UN members and civil society. They may also refer to internal limits among the great powers themselves, such as the compromise one of the Security Council's five permanent members (P5) must make to secure support for an initiative it favours and avoid another permanent member using the veto.[17] Krisch specifically stresses the benefits the great powers derive from Security Council approval of their initiatives, including more cooperation among them and increased acceptance of the relevant actions among UN members.[18]

[14] *Ibid.*
[15] See, e.g., Erika de Wet, *The Chapter VII Powers of the United Nations Security Council* (Oxford: Hart, 2004); David M. Malone, *The UN Security Council: From the Cold War to the 21st Century* (Boulder: Lynne Rienner, 2004); Niels Blokker and Nico Schrijver (eds), *The Security Council and the Use of Force* (Leiden: Nijhoff, 2005); Vaughan Lowe, Adam Roberts, Jennifer Welsh, and Dominik Zaum (eds), *The United Nations Security Council and War: The Evolution of Thought and Practice since 1945* (Oxford: Oxford University Press, 2008); Lise Morjé Howard, *UN Peacekeeping in Civil Wars* (Cambridge: Cambridge University Press, 2008); Hitoshi Nasu, *International Law on Peacekeeping: A Study of Article 40 of the UN Charter* (Leiden: Nijhoff, 2009); Tom Ruys, *'Armed Attack' and Article 51 of the UN Charter: Evolutions in Customary Law and Practice* (Cambridge: Cambridge University Press, 2010); Peter G. Danchin and Horst Fischer (eds), *United Nations Reform and the New Collective Security* (Cambridge: Cambridge University Press, 2010); Tamsin Phillipa Paige, *Petulant and Contrary: Approaches by the Permanent Five Members of the UN Security Council to the Concept of 'Threat to the Peace' under Article 39 of the UN Charter* (Leiden: Brill Nijoff, 2017); Tom Ruys, Olivier Corten, and Alexandra Hofer (eds), *The Use of Force in International Law: A Case-Based Approach* (Oxford: Oxford University Press, 2018).
[16] Nico Krisch, 'The Security Council and the Great Powers', in Lowe et al. (eds), *The United Nations Security Council and War* (n. 15), 133–53 (135–7).
[17] *Ibid.*, 142–9.
[18] *Ibid.*, 137–42.

Clearly, Krisch expects or believes that the great powers will pay respect to one another and to the Security Council. However, Krisch does not go further to illustrate whether those actions authorised by the Security Council are really justified or helpful in the long run, either from the perspective of targeted states or, more generally, for international peace and the international rule of law.

Krisch conducted his research in the early 2000s, when many people were still encouraged by unity among the P5 following the end of the Cold War.[19] Krisch might have reconsidered his arguments had he completed that work several years later, in the face of confrontations among the P5 disabling the Security Council, as though the Cold War were happening all over again.

By contrast, David L. Bosco – who published *Five To Rule Them All: The UN Security Council and the Making of the Modern World*[20] in the late 2000s, when confrontations among the P5 were again more prevalent – takes a more passive stance regarding the Security Council's role in the maintenance of international peace. He found that 'two distinct, and sometimes competing, visions' of the Security Council exist: in the first, the Security Council is expected to 'maintain international peace and security', while in the second, it is expected to 'help prevent conflict between the great powers'.[21] In Bosco's view, the first vision requires the Security Council to exercise the authority to 'govern', while the second vision requires 'concert' among the P5.[22] By investigating many situations and disputes, he found that the Security Council succeeded in avoiding sustained military clashes between the great powers but largely failed in maintaining peace, even though the great powers could reach consensus on particular occasions[23] – and hence Bosco suggested that observers should lower their expectations of the Security Council. He asked rhetorically: '[W]hy not abandon the conceit that is managing international peace and security?'[24] According to Bosco, power politics in the 21st century became more complex. He highlights the rise of China and the revival of Russia, arguing that the two non-Western powers are a challenge to US-led Western hegemony.[25]

---

[19] *Ibid.*, 136.
[20] David L. Bosco, *Five to Rule Them All: The UN Security and the Making of the Modern World* (Oxford: Oxford University Press, 2009).
[21] *Ibid.*, 4–5.
[22] *Ibid.*
[23] *Ibid.*, 5–6.
[24] *Ibid.*, 253.
[25] *Ibid.*, 256.

It is now, again, the right time to examine the relationship between law and politics – especially how interactions among great powers in the new power constellation may affect the Council-centred mechanism of maintaining international peace. This examination is helpful in rethinking both the action and inaction of the Security Council, as well as its impact on international peace during the Cold War and on the 'New World Order', respectively. It is also helpful in exploring a better approach to maintaining international peace in the new power constellation of the globalised world. And it is especially helpful to ponder whether a more powerful China will disable the Security Council, as the USSR once did, or instead enable it to better shoulder its responsibility.

While it is the common endeavour of international lawyers – including the authors of this Trialogue – to explore ways of enhancing the Security Council so it may better shoulder the responsibility of maintaining peace, it would be wise to stay open to different approaches. In this volume, Larissa van den Herik, like many other lawyers, continues to explore enhancing the institutional strength of the Security Council itself; in contrast, Tiyanjana Maluwa seeks more promises regarding regional arrangements outside the Security Council. In their chapters, both Van den Herik and Maluwa take a more generally legalist approach than I do.[26] Van den Herik seeks to enhance the institutional strength of the Security Council by advancing accountability mechanisms rooted in the rule of law, such as more participation from less powerful states in the Security Council's decision-making and stronger reporting requirements for actions authorised by the Security Council. In doing so, she expects to reduce the negative impact of power politics – especially that arising from struggles among great powers.

In contrast, Maluwa has high expectations of regional arrangements, hoping that they may be less susceptible to the struggles among the great powers that often disable the Security Council. This legally institutional approach is generally desirable. However, we should be aware that any legal designs concerning the Security Council cannot help but be deeply embedded in power politics itself, whether we like it or not. As the Security Council's history illustrates, the great powers can render the legal means available to the Security Council useless, or misuse or abuse them. From a theoretical perspective, some of the legal proposals aimed at enhancing the functionality of the Security Council could create tremendous risks that their advocates may not expect.

---

[26] See also Sherif A. Elgebeily, *The Rule of Law in the United Nations Security Council* (New York: Routledge, 2017).

Van den Herik's chapter elaborates the improvement of a more inclusive decision-making and reporting mechanism; it is interesting, however, that she does not discuss the impact of those more ambitious legal proposals. Meanwhile, since Maluwa confines himself to the African Union, he largely ignores the negative impacts of the regional approach, which are illustrated by the North Atlantic Treaty Organization (NATO). This implies that a purely legalist approach is not enough. Thus, in contrast with Van den Herik and Maluwa, I take a hybrid approach in this chapter, centring both politics and law.

This chapter consists of five sections in addition to this introduction (section I) and its conclusion (section VII).

- Section II examines the interactions between politics and law in the Security Council. It first deals with the relationship between politics and law at the international level; then, it examines the politics underlying the legal privileges granted to great powers and investigates the legal restraints on great powers that are already in existence. Furthermore, it deconstructs the tension between the institutional nature and actions of the Security Council. Bearing in mind the complexity of interactions between politics and law, I do not take a one-sided approach but instead seek to strike a balanced stance on the relationship between the two. This is the starting point from which I evaluate what the Security Council has done and what it has failed to do over the past decades.
- Section III portrays how global power shifts affected the workings of the Security Council during the Cold War, during the 'New World Order', and during what is arguably a 'new Cold War', respectively, illustrating how the law of peace and war is interpreted, enforced, and created within the Security Council. I respond here too to Bosco's bold support for a resetting of the mandate of the Security Council.
- Section IV investigates several novel threats that the Security Council faces and explores how it might address them. It illustrates how power politics can influence the Security Council to address such threats.
- Section V focuses on China's role in the Security Council. Many people are increasingly concerned with the implications of a more powerful China on the Security Council; I consider what China may bring about on the Security Council and in terms of international peace. After reviewing China's historical engagement with the Security Council, this section discusses how the new power setting and Chinese international legal policies influence China's behaviour in the Security Council. Furthermore, it examines China's normative role in relation to the law of peace and war.

- Section VI ponders the trajectory of Security Council reforms by reviewing some legal proposals made under the universal and regional approaches.

I present four core arguments in this chapter. First, the Security Council was, and continues to be, deeply embedded in power politics. Legal proposals to reform the Security Council should therefore give power politics due consideration; otherwise, some legal proposals aimed at helping the Security Council to better shoulder responsibility for the maintenance of international peace may instead create unexpected risks.

Second, the functioning of the Security Council still largely depends on the relations among the P5. It is not expected that the elected members of the Security Council will play a significant role, and hence the deteriorating relationships among the great powers of the past decade – expected to continue in the coming years – risks disabling the Security Council, much as they did during the Cold War.

Third, some actions that the Security Council has sanctioned are not necessarily legally sound and are not desirable in the long run. While struggles between the great powers are likely to disable the Security Council, might they not also prevent the Security Council from taking measures that are inconsistent with the UN Charter or prove undesirable?

Fourth, a more powerful China will play a larger role in the Security Council. China's normative role in the Security Council has multiple dimensions: as norm defender, as norm taker, as norm 'antipreneur', and as norm entrepreneur. Thus this chapter goes beyond the one-sided perspective that cannot fully explore the impact of a more powerful China on the workings of the Security Council.

II. THE UN SECURITY COUNCIL: BETWEEN POLITICS AND LAW

Despite centuries of debate, the relationship between politics and law remains unsettled. As Loughlin observes, such a relationship at the domestic level 'tends to be characterised as one of reason *versus* will, might *versus* right, or justice *versus* power, which not only highlights law's ideal qualities but also presents politics in a negative light'.[27] Implicit in such thinking is a belief that law 'seems to exist to control the exercise of politics – understood as an arena of power – and to direct it towards the pursuit of the good'.[28] In other words, the

---

[27] Martin Loughlin, *Sword and Scales: An Examination of the Relation between Law and Politics* (Oxford: Hart, 2001), 12.
[28] *Ibid.*, 13.

triumph of law over politics has been deemed a worthwhile pursuit. Such thinking is also popular among international lawyers. In this volume, Van den Herik explores the institutional strength of the Security Council based on her conception of rule of law. Yet, based on his examination of what law really is and how it is created at the national level, Martin Loughlin has suggested that the predominant thinking on the relationship between politics and law is highly polarised.[29] It is, according to Loughlin, based on a simplified conception of law whose meaning, creation, and function should rather be understood in multiple directions.

As illustrated through this section, the interaction between politics and law at the international level – including in the Security Council – is far more complicated than that at the national level. People should therefore be more sensitive to the political logic underlying legal arrangements and initiatives in connection with the Security Council, and should not take for granted the actions that the Security Council has taken or authorised. This section first reviews the relationship between politics and law at the international level, and then examines the political logic underlying the legal arrangements in connection with the Security Council.

A. *The Relationship between Politics and Law at the International Level*

According to Loughlin's observation, divergent understandings of the relationship between law and politics exist. For instance, the end of law arguably means the beginning of tyranny, but it may also mean the end of liberty,[30] depending on differing conceptions of law.[31] While law has been increasingly influential in the conducting of politics, this 'does not mean that law is replacing politics, but it is indicative of a change in the role and function of politics in the modern era'.[32] Notably, a process toward the 'legalization of politics has led primarily to a politicization of law'.[33] Nevertheless, a critique of politics is not absolutely unfounded. In practice, decisions influencing social life are commonly irrational or self-interested in that they may be made based on the decision-makers' own particular understanding of human conditions.[34] Yet politics should also be understood as an activity

---

[29]   *Ibid.*, 12, 225.
[30]   *Ibid.*
[31]   *Ibid.*, 9–12, 218–25.
[32]   *Ibid.*, 231.
[33]   *Ibid.*, 233.
[34]   *Ibid.*, 7–8.

closely linked to the virtues of freedom and civilisation.[35] It may be a vocation tied to exploring appropriate patterns of collective life.[36] Thus, sometimes, politics are necessary to produce shared norms and to make the law work as expected.[37] Some political values should be respected and pursued, as is necessary to make 'good' laws.[38] Loughlin concludes by stressing that, 'rather than existing in opposition to one another, politics and law can be understood as each performing important roles in the activity of creating and maintaining a normative universe'.[39]

In terms of structure and governance, because of the differences between domestic and international society, law's relationship to politics in the domestic context is not the same as it is in the international context. Nevertheless, divergent conceptions of the relationship between law and politics provide a spectrum on which to understand the history and reality of such a relationship in international society.

In domestic society, a common consensus has existed among constituents on building an advanced and hierarchical organism based on law instead of politics. This explains what people have long debated: whether law has triumphed over politics and, if not, how to achieve this end, rather than whether law *should* triumph over politics. While today is still not the right time to announce the 'end of politics and the triumph of law', law has been firmly recognised as 'a cordon' within which power politics is conducted.[40] As a result, the influence of power – the core of politics – on the creation and enforcement of law has been well controlled to the extent that constituents of domestic society find it acceptable, if not wholly satisfactory. The wealthy can lobby legislators to approve laws in their favour, but their influence is limited. Legislators are not easy to capture. The adoption of laws must comply with sophisticated procedures, including internal deliberations and public participation, thereby ensuring that competing arguments and interests receive fair consideration. Furthermore, the legislature may make timely updates to laws in light of new circumstances. The executive branch, which enforces laws, is subject to legal scrutiny, especially from judges. In short, at the domestic level, law is fairly reliable and giving too much regard to politics is often considered threatening to the rule of law.

---

[35] *Ibid.*, 112.
[36] *Ibid.*, 7.
[37] Robert Post, 'Theorizing Disagreement: Reconceiving the Relationship between Law and Politics', *California Law Review* 98 (2010), 1319–50 (1340–3).
[38] Thomas Hobbes, *Leviathan* (Cambridge: Cambridge University Press, 1996 [1651]), 239–40.
[39] Loughlin, *Sword and Scales* (n. 27), 17.
[40] *Ibid.*, 232–3.

However, we see quite a different picture in international society. There is a fundamental distinction between international and domestic society that should serve as a starting point from which to understand the relationship between law and politics in the former[41] – namely, sovereign states, both strong and weak, are unlikely to intend to organise international society as a state-like organism. There may be two major reasons for this: first, such an organism would impose undue constraints on sovereignty, to an extent that sovereign states would find unacceptable; and second, such an organism would be no more effective than sovereign states themselves in achieving their state interests. Consequently, power is far less regulated at the international level than it is at the domestic – which, in some sense, is precisely what sovereign states want. While there have been attempts to extend the concept and practice of the rule of law from the domestic level to the international level,[42] international rule of law therefore 'remains a contested concept and barely more than a hopeful project in the making'.[43]

This distinction brings about two additional consequences. First, those states with prominent power are often the major sources of threats to international peace. Like less powerful states, they inevitably prioritise their own state interests. They are reluctant to act in a manner that disadvantages them. They may further abuse their power to pursue their own interests. This is not to say that they do not care at all about the interests of other states or of international society; rather, they are often willing to shoulder the responsibility of promoting and protecting interests beyond their own. This is mainly because, unlike those who are less powerful, great powers have more resources to internalise the costs that may arise from actions protecting interests other than their own. Moreover, in a closely interconnected world in which no one actor can fully isolate from another, great powers have more resources and breath to invest in seeking long-term advantages, even at immediate cost. They are capable of renouncing short-term advantages that they calculate may become boomerangs against them later. Thus they may act with a long-term perspective rather than short-sightedly.

---

[41] See further Matthieu Burnay, *Chinese Perspectives on the International Rule of Law* (Cheltenham: Edward Elgar, 2018), 47–52.

[42] See, e.g., GA Res. 60/1 of 24 October 2005, UN Doc. A/RES/60/1, para. 11; GA Res. 67/1 of 30 November 2012, UN Doc. A/RES/67/1.

[43] Burnay, *Chinese Perspectives* (n. 41), 55; Machiko Kanetake, 'The Interfaces between the National and International Rule of Law: A Framework Paper', in Machiko Kanetake and André Nollkaemper (eds), *The Rule of Law at the National and International Levels* (Oxford: Hart, 2016), 11–41 (18–22).

Second, given that nearly all states, whether powerful or not, prefer to cater to their own interests, international law often fails to be well made, duly updated, or effectively enforced. Great powers often have little interest in initiatives constraining the exercise of their prominent power.[44] They also attempt to seek de jure privilege, or 'legalized hegemony',[45] and de facto privileges in their favour.[46] The Covenant of the League of Nations was the first universal treaty that legally privileged great powers. Several great powers acquired permanent membership of the Council of the League of Nations.[47] The UN Charter goes even further. In addition to granting permanent Security Council membership to the P5, the UN Charter provides them with veto power, whereby each can block any non-procedural initiatives proposed in the Security Council.[48] More generally, great powers are used to taking a selective approach to international law. While nearly all states treat international law in a selective way, the great powers' selective approach is far more consequential.

Because of the unique structure and governance of international society, the focus has long been on how to induce great powers, individually or collectively, to respect international law rather than on how to try to control them. Implicit in the legal privilege granted to great powers is that they are expected to take advantage of their power 'for the common good and promote and [to] obey international law'.[49] This does not mean, however, that there has been no important legal progress achieved in constraining the great powers. The UN Charter, while privileging great powers, also represents great achievements in this regard. It is the first multilateral treaty that provides the principle of sovereign equality. The United Nations, in accordance with Article 2 UN Charter, is based on the principle of sovereign equality for 'all its Members'. This principle was reaffirmed and clarified in the Declaration on Principles of International Law concerning Friendly Relations and Co-operation among

---

[44] For example, none of the P5 participated or joined the UN Treaty on the Prohibition of Nuclear Weapons of 7 July 2017, 3380 UNTS (TPNW), adopted with the approval of 122 UN Members at the General Assembly in July 2017 and, as of 11 May 2023, signed by 92 UN Members with ratifications or accessions from 68 Contracting Parties.

[45] Gerry Simpson, *Great Powers and Outlaw States: Unequal Sovereigns in the International Legal Order* (Cambridge: Cambridge University Press, 2004), x.

[46] See generally Jacob Katz Cogan, 'Representation and Power in International Organization: The Operational Constitution and its Critics', *The American Journal of International Law* 103 (2009), 209–63.

[47] Art. 4(2) Covenant of League of Nations.

[48] Arts 23 and 27 UN Charter.

[49] *A More Secure World: Our Shared Responsibility, Report of the High–Level Panel on Threats, Challenges and Change*, 2 December 2004, UN Doc. A/59/565, 4.

States, adopted by the UN General Assembly in 1970.[50] These achievements arguably comfort people, like Emer de Vattel, who conceive of the relationship between politics and law thus: '[P]ower or weakness does not in this respect produce any difference ... a dwarf is as much a man as a giant; a small republic is no less a sovereign state than the most powerful kingdom.'[51] Importantly, as indicated by Van den Herik's examination in this volume of numerous proposals aiming to refine the decision-making procedure regarding the use of force,[52] many states – especially those that are less powerful – continue their efforts to infuse more law into politics in the Security Council.

B. *The Politics of Legal Privileges and the Great Powers*

Debates on the relationship between politics and law in the Security Council, first and foremost, refer to how the political rationale underlying legal privileges granted to the great powers can be understood, and whether the conventional assumptions about the relationship between politics and law still holds. This issue can be illustrated from two different angles.

First, while great powers are the major sources for threats to peace, they are also guardians of that same international peace. This functional advantage is often invoked to justify great powers' seeking privileges, de jure and de facto. The Permanent Court of International Justice (PCIJ) once admitted that:

> [I]t is hardly conceivable that resolution on questions affecting the peace of the world could be adopted against the will of those among the Member of the Council who, although in a minority, would by reason of their position, have to bear the larger share of the responsibility and consequences ensuing therefrom.[53]

This indicates that, given their prominent state power, great powers may act without due regard for the interests of other states and international society.

However, the PCIJ pointed out an important fact: while great powers make up a minority of the international society, they can provide huge resources to maintain peace that less powerful states cannot. For example, from 2019 to 2021, the effective rate of assessment for the peacekeeping operations of the P5 accounted for more than half of the total UN peacekeeping budget, while the

---

[50]   GA Res. 2625 (XXV) of 24 October 1970, UN Doc. A/RES/2625(XXV).
[51]   Emer de Vattel, *The Law of Nations* (Indianapolis: Liberty Fund, 2008), 75.
[52]   See Larissa van den Herik, 'The UN Security Council: A Reflection on Institutional Strength', Chapter 2 in this volume, section II.B.
[53]   PCIJ, *Article 3, Paragraph 2 of the Treaty of Lausanne*, advisory opinion no. 12 of 21 November 1925 (Ser. B), 29.

other 188 UN member states contributed the remaining portion.[54] It is unlikely that the contribution of the great powers to the maintenance of peace will considerably diminish in the near future.

Indeed, great powers have made some promises to justify their privileges. In explaining the justification for the veto power arrangement in the Security Council in the 1940s, the great powers stated that:

> [I]n view of the primary responsibilities of the permanent members, they could not be expected, in the present condition of the world, to assume the obligation to act in so serious a matter as the maintenance of international peace and security in consequence of a decision in which they had not concurred.[55]

Implicit in this statement is that they would act in the interest of international peace if they were granted the veto power. In its report *A More Secure World*, submitted in 2004, the UN High-Level Panel on Threats, Challenges, and Change frankly stated that the great powers' privilege was an 'exchange' granted to them, and that it implied their promise to use their overwhelming power in the interests of international society.[56]

The difference between the promises the great powers have made and the privileges they have attained should be noted. What the great powers have seized are 'legal' privileges; by contrast, apart from those legal obligations universally applicable to UN member states (e.g., the obligation of non-intervention), what the great powers have promised are not legal obligations as prescribed in the UN Charter but political obligations. Some negotiating states already took note of this problem at the San Francisco Conference. The representative from New Zealand, who was very concerned with potential abuse of the veto power, warned that the great powers 'have so recognised their great responsibility, their pledge, not written, not entered into the Charter but spoken as of good faith'.[57] He added: 'I don't think the possible effects of the veto were exaggerated at all.'[58] While aware of concerns raised by states such as New Zealand, the great powers did not express any intention to commit, in the exercise of the veto power, to any legal obligations; rather, they merely stated that '[i]t is not to be assumed, however, that the

---

[54] *Implementation of General Assembly Resolutions 55/235 and 55/236*, Report of the Secretary-General to the 73rd Session, 24 December 2018, UN Doc. A/73/350/Add.1, Annex.

[55] Statement by the Delegations of the Four Sponsoring Governments on Voting Procedure in the Security Council, 7 June 1945, available at www.hamamoto.law.kyoto-u.ac.jp/kogi/2005k iko/Statement%20of%20four%20sponsoring%20states.pdf, para. 9.

[56] *A More Secure World* (n. 49), 4.

[57] UN Conference on International Organization (UNCIO), Verbatim Minutes of the Fifth Meeting of Commission III, 22 June 1945, UN Doc. 1150, III/12, 9, reprinted in 11 Doc. U.N. Conf. on Int'l Org. 170 1945, 171.

[58] *Ibid.*

permanent members, any more than the non-permanent members, would use their "veto" power maliciously to obstruct the operation of the Council'.[59]

Second, while less powerful states often complain that the great powers use and abuse their legal privileges, in addition to their raw power, the great powers in turn are gravely concerned about a 'tyranny of the majority' in international society.[60] As noted above, both powerful and less powerful states prioritise their own state interests in international dealings. Thus, while less powerful states are particularly susceptible to coercion from powerful states in whatever form, they are not necessarily 'good citizens' in international society. Arguably, the major difference between powerful states and less powerful states is that the former often are more efficient in simply employing their prominent raw power. In contrast, the latter are more likely – perhaps have no other choice but – to rely on the legal principle of sovereign equality, whereby they disfavour any kind of weighed voting arrangement in international decision-making. The great powers' concern with a tyranny of the majority is therefore not totally unfounded on 'one country, one vote' occasions, such as in the General Assembly. In fact, the UN High-Level Panel states frankly that it 'recognise[s] that the veto had an important function in reassuring the United Nations' most powerful members that their interests would be safeguarded'.[61] For the great powers' part, their claim of legal privileges, arguably, does not (only) purport to acquire legal advantage over less powerful states but also ensures that their state interests are not threatened by those states who, albeit less powerful, constitute a majority in international society and who, like the great powers, prioritise their own state interests.

C. *Legal Restraints on the Great Powers*

Given the long-standing and widely accepted assumption that the great powers are dangerous to international peace inside or outside of the Security Council, actors have constantly reflected on how to best conceive meaningful constraints on them. In fact, legal restraints on the veto power have long been a major agenda item for those less powerful states. During the San Francisco Conference, they expressed a grave concern that the great powers would use their legal privileges 'unthinkingly or unjustly or tyrannically', but their efforts to constrain those privileges have largely failed.[62]

---

[59] 1945 Statement by the Four Sponsoring Governments (n. 55), para. 8.
[60] Bardo Fassbender, *UN Security Council Reform and the Right of Veto: A Constitutional Perspective* (The Hague: Kluwer Law International, 1998), 165.
[61] *A More Secure World* (n. 49), 82.
[62] See UNCIO, Verbatim Minutes (n. 57), 171.

Nevertheless, a number of political and legal restraints on the great powers exist. We cannot say that these restraints do not make any difference at all, but it is fair to say that they do not work as expected. One example is the 'group veto'. In arguing for veto power in the 1940s, the great powers suggested that they could not act 'by themselves'; rather, elected members, 'as a group', could block any actions that the P5 initiated with unanimity.[63] In practice, however, this legal constraint is of little relevance. Legally, elected members of the Security Council, if they unite, can block any initiatives proposed by the great powers. Unfortunately, there is no evidence that the elected members have the willingness to unite. In fact, the right of 'group veto' of the elected members has never been used in the history of the Security Council.

Some commentators argue that the elected members could shift from 'lame ducks' to become key players.[64] In this volume, Van den Herik takes a similar stance. For her, the less powerful states do not only play a secondary role.[65] Van den Herik notes that those less powerful but democratic Western states may form a democratic alliance with the United States, France, and the United Kingdom. In particular, she would expect this alliance to resist 'a move away from current structures and liberal values'.[66]

In my view, the idea of a democratic alliance is a major source of confrontations, disabling the Security Council, whose primary responsibility is to maintain international peace and not to enhance domestic democracy. This is not to say that the Security Council can do nothing to enhance domestic democracy, but when domestic democracy gives rise to a situation or event that endangers international peace, calls for the Security Council to take enforcement action are likely to little more than exacerbate international confrontations and disrupt international peace. More importantly, other than by blocking the great powers' initiative and uniting themselves to exercise the 'group veto', elected members of the Security Council cannot legally compel any of the P5 to take any action, because every P5 can exercise its veto power. Nevertheless, the elected members may put great political pressure on the P5. From the perspective of power politics, the P5 may find that they have to take this political pressure into serious consideration.

---

[63] 1945 Statement by the Four Sponsoring Governments (n. 55), para. 8.
[64] Blocker and Schrijver, *The Security Council and the Use of Force* (n. 15), 9.
[65] Van den Herik 'A Reflection on Institutional Strength', Chapter 2 in this volume, section I.
[66] *Ibid.*

D. *A Politicised Institution and Legalised Actions*

Even though the Security Council was established in accordance with the UN Charter, a legal instrument, this UN organ is traditionally considered to be a political organ rather than a legal one. People in favour of this argument suggest generally that there is no conflict between the nature and activities of the Security Council. For example, Andreas S. Kolb submits that 'there is no contradiction per se between the observation that the Security Council is a political body in that its decisions are shaped by political considerations and the possibility that international law may still define boundaries for its conduct'.[67] Such a general argument is unhelpful – especially considering the fact that political considerations regularly prevail over law in the workings of the Security Council. Indeed, as illustrated above, politics interact with law in both negative and positive ways.[68]

In examining many meeting records of the Security Council, I have found that many Security Council members – especially the great powers – are accustomed to blaming each other, using very diplomatic but hypocritical language. They show little interest in identifying the relevant facts in legal terms – apart from rhetorically referring to UN Charter provisions or abstract values.[69]

Indeed, the first and foremost mission of the Security Council is to maintain international peace, which, on some occasions, implies sacrificing justice. This reminds us of the argument of Judge Stephen M. Schwebel in the International Court of Justice (ICJ), in the *Nicaragua* case, which has frustrated many international lawyers. Judge Schwebel suggested that, '[i]n short, the Security Council is a political organ which acts for political reasons. It may take legal considerations into account but, unlike a court, it is not bound to

---

[67] Andreas S. Kolb, *The UN Security Council Member's Responsibility to Protect* (Berlin: Springer, 2018), 146.

[68] See below, sections II.A and II.B.

[69] During the debates on SC Res. 189 concerning the Ukrainian situation, Rwanda's representative stated:

> The situation in Ukraine has rapidly unfolded. We are concerned that the rhetoric of, and pressure from, many actors have blinded us from carefully analysing the situation and understanding the root causes, thereby preventing us from finding a suitable solution and, in the process, de-escalating the crisis. Why, then, did we vote in favour? The draft resolution contains important principles on which we all agree: respect for the independence, sovereignty and territorial integrity of countries and the need for a de-escalation of the crisis. Most important to us is the fact that the draft text calls for a Ukrainian inclusive political dialogue.

See UN Doc. S/PV.7138, 15 March 2014, 7.

apply them.'[70] Specifically, he supported the way in which the Security Council addressed a particular asserted aggression. He said that, '[h]owever compelling the facts which could give rise to a determination of aggression, the Security Council acts within its rights when it decides that to make such a determination will set back the cause of peace rather than advance it'.[71]

However, it should be stressed that the 'decisions' adopted by the Security Council are legally binding for all UN members, whether they are in agreement or not.[72] These Security Council resolutions may also apply to non-UN member states if they are deemed 'necessary for the maintenance of international peace and security'.[73] Thus it is justified to inquire what role law, or rule of law, can and should play in enhancing the accountability of the Security Council.

Since the end of Cold War, accountability has become more important for the Security Council. Noticeably, the requirement of accountability is invoked unevenly. The Security Council, by referring to accountability, often requires a targeted state to enforce Council measures.[74] It also requires that individuals in peacemaking operations be held accountable for any sexual exploitation and abuse they perpetrate.[75] However, the Security Council hardly specifies what 'accountability' means – that is, what the Security Council has done to make its decision-making processes more inclusive or to establish a more participatory process, as Van den Herik highlights in this volume.[76]

---

[70] ICJ, *Case Concerning Military and Paramilitary Activities in and against Nicaragua* (Nicaragua v. United States of America), merits, judgment of 27 June 1986, ICJ Reports 1986, dissenting opinion of Judge Schwebel, 259, 290.

[71] *Ibid.*

[72] Art. 25 UN Charter provides that '[t]he Members of the United Nations agree to accept and carry out the decisions of the Security Council in accordance with the present Chapter'.

[73] Art. 2(6) UN Charter. The ICJ once held that, 'when the Security Council adopts a decision under Article 25 in accordance with the Charter, it is for member States to comply with that decision [...] To hold otherwise would be to deprive this principal organ of its essential functions and powers under the Charter': ICJ, *Legal Consequences for States of the Continued Presence of South Africa in Namibia (South-West Africa) Notwithstanding Security Council Resolution 276 (1970)*, advisory opinion of 21 June 1971, ICJ Reports 1971, 16, para. 116.

[74] As to the examination of the Security Council's resolutions with reference to accountability, see Jeremy M. Farrall, 'Rule of Accountability or Rule of Law? Regulating the UN Security Council's Accountability Deficits', *Journal of Conflict and Security Law* 19 (2014), 389–408 (398–402).

[75] For example, SC Res. 2135 of 30 January 2014, UN Doc. S/RES/2135(2014), para. 12; SC Res. 2109 of 11 July 2013, UN Doc. S/RES/2109(2013), para. 39. See also Farrall, 'Rule of Accountability or Rule of Law?' (n. 74), 389.

[76] See Van den Herik, 'A Reflection on Institutional Strength', Chapter 2 in this volume, section II.

This inquiry is warranted because of the revival of the Security Council in the wake of the Cold War, which demonstrated its strength while increasing the risks arising from its institutional weakness.

First, it has been generally recognised that a threat to peace does not necessarily indicate an act that is in violation of international law. Unlike the League of Nations, the United Nations' collective security mechanism is 'not conceived as a reaction to a violation of international law, but as a preventive tool to ensure the maintenance of peace', and hence it primarily assumes a 'police function' under Chapter VII UN Charter.[77] Hans Kelsen suggests that an act without breach of international law may also trigger the application of Article 39.[78] Furthermore, Kelsen argues that the Security Council has the power to adopt and enforce 'a decision which it considered to be just though not in conformity with existing law' if it finds the existing law unsatisfactory.[79] Given that international law was less developed in the 1940s, Kelsen's argument is sound. Perhaps inspired by the dual nature of the UN's collective security mechanism, some authors go further and distinguish 'law enforcement', which targets acts in violation of international law, from 'peace enforcement', which targets acts not inconsistent with international law.[80] However, we should bear in mind an important fact: while 'peace enforcement' is not triggered by a wrong act, relevant legal measures or actions may also be adopted and enforced. Obviously, the sovereignty of a state is more likely to be unduly compromised by 'peace enforcement' than by 'law enforcement'. A cautious approach should therefore be taken when peace enforcement is enacted against a state that has not violated any primary rules of international law (perhaps because such rules did not exist at the time of the impugned behaviour).

Such a cautious approach has already been adopted in the International Law Commission's Draft Articles on the Responsibility of States for Internationally Wrongful Acts, adopted in 2001. Under the Draft Articles, some legal burdens may be imposed on a state that acts in ways not prohibited by international law. The consequences on this occasion would be distinct from those arising from an international wrongful act – that is, what is incurred

---

[77] Nico Krisch, 'Article 39', in Bruno Simma, Daniel-Erasmus Khan, Georg Nolte, and Andreas Paulus (eds), *The Charter of the United Nations: A Commentary* (Oxford: Oxford University Press, 3rd edn, 2012), 1272–96 MN 10, (p. 1278).

[78] Hans Kelsen, *The Law of the United Nations: A Critical Analysis of its Fundamental Problems* (London: Stevens, 1950).

[79] Kelsen, *The Law of the United Nations* (n. 78), 295.

[80] See Krisch, 'Article 39' (n. 77), MN 10–11 (p. 1278).

on the former occasion refers to 'international liability', while, in the latter situation, it is 'international responsibility'. Furthermore, the loss incurred on the first occasion may be divided between the relevant states in the dispute.[81] This is indeed significant since the international law of peace has been far more developed in the 21st century than in Kelsen's time. The distinction between 'law enforcement' and 'peace enforcement' is less important. Yet it is still meaningful for two reasons: first, novel international threats continue to emerge,[82] but the relevant international law is not created or updated in a timely fashion; second, some states do not accept the relevant extant international law or they withdraw from their international commitments.

Second, some authors seem to assume that the measures provided in Article 39 UN Charter can be taken in disregard of international law.[83] Kelsen was a leading proponent of this view. Based on his understanding of 'measures' in Article 39, Kelsen suggests that enforcement measures were not designed 'to maintain or restore the law, but to maintain, or restore peace'.[84] Thus they are 'purely political measures ... which the Security Council may apply at its discretion for the purpose to maintain international peace and security'.[85] Kelsen further argues that the requirement 'in conformity with the principles of justice and international law' in Article 1(1), which the Security Council shall comply with when it acts in accordance with Article 24, did not apply to the Security Council measures under Chapter VII but only to those under Chapter VI.[86] In Kelsen's view, to interpret measures under Chapter VII not as 'sanctions' (i.e., as responses to a prior breach of the law) subject to general international law but instead as measures at the discretion of the Security Council 'would be in conformity with the general tendency which prevailed in drafting the Charter: the predominance of the political over the legal approach'.[87] Notwithstanding, Kelsen is aware of the weakness of such interpretation, recognising that it 'lead[s] to the consequence that with respect to enforcement measures there is no difference between a Member which has violated its obligations under the Charter, and a Member which is

---

[81] James Crawford, Alain Pellet, and Simon Olleson (eds), *The Law of International Responsibility* (Oxford: Oxford University Press, 2013), 95–104 and 503–20.

[82] See below, section IV.

[83] According to Krisch, the Security Council's effective action 'shall not be delayed by time-consuming procedures to determine the responsibility of the parties': Krisch, 'Article 39' (n. 77), 1278.

[84] Kelsen, *The Law of the United Nations* (n. 78), 294 and 733.

[85] *Ibid.*, 733.

[86] *Ibid.*, 295.

[87] *Ibid.*, 735.

not guilty of any such violation'.[88] Thus Kelsen admits that such interpretation is 'not the only possible one'.[89] An alternative exists: '[I]n accordance with general international law, a forcible interference in the sphere of interest of a state, that is reprisals or war, is permitted only as a reaction against a violation of law, that is to say as sanction.'[90] Interpreted thus, the enforcement measures under Chapter VII – given that they constitute forcible interferences – 'must be interpreted as sanctions if the Charter is supposed to be in conformity with general international law'.[91]

Kelsen further distinguishes the situations under Articles 41 and 42. He appears confident on the alternative interpretation of the Article 41 measures as sanctions: 'No other interpretation is possible with respect to the enforcement measures not involving the use of armed force as determined in Article 41', because those measures 'have the character of reprisals; and according to a generally accepted opinion, reprisals are permissible only as reaction against a violation of international law, that is to say, as sanctions'.[92] By contrast, Kelsen is less confident of the interpretation of measures under Article 42 as sanctions (requiring a prior breach). Under Article 42, the use of armed force may be initiated when the Security Council finds the Article 41 measures inadequate. Kelsen contends that 'whether such action is always possible without constituting a violation of general international law' remains debatable.[93]

The requirement of 'prompt and effective' UN action, as demanded by Article 24 UN Charter, is another factor invoked to support the enforcement of Security Council measures without regard for international law. According to Krisch, Security Council actions shall not be delayed by time-consuming procedures to ensure their effectiveness.[94] Because of the United Nations' shameful failure to respond to the Rwanda genocide in 1994, it is absolutely necessary that the Security Council act promptly and effectively. However, the criteria of 'prompt and effective' is a major source of disagreement among Council members. Looking into the meeting records of the Security Council, we readily find that members often disagree not over what measures should be taken but over when they should be taken. Comparatively speaking, the Western powers generally insist that coercive enforcement measures be

[88] *Ibid.*
[89] *Ibid.*
[90] *Ibid.*
[91] *Ibid.*
[92] *Ibid.*
[93] *Ibid.*
[94] Krisch, 'Article 39' (n. 77), 94.

taken as soon as possible, while some others argue that hasty measures are not helpful in maintaining the peace. Actually, the requirement 'prompt and effective' is not only a legal issue but also a factual one. Thus the understanding of 'prompt and effective' on a particular occasion largely depends on whether the relevant situations or disputes can be assessed and verified credibly. Unfortunately, as many Security Council meeting records show, the Security Council members often quarrel with each other over what has really happened.

Third, the Security Council undertook some significant legislative activities. They affected particular states targeted by Security Council measures and also broadly impacted international law. In Kelsen's view, when the Security Council makes and enforces 'a decision which it considered to be just though not in conformity with existing law' that it finds unsatisfactory, it seeks to remedy the situation by 'creat[ing] new law for the concrete case'.[95]

It has been suggested that the Security Council, in accordance with the UN Charter, is not prevented from undertaking legislative activities. In the *Tadić* case, the Appeal Chamber of the International Criminal Tribunal for the former Yugoslavia (ICTY) held that judicial, executive, and legislative functions were not clearly divided among the UN organs.[96] Anne Peters submits that, while the UN Charter drafters might have conceived of a 'police function', it was not explicitly provided for by the UN Charter. The 'measures' provided for in Article 39 are sufficiently broad so as to include legislative measures. It can therefore be assumed that while nothing in the Charter explicitly authorises the Security Council to adopt resolutions with legislative content, 'it does not rule it out, either'.[97] Peters observes that the majority of the UN members appear to be in support of the Security Council's legislative activities.[98]

Fourth, the determination of relevant facts faces a high risk of manipulation in the context of politicised institutions and legalised actions. Whether the legal actions approved by the Security Council or in the name of the Security Council resolutions are justified or not depends on whether a situation or dispute can be duly determined, which is particularly significant for those outside the Security Council. The Iraq war is a strong example. No one argued that the Security Council was not entitled to authorise enforcement measures

---

[95]   Kelsen, *The Law of the United Nations* (n. 78), 294.
[96]   ICTY, *Prosecutor v. Duško Tadić*, Appeal Chamber decision on the defence motion for interlocutory appeal on jurisdiction of 2 October 1995, case no. IT-94-1-A, para. 43.
[97]   Anne Peters, 'Article 24', in Bruno Simma, Daniel-Erasmus Khan, Georg Nolte, and Andreas Paulus (eds), *The Charter of the United Nations: A Commentary* (Oxford: Oxford University Press, 4th edn, 2024 forthcoming), MN 70–84 (MN 74).
[98]   *Ibid.*, MN 73.

should Iraq have been found to have gravely violated Resolutions 687 and 1441; rather, the debate very much focused on whether Iraq had indeed gravely violated those resolutions.

On 5 February 2003, then US Secretary of State Colin Powell presented evidence before the Security Council – 'some are United States sources and some are those of other countries' – firmly asserting that the United States 'know[s] about Iraq's weapons of mass destruction as well as Iraq's involvement in terrorism', and thus Powell accused Iraq of grave breaches of Resolutions 687 and 1441.[99] The United Kingdom supported the US 'evidence'.[100] China, while welcoming the information presented by the United States, supported the UN Monitoring, Verifying and Inspection Commission (UNMVIC), which, together with the International Atomic Energy Agency (IAEA), wanted to progress its work.[101] Russia held a similar position.[102] Interestingly, unlike the United Kingdom, France – while noting there were some grey areas in Iraq's cooperation with the UNMVIC – did not support the United States' accusations.[103] In other words, the Security Council members could not agree on whether Iraq gravely violated Resolutions 687 and 1441. For the United States' part, the important thing was that it had already presented 'evidence' before the Security Council, not whether the asserted evidence would be verified by the UNMVIC or other Security Council members.

Based on its self-identified 'evidence', the United States, together with the United Kingdom, launched 'Operation Iraqi Freedom' on 20 March 2003.

On 30 May, when the Iraq war ended, the UNMVIC submitted a report to the Security Council, stating that it 'did not find evidence of the continuation or resumption of programmes of weapons of mass destruction or significant quantities of proscribed items from before the adoption of Resolution 687 (1991)'.[104]

Again, in reviewing the United Kingdom's intervention in Libya in 2011, which was based on Security Council Resolution 1973, the Foreign Affairs Committee of the UK House Commons admitted that the evidence of the threat to civilians in Libya was presented with 'unjustified certainty' and thus intervention in Libya was a 'intelligence-light decision'.[105] However, the great

---

[99] UN Doc. S/PV.4701, 5 February 2003, 2–17.
[100] *Ibid.*, 18–20.
[101] *Ibid.*, 18.
[102] *Ibid.*, 20–1.
[103] *Ibid.*, 23–4.
[104] Note by Secretary-General, UN Doc. S/2003/580, 30 May 2003, Annex, para. 8.
[105] House of Commons Foreign Affairs Committee, *Libya: Examination of Intervention and Collapse and the UK's Future Policy Options*, Third Report of Session 2016–17, September 2016, HC 119, para. 37.

powers who justified their actions with the relevant Security Council resolutions were not held accountable for their actions. Nor did the Security Council later announce that the use of force against Iraq in 2003 and Libya in 2011 were in breach of the UN Charter and the relevant Security Council resolutions.

These cases show that serious long-term consequences often occur other than might be expected by the Security Council and those states actively supporting or seeking the Security Council actions. Based on his observation on UN peacekeeping operations, Martti Koskenniemi suggests that 'there is very little that is predictable about such operations'.[106] Indeed, the UK Foreign Affairs Committee acknowledged that the intervention brought about in Libya 'political and economic collapse, inter-militia and inter-tribal warfare, humanitarian and migrant crises, widespread human rights violations, the spread of Gaddafi regime weapons across the region and the growth of ISIL in North Africa'.[107]

All this notwithstanding, international law is absolutely relevant to the workings of the Security Council. In the *Conditions of Admission Case*, the majority of the ICJ judges suggested that 'the political character of an organ cannot release it from the observance of the treaty provisions established by the Charter when they constitute limitations on its powers or criteria for its judgment'.[108] They argued that, '[t]o ascertain whether an organ has freedom of choice for its decisions, reference must be made to the terms of its constitution'.[109] In that case, the ICJ noted that 'the limits of this freedom are fixed by Article 4, and allow for a wide liberty of appreciation. There is therefore no conflict between the functions of the political organs and the exhaustive character of the prescribed conditions'.[110] In other words, the Security Council can exercise discretion out of political considerations only to the extent that Article 4 allows. The ICJ concluded that the requirements specified in Article 4(1) were exhaustive and that any additional requirements were unjustified.[111] Unfortunately, many of the UN Charter provisions are so broad that a definite clarification cannot be made. Thus they are susceptible to misuse and abuse by either the Security Council or particular UN members. Furthermore, the ICJ is not often sought out for advisory opinions to clarify

---

[106] Martti Koskenniemi, *The Politics of International Law* (Oxford: Hart, 2011), 85.
[107] *Ibid.*, 3.
[108] ICJ, *Conditions of Admission of a State to Membership in the United Nations (Article 4 of the Charter)*, advisory opinion of 28 May 1948, ICJ Reports 1948, 57 (64).
[109] *Ibid.*
[110] *Ibid.*
[111] *Ibid.*

UN Charter provisions and few of the advisory opinions it has delivered concern the workings of the Security Council.[112]

Since the 1990s, propositions have emerged that more legal limits on the workings of the Security Council should be considered, thereby enhancing the accountability of this UN organ. Like many others, Peters agrees that peace may not necessarily be brought about through lawful actions. However, she stresses that:

> [T]he mere fact that the purpose (end) of Security Council action is not as such to secure compliance (of States) with the law does not automatically relieve the Council from observing the law when applying specific means to that end. The means (peace) must be distinguished from the ends (Council action) to reach it.[113]

In her view, the fact that the Security Council takes actions under Chapter VII in emergency situations 'does not justify any move to place the decisions as such outside the law'.[114]

Peters further suggests that the legislative activities of the Security Council should be subject to substantive and procedural constraints. The former mainly include the following.

(i) The Security Council should limit its legislative activities on occasions of 'significant, new and urgent threat in an emergency situation', which amount to a threat to peace as provided for in Article 39.

(ii) The Security Council should respect the institutional balance between the main UN organs and, especially, should not adopt legislative resolutions inconsistent with General Assembly resolutions.

(iii) The legislative measures should intrude as little as possible.

(iv) The Security Council should respect general international law as much as possible.

As a rule, the Security Council should legislate only when there is a gap in the existing international law and the legislative resolutions should not contradict international law.

As for procedural constrains, Peters suggests that the Security Council subject deliberations to the requirement of transparency, seek a broad consensus among

---

[112] For the number and subject of the ICJ advisory cases as of January 2021, see 'Advisory Proceedings', available at www.icj-cij.org/en/advisory-proceedings.

[113] Anne Peters, 'Article 25', in Simma et al. (eds), *The Charter of the United Nations* (n. 97), MN 73.

[114] *Ibid.*, MN 70.

states, and consider leeway to relevant states and help them to carry out legal measures.[115]

Ius cogens has also been invoked to impose constraints on the Security Council.[116] However, the great powers tend to resist these attempts. For example, Van den Herik observes that while many middle-class states support the idea of extending the ius cogens to the Security Council, the P5 discourage such an attempt.[117] It is the great powers' resistance that has sidelined some legal arrangements already existing in the UN Charter that would help to enhance the Security Council's accountability. Under Article 43, an agreement should be negotiated between the Security Council and a particular UN member, or a group of UN members, in the maintenance of international peace. Furthermore, under Article 47, a military staff committee could and should be established. Unfortunately, these two Articles have remained dead letter for decades.

III. HOW POWER POLITICS INFLUENCE THE WORKINGS OF THE SECURITY COUNCIL

In terms of the rise and fall of great powers since the 1940s, power politics can be roughly divided into three periods: the Cold War, the 'New World Order', and the 'new Cold War'.

In this section, I do not argue for or against particular Security Council actions or inaction; I instead seek to unpack the law and the political dynamics underlying its workings, calling for reflection on what the Security Council has done. This is helpful as we think about how best to reform the Security Council.

A. *The Cold War*

In World War II, the Allied forces – especially the great powers – exhibited unity in fighting the Axis alliance. In Tehran, in 1943, Roosevelt, Churchill, and Stalin stated: 'We came here with hope and determination. We leave

---

[115] Peters, 'Article 24' (n. 97), MN 80–82.
[116] Erika de Wet, *The Chapter VII Power of the United Nations Security Council* (London: Hart, 2024 forthcoming), ch. 5.
[117] Van den Herik, 'A Reflection on Institutional Strength', Chapter 2 in this volume, section II.

here, friends in fact, in spirit and in purpose.'[118] During their negotiations for establishing the United Nations, almost all participating states agreed that unity among the great powers was a precondition to the would-be organisation making a difference in the maintenance of peace.

As its 'chief designer', the United States' vision of world unity was particularly significant.[119] During the San Francisco Conference, Senator Connally, an American representative, affirmed a belief that 'the Security Council when united, can preserve peace; we fear that if it is not united, it cannot preserve peace'.[120] He applauded participants, saying: 'Now we are united. Now we are marching forward under the same banner on behalf of peace and security and with the same unity, the same harmony, the same purposes, and the same resources.'[121] Connally stated: '[W]e are voting and did vote for those measures that would contribute to the continued unity and harmony among permanent members of the Security Council.'[122] Arguably, it was that vision of unity, together with overwhelming state power, that made US President Roosevelt change his mind, shifting from a regional approach to a global approach to world peace. As a result, the United States strongly recommended that the UN Security Council be conferred with the primary responsibility of maintaining peace and, to this end, be entrusted with extensive authority, while the great powers be granted legal privileges.

However, that rosy vision of international unity was questioned from the very beginning. Some British elites warned that their country should not have high expectations of the United Nations. They doubted that the USSR would be a reliable partner: the United Kingdom was cautious that the USSR may be more dangerous than Nazi Germany.[123] For its part, the USSR was similarly suspicious of the new organisation. Thus it insisted on the principle of unanimity among the P5 in Security Council decision-making and threatened that, without veto power, 'there would simply be no United Nations'.[124]

The Cold War emerged in 1947. During the next four decades, the USSR-led East/socialist bloc and the US-led West/capitalist bloc struggled with each other – largely because of ideological and strategic considerations. In 1945,

---

[118]   Declaration of the Three Powers, 1 December 1943, available at https://avalon.law.yale.edu/wwii/tehran.asp.

[119]   José E. Alvarez, *International Organizations as Law-Makers* (Oxford: Oxford University Press, 2005), 67.

[120]   UNCIO, Verbatim Minutes of the Fourth Meeting of Commission III, 22 June 1945, UN Doc. 1149, III/11, 29.

[121]   *Ibid.*, 30.

[122]   *Ibid.*, 29.

[123]   Bosco, *Five to Rule Them All* (n. 20), 18–19, 39.

[124]   *Ibid.*, 23–4.

when the United Nations was founded, and during the Cold War, only the United States and the USSR qualified as world powers. While these two enjoyed this privilege on the Security Council, the United Kingdom, France, and China were merely the 'middle' great powers. They could only 'expect to be consulted on any issue within the radius of their actual power'.[125] How the Security Council worked largely depended on relations between the two world powers.

The Cold War had multiple implications for international law[126] – particularly for the working of the Security Council and, even more specifically, for the undue exercise of the veto power. Between 1946 and 1989, the Security Council debated 646 draft resolutions, 189 of which were vetoed. Nearly 50 per cent of these vetoes happened in the 1950s. Most vetoes were cast by the USSR and thus the exercise of the veto power was considered 'almost synonymous with Soviet foreign policy'.[127] Because of the conspicuous abuse of the veto power,[128] a call emerged for the renegotiation of the UN Charter and the reconstruction of the Security Council.[129] Since the 1970s, however, the United States and the United Kingdom have overtaken the USSR: between 1970 and 1989, the USSR vetoed on only 16 occasions, while the United States and the United Kingdom exercised their veto power 80 times and 30 times, respectively.[130]

The result of these struggles among the great powers – especially between the United States and the USSR – was that the Security Council is generally said to have been fundamentally disabled, except for peacekeeping operations.[131] Such an assessment is sound, if a bit too general. Here, I would like to discuss the influence of power politics on particular legal

---

[125]   Schwarzenberger, Power Politics (n. 3), 119–20.
[126]   See generally Matthew Craven, Sundhya Pahuja, and Gerry Simpson (eds), International Law and the Cold War (Cambridge: Cambridge University Press, 2020).
[127]   Thomas Schindlmayr, 'Obstructing the Security Council: The Use of the Veto in the Twentieth Century', Journal of the History of International Law 3 (2001), 218–34 (226, 227).
[128]   These abuses often happened on the occasion of voting on UN membership. In 1948, the ICJ decided that the requirements as provided for UN membership in Art. 4(1) were exhaustive and any additional requirements were therefore unjustified: ICJ, Admission of a State to the United Nations (n. 108), 65. However, the United States and the USSR vetoed applications for UN membership again and again. In fact, most vetoes cast in the 1950s concerned UN membership. It should be noted that while those vetoes damaged the universality of the United Nations, they were not very harmful to international peace and security.
[129]   Bosco, Five to Rule Them All (n. 20), 46–7.
[130]   Schindlmayr, 'Obstructing the Security Council' (n. 127), 228.
[131]   Mats Berdal, 'The Security Council and Peacekeeping', in Lowe et al. (eds), The United Nations Security Council and War (n. 15), 175–204.

arguments that were expounded in the Security Council by examining the
P5's position on the humanity and sovereignty of Viet Nam's intervention in
Cambodia in the late 1970s.[132]

It is well known that, since the 1990s, some states have relied on humanitarian concerns to justify their initiatives or actions within or outside the Security
Council, while some other states have invoked the principle of sovereignty to
oppose humanitarian interventions. That landscape was different during the
Cold War.

In December 1978, Viet Nam waged a military intervention against
Cambodia and soon controlled most of the Cambodian territory. Viet
Nam's intervention led to the collapse of Pol Pot's regime. As a major
justification for its intervention, Viet Nam asserted that the regime had
massacred some 3 million civilians in Cambodia.[133] While condemning
the regime's consistent and grave human rights violations, France and the
United Kingdom's arguments marked a sharp contrast with their position
after the end of the Cold War. France stated:

> The notion that because a regime is detestable foreign intervention is justified
> and forcible overthrow is legitimate is extremely dangerous. That could
> ultimately jeopardise the very maintenance of international law and order
> and make the continued existence of various regimes dependent on the
> judgement of their neighbours. It is important for the Council to affirm,
> without any ambiguity, that it cannot condone the occupation of a sovereign
> country by a foreign Power.[134]

The United Kingdom took a similar stance. It stated that:

> Whatever is said about human rights in Kampuchea, it cannot excuse
> Viet Nam, whose own human rights record is deplorable, for violating
> the territorial integrity of Democratic Kampuchea, an independent
> State Member of the United Nations … Respect for the sovereignty,
> territorial integrity and political independence of Member States is one
> of the cornerstones of the Charter and of the United Nations system.[135]

The USSR expressed a totally different position. In its view, the gross violation
of human rights deprived the Pol Pot regime of legitimacy; thus it was the

---

[132] See, in detail, Gregory H. Fox, 'The Vietnamese Intervention in Cambodia – 1978', in Ruys
et al. (eds), *The Use of Force in International Law* (n. 15), 242–54.

[133] *Ibid.*, 250–3.

[134] UN Doc. S/PV.2109, 12 January 1979, 4.

[135] *Ibid.*, 6–7.

Cambodian people that overthrew the vicious Pol Pot regime. The USSR
stated that:

> It would appear that in this way certain persons are attempting to divert the
> attention of the world public opinion from the monstrous crimes committed
> by this clique against people of their own country and their acts of aggression
> against neighbouring states, which have led to the undermining of stability in
> international security in the area ... In a country with a population of
> 8 million, the rulers destroyed, according to statistics reported in, among
> others, the Western press, from 2 to 3 million people. The vocabulary used in
> international practice to describe mass violations of human rights is simply
> inadequate to describe these monstrous crimes.[136]

In contrast with these three states, the United States held a moderate position.
Intriguingly, the US position reminds many people of China's more recent
statements in the Security Council.[137] The United States argued that:

> The invasion by Viet Nam of Kampuchea presents to the Council *difficult
> political and moral questions. The issue is affected by history, rival claims and
> Charter principles. It appears complex because several different provisions of
> the Charter are directly relevant to deliberations.* These are that: the funda-
> mental principles of human rights must be respected by all governments, one
> State must not use force against the territory of another State, a State must not
> interfere in the affairs of another State, and, if there is a dispute between
> States that must be settled peaceably.[138]

Unlike France and the United Kingdom, and particularly the USSR, China did
not mention the gross violations of human rights committed by the Pol Pot
regime. However, it did – as did France and the United Kingdom – argue that
Viet Nam's action constituted aggression against Cambodia. Thus China
appealed that 'it is the incumbent duty of all peace-loving and justice-
upholding countries to stop Viet Nam's aggression, support the Kampuchean
people's struggle and save peace in South-East Asia'.[139]

The P5's positions on humanitarian concern and sovereignty were heavily
influenced in this case by considerations of power politics. The USSR's
support for Viet Nam comes as no surprise, because it was an ally of Viet
Nam, and its condemnation of the Pol Pot regime's atrocities was obviously
hypocritical. The United States', the United Kingdom's, and France's opposition is understandable, for they opposed the action of Viet Nam, and they

---

[136] UN Doc. S/PV.2108, 11 January 1979, 14–15.
[137] See, e.g., UN Doc. S/PV.7138, 15 March 2014, 7.
[138] UN Doc. S/PV.2110, 13 January 1979, 7 (emphasis added).
[139] UN Doc. S/PV.2108, 11 January 1979, 10.

sided with the USSR even though they acknowledged the humanitarian disaster in Cambodia. In contrast, China's position is more complicated. On the one hand, the relations between China, the USSR, and Viet Nam were very bad in the 1970s, and there were actually occasional military conflicts between China and Viet Nam. On the other hand, China maintained close relations with the Pol Pot regime. Therefore, while China condemned Viet Nam's aggression, it was silent on the regime's atrocities. Thus each permanent member interpreted humanity and sovereignty in ways that served their own state interests.

Although power politics largely disabled the Security Council in the Cold War, they did not totally prevent the UN members from seeking new arrangements to maintain international peace. A significant example is the 'Uniting for Peace' (UFP) procedure. The idea for the procedure came from the United States. According to the UFP procedure, if a threat to peace could not be addressed by the Security Council because of a lack of unanimity among the P5, it should be referred to the UN General Assembly and the Assembly should make an appropriate recommendation for collective measures.[140]

In the early months after the outbreak of the Korean War, the USSR was absent from the Security Council. As a result, the Security Council successfully adopted three resolutions declaring that North Korea's armed attack against South Korea constituted a 'breach of the peace'; these resolutions authorised UN members to provide assistance to South Korea and to restore peace in the Korean Peninsula.[141] Aware that the USSR's return would make it impossible to adopt any new resolutions in the Security Council, the United States sought an alternative path. It succeeded in convincing the General Assembly to approve a UFP resolution, since, in the United Nations' early years, the majority of Members had an affinity with the Western world.[142] That resolution stated that if the Security Council, 'because of lack of unanimity of the permanent members', were to fail to exercise its primary responsibility for the maintenance of peace in the case of a breach of the peace or acts of aggression, the General Assembly would consider the matter immediately with a view to making appropriate recommendations to the UN members for collective measures, including the use of armed force when it is necessary

---

[140] Dominik Zaum, 'The Security Council, The General Assembly, and War: The Uniting for Peace Resolution', in Lowe et al. (eds), The *United Nations Security Council and War* (n. 15), 154–74.

[141] SC Res. 82 of 25 June 1950, UN Doc. S/RES/82(1950); SC Res. 83 of 27 June 1950, UN Doc. S/RES/83(1950); SC Res. 84 of 7 July 1950, UN Doc. S/RES/84(1950).

[142] GA Res. 377 (V) of 3 December 1950, UN Doc. A/RES/377(V).

to maintain or restore peace and security.[143] In other words, the General Assembly, on these occasions, would assume the 'primary' responsibility for the maintenance of peace.

Actions under the UFP procedure were taken four times in the 1950s.[144] However, it was rarely used in the following decades[145] – until it was again applied in response to the Russian invasion in Ukraine.

B. *The 'New World Order'*

The 'New World Order' was a fashionable political discourse in the 1990s and 2000s. In his address delivered before the US Congress on 11 September 1990, President George W. Bush introduced his conception of the 'New World Order':

> [O]ur fifth objective – a new world order – can emerge; a new era – freer from the threat of terror, stronger in the pursuit of justice, and more secure in the quest for peace, an era in which the nations of the world, East and West, North and South, can prosper and live in harmony. A hundred generations have searched for this elusive path to peace, while a thousand wars raged across the span of human endeavour. Today, that new world is struggling to be born, a world quite different from the one we have known, a world where the rule of law supplants the rule of the jungle, a world in which nations recognize the shared responsibility for freedom and justice, a world where the strong respect the rights of the weak.[146]

While there were debates, at the outset, as to what it really meant[147] and whether it would come to fruition, the 'New World Order' betokened a less confrontational and more harmonious world for many states. Indeed, China and Russia were optimistic about what the world might look like after the Cold War. In a declaration issued jointly in 1997, Russia and China stated:

> The Parties believe that profound changes in international relations have taken place at the end of the twentieth century. The cold war is over. The

---

[143]   *Ibid.*, para. 1: 'If not in session at the time the General Assembly may meet in emergency special session within twenty four hours of the request thereof. Such emergency special session may be called if requested by the Security Council on the vote of any seven members, or by a majority of the United Nations.'

[144]   Lowe et al. (eds), *The United Nations Security Council and War* (n. 15), appx 6.

[145]   Zaum, 'The Uniting for Peace Resolution' (n. 140), 160, 166.

[146]   George H. W. Bush, 'Toward a New World Order', *US Department of State Dispatch* 1 (1990), 91–4.

[147]   Joseph S. Nye, Jr., 'What New World Order', *Foreign Affairs* 71 (1992), 83–96; Anne-Marie Slaughter, 'The Real New World Order', *Foreign Affairs* 76 (1997), 183–97.

bipolar system has vanished. A positive trend towards a multipolar world is gaining momentum, and relations between major States, including former cold-war adversaries, are changing.[148]

The New World Order had two major features: first, democracy and human rights attained greater importance in the foreign policy of the Western states than they had during the Cold War; second – and more importantly – the Western states acquired overwhelming power to pursue their foreign policy agendas and the world entered a 'unipolar' era. The United States became 'the first and the only truly global power' in the wake of the Cold War.[149] The USSR disappeared in December 1991. Yeltsin-led Russia struggled to rebuild the nation and was neither powerful enough nor willing to challenge the US-led international order; rather, Russia adopted a pro-Western policy. China, meanwhile, was under a wide range of sanctions imposed by Western states who accused China of forcefully suppressing protests in Tiananmen Square in 1989.[150] For China, release from international sanctions and improved relations with the Western world were a priority, and hence China maintained a policy of 'keeping a low profile' in international relations.[151]

This context has significantly shaped the workings of the Security Council since the 1990s. Now with unrivalled power, the United States and like-minded states felt comfortable reshaping the world order – in particular, the workings of the Security Council – to meet their own expectations. They encountered few difficulties in pursuit of the Security Council's approval for measures they favoured. While Russia and China were not supportive of many of these measures, they were reluctant to exercise their veto power; their abstention votes grew significantly in the 1990s, compared with the 1980s – Russia, from 15 to 20, and China, from 13 to 42.[152] This gave many people the impression that unity existed among the great powers of the Security Council.

In this new context, the Security Council played a more complicated role in the maintenance of peace. On the one hand, it succeeded more often in taking

---

[148]   Annex to letter dated 15 May 1997 from the Permanent Representatives of China and the Russian Federation to the United Nations addressed to the Secretary-General, UN Doc. S/1997/384 ('Russian-Chinese Joint Declaration on a Multipolar World and the Establishment of a New International Order, adopted in Moscow on 23 April 1997').

[149]   Zbigniew Brzezinski, *The Grand Chessboard: American Primacy and its Geostrategic Imperatives* (New York: Basic Books, 1997), 3–29.

[150]   See Rosemary Foot, *Rights beyond Borders: The Global Community and the Struggle over Human Rights in China* (Oxford: Oxford University Press, 2000), 113–49.

[151]   John W. Garver, *China's Quest: The History of the Foreign Relations of the People's Republic of China* (Oxford: Oxford University Press, 2016), 486–7.

[152]   Joel Wuthnow, *Chinese Diplomacy and the UN Security Council: Beyond the Veto* (London: Routledge, 2013), 19, 21.

'prompt and effective measures' to address threats to international peace, increasing international confidence in the UN collective security system and defending an international order centred on the UN Charter. On the other hand, some measures that the Security Council adopted were controversial both within or outside the Security Council and opened the door to different interpretations, risking misuse and abuse.

After Iraq invaded Kuwait on 2 August 1990, the Security Council adopted six resolutions within four months.[153] Resolution 660, for example, condemned the Iraq invasion of Kuwait, demanding 'that Iraq withdraw immediately and unconditionally all its forces' from Kuwait. Resolution 678, in particular, authorised UN members to use 'all necessary measures' to enforce Resolution 660 unless Iraq implemented it. The permanent members vetoed only one Security Council resolution concerning the Gulf War in 1990 – that one a resolution concerning humanitarian need proposed by Cuba but vetoed by the United States, the United Kingdom, and France.[154] On 17 January 1991, in accordance with Resolution 678, a US-led coalition of states initiated collective action against Iraq and soon expelled the Iraqi forces from Kuwait. Resolution 687 acknowledged 'the restoration to Kuwait of its sovereignty, independence and territorial integrity and the return of its legitimate Government'.

Ten years later, the Security Council acted promptly after terrorist attacks against the World Trade Centre in New York on 11 September 2001. One day after the attack, the Security Council members unanimously adopted Resolution 1368 to combat 'by all means' threats to international peace and security caused by terrorist acts.[155] More importantly, the Resolution mentioned in its Preamble 'the inherent right of individual or collective self-defence in accordance with the Charter'. Thus Resolution 1368 implied that non-state actors could trigger Article 51 UN Charter, which had traditionally been understood as being applicable to attacks by sovereign states.[156]

---

[153] SC Res. 660 of 2 August 1990, UN Doc. S/RES/660(1990); SC Res. 661 of 6 August 1990, UN Doc. S/RES/661(1990); SC Res. 662 of 9 August 1990, UN Doc. S/RES/662(1990); SC Res. 664 of 18 August 1990, UN Doc. S/RES/664(1990); SC Res. 665 of 25 August 1990, UN Doc. S/RES/665(1990); SC Res. 666 of 13 September 1990, UN Doc. S/RES/666(1990); SC Res. 667 of 16 September 1990, UN Doc. S/RES/667(1990); SC Res. 669 of 24 September 1990, UN Doc. S/RES/669(1990); SC Res. 670 of 25 September 1990, UN Doc. S/RES/670(1990); SC Res. 674 of 29 October 1990, UN Doc. S/RES/674(1990); SC Res. 678 of 28 November 1990, UN Doc. S/RES/678(1990).

[154] UN Doc. S/PV.2939, 14 September 1990, 6.

[155] SC Res. 1368 of 12 September 2001, UN Doc. S/RES/1368(2001), cons. 2.

[156] According to Christian J. Tams, a state's self-defence against a non-state actor 'ostensibly seems to fall foul of the prohibition against the use of force in international relations,

Surprisingly, such a significant legal breakthrough met with no challenge in the Security Council when the draft resolution was debated. It should be noted, however, that not all UN members were in support of it. Specifically, members were divided in the UN General Assembly debate on terrorism in early 2001 as to whether the provision of self-defence could serve as a legal basis to combat terrorism. The legal propriety and consequence of Resolution 1368 remains open to debate.[157]

Nevertheless, the Security Council after the Cold War seemed more susceptible to power politics. Significantly, it has sometimes had to legitimise, in some sense, those actions that were taken by several great powers but opposed by many of the other members. The 1999 Kosovo War is an example.[158] The Security Council did not authorise NATO's use of force against the Federal Republic of Yugoslavia (FRY) and some of NATO's members recognised that there was no legal basis for the use of force. Yet NATO conducted airstrikes against the FRY for 70 days in the name of a humanitarian emergency in the FRY.[159] It should be stressed that few UN members accepted this explanation and many contended that NATO's actions were categorically unlawful under the UN Charter.[160] While Russia and China condemned NATO's flagrant violation of the Charter provision prohibiting the use of force, they could not stop NATO's actions inside or outside of the Security Council. Ultimately, they had to accept that Resolution 1244 mapped a way out of the Kosovo crisis in line with the principles established by the then Group of Eight (G8) foreign ministers.[161]

---

enshrined in Art. 2(4) of the UN Charter and customary international law': Christian J. Tams, 'Self-Defence against Non-State Actors: Making Sense of the "Armed Attack" Requirement', in Mary-Ellen O'Connell, Christian Tams, and Dire Tladi, *Self-Defence against Non-State Actors*, Max Planck Trialogues on the Law of Peace and War (Anne Peters and Christian Marxsen, series eds), vol. 1 (Cambridge: Cambridge University Press, 2019), 90–173 (95). Tams appears to admit that an extension of self-defence does not find support from the literal provision of Art. 51 or conventional understanding of Art. 2(4): *ibid.*, 112–16. He argues that '[w]hile the Charter does not stipulate that the armed attack must be by "a State", this has, until recently, been the generally accepted interpretation of Article 51', and that this interpretation 'is consistent with the context of the Charter provisions': *ibid.* In contrast, the arguments based on 'practice' that international law permits the unilateral use of force in self-defence against non-state actors are 'at best unconvincing and, at worst, dangerous': *ibid.*, 87–8.

[157] *Ibid.*, 36–52; Michael Byers, 'The Intervention in Afghanistan – 2001', in Ruys et al. (eds), *The Use of Force in International Law* (n. 15), 625–38.

[158] Daniel Franchini and Antonios Tzanakopoulos, 'The Kosovo Crisis – 1999', in Ruys et al. (eds), *The Use of Force in International Law* (n. 15), 594–622 (594–7).

[159] *Ibid.*, 598–603.

[160] *Ibid.*, 603–4.

[161] SC Res. 1244 of 10 June 1999, UN Doc. S/RES/1244(1999). Russia cast an affirmative vote, while China abstained. The G8 comprised the United States, the United Kingdom, France, Germany, Italy, Canada, Japan, and Russia.

We can also see some evidence of the Security Council legitimising the consequences of a use of force in the context of the 2003 Iraq War. Resolution 687 included disarmament obligations for Iraq in the package of measures targeting threats to peace arising from Iraq's invasion of Kuwait. Given Iraq's failure to fully implement those obligations, the Security Council adopted several resolutions in the following years. Resolution 1441, for example, offered Iraq 'a final opportunity' to comply with its disarmament obligations.[162] Some Security Council members recognised that Iraq had made progress towards compliance with those obligations. However, the United States, the United Kingdom, and like-minded states asserted that Iraq had cheated the world again and again. On 18 March 2003, they launched 'Operation Iraqi Freedom' and overturned the regime of Saddam Hussein – even though the United States and the United Kingdom disagreed somewhat over the legal basis of their operation. The United States argued that if Resolution 1441 were not effectively enforced, the use of force would be justified.[163] In contrast, the United Kingdom's legal advisers have tended to believe that they needed a new Security Council resolution to authorise the use of force.[164]

It was later found that there was no evidence that Iraq had violated the disarmament obligations.[165] In addition to ruining Iraq, 'Operation Iraqi Freedom' had other serious consequences – not least that an enfeebled Iraq became a breeding ground for terrorism, including the so-called Islamic State of Iraq and Syria (ISIS), which constituted a new threat to international peace in the Middle East. All across the world 'Operation Iraqi Freedom' was condemned as unlawful, and the United States and its allies were accused of having committed an aggression.[166] Yet the United States and the United Kingdom were not held accountable for their actions.

---

[162] SC Res. 1441 of 8 November 2002, UN Doc. S/RES/1441(2002).

[163] The United States stated that '[i]f the Security Council fails to act decisively in the event of further Iraqi violation, this resolution does not constrain any Member State from acting to defend itself against the threat posed by Iraq or to enforce relevant United Nations resolutions and protect world peace and security': UN Doc. S/PV.4633, 8 November 2002, 3.

[164] Michael Wood, legal adviser to the UK Foreign and Commonwealth Office, warned that, 'without a further decision by the Council, and absent extraordinary circumstances', the United Kingdom would not be able to lawfully use force against Iraq: *The Report of the Iraq Inquiry*, Report of a Committee of Privy Counsellors, vol. 5, HC 265-V, Pt 5 ('Advice on the Legal Basis for Military Action, November 2002 to March 2003'), 65.

[165] UN Doc. S/PV.4768, 3 June 2003, 2.

[166] Marc Weller, 'The Iraq War – 2003', in Ruys et al. (eds), *The Use of Force in International Law* (n. 15), 639–61 (647–50).

C. A 'New Cold War'?

Given the deteriorating relations between the Western world and Russia and China during the past decade, there has been a growing concern that the world is at risk of sinking into a 'new Cold War'.[167] Speaking at a China–US think tanks media forum, China's Foreign Minister Wang Yi refused to give a direct answer when asked about the possibility of a 'new Cold War' brewing between China and the United States; instead, he cautioned that if the United States 'chooses to conjure up "China Threats" of various kinds, its paranoia may turn into self-fulfilling prophecies at the end of the day.'[168] In contrast, Russia's attitude is frank. Russian Foreign Minister Sergey Lavrov has explicitly warned of the start of a 'new Cold War'.[169] Either way, it appears certain that the world now faces a power constellation similar to that of the Cold War, which may again significantly affect the workings of the Security Council.

As already noted, Russia had adopted a pro-Western policy in the 1990s, with the expectation that it would be welcomed as a partner to or member of the Western world. Russia was soon disappointed. Not only did NATO not disband when the Warsaw Treaty Organization ceased to exist, but also it expanded eastward to include several Eastern European countries that had been members of the former USSR. NATO constantly expanded its influence over other Eastern European countries and over former USSR members, some of whom sought NATO membership.[170] From the perspective of international law, NATO had the right to expand and the relevant states had the right to apply for NATO membership. From the perspective of power politics, however, these actions placed Russian strategic interests at stake.[171] Russia claimed that NATO's expansion – along with an increased NATO military presence and activities approaching the Russian border – constituted 'a violation of the principle of equal and indivisible security and [led]

---

[167] Eric Engle, 'A New Cold War? Cold Peace, Russia, Ukraine, and NATO', *Saint Louis University Law Journal* 59 (2014), 97–174.

[168] Wang Yi, 'Stay on the Right Track and Keep Pace with the Times to Ensure the Right Direction for China–US Relations', 9 July 2020, available at www.fmprc.gov.cn/mfa_eng/wjb_663304/wjbz_663308/2461_663310/202007/t20200709_468780.html.

[169] Andrea Peters, 'Russian Foreign Minister Warns of a New "Cold War"', *World Socialist Website*, 28 April 2021, available at www.wsws.org/en/articles/2021/04/29/rutr-a29.html.

[170] Andrey Makarychev, 'Russia, NAFTA, and the "Color Revolution"', *Russian Politics and Law* 47 (2009), 40–51.

[171] J. L. Black, 'Russia and NATO Expansion Eastward: Red-Lining the Baltic States', *International Journal* 54 (1999), 249–66.

to the deepening of old dividing lines in Europe and to the emergence of new ones'.[172]

In fact, some Western strategic analysts had already warned of the potential negative impact of NATO's expansion.[173] After Vladimir Putin became president in 2000, Russia began to 'leave ... the West'[174] and turned to a more aggressive foreign policy. The Syrian crisis is an example.[175] Unlike Ukraine, Syria is not a part of the former USSR, but it is one of few places where Russia can still exercise strategic deterrence in lieu of the Western powers. The struggle between Russia and the Western powers is a major cause of the Syrian crisis that has already lasted more than ten years. Notably, UN Secretary-General António Guterres has explicitly referred to it as a 'proxy war': in Syria, 'we see confrontations and proxy wars involving several national armies, a number of armed opposition groups, many national and international militias, foreign fighters from all over the world and various terrorist organizations'.[176]

The Ukrainian crisis, however, could have a more destructive impact on international peace. People are not shy in talking about it in Cold War terms. From the Russian perspective, NATO's eastern expansion to include Ukraine constitutes a strategic threat to Russia; thus Russia asserts that Ukraine 'is merely a geopolitical playground for some Western politicians'.[177] In contrast, Western powers suggest that Russia is the very source of rebels and the secessionist movement in the eastern part of Ukraine.

An event crucial to the crisis occurred in 2014, after the local Crimean government held an independence referendum in March that was unconstitutional under Ukrainian law and Russia immediately accepted Crimea's application to become a part of Russia. The Western powers condemned Russia's action as an annexation. They explicitly compared the Crimean crisis with what the USSR once did to Hungary and Czechoslovakia. The United Kingdom stated: 'This is not 1968 or 1956. The era in which one country can suppress democratisation in a neighbouring state through military intervention on the

[172] Foreign Policy Concept of the Russian Federation, 30 November 2016, available at https://interkomitet.com/foreign-policy/basic-documents/foreign-policy-concept-of-the-russian-federation-approved-by-president-of-the-russian-federation-vladimir-putin-on-november-30-2016/, para. 70.
[173] See, e.g., John J. Mearsheimer, 'Why the Ukraine Crisis is the West's Fault: The Liberal Delusions that Provoked Putin', *Foreign Affairs* 93 (2014), 1–12.
[174] Dmitri Trenin, 'Russia Leaves the West', *Foreign Affairs* 85 (2006), 87–96.
[175] Anne Lagerwall, 'Threats of and Actual Military Strike against Syria – 2013 and 2017', in Ruys et al. (eds), *The Use of Force in International Law* (n. 15), 828–54 (828–33).
[176] UN Doc. S/PV.8233, 14 April 2018, 2.
[177] UN Doc. S/PV.7125, 3 March 2014, 4.

basis of transparently trumped-up pretexts is over."[178] Similarly, France's representative argued: 'It is in fact the voice of the past that we have just heard. I was 15 years old in August 1968, when the USSR forces entered Czechoslovakia. We heard the same justifications, the same documents being flaunted and the same allegations."[179] On 1 April 2014, the General Assembly adopted Resolution 262 calling for all states 'to desist and refrain from actions aimed at the partial or total disruption of the national unity and territorial integrity of Ukraine, including any attempts to modify Ukraine's borders through the threat or use of force or other unlawful means'.[180] It is noteworthy, however, that only 100 states supported the Resolution, while 58 states abstained and 11 states opposed it. Nearly all of the states, including those that cast abstention votes, expressed their support for the principle of sovereignty and territorial integrity. It seems as though some of them considered the annexation partly attributable to the Western powers. For example, Ecuador stated that the 'irresponsible presence of foreign politicians' aggregated violence in Ukraine, which were the 'precedents' for the referendum taking place in Crimea and the basis for Russia consenting to Crimea's application to join Russia.[181]

The Ukrainian crisis deteriorated into the so-called SMO that Russia waged on 22 February 2022. The UN General Assembly, by convening an Emergency Special Session, adopted a resolution on 2 March 2022[182] – after 141 states voted in favour of it, 5 opposed it, 35 abstained, and 12 states did not vote. Resolution ES-11/1 states that the SMO constitutes an aggression against Ukraine. The Resolution recognises that the SMO is 'on a scale that the international community has not seen in Europe in decades' and that urgent action is needed to 'save this generation from the scourge of war'.[183] It condemns the SMO and states that 'no territorial acquisition resulting from the threat or use of force shall be recognized as legal'.[184]

Two additional points are worth mentioning. First, while the European Union, most NATO members, and some of the United States' allies (i.e., some 50 states or so) have imposed a wide range of sanctions on Russia, and have provided economic and military assistance to Ukraine, most states have maintained normal relations with Russia, even though they supported the General Assembly's Resolution ES-11/1. Second, while it is clearly impossible to adopt any meaningful actions through the Security Council, NATO has not

---

[178] *Ibid.*, 7. See also UN Doc. S/PV.7138, 15 March 2014, 3.
[179] UN Doc. S/PV.7125, 3 March 2014, 5.
[180] GA Res. 68/262 of 1 April 2014, UN Doc. A/RES/262(2014), 2.
[181] UN Doc. A/68/PV.80, 7 March 2014, 124–5.
[182] GA Res. ES-11/1 of 1 March 2022 on aggression against Ukraine, UN Doc. A/RES/ES-11/1.
[183] *Ibid.*
[184] *Ibid.*

directly undertaken intervention as the United States did in the Kosovo War. Furthermore, although the UFP procedure was triggered because the General Assembly convened an Emergency Special Session, the General Assembly, in Resolution ES-11/1, did not take strong action as it had done on the occasion of the Korean War in the 1950s.[185] This partly supports an argument proposed a decade ago: that what has occurred in Ukraine is a 'proxy war'.[186]

There is also a growing concern that a 'new Cold War' will occur between China and the United States.[187] This has been betokened by the fact that the United States identifies China both as the only country with the intent to reshape the international order[188] and, in particular, as a country attempting to 'challenge American power, influence, and interests, attempting to erode American security and prosperity'.[189] As a result, in 2020, the United States announced its plans to compete with China 'through a whole-government approach and guided by a return to principled realism'.[190]

In this context, it is of grave concern to the Western powers that Russia and China might develop an alliance, since both are in a strategic struggle with the US-led Western powers. Currently, the two states define their relationship as a 'comprehensive strategic partnership'.[191] While China has established comprehensive strategic partnerships with many other states, that between China and Russia is far more profound given their leading role in international relations, including their permanent membership on the Security Council. In recent years, the two states have issued a number of significant statements

[185] Michael Ramsden, 'Uniting for Peace: The Emergency Special Session on Ukraine', *Harvard Journal of International Law*, April 2022, available at https://journals.law.harvard.edu/ilj/2022/04/uniting-for-peace-the-emergency-special-session-on-ukraine/.

[186] Geraint Hughes, 'Ukraine: Europe's New Proxy War', *Fletcher Security Review* 1 (2014), 105–18; Robert Heinsch, 'Conflict Classification in Ukraine: The Return of the Proxy War', *International Law Studies Series* 91 (2015), 323–60.

[187] Odd Arne Westad, 'The Sources of Chinese Conduct: Are Washington and Beijing Fighting a New Cold War?', *Foreign Affairs* 98 (2019), 86–95 (87).

[188] Antony J. Blinken, 'The Administration's Approach to the People's Republic of China', 26 May 2022, available at www.state.gov/the-administrations-approach-to-the-peoples-republic-of-china/.

[189] National Security Strategy of the United States of America, December 2017, available at https://trumpwhitehouse.archives.gov/wp-content/uploads/2017/12/NSS-Final-12-18-2017-0905.pdf, 2.

[190] United States Strategic Approach to the People's Republic of China, 26 May 2020, available at https://trumpwhitehouse.archives.gov/wp-content/uploads/2020/05/U.S.-Strategic-Approach-to-The-Peoples-Republic-of-China-Report-5.24v1.pdf, 16.

[191] See, e.g., Joint Statement of the People's Republic of China and the Russian Federation on the Development of a Comprehensive Strategic Partnership for Collaboration in the New Era, 5 June 2019; Joint Statement between the People's Republic of China and the Federation of Russia, 8 June 2018.

regarding their common stances on international relations and international law. On 25 June 2016, the two states released a joint declaration on international law, in which they elaborated their common stances on several crucial issues.[192] For example, they argued that any attempts of 'regime change' and extraterritorial application of national law violate the principle of non-intervention.[193] They also submitted that international dispute settlement means and mechanisms should be based on consent, and used in good faith and in the spirit of cooperation (i.e., that they should not be abused).[194] In addition, they suggested that the imposition of unilateral coercive measures 'defeat[s] the objects and purposes of measures imposed by the Security Council, and undermine[s] their integrity and effectiveness'.[195]

In March 2021, the two issued a joint statement on global governance.[196] This statement highlighted the significance of good relations among states – especially among the 'major global powers'. It urged them 'to strengthen mutual trust and to be in the forefront of defending international law as well as the world order based on it'.[197] For this purpose, it called for dialogues 'aimed at rapprochement of all countries, not disunion; at cooperation, not confrontation'.[198] On the one hand, this statement, as Achilles Skordas observes, indicates that the two states have turned to a concerted approach to global governance, which include several other leading powers beyond the P5, and may thus please those states.[199] On the other hand, because of the two states' stance on human rights and democracy, which Skordas characterises as pro-sovereignty, he suggests that the two states seem to promote or induce an 'authoritarian' global governance.[200]

Compared with these previous statements, the joint statement that China and Russia issued on 4 February 2022 – after Russia's SMO against Ukraine – seemed to stir more caution among the Western powers.[201] In addition to reaffirming many common positions that had already been formulated in prior

---

[192] Declaration of the Russian Federation and the People's Republic of China on the Promotion of International Law, 25 June 2016.

[193] *Ibid.*, para. 4.

[194] *Ibid.*, para. 5.

[195] *Ibid.*, para. 6.

[196] Joint Statement by the Foreign Ministers of China and Russia on Certain Aspects of Global Governance in Modern Conditions, 23 March 2021.

[197] *Ibid.*

[198] *Ibid.*

[199] Achilles Skordas, 'Authoritarian Global Governance? The Russian-Chinese Joint Statement of March 2021', *Heidelberg Journal of International Law* 81 (2021), 293–302 (299, 301).

[200] *Ibid.*, 295–6, 302.

[201] Joint Statement of the Russian Federation and the People's Republic of China on the International Relations Entering a New Era and the Global Sustainable Development, 4 February 2022, available at http://en.kremlin.ru/supplement/5770.

documents, this statement included a sentence with distinctly Chinese characteristics: 'Friendship between the two States has no limits, there are no "forbidden" areas of cooperation.'[202] Some Western powers may have experienced this sentence as provocative, aggravating their concerns about whether the partnership between China and Russia may become an alliance. In my view, however, this diplomatic language does not mean that a substantial change to China's foreign policy is forthcoming, including for its policy on Russia. We can look, for evidence, at the 'Five Points' on the SMO that China announced on 25 February 2022.[203]

Many Western powers are unhappy with the 'Five Points' because China neither joined them in condemning the SMO nor imposed sanctions on Russia[204] – but China's position is not exceptional. As already noted, 52 UN members – including China and India – either opposed, abstained, or did not vote on General Assembly Resolution ES-11/1 condemning Russia's SMO. More importantly, few states imposed sanctions on Russia. As a matter of fact, in its 'Five Points', China expressed its support for Ukraine by reaffirming its long-standing policy of respect for the sovereignty and territorial integrity of all countries, including for the purposes and principles of the UN Charter. In particular, the 'Five Points' explicitly stated that the position 'applies equally to the Ukraine issue'.[205] China neither said the SMO was lawful nor did it provide assistance to Russia.

Nevertheless, it is also obvious that China shares stances with Russia on other issues because both states face hostility from some Western powers. For instance, in the 'Five Points', China argues that states should pursue a policy of 'common, comprehensive, cooperative and sustainable security', which is threatened by military alliances.[206] This statement has been made not only because China considers the Ukrainian crisis, including the SMO, largely attributable to NATO's expansion[207] – an idea shared by some Western observers[208] – but also because NATO, which identifies China as posing

[202] *Ibid.*
[203] Ministry of Foreign Affairs of the People's Republic of China, 'Wang Yi Expounds China's Five-Point Position on the Current Ukraine Issue', 26 February 2022, available at www.fmprc.gov.cn/eng/zxxx_662805/202202/t20220226_10645855.html.
[204] *Ibid.*
[205] *Ibid.*
[206] *Ibid.*
[207] *Ibid.*
[208] See, e.g., The Robert Schuman Centre of Advanced Studies, 'The Causes and Consequences of the Ukraine War: A Lecture by John J. Mearsheimer', 6 June 2022, available at www.youtube.com/watch?v=qciVozNtCDM. See also Mearsheimer, 'Why the Ukraine Crisis is the West's Fault' (n. 173).

systematic challenges to Euro-Atlantic security,[209] has encroached upon the Asia-Pacific region in recent years, thereby increasing security pressures on China. In short, given their common challenges and threats, it is unsurprising that China has deepened its comprehensive strategic partnership with Russia. However, China has not changed, and is not expected to substantially change, its long-standing foreign policy. The conception of common security and comprehensive security, under which China is always critical of military alliance, was not first stated in the 'Five Points'; it was expounded on as early as 20 years ago.[210]

This new constellation of power has brought the Security Council into a more troubled position. Consider the role of the Security Council in the Syrian and Ukrainian crisis as examples. Seventeen draft resolutions concerning the Syrian crisis were vetoed between 2011 and 2019.[211] By contrast, while the Security Council held many meetings on the Ukrainian crisis, only one draft resolution has been co-sponsored by 42 UN members between 2014 and 2021, and it was vetoed by Russia.[212] This indicates that the UN members have no expectation that the Security Council can make a difference in handling the Ukrainian crisis and thus they have no intention of proposing more draft resolutions for debate. As of August 2022, the Security Council had held more than 15 meetings discussing peace and security in Ukraine arising from Russia's SMO, but no other resolutions had been adopted other than one calling for an emergency special session of the General Assembly.[213]

Accordingly, actions outside the Security Council are expected to increase. Efforts aiming to end the Ukrainian crisis are undertaken outside the Security Council, such as the international sanctions on Russia imposed by individual

---

[209]   NATO 2022 Strategic Concept, 29 June 2022, available at www.nato.int/cps/en/natohq/topi cs_210907.htm, para. 14.

[210]   Ministry of Foreign Affairs of the People's Republic of China, 'China's Position Paper on the New Security Concept', 31 July 2002, available at www.fmprc.gov.cn/mfa_eng/wjb_663304/ zzjg_663340/gjs_665170/gjzzyhy_665174/2612_665212/2614_665216/200208/t20020806_598568 .html, Pt III.

[211]   Draft SC Res. S/2019/962 of 20 December 2019; Draft SC Res. S/2019/757 of 19 September 2019; Draft SC Res. S/2019/756 of 19 September 2019; Draft SC Res. S/2019/961 of 20 December 2019; Draft SC Res. S/2018/355 of 14 April 2018; Draft SC Res. S/2018/322 of 10 April 2018; Draft SC Res. S/2018/321 of 10 April 2018; Draft SC Res. S/2017/172 of 28 February 2017; Draft SC Res. S/2017/315 of 12 April; Draft SC Res. S/2016/1026 of 5 December 2016; Draft SC Res. S/2016/1026 of 5 December 2016; Draft SC Res. S/2016/846 of 8 October 2016; Draft SC Res. S/2016/847 of 8 October 2016; Draft SC Res. S/2014/348 of 22 May 2014; Draft SC Res. S/2012/538 of 19 July 2012; Draft SC Res. S/2012/77 of 4 February 2012; Draft SC Res. S/2011/612 of 4 October 2011.

[212]   Draft SC Res. S/2014/189 of 15 March 2014.

[213]   SC Res. 2623 of 27 February 2022, UN Doc. S/RES/2623(2022).

states and the European Union without the Council's approval. According to Van den Herik, in this volume, these unilateral sanctions 'should not be regarded as a challenge to the UN Security Council but rather as a correction in the event of inactivity'.[214] This position is arguably right in the unique instance of the SMO. On the one hand, Russia absolutely would not allow the Security Council to approve any actions that aim to end the SMO, which means that the Security Council can do nothing. On the other hand, while many states do not explicitly condemn the SMO, few, if any, states regard the SMO to be lawful. More importantly, the General Assembly adopted Resolution ES-11/1 identifying Russia's aggression against Ukraine. However, we should not be blind to the possibility that these sanctions may be abused. As Van den Herik notes, some legal regimes and mechanisms at the international and domestic levels are already in place to scrutinise the enforcement of the UN sanctions, even though they are not yet perfect.[215] Nevertheless, unilateral sanctions, as a general matter, are likely to be abused by the great powers.

D. *The Security Council for International Peace – or for Peace between Only the Great Powers?*

As noted in section I, Bosco thinks the Security Council has demonstrated that it is unable to effectively address threats to peace, and that the vision of maintaining international peace should therefore be abandoned and priority given to tactics that avoid military conflicts between the great powers. Bosco has observed that while, on several occasions, military conflicts occurred between the United States and the USSR, the two always managed to 'pull back in time', and that there have never been prolonged military clashes between permanent members of the Security Council.[216] Not only does Bosco's proposition run counter to the Security Council's primary responsibility for maintaining international peace but also it dismantles the very rationale for the founding of the United Nations, which aimed to save the world from 'the scourge of war'.[217] In fact, it is hard to say to what extent the Security Council matters in keeping peace between the great powers. A major reason behind the great powers' avoidance of sustained military conflict

---

[214] Van den Herik, 'A Reflection on Institutional Strength', Chapter 2 in this volume, section IV.A.
[215] *Ibid.*, section IV.B.
[216] Bosco, *Five to Rule Them All* (n. 20), 6.
[217] UN Charter, Preamble.

between them is that each of them has a powerful military and hence none can afford sustained or large-scale military conflict with another great power.

Nevertheless, Bosco's heretical argument is meaningful. It is indeed necessary to improve the functionality of the Security Council – especially by finding ways of reducing the negative impact of power politics among the great powers. All of the contributors to this volume seek to achieve this purpose from different perspectives.

IV. NOVEL THREATS AND THE RESPONSE OF THE SECURITY COUNCIL

From the perspective of the UN Charter and more importantly, in international relations when the UN Charter was initially drafted in the 1940s, 'threat to the peace' in Article 39 referred to military threats to international peace among states.[218] This fundamentally determined the Security Council's institutional structure and culture.

The world has changed significantly since the UN Charter was initially drafted – especially since the 1990s, which witnessed the end of Cold War and the acceleration of globalisation. In a globalised world, new risks and threats have emerged, and some of them are too grave to be effectively addressed by states individually. To address them effectively, states have needed to seek more involvement from international institutions, including the United Nations. As a result, it has been recognised that the very meaning of 'threat to the peace' should be updated. In its report *A More Secure World*, UN High-Level Panel on Threats, Challenges, and Change advised that the Security Council is fully empowered under Chapter VII to address 'the full range of security threats with which States are concerned'.[219] Indeed, 'threat to the peace' has been interpreted more broadly over time – but while the UN members generally support a more liberal interpretation of 'threat to the peace', disagreements remain. Even though threats such as HIV/AIDS, for example, may not be less dangerous than wars, whether they should be addressed as threats under the terms of Article 39 remains a contentious issue.

Many studies have been done to determine what constitutes a 'threat to the peace'.[220] Here, I examine how the Security Council addresses novel threats by focusing on public health, extremism, and cyber-attacks, elaborating on

---

[218] Kelsen, *The Law of the United Nations* (n. 78), 930.

[219] *A More Secure World* (n. 26), para. 198.

[220] See, e.g., Inger Österdahl, *Threat to the Peace: The Interpretation by the Security Council of Article 39 of the UN Charter* (Uppsala: Och Justus Forlag, 1998).

whether it is desirable for the Security Council to expand its authority as much as possible, what side-effects its activities aiming to protect the peace may have, and whether a purely legalist approach is feasible to address threats to the peace.

A. *International Public Health Crisis*

At time of writing, COVID-19 is one of the most significant new international threats international society has encountered. The UN Security Council was criticised for its silence in response to the threat – a silence that lasted several months after the outbreak of the pandemic.[221] From April 2020 to May 2021, the Security Council held 15 meetings discussing issues related to the virus, including the implications of the pandemic for sustaining peace, equitable access to vaccines, and the cessation of hostilities.[222] In Resolution 2532, adopted on 1 July 2020, the Security Council stated that 'the unprecedent extent of COVID-19 pandemic is likely to endanger the maintenance of international peace and security', and it thus demanded 'a general and immediate cessation of hostilities in all situations'. While, in that Resolution, the Security Council did not mention any particular provisions of the UN Charter, it decided to 'remain seized of the matter'.

COVID-19 is not the first public health issue to be brought before the Security Council. The Security Council debated the AIDS pandemic in Africa between 2000 to 2005. During that time, the United States observed that '[w]e tend to think of a threat to security in terms of war and peace. Yet no one can doubt that they havoc wreaked and the toll exacted by HIV/AIDS do threaten our security.'[223] In its view, AIDS was 'a global aggressor'.[224] Given that the United Nations was created to stop wars, the United States suggested that '[n]ow we must wage and win a great and peaceful war of our time – the war against AIDS',[225] asking, '[H]ow could it not be a threat to international peace and security?'[226] Clearly, in the United States' view, the grave impact of AIDS qualified it as a 'threat to peace'. However, the United States did not

[221] Security Council Report, 'International Peace and Security, and Pandemics: Security Council Precedents and Options', 5 April 2020, available at www.securitycouncilreport.org/whatsinblue/2020/04/international-peace-and-security-and-the-covid-19-pandemic-security-council-precedents-and-options.php.
[222] For a list, see Security Council Report, 'Health Crises', available at www.securitycouncilreport.org/health-crises/page/2.
[223] UN Doc. S/PV.4087, 10 January 2000, 2.
[224] *Ibid.*, 5.
[225] *Ibid.*, 7.
[226] UN Doc. S/PV.4227, 17 November 2000, 10.

suggest what the Security Council could do to combat the threat. By contrast, the other four permanent members of the Security Council held a different position.[227] China acknowledged that AIDS 'has not only constituted a major threat to human life and health, but seriously affected the economic development and social stability of the countries and regions concerned. Thus it has become one of the most important non-traditional security issues.'[228] However, China suggested that fighting the AIDS epidemic should be left to other 'relevant international bodies'.[229] This does not mean, however, that China thought a public health crisis such as AIDS irrelevant to international peace. China supported the Security Council in accordance with its mandate and devoted increased attention to the issue of peacekeepers and HIV/AIDS, as well as the impact of AIDS on peace and security.[230] The United Kingdom too argued that an effective response to AIDS 'needs the coordinating response of the United Nations bodies, including the Security Council'.[231] Russia thought AIDS, generally, was an issue for other UN organs – especially the General Assembly, the Economic and Social Council, and the Secretariat.[232] Similarly, France suggested that AIDS, as a whole, was an issue that fell outside the Security Council and landed with the Secretariat.[233] Ultimately, while it held many meetings, the Security Council did not adopt any resolutions on AIDS.

In short, some novel international issues are indeed relevant to international peace. Especially when they affect certain of its measures, the Security Council needs to consider taking action to prevent its mission from being disrupted by threats such as COVID-19, even if they may not constitute 'threats to peace' as such. The alternative, as illustrated shortly, is that such attempts may mean little and risk exacerbating disagreements between the UN members, while disrupting international efforts to address specific international matters. Based on her observations of the attitudes of some states – especially developing states – Van den Herik is also cautious about the consequences of treating matters such as public health as security issues within the reach of the Security Council.[234]

---

227   Tamsin Phillipa Paige, *Petulant and Contrary: Approaches by the Permanent Five Members of the UN Security Council to the Concept of 'Threat to the Peace' under Article 39 of the UN Charter* (Leiden: Brill Nijhoff, 2017), 164–6.
228   UN Doc. S/PV.5228, 18 July 2005, 14.
229   UN Doc. S/PV.4859, 17 November 2003, 16.
230   UN Doc. S/PV.5228, 18 July 2005, 14.
231   UN Doc. S/PV.4259, 19 January 2001, 20.
232   UN Doc. S/PV.4859, 17 November 2000, 13.
233   *Ibid.*, 17–18.
234   Van den Herik, 'A Reflection on Institutional Strength', Chapter 2 in this volume, section V.

Still, the possibility that threats such as COVID-19 will be identified as a 'threat to the peace' ought not to be totally precluded. As the debates on AIDS and COVID-19 in the Security Council suggest, there are several factors that the Security Council may consider when identifying a 'threat to the peace'. One is whether the relevant impact is on the same level as those that have already been identified as threats to the peace. A second is whether the Security Council can take meaningful measures. As noted above, although the United States argued that AIDS should be identified as a 'threat to the peace', it did not explain what the Security Council – and the United States itself – could do to combat it. If what the Security Council or the United Nations can do, or promise to do, is mere rhetoric, it is meaningless to identify a threat such as COVID-19 as a 'threat to the peace'. Arguably, doing so merely increases quarrels among the members of the Security Council. And given that the United States frequently advocates the securitising of matters such as public health, it is not unreasonable to suggest that the United States might leverage such action to pursue its own interests. A third factor of relevance is whether a threat is already addressed by other international institutions. In the case of COVID-19, for example, the World Health Organization (WHO) undoubtedly has the competence to address the pandemic and it, together with its members, has extended great efforts. As a consequence, the WHO's leadership in this field should be respected. If the Security Council were to intervene in fighting COVID-19 by identifying it as a 'threat to the peace', it could undermine the leadership of the WHO and disrupt international efforts to fight the virus.

B. *Extremism*

Since the 1990s, terrorism has emerged as a threat that often causes devastating casualties. As a result, the UN organs, in addition to individual states, have listed counter-terrorism as a major item on their agendas again and again. On 20 September 2006, the General Assembly approved the Global Counter-Terrorism Strategy, guiding the counter-terrorism efforts of states and the UN organs.[235] More importantly, the Security Council adopted successive resolutions identifying terrorism as a 'threat to the peace' and authorising or requiring measures aimed to tackle terrorism.[236] Over time, however, these

---

[235] GA Res. 60/288 of 20 September 2006, UN Doc. A/RES/60/288.
[236] See, e.g., SC Res. 1267 of 15 October 1999, UN Doc. S/RES/1267(1999); SC Res. 1269 of 19 October 1999, UN Doc. S/RES/1269(1999); SC Res. 1368 of 12 September 2001, UN Doc. S/RES/1368(2001); SC Res. 1373 of 28 September 2001, UN Doc. S/RES/1373(2001).

efforts were found to be insufficient. Many states came to recognise that the approach adopted in the 2006 Global Counter-Terrorism Strategy needed improving upon. In 2013, the General Assembly adopted Resolution 68/127, which was concerned with the broader issue of combating 'violence and violent extremism'.[237] That Resolution does not explicitly incorporate counter-extremism into the framework of counter-terrorism, but it foreshadows this trend. Resolution 2178, adopted by the Security Council in 2014, indicates the close linkage between terrorism and extremism. That Resolution takes note of 'terrorist acts including those motivated by intolerance or extremism', and it recognises that 'terrorism will not be defeated by military force, law enforcement measures, and intelligence operations alone', underlining 'the need to address the conditions conducive to the spread of terrorism'. It therefore calls for collective efforts, 'including preventing radicalization, recruitment and mobilization of individuals into terrorist groups and becoming foreign terrorist fighters'.[238]

From that time on, counter-extremism received more attention. As then UN Secretary-General Ban Ki-moon noted, traditional 'security-based' counter-terrorism measures came to be understood as insufficient in preventing the spread of violent extremism, which encompasses 'a wider category of manifestations'.[239] Ban Ki-moon also warned of the risk that 'a conflation of the two terms may lead to the justification of an overly broad application of counter-terrorism measures, including against forms of conduct that should not qualify as terrorist acts'.[240] In 2016, the General Assembly adopted Resolution 291. This Resolution acknowledged the difficulty of preventing the violent extremism conducive to terrorism.[241] Thus it proposed a new Global Counter-Terrorism Strategy, under which the United Nations and its members were urged to 'unite against violent extremism as and when conducive to terrorism, encourage the efforts of leaders to discuss within their communities the drivers of violent extremism conducive to terrorism and to evolve strategies to address them', as well as to 'take measures, pursuant to international law and while ensuring national ownership, to address all drivers of violent extremism conducive to terrorism, both internal and external, in a balanced manner'.[242] For this purpose, the UN members are expected to

---

[237]   GA Res. 68/127 of 13 February 2013, UN Doc. A/RES/68/127.
[238]   SC Res. 2178 of 24 September 2014, UN Doc. S/RES/2178(2014).
[239]   *Plan of Action to Prevent Violent Extremism*, Report of the Secretary-General, UN Doc. A/70/674, 24 December 2015, para. 4.
[240]   *Ibid.*
[241]   GA Res. 70/291 of 19 July 2016, UN Doc. A/RES/70/291, para. 40.
[242]   *Ibid.*, para. 38.

consider, 'in the national context', the implementation of recommendations suggested in the Plan of Action to Prevent Violent Extremism.[243] It should be stressed that none of these UN instruments define the meaning of extremism. Furthermore, they focus only on 'violent' extremism. However, extremism, in the previously adopted UN resolutions, was not confined to only its 'violent' type. Moreover, as Van den Herik observes in this volume, there is not yet a definition of 'violent extremism' either.[244] In a nutshell, neither the General Assembly nor the Security Council has developed any meaningful rules on counter-extremism. The ambiguities around extremism may therefore become a new source for division among the members of the Security Council.

On the one hand, counter-extremism again indicates the complexity of national circumstances in the context of international peace. The tension between the Security Council's authority to maintain the peace and the principle of non-intervention is expected to increase. On the other hand, as already noted, a state may decide the counter-extremism measure 'in the national context'. Based on the principle of non-intervention and the New Global Counter-Terrorism Strategy, a state may be encouraged to claim the legitimacy and legality of its actions to defend particular measures that aim to combat extremism. Furthermore, given that extremism refers not only to particular acts but also to a 'source' conducive to terrorism, which is clearly broader in terms of content and scope, those measures aimed at combating extremism are at a high risk of misuse or abuse. This is especially true of the international obligations entered into by a state. For example, human rights obligations are susceptible to violations. Such risks have been recognised. And while stating that counter-terrorism measures, the protection of human rights, fundamental freedoms, and the rule of law 'are not conflicting goals, but complementary and mutually reinforcing, and are an essential part of a successful effort to counter violent extremism', Resolution 68/217 requires a state to ensure that the relevant measure complies with its obligations under international law, as well as refugee and humanitarian law.[245] Yet the risk of the Security Council and the UN members unduly intervening in domestic affairs may increase. Several commentators have acknowledged the uncertainties in the New Global Counter-Terrorism Strategy.[246] Similarly, Van den

---

[243]   *Ibid.*, para. 40.
[244]   Van den Herik, 'A Reflection on Institutional Strength', Chapter 2 in this volume, section IV.
[245]   GA Res. 68/127 of 13 February 2013, UN Doc. A/RES/68/127, cons. 13.
[246]   David H. Ucko, 'Preventing Violent Extremism through the United Nations: The Rise and Fall of a Good Idea', *International Affairs* 94 (2018), 251–70. See also Naz Modirzadeh, 'If it's

Herik suggests that there is a risk of the 'securitisation of development and the politicisation of the humanitarian space'.[247]

From China's perspective, the United States, together with some other Western states, already seeks to intervene in Chinese domestic affairs by limiting China's efforts to fight terrorism and extremism in Xinjiang, an area inhabited by Chinese Uygur Muslims. According to China, people living in Xinjiang, including the Uygur, face grave terrorist threats and extremism.[248] Based on a preventive approach, it has taken a wide range of measures.[249] China claims that these measures aim to tackle terrorism and extremism, and to protect human rights in Xinjiang. Thus it claims that they do not violate but in fact protect human rights.[250] Several Western states hold a totally different view of these measures. They condemn China's government, arguing that, by enforcing the measures, commit gross violations of human rights against the Uygur[251] – some even alleging 'genocide'.[252] Several sanction laws have been adopted against China[253] and, in a closed-door consultation, several Western states raised the issue of China's counter-extremist measures before the Security Council in 2019.[254]

I do not want to debate here what has really happened in Xinjiang; instead, I would prefer to stress two normative issues. First, given the new UN Global Counter-Terrorism Strategy,[255] as well as the relevant Shanghai Cooperation Organization (SCO) conventions on counter-terrorism and extremism, China

Broke, Don't Make it Worse: A Critique of the UN Secretary-General's Plan of Action to Prevent Violent Extremism', *Lawfare*, 23 January 2016, available at www.lawfaremedia.org/article/if-its-broke-dont-make-it-worse-critique-un-secretary-generals-plan-action-prevent-violent-extremism.

[247] Van den Herik, 'A Reflection on Institutional Strength', Chapter 2 in this volume, section IV.

[248] The State Council Information Office of China, *The Fight against Terrorism and Extremism and Human Rights Protection in Xinjiang* [White Paper], March 2019, available at http://geneva.china-mission.gov.cn/eng/ztjs/aghj12wnew/Whitepaper/202110/t20211014_9587980.htm, March 2019, Preamble, Pts II and III.

[249] *Ibid.*, Pt V; Xinjiang Uygur Autonomous Region Regulation on De-radicalization, adopted 29 March 2017, chs III–V.

[250] State Council Information Office of China, *The Fight against Terrorism* (n. 248), Preamble.

[251] See, e.g., Joint Statement [of the Foreign Minister of Canada, Foreign Secretary of the United Kingdom, and United States Secretary of State] on Xinjiang, 22 March 2021, available at www.state.gov/joint-statement-on-xinjiang/.

[252] See, e.g., Michael R. Pompeo, 'Determination of the Secretary of State on Atrocities in Xinjiang', 19 January 2021, available at https://2017-2021.state.gov/determination-of-the-secretary-of-state-on-atrocities-in-xinjiang/index.html.

[253] See, e.g., the US Uyghur Human Rights Policy Act of 17 June 2020.

[254] The closed-door consultation is not documented. China was unhappy with how the consultation was leaked. See, e.g., Reuters, 'U.S., Germany Slam China at U.N. Security Council over Xinjiang: Diplomats', 3 July 2019, available at www.reuters.com/article/us-china-usa-rights/us-germany-slam-china-at-un-security-council-over-xinjiang-diplomats-idUSKCN1TX2YZ.

[255] See below, section V.D.4.

has a legal basis on which to consider, in its national context, measures to tackle extremism. Second, given that international laws setting standards on how to conduct counter-extremism are not yet well developed, those measures that are asserted to contain counter-extremism are at risk of being misused or abused, thereby leading to violations of human rights of particular populations.

C. *Cyber-Attacks*

Cyber-security is one of most prominent issues facing the Security Council in the 21st century and it is particularly challenging to the application of the UN Charter – especially of Article 51 on self-defence. From the perspective of the UN Secretary-General, cyber warfare has become a first-order threat to international peace, but the methods of cyber warfare are not yet fully understood.[256] As a peace and security issue, cyber-security has been hotly debated.[257] There have been numerous news reports of cyber-attacks, and some member states, such as the United States and China, accuse each other of initiating cyber-attacks.[258] In fact, several powerful countries have established cyber forces, for example the United States' Cyber Command, established in 2010. China, too, has included the topic of strengthening its capability in cyberspace in its military strategy.[259] In its view, some countries are 'strengthening a cyber deterrence strategy, aggravating an arms race in cyberspace, and bringing new challenges to global peace'.[260]

At the core of cyber-security concerns is the debate about whether cyber-attacks constitute an 'armed attack', as provided for in Article 51 UN Charter. By referring to the ICJ's decision in *The Legality of the Threat or Use of Nuclear Weapons*, in which the Court opined that the right of self-defence does not depend on the type of weapon used in an attack,[261] some commentators have

---

[256] Annex to the letter dated 30 April 2018 from the Permanent Representative of Finland to the United Nations addressed to the President of the Security Council, UN Doc. S/2018/404, 3 May 2018, 3.

[257] See, in particular, Michael N. Schmitt (ed.), *Tallinn Manual on the International Law Applicable to Cyber Warfare* (Cambridge: Cambridge University Press, 2013).

[258] Zhixiong Huang and Kubo Macák, 'Towards the International Rule of Law in Cyberspace: Contrasting Chinese and Western Approaches', *Chinese Journal of International Law* 16 (2017) 271–310 (272–3).

[259] Cyberspace Administration of China, 'International Strategy of Cooperation on Cyberspace', 1 March 2017, available at www.xinhuanet.com/english/china/2017-03/01/c_136094371.htm, sect. 3.1.

[260] Cyberspace Administration of China, 'National Cybersecurity Strategy', December 2016, available at www.cac.gov.cn/2016-12/27/c_1120195926, sect. I.2.

[261] ICJ, *The Legality of the Threat or Use of Nuclear Weapons*, advisory opinion of 8 July 1996, ICJ Reports 1996, 226, para. 39.

suggested that, despite their novelty and specific character, cyber-attacks could be identified as armed attacks and thus trigger the right of self-defence.[262]

The United States is a major advocate of the right to self-defence against cyber-attacks. It argues that, 'consistent with the United Nations Charter', states 'have an inherent right to self-defense that may be triggered by certain aggressive acts in cyberspace'.[263] The United States has worked with NATO partners to develop means and methods of collective self-defence in cyberspace.[264] By contrast, China's position appears a bit ambivalent. Illustrated below are some of the debates that have occurred within the UN Group of Governmental Experts (UNGGE) on information technology.

On the one hand, China opposes the United States' argument for directly referring to the right of self-defence towards cyber-attacks; on the other hand, it supports the application of the UN Charter in cyberspace. China especially highlights the principles of sovereignty and the peaceful settlement of disputes.[265] Clearly, there is some contradiction in China's policy, in that while China intentionally avoids directly referring to the right of self-defence, it does not openly preclude the application of Article 51 UN Charter in cyberspace. There might be two explanations why. First, China's cyber capability is perhaps not yet comparable with that of the United States and hence China may be afraid of potential cyber-attacks from the United States under the guise of self-defence. Second, open agreement on the application of Article 51 in cyberspace increases the risk that prominent cyber actors may abuse this provision. It remains to be seen how long China will maintain such ambiguous gestures, and how it will frame a clearer position on the relationship between the right of self-defence and cyber-attacks.

One interesting proposition was made on 24 October 2020, when several Chinese academic institutions and think tanks jointly issued the report, *Sovereignty in Cyberspace: Theory and Practice* (version 2.0).[266] The report suggests that sovereignty in cyberspace includes the rights of independence,

---

[262]   Schmitt, *Tallinn Manual* (n. 257), 54–68.
[263]   See, e.g., International Strategy for Cyberspace: Prosperity, Security, and Openness in a Networked World, 10 May 2011, available at https://obamawhitehouse.archives.gov/sites/d efault/files/rss_viewer/international_strategy_for_cyberspace.pdf.
[264]   *Ibid.*, 20.
[265]   Cyberspace Administration of China, 'International Strategy' (n. 259), sects 2.1 and 2.2.
[266]   Chinese Academy of Social Sciences, Tsinghua University, Fudan University, Nanjing University, University of International Business and Economics, and Cybersecurity Association of China, *Sovereignty in Cyberspace: Theory and Practice* (Version 2.0), 25 November 2020, available at www.wicinternet.org/2020-11/26/c_808744.htm.

equality, jurisdiction, and 'cyber-defence'.[267] The right of cyber-defence, according to the report, means that each state has the right to 'conduct capacity building on cyber security and adopt lawful and reasonable measures under the framework of the UN Charter to protect its legitimate rights and interests in cyberspace from external infringement'.[268] The report refers to Article 51 UN Charter, but it intentionally uses the term 'cyber-defence' instead of 'self-defence'. Arguably, the report is cautious in justifying the use of force to combat cyber-attacks. It seems that China's cyber authority, the Cyberspace Administration of China, is sympathetic with the report,[269] even though it does not yet explicitly endorse it. This includes the Chinese use of the term 'cyber-defence'.

In the General Assembly, cyber-security has been a hot topic in international peace. Adopted in 2011, Resolution 66/24 required that a group of government experts be established to study threats in the sphere of information security and possible measures to address them, which included 'norms, rules or principles of responsible behaviour of States'.[270] The UN Group of Governmental Experts on Developments in the Field of Information and Telecommunications (ITC) in the Context of International Security was duly appointed in 2012. The Group completed its first report in 2013, suggesting that international law – 'in particular, the UN Charter' – should be applicable in cyberspace, which is 'essential to maintaining peace and stability and promoting an open, secure, peaceful and accessible ITC environment'.[271] According to the Group's second report of 2015, states, in their use of ITC, 'must observe, among other principles of international law, state sovereignty, sovereign equality, the settlement of disputes by peaceful means and non-intervention in the internal affairs of other States'.[272] In addition, the Group suggested, given the unique attributes of ITC, 'new norms' could be developed.[273] Clearly, whether cyber-attacks can trigger the right of self-defence is a crucial issue in the Group's deliberations. Because of strong opposition from China and some other countries, however, the 2015 report merely 'noted' the inherent right of states to take measures consistent with international law and as

---

[267] *Ibid.*, sect. I.1.
[268] *Ibid.*, sect. I.1.4.
[269] The official website of the Cyberspace Administration of China publishes the report.
[270] GA Res. 66/24 of 13 December 2011, UN Doc. A/RES/66/24.
[271] Report of the Group of Governmental Experts on Developments in the Field of Information and Telecommunications in the Context of International Security, UN Doc. A/68/98, 24 June 2013 (hereinafter 2013 UNGGE Report), 8.
[272] Report of the Group of Governmental Experts on Developments in the Field of Information and Telecommunications in the Context of International Security, UN Doc. A/70/174, 22 July 2015 (hereinafter 2015 UNGGE Report), 12.
[273] 2013 UNGGE Report (n. 271), 8; 2015 UNGGE Report (n. 272).

recognised in the UN Charter.[274] It did not explicitly refer to the right of self-defence; rather, it suggested that 'further study on this matter' was needed.[275]

The United States' attempt to reach a consensus on the right of self-defence within the Group failed again at its 2017 meeting.[276] To make debates on cyber-security 'more democratic, inclusive and transparent', the General Assembly adopted – upon Russian initiative – Resolution 73/27 to establish an Open-Ended Working Group (OEWG).[277] In 2021, the duly convened OEWG submitted its first substantive report to the General Assembly.[278] While affirming international law – especially the UN Charter – to be applicable in maintaining peace and security, and promoting an open, secure, stable, accessible, and peaceful ITC,[279] the report said nothing about the application of Chapter VII. It instead urged states to seek the settlement of disputes with peaceful means.[280] It comes as no surprise that China was happy with this report.[281] The United States, which voted against Resolution 73/27, was frustrated. From its perspective, the OEWG, while identifying some state obligations, had failed to mention that states may respond to unlawful actions consistent with the right of self-defence.[282] The United States therefore labelled the report 'not perfect'.[283]

In contrast with the General Assembly, the Security Council remains inactive in this field, even though the Secretary-General urged it to find ways of dealing with cyber warfare as soon as possible.[284] In 2020, the Security Council held an

---

[274] 2015 UNGGE Report (n. 272), 12.

[275] *Ibid.*

[276] See Michele G. Markoff, 'Explanation of Position at the Conclusion of the 2016–2017 Group of Governmental Experts (GGE) on Developments in the Field of Information and Telecommunications in the Context of International Security', 23 June 2017, available at ht tps://2017-2021.state.gov/explanation-of-position-at-the-conclusion-of-the-2016-2017-un-group-of-governmental-experts-gge-on-developments-in-the-field-of-information-and-telecommuni cations-in-the-context-of-international-sec/.

[277] GA Res. 73/27 of 11 December 2018, UN Doc. A/RES/73/27.

[278] Final Substantive Report of the Open-Ended Working Group on Developments in the Field of Information and Telecommunications in the Context of International Security, UN Doc. A/AC. 290/2021/CRP.2, 10 March 2021.

[279] *Ibid.*, para. 34.

[280] *Ibid.*, para. 35.

[281] Open-Ended Working Group on Developments in the Field of Information and Telecommunications in the Context of International Security, Compendium of Statements in Explanation of Position on the Final Report, UN Doc. A/AC.290/2021/INF/2, 25 March 2021, 25.

[282] United States Comments on the Chair's Pre-Draft of the Report of the UN Open Ended Working Group (OEWG), available at https://front.un-arm.org/wp-content/uploads/2020/04/oewg-pre-draft-usg-comments-4-6-2020.pdf, 3.

[283] OEWG, Compendium of Statements (n. 281), 85.

[284] Annex to the letter dated 30 April 2018 from the Permanent Representative of Finland to the United Nations addressed to the President of the Security Council, UN Doc. S/2018/404, 3 May 2018, 3.

informal meeting concerning the protection of civilians and humanitarian efforts related to cyber-attacks on critical infrastructure during the COVID-19 pandemic.[285] This was, perhaps, the sole occasion on which the Security Council has addressed cyber-attacks, but the topic of the meeting had nothing to do with international peace. Van den Herik argues, in this volume, that the inaction of the Security Council on cyber-security can be attributed to the P5, who are the most prominent cyber actors.[286] This explanation is reasonable. As already noted, the P5 – or, at least, the United States and China – tend to consider Chapter VII applicable to cyber-attacks. Cyber-security, including cyber warfare, will therefore be tabled in the Security Council sooner or later.

Arising from technology, cyber-attacks represent a unique threat to peace. New technologies bring with them huge benefits, but they may cause tremendous threats to international peace. Compared with threats arising from other technologies, cyber-attacks reveal an unpredictable dimension of technology. If we say that nuclear weapons astonish people with their horribly destructive effects, we can say that cyber-attacks beset people with their high degree of uncertainty. It is often difficult to locate where cyber-attacks have been initiated, and by whom. Even worse, it is often hard to verify whether they have done damage.[287] There is an established presumption that any legal determination should be fact-based, but it seems that such presumption does not apply in the context of cyber-attacks. As a result, legal determination and action in the face of alleged cyber-attacks might not have a solid factual basis, and there is a high risk that their origin may be misidentified. In this unique context, in the absence of trust between the major cyber actors, including the United States and China, it is impossible to effectively address the issue of cyber-attacks inside or outside of the Security Council.

V. CHINA'S ASCENSION AND THE UN SECURITY COUNCIL

In the first thirty years since the People's Republic of China (PRC) – in accordance with General Assembly Resolution 2758, adopted in 1971[288] – began to sit on the Security Council, it has attracted little attention in this

[285] OCHA, 'Acting Assistant Secretary-General for Humanitarian Affairs, Ramesh Rajasingham's Opening Remarks on Contemporary Challenges for the Protection of Civilians and the Humanitarian Aspects Related to Cyber-Attacks at the Arria-Formula Meeting on Cyber-Attacks', 26 August 2020, available at https://reliefweb.int/report/world/acting-assistant-secretary-general-humanitarian-affairs-ramesh-rajasingham-opening.
[286] Van den Herik, 'A Reflection on Institutional Strength', Chapter 2 in this volume, section V.
[287] See, e.g., Reuters, 'Suspicions Cyber Sabotage behind Fire at Iran Nuclear Facility, but Israel Says It's "Not Necessarily" Involved', *ABC News*, 5 July 2020, available at www.abc.net.au/news/2020-07-06/iran-nuclear-site-fire-causes-significant-damage,-official-says/12424586.
[288] GA Res. 2758 (XXVI) of 25 October 1971, UN Doc. A/RES/2758(XXVI).

most powerful UN organ. China, again and again, has pronounced a firm defence of the UN Charter, condemning blatant violations by some Western powers. However, this highly rhetorical gesture has rarely been followed by strong actions. China did not veto resolutions that it did not like; it instead abstained or did not participate in voting. Furthermore, China did not propose any provocative initiatives. Thus China was not a 'trouble-maker', in the eyes of the Western powers. They were happy to find that China has gradually become internationally socialised since the 1980s and hence has been sympathetic with many of the initiatives they sponsored. By contrast, developing states, with whom China always highlighted its affinity, might have been a bit frustrated: what they got from China was often merely rhetorical blessing, rather than any firm action. Neither did the Security Council benefit much from China: in terms of budget and personnel, China made only small contributions to UN peacekeeping missions. More recently, however, many people have come to recognise a change in China's approach, in the shape of its increased commitment to international peace and its more aggressive behaviour in the Security Council.

Because China is already a key player on the Security Council, several concerns have been raised.

- Will China be prepared to commit more to international peace through the Security Council?
- Will China reshape the institutional culture and methodology of the workings of the Security Council, helping it to better perform its mission?
- Will China use the Security Council as an instrument to engage with the Western world?
- Does China seek to reframe or reverse the law of peace and war favoured by Western powers through the Security Council mechanism?
- Is China keen to pursue its own normative agenda?

The potential normative impact that a more powerful China will have on the international legal order has attracted much attention. Generally speaking, most Western commentators consider the normative impact from China negative.[289] Some exceptions exist, however. For example, Scott Kennedy has argued that, given the unfairness of the current international order, the concern should not be that China has disrupted or will be

---

[289] See, e.g., Katrin Kinzelbach, 'Will China's Rise Lead to a New Normative Order? An Analysis of China's Statements on Human Rights at the United Nations (2000–2010)', *Netherlands Quarterly of Human Rights* 30 (2012), 299–332.

a disruptor of the status quo, but that 'it won't be, that it is so wedded to the status quo that China will forestall important reforms that are desperately needed'.[290] Through an investigation of China's recent engagement with UN peacekeeping operations, Lisa MacLeod has suggested that, as China ascends, its own global outlook and national priorities will be of foremost importance. Western powers 'can no longer expect that China will refrain from demanding that Council resolutions reflect its causal and principled beliefs'.[291]

It has also been suggested that China has come to seek more delicate normative arguments to justify its Security Council votes. Courtney J. Fung observes that China – especially in addressing the Syrian crisis – has innovated the discourse by introducing regime change rhetoric to oppose interventions, which appears to have won international support.[292] Similarly, according to three other scholars, China's engagement with the Darfur crisis has indicated 'a new Chinese approach to conflict resolution is in the making'.[293] They found that, instead of embracing the Western conception of humanitarian intervention, China advocated a new rule of 'conditional intervention', whereby an intervention is undertaken by 'actors at three levels: the host country at the national level; a pertinent intergovernmental organisation at the regional level; and the UN at the global level'.[294] This 'is likely to set a precedent for future interventions'.[295] While Larissa van den Herik does not discuss the role of a more powerful China in the Security Council at length in her chapter in this volume, her outlook does not seem positive.[296]

As a Chinese lawyer, I would like to note two starting points that are helpful when conducting a proper evaluation of China's potential impact on the law

---

[290] Scott Kennedy, 'China in Global Governance: What Kind of Status Quo Power?', in Scott Kennedy and Shuaihua Cheng (eds), *From Rule Takers to Rule Makers: The Growing Role of Chinese in Global Governance* (Bloomington, IN, Geneva: Research Center for Chinese Politics & Business [Indiana University] and International Centre for Trade & Sustainment Development, 2012), 9–22 (11).

[291] Lisa MacLeod, 'China's Security Council Engagement: The Impact of Normative and Causal Beliefs', *Global Governance* 23 (2017), 383–401.

[292] Courtney J. Fung, 'Separating Intervention from Regime Change: China's Diplomatic Innovations at the UN Security Council Regarding the Syria Crisis', *The China Quarterly* 235 (2018), 693–712 (699, 702). See also Matthias Vanhullebusch, 'Regime Change, the Security Council and China', *Chinese Journal of International Law* 14 (2015), 665–707.

[293] Pak K. Lee, Gerald Chan, and Lai-Ha Chan, 'China in Darfur: Humanitarian Rule-Maker or Rule-Taker?', *Review of International Studies* 38 (2012), 423–44 (440). See also Andrew Garwood-Gowers, 'China's Responsible Protection Concept: Reinterpreting the Responsibility to Protect (R2P) and Military Intervention for Humanitarian Purposes', *Asian Journal of International Law* 6 (2016), 89–118.

[294] Lee et al. (eds), 'China in Darfur' (n. 293), 437.

[295] *Ibid.*, 437.

[296] Van den Herik, 'A Reflection on Institutional Strength', Chapter 2 in this volume, section I.

of peace and war through the Security Council. First, as illustrated in previous sections, we should bear in mind that the measures that the Security Council has adopted in the past decades – especially during the 'New World Order' period – are open to debate. Second, China needs to be accurately understood. In the absence of such understanding, we may misjudge how China behaves in the Security Council in the coming years. From my perspective, China's previous engagement with the Security Council, China's increased power in the world, Chinese foreign policies and international legal policies, and even Chinese philosophy are relevant to China's behaviour in the Security Council.

A. A General Observation

Socialist China's presence in the United Nations was cause for global concern from the very outset. Would it disrupt the Security Council by exercising the veto power in the same way the USSR did?[297] In the subsequent three decades or so, China demonstrated instead that it was a team player – a 'silent power'.[298]

Between 1971 and 1979, China cast 130 affirmative votes out of a possible 195, in comparison to 149, 166, 172, and 163 by the United States, the USSR, France, and the United Kingdom, respectively. China exercised the veto power only twice – far less than the 18, 7, 7, and 12 instances on which the United States, the USSR, France, and the United Kingdom, respectively, did so. By contrast, China abstained or did not participate in voting on 63 occasions, which was in sharp contrast with the 28, 22, 16, and 20 abstentions by the United States, the USSR, France, and the United Kingdom, respectively.[299]

Two major factors influenced China's voting pattern. First, Chinese diplomats were not well acquainted with the Security Council in their early years of membership. Qiao Guanhua, China's first ambassador to the United Nations, admitted: 'To tell the truth, we're quite unfamiliar with this institution. We need to honestly study and become familiar as soon as possible, so that China can carry out its duties as permanent member of the Security Council.'[300] Chairman Mao Zedong, in a meeting with Chinese diplomats on the eve of their departure to New York, required each to assume the attitudes of a 'student' and to avoid 'rushing into battle unprepared'.[301] As a consequence, Chinese

---

[297] Samuel S. Kim, *China, the United Nations, and World Order* (Princeton: Princeton University Press, 1979), 195.
[298] Wuthnow, *Chinese Diplomacy* (n. 152), 18.
[299] *Ibid.*, 16.
[300] *Ibid.*, 15.
[301] *Ibid.*

diplomats did not speak much in the Security Council. Second, as a socialist country, China distanced itself from the Western states. As a result, China's voting affinity with the United States during this period was only 46 per cent.[302] Nevertheless, it was observed that Chinese diplomats gave respect to other countries. They did not use provocative language nor did they sponsor any propaganda-induced proposals, like the USSR did. According to Samuel S. Kim, Chinese diplomats behaved 'more like a workhorse than a showhorse'.[303]

In the 1980s, China became more willing to involve itself in the workings of the Security Council. Out of a total 209, China cast 196 affirmative votes – second only to those of France (200) and more than those of the United States (162), the USSR (192), and the United Kingdom (189). All of China's votes from September 1983 on were affirmative. Specifically, China's abstentions or non-participation in voting dropped significantly to only 13 – less than those of the United States (27), the USSR (22), and the United Kingdom (14), and more only than those of France (5). China was the only permanent member of the Security Council that did not use the veto power throughout the 1980s. In addition, China's voting affinity with the United States grew, during this time, to 73 per cent.[304]

These developments were mainly induced by China's new foreign policy. In the late 1970s, China commenced its Reforming and Opening Up Policy, a key aim of which was to develop trading relations with and to attract investment from Western states. Thus it sought to improve relations with Western states both outside and inside the Security Council. Deng Xiaoping, the 'chief designer of the Reforming and Opening-up policy', set the tone for the Chinese foreign policy of 'keeping a low profile' in international relations. While, in the 1980s, some developing states expected China to act as 'a leader of the Third World', Deng clearly stated that China could not 'qualify as the leader in that we are not powerful enough to do that'.[305] According to Deng, China should insist on a fundamental national policy. It should not take on a leadership role – although this did not mean that China should do nothing to promote a fair international political and economic order.[306] In fact, given that Chinese diplomats became more familiar with the workings of the Security Council over time, China participated much more in voting and abstained much less frequently than before.

[302] *Ibid.*, 17.
[303] Kim, *China, the United Nations, and World Order* (n. 297), 196.
[304] Wuthnow, *Chinese Diplomacy* (n. 152), 19.
[305] Literature Office of the Central Committee of the CCP (ed.), *Selected Works of Deng Xiaoping*, vol. 3 (Beijing: People's Press, 1993), 363.
[306] *Ibid.*

During the 1990s, China's rate of affirmative voting was 93.1 per cent – the lowest among the P5, the rates of which were 98.9 per cent, 96.4 per cent, 99.7 per cent, and 100 per cent for the United States, the USSR/Russia, France, and the United Kingdom, respectively. China continued its highly self-constrained approach to the veto power and blocked only two resolutions.[307] Nevertheless, China's abstention pattern was noticeably revived in the 1990s: it abstained on 42 occasions – three times as many as it had done so in the 1980s.[308] It should be stressed that a large portion of these abstentions were cast on sanctions-related resolutions[309] – the most innovative practice of the Security Council in the 1990s. Western powers introduced new causes for triggering sanctions and included new contents in the sanctions, which had significant normative impacts.[310] China, like many other states, was concerned with whether those sanctions were consistent with the UN Charter – especially with Chapter VII.[311] While China was reluctant to offend the Western powers by exercising the veto power, it did not explicitly endorse the relevant sanctions. This explains why China, after casting abstention votes on the sanctions-related resolutions, often gave explanations for its voting.[312] In addition, China's voting affinity with the United States jumped up to 92.1 per cent from 73 per cent in the previous decade.[313]

Generally speaking, China sustained the same voting pattern in the first ten years of the 21st century. It cast 622 affirmative votes out of a total of 636, while exercising only the veto power twice. Importantly, China became more open to UN sanctions, leading to a considerable decrease in its abstentions.[314] Moreover, during this period, China's voting affinity with the United States rose to a new high of 95.3 per cent.[315]

Since the 2010s, however, China's behaviour in the Security Council has begun to make many Western states and observers unhappy. The most conspicuous change has been its increased use of the veto power. In the 2010s,

---

[307] Wuthnow, *Chinese Diplomacy* (n. 152), 21.

[308] *Ibid.*, 21, 19.

[309] *Ibid.*, 26. China abstained in 16 sanction-related votes in the 1990s, accounting for over a third of its total abstentions in this period.

[310] See generally Jeremy Matam Farral, *The United Nations Sanctions and the Rule of Law* (Cambridge: Cambridge University Press, 2007).

[311] See, e.g., UN Doc. S/PV.3238, 16 June 1993, 21. See also Richard Falk, 'The Haiti Intervention: A Dangerous World Order Precedent for the United Nations', *Harvard International Law Journal* 36 (1995), 341–58.

[312] China's UN mission issued remarks in 43 out 52 votes on sanctions: Wuthnow, *Chinese Diplomacy* (n. 152), 29.

[313] *Ibid.*, 20.

[314] China cast only 12 abstentions during this period – far less than those in the 1990s: *ibid.*, 29.

[315] *Ibid.*

China vetoed nine draft resolutions authorising sanctions and other coercive measures – far more than those in any previous period. Among those were eight vetoes cast on resolutions against Syria.[316] China's vetoes of resolutions relating to Syria enraged some Security Council members – especially those from the West. They blamed China, together with Russia, for the Security Council's repeated failure to address the humanitarian disaster in Syria. After Russia and China blocked Resolution 538,[317] for example, the UK representative condemned them: 'for the third time', they had blocked an attempt by the majority of the Security Council – supported by most states – to try a new approach, choosing instead 'to put their national interests ahead of the lives of millions of Syrians'.[318] He argued that the voting of Russia and China served to protect a brutal regime. The US representative expressed a similar position.[319] China firmly denied such accusations and affirmed that it upheld the UN Charter. Specifically, China emphasised that it had 'no self-interest' in addressing the Syrian crisis.[320] It argued further that the current situation in Syria was 'precisely the result of the wrongful conduct of some countries, and it is those countries that should reflect on their behaviour'.[321]

China has also significantly increased its financial and personnel contributions to the work of the Security Council. During 2010–12, China's contribution to UN peacekeeping operations amounted to 3.189 per cent of the total peacekeeping budget – far less than that of the United Kingdom (6.604 per cent) and France (6.623 per cent).[322] However, during 2019–21, China became the second largest contributor to the regular budget of UN peacekeeping operations, next to only the United States. During this period, the rate of assessment for China reached over 12 per cent – far more than the United Kingdom (4.567 per cent) and France (4.427 per cent).[323] In 2016, China established the China–UN Peace and Development Fund,

---

[316] Draft SC Res. S/2019/756 of 19 September 2019; Draft SC Res. S/2016/1026 of 5 December 2016; Draft SC Res. S/2019/961 of 20 December 2019; Draft SC Res. S/2017/172 of 28 February 2017; Draft SC Res. S/2016/1026 of 5 December 2016; Draft SC Res. S/2014/348 of 22 May 2014; Draft SC Res. S/2012/538 of 19 July 2012; Draft SC Res. S/2012/77 of 4 February 2012; Draft SC Res. S/2011/612 of 4 October 2011.

[317] Draft SC Res. S/2012/538 of 19 July 2012. Eleven Council members were in favour of that resolution, two (Pakistan and South Africa) abstained, and two (Russia and China) vetoed.

[318] UN Doc. S/PV.6810, 19 July 2012, 3.

[319] *Ibid.*, 10.

[320] *Ibid.*, 13.

[321] UN Doc. S/PV.8263, 19 September 2019, 9.

[322] *Implementation of General Assembly Resolutions 55/235 and 55/236*, Report of the Secretary-General, UN Doc. A/64/220/Add.1, 31 December 2009, Annex.

[323] *Implementation of General Assembly Resolutions 55/235 and 55/236*, Report of the Secretary-General, UN Doc. A/73/350/Add.1, 24 December 2018, Annex.

contributing US\$1 billion to it in the ten years that would follow. In 2015, China decided to join the UN Peacekeeping Capability Readiness System and, for this purpose, built a standby peacekeeping force of 8,000 troops. China was also the largest source country for peacekeeping forces among the P5. By December 2018, China had participated in 24 UN peacekeeping operations and dispatched more than 39,000 troops.[324]

B. *How the New Power Constellation Influences China's Behaviour in the Security Council*

As illustrated by section IV, great powers may adjust their policy of international peace in the Security Council in light of the power shift.

From the perspective of power politics – with special reference to the growing state power of China and the accelerating hostilities of some Western powers – Resolution 1973 against Libya perhaps represents a turning point in China's Security Council voting. The Resolution strengthened the sanctions that had previously been approved in Resolution 1970.[325] The new Resolution explicitly established a 'no-fly zone'.[326] It also allowed UN members to take 'all necessary measures' to protect civilians.[327] Conscious of the high levels of uncertainty implicit in that provision, several Security Council members, including China, Germany, Brazil, India, and Russia, abstained from voting on the Resolution.[328] According to China, they and several other countries had raised serious concerns, but 'unfortunately, many of those questions failed to be clarified or answered', and therefore China had 'serious difficulty with parts of the resolution'.[329] Notwithstanding this, given the grave circumstances in Libya and especially the supportive position of the Arab League on the 'no-fly zone' provision,[330] China cast its vote in abstention on Resolution 1973. Similarly, Germany 'decided not to support a military option, as foreseen in paragraphs 4 and 8 of the resolution', and therefore abstained from voting on the draft resolution.[331] Obviously, at least five Security Council members did not support the military attacks authorised under Resolution 1973.

---

[324] State Council Information Office of China, *China and the World in the New Era* [White Paper], September 2019, available at http://english.scio.gov.cn/2019-09/28/content_75252746.htm, sect. I.3.

[325] SC Res. 1970 of 26 February 2011, UN Doc. S/RES/1970(2011).

[326] *Ibid.*, paras 6–12.

[327] *Ibid.*, para. 4.

[328] UN Doc. S/PV.6498, 17 March 2011, 5, 6, 8.

[329] *Ibid.*, 10.

[330] *Ibid.*

[331] *Ibid.*, 5.

Two days after the adoption of Resolution 1973, however, a multi-state, NATO-led coalition launched airstrikes against Libya with the asserted aim of enforcing Resolution 1973. Given the provision for 'all necessary measures' in the Resolution, the military intervention was justified. During a Security Council meeting, China stated that the 'original intention' of Resolutions 1973 and 1970 'was to put an end to violence and to protect civilians', and it claimed that NATO had wilfully interpreted the two resolutions to justify its military actions.[332] Clearly, the literal provision of Resolution 1973 should prevail over the 'original intention', as understood by China, and hence Sun suggests that China's acquiescence to Resolution 1973 was 'a complete loss'.[333]

Arguably, China has learned two lessons from Resolution 1973. First, the Western great powers still paid little regard to its concerns and interests, even though China had never been more powerful. China had huge economic interests in Libya.[334] It was also reported that the Chinese government evacuated more than 30,000 Chinese citizens from Libya and that Chinese companies incurred more than US$20 billion in losses. Second, China learned not to leave any loopholes in the relevant Security Council resolutions that some Western powers could use to justify their interventions. In short, the enforcement of Resolution 1973 made China realise that it needed to take a tougher stance on the Security Council. China's experience concerning Libya had a direct impact on its behaviour regarding Syria.[335]

It may therefore come as no surprise that China has repeatedly exercised the veto power on draft resolutions relating to the situation in Syria, where Russia has strategic interests but China has no substantial interests. China maintains a high affinity for voting with Russia, with one exception when China cast an abstention.[336] China, together with Russia, exercised the veto power on another eight resolutions. In particular, China vetoed draft Resolutions 348[337] and 172,[338] on Syria – resolutions co-sponsored by 65 and 45 states,

---

[332] UN Doc. S/PV.6531, 10 May 2011, 20–1.
[333] Yun Sun, 'Syria: What China Has Learned from its Libya Experience', *Asia Pacific Bulletin*, 152, 27 February 2012, 2.
[334] Deborah Brautigam, 'China and Libya: What's the Real Story?', *The China*Africa Research Initiative Blog*, 4 March 2011, available at www.chinaafricarealstory.com/2011/03/china-and-libya-whats-real-story.html.
[335] Yun Sun, 'Syria' (n. 333), 1.
[336] Draft SC Res. S/2016/846 of 8 October 2016; Draft SC Res. S/2017/315 of 12 April 2017.
[337] Draft SC Res. S/2014/348 of 22 May 2014. The most important point in this draft is to refer the situation in Syria to the International Criminal Court.
[338] Draft SC Res. S/2017/172 of 27 February 2017. This draft, among others, decided to establish a Committee of the Security Council to undertake tasks in relation to chemical weapons in Syria.

respectively. This had never happened in the history of China's Security Council votes. While this radical turn reflected China's thinking that legal loopholes should no longer be left open to the Western powers, as had been the case with Resolution 1973 on Libya,[339] it is reasonable to assume that growing hostilities from the Western world prompted China and Russia to support each other both outside and inside of the Security Council.

As has been noted, in its disabling of the Security Council, some Western states considered China an accomplice of Russia in the Syrian crisis. We should bear in mind, however, that those resolutions would undoubtedly have been vetoed by Russia whether or not China supported them. Furthermore, there is another angle from which to view China's more aggressive behaviour on the Security Council. While, in the era of the 'New World Order', Western powers rarely found the initiatives they favoured challenged in the Security Council, some of them were legally controversial or did not work as expected in practice.[340] It is therefore not totally unsound to say that a more aggressive China might prevent the Security Council from being dominated by Western hegemony.

Additionally, a more powerful China might enable the Security Council in a unique way. Consider how China engaged in the Darfur crisis. In Resolution 1706, the Security Council 'invited' Sudan to give the United Nations consent to deploy a peacekeeping force[341] and China abstained in the voting. China supported the idea of a UN peacekeeping deployment, but the push for adoption of a Security Council resolution, in China's view, 'would not contribute to the smooth implementation of the resolution nor help to stop further deterioration of the situation in Darfur'.[342] After Sudan's government expressed opposition to the 'invitation' extended by Resolution 1706, the United States and several other Western states imposed economic sanctions on Sudan – sanctions that made no difference. Western powers then urged China – Sudan's largest economic partner – to encourage Sudan to comply with Resolution 1706. It was reported that, to persuade Sudan to accept the UN's peacekeeping mission, China threatened to remove its

---

[339] China stressed that it had 'no self-interest' in addressing the Syrian crisis, alleging that those accusations against China were 'completely mistaken and are based on ulterior motives': UN Doc. S/PV.6810, 19 July 2012, 14.

[340] An important case is SC Res. 1970 and SC Res. 1973 against Libya, adopted in 2011. The Foreign Affairs Committee of the UK House of Commons could not help but admit that the interventions based on the two resolutions largely failed in bringing peace and order to Libya: House of Commons Foreign Affairs Committee, 'Libya' (n. 105).

[341] SC Res. 1706 of 31 August 2006, UN Doc. S/RES/1706(2006).

[342] UN Doc. S/PV.5519, 31 August 2006, 5.

preferred trade status and to discourage Chinese companies from investing in Sudan.[343] Sudan accepted the peacekeeping deployment. Since China has maintained close economic relationships with other states who are plagued by national disorders, it may be better positioned than Western powers to enhance the measures adopted by the Security Council when relevant situations in these states are identified as threats to the peace. Indeed, Maluwa has suggested, in this volume, that China's economic and ideological affinity with many African states has been helpful to the maintenance of peace in Africa.[344] However, it remains to be seen to what extent that this unique leverage might be sacrificed to the growing hostilities between China and several Western powers.

C. *How Chinese International Legal Policies Influence China's Security Council Behaviour*

How China engages with the Security Council largely depends on Chinese international legal policies. Since I have examined in depth the evolution of Chinese international legal policies elsewhere,[345] here I will focus on how they influence China's behaviour in the Security Council setting.

1. Shouldering More International Responsibility

As China adopts the policies of a 'responsible' great power, it is willing to make more commitments to international peace. There is a growing expectation among states that China could and should shoulder more international responsibilities. Robert B. Zoellick, a former US trade representative, has urged China to behave as a 'responsible stakeholder' and to do more to sustain the international system's peaceful prosperity.[346]

China has already established its policy of 'responsible' power. In a 2011 White Paper on Chinese foreign policy, China stated that it was a 'responsible' state and would shoulder more international responsibility

---

[343] Chin-Hao Huang, 'U.S.–China Relations and Darfur', *Fordham International Law Journal* 31 (2007–8), 827–42 (837–8).

[344] Tiyanjana Maluwa, 'The UN Security Council: Between Centralism and Regionalism', Chapter 3 in this volume, section III.C.

[345] Cai, *The Rise of China and International Law* (n. 8), 41–100.

[346] Robert B. Zoellick, 'Whither China: From Membership to Responsibility?', 21 September 2005, available at https://2001-2009.state.gov/s/d/former/zoellick/rem/53682.htm.

because its capabilities allowed it to do so.[347] The concept of 'public goods' was officially introduced into Chinese foreign policy in the 2010s. President Xi Jinping has stated, in particular, that China is willing to provide more 'international public goods' to the international community.[348]

A turn towards the policies of a 'responsible' great power explains the significant growth of China's contributions to UN peacekeeping missions. More importantly, this shift induces China to refine its conception of sovereignty – a major factor influencing its behaviour on the Security Council. Given the constant suppression of Western powers since the 19th century, China is 'a most enthusiastic champion' of sovereignty.[349] As a result, Five Principles of Peaceful Coexistence[350] – the core element of which is sovereignty – have been firmly established as a cornerstone of Chinese diplomacy.[351] However, China's conception of sovereignty tends to be flexible. In 2014, on the 60th anniversary of the Five Principles, President Xi Jinping reaffirmed that the 'spirit of the Five Principles of Peaceful Coexistence, instead of being outdated, remains as relevant as ever; its significance, rather than diminishing, remains as important as ever; and its role, rather than being weakened, has continued to grow', and he asserted that the Five Principles are 'open and inclusive'.[352] Moreover, the Five Principles have evolved over time: in addition to 'peaceful coexistence', new elements of 'peaceful development', a 'harmonious world', and a 'community of shared future for mankind' are now

---

[347] State Council of the People's Republic of China, *China's Peaceful Development* [White Paper], 2011, available at http://english.www.gov.cn/archive/white_paper/2014/09/09/con tent_281474986284646.htm, Pt III.

[348] Xi Jinping, 'Having Full Confidence in China's Economic Development Prospects to Build a Better Asia-Pacific that Will Guide the World and Benefit all Parties and the Offspring', 7 October 2013, quoted in Embassy of The People's Republic of China in the Republic of Indonesia, 'Xi Jinping Attends APEC CEO Summit and Delivers Important Speech', 16 October 2013, available at http://id.china-embassy.gov.cn/eng/ztbd/001288pyb/201310/t201 31016_2345452.htm.

[349] Tieya Wang, 'International Law in China: Historical and Contemporary Perspectives', *Recueil des Cours* 221 (1990), 199–369 (288, 290, 297).

[350] The 'Five Principles' include: (a) mutual respect for each other's territorial integrity and sovereignty; (b) mutual non-aggression; (c) mutual non-interference in each other's internal affairs; (d) equality and mutual benefit; and (e) peaceful coexistence: Agreement between the Republic of India and the People's Republic of China on Trade and Intercourse between Tibet Region of China and India, 29 April 1954, Preamble.

[351] Constitution of the People's Republic of China, 1975, as amended in 2018, Preamble.

[352] President of the People's Republic of China Xi Jinping, 'Carry Forward the Five Principles of Peaceful Coexistence to Build a Better World through Win-Win Cooperation', Address at Meeting Marking the 60th Anniversary of the Initiation of the Five Principles of Peaceful Coexistence, 28 June 2014, available at www.fmprc.gov.cn/mfa_eng/wjdt_665385/zyj h_665391/201407/t20140701_678184.html.

included.[353] Such illustrations are general, but they are meaningful in that they represent China's new conception of the world order, which may influence China's diplomacy to a greater or lesser extent. China should not be expected to embrace the same liberal conception of sovereignty that Western powers cling to. In fact, sovereignty remains a basic legal shield in China's struggles with Western powers on issues such as Tibet, Xingjiang, Taiwan, and Hong Kong.[354] Nevertheless, China has softened its conception of sovereignty on many matters related to international peace, as evidenced by its stance on the Responsibility to Protect (R2P), as will be discussed later in the chapter.[355]

2. Seeking a Larger Role in International Law-Making

China's new strategy of international normativity makes it more cautious of initiatives proposed in the Security Council that could have normative impacts in the future. For a long period, China's priority was to convince international society that it was a 'good citizen' in terms of compliance with international law.[356] Thus China has long been a 'taker' of international law. More recently, China has recognised that competition in international rule-making is fundamental to international relations. China has realised that unless it increases its role in international law-making, what it will be able to do, at best, is either comply with or violate international laws.[357] Thus China has begun to change its traditional strategy of normativity by shifting away from international law compliance towards international law-making.

This new strategy was evident in the Decision on Several Major Issues Concerning Comprehensively Enhancing Governance to Rule the State by

---

[353] Vice Minister of Foreign Affairs of the People's Republic of China Liu Zhengming, 'Following the Five Principles of Peaceful Coexistence and Jointly Building a Community of Common Destiny', Speech at the International Colloquium Commemorating the 60th Anniversary of the Five Principles of Peaceful Coexistence, 27 May 2014, available at www.fmprc.gov.cn/mfa_eng/wjdt_665385/zyjh_665391/201405/t20140528_678165.html.

[354] Phil C. W. Chan, *China: State Sovereignty and International Legal Order* (Leiden: Brill, 2015), 179–233; Randall Peerenboom, 'China Stands up: 100 Years of Humiliation, Sovereignty Concern, and Resistance to Foreign Pressure on PRC Courts', *Emory International Law Review* 24 (2010), 657–68.

[355] See below, section V.D.2.

[356] See, in detail, Cai, *The Rise of China and International Law* (n. 8), 102–12.

[357] Wang Yang, 'To Construct Open-Oriented New Economic Regime', *People's Daily*, 22 November 2013. See also Joint Statement by the Foreign Ministers of China and Russia on Certain Aspects of Global Governance in Modern Conditions, 23 March 2021.

Law, approved by the Chinese Communist Party (CCP) in 2014.[358] The decision outlined China's legal reform under Xi Jinping's presidency. It stated that China would 'actively participate in international rule-making ... [to] increase China's power of discourse and influence in international legal affairs'.[359] For China, its growing role in international law-making not only promotes and protects its state interests but also enhances the fairness of the international order. President Xi noted that, 'with the increase in global challenges and constant changes in the international balance of power, there is a growing demand for strengthening global governance and transforming the global governance system'.[360] He therefore urged China to 'seize the opportunity and take appropriate actions'.[361] He further required that China improve its ability to 'make rules and set agendas' in global governance.[362] As a result, China has recently been active in advocating 'Chinese wisdom' or 'Chinese proposals' on a range of international affairs, such as reform of the World Trade Organization (WTO).[363]

Such new strategy regarding international normativity may also influence China's behaviour on the Security Council. As will be highlighted later in the chapter,[364] China is alert to the emergence of any rule pertaining to regime change created by Security Council practice. This is perhaps a major consideration as China exercises, again and again, the veto power over the draft resolutions against Syria in the Security Council.

3. Maintaining the Friendly Policy towards Developing Countries

China's affinity with the developing world remains highly relevant to China's behaviour in the Security Council. China has sustained a foreign policy that it believes is beneficial to the developing world. As early as the 1970s, Deng Xiaoping stated before the UN General Assembly that China 'shall always belong to the Third World and shall never seek hegemony'.[365] Three decades

---

[358] See Central Committee of the Chinese Communist Party (CCP), Decision on Several Major Issues concerning Comprehensively Advancing Governance According to Law, 23 October 2014, available at www.gov.cn/zhengce/2014-10/28/content_2771946.htm.

[359] *Ibid.*, sect. VII.7.

[360] Xi Jinping, *The Governance of China (II)* (Beijing: Foreign Language Press, 2017), 487.

[361] *Ibid.*

[362] *Ibid.*, 490; Cai, *The Rise of China and International Law* (n. 8), 113–51.

[363] See World Trade Organization (WTO), China's Proposal on WTO Reform, Doc. WT/GC/W/773, 13 May 2019.

[364] See below, section V.D.3.

[365] Literature Office of the Central Committee of the CCP (ed.), *Selected Works of Deng Xiaoping*, vol. 2 (Beijing: People's Press, 2nd edn, 1994), 112.

later, President Xi reaffirmed that China 'will always belong to the developing countries'.[366] On numerous occasions, China has explained its position to the Security Council by referring to the situations and concerns of developing states.

China's emphasis of its affinity with developing states may be understood from different angles. Its friendly policy toward developing states – the majority among UN members – helps to make the Security Council more attentive to their situations and concerns. This explains why China always suggests that the Security Council should be highly constrained in approving sanctions, most of which target developing states. This is also demonstrated by Maluwa's examination of China's engagement with African countries in this volume.[367] There may be another explanation, however – namely, that its affinity with developing states may merely be a pretext for China's struggles with the Western powers.

4. Upholding the Universal International Legal Order

China insists on the universality of international law centred and based on the UN Charter. China has always stated that the authority of the UN Charter – and especially the authority of the Security Council in pursuit of international peace – should be maintained. It further disfavours broad readings of those UN Charter provisions that not only expand the United Nations' mission but also, and more importantly, allow for more interventive actions by the UN members, potentially damaging the authority of the United Nations and the universality of international law. This legal policy has seen growing tensions in the 'rules-based international order'(RBIO), which the Western powers have zealously advocated in recent years.[368]

It is generally acknowledged that the RBIO is poorly defined.[369] Van den Herik argues, in this volume. that the RBIO risks compromising the universality

---

[366] Xi Jinping, *The Governance of China (II)* (n. 360), 572. See also Information Office of the State Council (China), *China's Peaceful Development* (n. 347), Pt III.

[367] Maluwa, 'Between Centralism and Regionalism', Chapter 3 in this volume, section III.

[368] See, e.g., Leader's Declaration, G7 Summit, 7–8 June 2015, available at https://sustainable development.un.org/content/documents/7320LEADERS%20STATEMENT_FINAL_CLE AN.pdf, 4, 7; US Department of State, 'Secretary Antony J. Blinken Virtual Remarks at the UN Security Council Open Debate on Multilateralism', 7 May 2021, available at www.state .gov/secretary-antony-j-blinken-virtual-remarks-at-the-un-security-council-open-debate-on-m ultilateralism/.

[369] Shirley Scott, 'In Defense of the International Law-Based Order', *Australian Outlook*, 7 June 2018, available at www.internationalaffairs.org.au/australianoutlook/in-defense-of-th e-international-law-based-order/; Stefan Talmon, 'Rules-Based Order v. International Law?',

of international law.[370] Indeed, both Russia and China are critical of the RBIO. Russian Foreign Minister Lavrov has alleged that some Western powers, by advocating for the RBIO, sought to displace the multilateral legal framework, including the UN Charter, to make room for rules they favour.[371] China holds a similar position. On 26 July 2021, during talks with US Deputy Secretary of State Wendy Sherman, China's Vice Foreign Minister Xie Feng argued that the RBIO was an effort by the United States and a few other Western countries to frame their own rules as international rules and to impose them on other countries. If this is the case, the United States would thereby damage universally recognised international law and order, and it would damage the international system that it helped to build.[372] As a response, China explicitly proposed a conception of 'international law-based international order' (ILBIO). President Xi Jinping, in the general debate of the 76th session of the UN General Assembly in 2021, asserted: 'There is only one international order, i.e. the international order under-pinned by international law. And there is only one set of rules, i.e. the basic norms governing international relations underpinned by the pur-poses and principles of the UN Charter.'[373] The ILBIO was explicitly included in China's Countering Foreign Sanctions, adopted in 2021.[374]

Perhaps the ILBIO vs the RBIO will become a new source of struggle between China and the Western powers, both inside and outside of the Security Council.

D. *China's Normative Role in the Security Council*

Western states and observers have been concerned about the potential norma-tive impact a more powerful and aggressive China may bring to the workings

---

GPIL Blog, 20 January 2019, available at https://gpil.jura.uni-bonn.de/2019/01/rules-based-or der-v-international-law/.

[370] Van den Herik, 'A Reflection on Institutional Strength', Chapter 2 in this volume.

[371] Sergei V. Lavrov, 'The World at a Crossroads and a System of International Relations for the Future', *Russia in Global Affairs* 17 (2019), 8–18 (11–12).

[372] Xie Feng, 'The U.S. Side's So-Called "Rules-Based International Order" is Designed to Benefit Itself at Others' Expense, Hold Other Countries Back and Introduce "the Law of the Jungle"', 27 July 2021, available at www.fmprc.gov.cn/mfa_eng/gjhdq_665435/3376_665 447/3432_664920/3435_664926/202107/t20210726_9169451.htm.

[373] Xi Jinping, 'Bolstering Confidence and Jointly Overcoming Difficulties: To Build a Better World', General Debate of the 76th Session of the United Nations General Assembly, 21 September 2021, available at www.fmprc.gov.cn/mfa_eng/wjdt_665385/zyjh_665391/20210 9/t20210922_9580293.html.

[374] Art. 2 China's Countering Foreign Sanctions (2021), which provides that China maintains 'the international order that is based on international law with the United Nations as its core'.

of the Security Council. Generally speaking, they consider China's normative role to be negative. However, such one-sided thinking is not
helpful in accurately demonstrating what role China plays in the
Security Council and in the maintenance of international peace. As
a matter of fact, China's normative role in the Security Council has
diverse dimensions: as norm-defender, as norm-taker, as norm 'antipreneur', and as norm entrepreneur.

1. China as Norm-Defender

China has proclaimed itself a 'staunch defender' of the international order
centred on the UN Charter.[375] It has stated that the purposes and principles
enshrined in that instrument – especially those of sovereign equality, non-
interference in internal affairs, and the peaceful resolution of disputes – should
always be upheld.[376] For China, these purposes and principles constitute 'the
foundation stones upon which modern international law and conduct of international relations'.[377] Thus China often insists that these purposes and principles
be included in relevant Security Council resolutions. For example, during the
process of drafting Resolution 1244 against the Federal Republic of Yugoslavia
(FRY), China proposed the addition of a preambular paragraph, 'bearing in
mind the purposes and principles of the Charter of the United Nations, and the
primary responsibility of the Security Council for the maintenance of international peace and security'. This proposed amendment was accepted. By
proposing this amendment, China intended to emphasise respect for the sovereignty and territorial integrity of FRY, and to oppose the use of force.[378]

For China, defending an international order centred on the UN Charter
demands its opposition of the broad interpretations of the UN Chapter that
some Western powers favour. How to interpret Article 51 is worth special
attention. In 2002, the United States announced a strategy of 'preemptive

---

[375] Yi Wang, 'China, a Staunch Defender and Builder of International Rule of Law', *Chinese Journal of International Law* 13 (2014), 635–8.
[376] See, e.g., China's Position Paper on the UN Reform (2005), Preamble, available at www.ch ina.org.cn/english/government/131308.htm; The State Council Information Office of China, 'China and the World in the New Era', September 2019, available at www.scio.gov.cn/zfbps/ 32832/Document/1665443/1665443.htm, sect. III.5.
[377] Wang, 'China, a Staunch Defender' (n. 375), 637.
[378] See ICJ, *Accordance with International Law of the Unilateral Declaration of Independence in Respect of Kosovo*, Advisory Opinion of 22 July 2010, oral statements, verbatim record 2009/29, 30.

self-defense',[379] which would relax the threshold triggering Article 51.[380] China opposes such a trend, stating at the time:

> We are of the view that Article 51 of the Charter should neither be amended nor reinterpreted. The Charter lays down explicit provisions on the use of force, i.e., use of force shall not be resorted to without the authorization of the Security Council with the exception of self-defense under armed attack. Whether an urgent threat exists should be determined and handled with prudence by the Security Council in accordance with Chapter 7 of the Charter and in light of the specific situation.[381]

It might be suspected that, in light of new threats to the peace, China's self-proclaimed role as norm-defender does not enable but rather disables the Security Council in the maintenance of international peace. It is especially likely that China, by 'defending' the UN Charter, instrumentalises the Security Council in engaging with the new distribution of power. However, we should remember that the majority of UN members are less powerful states whose sovereignty – as history shows – is particularly susceptible to infringement by the great powers and who are unable to hold the great powers accountable for wrongdoing. Then UN Secretary-General Kofi Annan, while arguing for humanitarian interventions, admitted that the principles of sovereignty and non-interference could 'offer vital protection to small and weak states'.[382] During debates on draft Resolution 612 against Syria, China also stated that the principle of non-interference in the internal affairs of states 'has a bearing upon the security and survival of developing countries, in particular small and medium sized countries'.[383]

2. China as Norm-Taker

China has long been an international norm-taker and it is rarely alone in advocating new international norms. From another angle, it can be said that China continues to be internationally socialised to embrace international law. In this regard, China's attitude towards the R2P – a variant of humanitarian intervention that China has always firmly opposed – is telling as an illustration of how China 'takes' new norms mainly advocated by the Western states.

---

[379] See Christine Gray, 'The US National Security Strategy and the New Bush Doctrine of Preemptive Self-Defense', *Chinese Journal of International Law* 1 (2002), 437–47.

[380] Tom Ruys, *'Armed Attack' and Article 51 of the UN Charter: Evolution in Customary Law and Practice* (Cambridge: Cambridge University Press, 2010), 305–41.

[381] China's Position Paper (n. 376), sect. II.7.

[382] See UN Doc. A/54/2000, 27 March 2000, para. 217.

[383] UN Doc. S/PV.6627, 4 October 2011, 5.

There have long been disputes between states over issues such as the legality, legitimacy, and consequences of humanitarian interventions.[384] For many states – especially less powerful ones – humanitarian intervention contravenes the principles of non-intervention, the peaceful settlement of international disputes, and the prohibition of the threat or use of force. And, in practice, most humanitarian interventions are initiated by the powerful states against the less powerful. China, like many other developing countries, therefore firmly opposes humanitarian intervention.[385]

In the 1990s, genocides and other gross and systematic violations of human rights committed in Rwanda and the former Yugoslavia changed many states' attitudes. While acknowledging that humanitarian intervention was 'a sensitive issue, fraught with political difficulty and not susceptible to easy answers',[386] then UN Secretary-General Kofi Annan proposed that:

> [S]urely no legal principle – not even sovereignty – can ever shield crimes against humanity. Where such crimes occur and peaceful attempts to halt them have been exhausted, the Security Council has a moral duty to act on behalf of the international community ... Armed intervention must always remain the option of last resort, but in the face of mass murder it is an option that cannot be relinquished'.[387]

To 'build a broader understanding of the problem of reconciling intervention for human protection purpose and sovereignty',[388] the International Commission on Intervention and State Sovereignty (ICISS) introduced the concept of R2P. As the ICISS suggested, in cases in which the Security Council fails to act in a timely or effective manner, regional organisations should have the power to initiate the R2P, including the use of force.[389] The R2P was included in the 2005 World Summit Outcome, but with several limitations. Importantly, and in deviation from the ICISS report, the authorisation of military action was reserved for the Security Council.[390] Although the Security Council has referred to the R2P in only a few resolutions,[391] it is important that it has embraced the R2P.

---

[384] See generally J. L. Holzgrefe and Robert O. Keohane (eds), *Humanitarian Intervention: Ethnic, Legal and Political Dilemmas* (Cambridge: Cambridge University Press, 2003).

[385] See UN Doc. A/63/PV.98, 24 July 2009, 23.

[386] See UN Doc. A/54/2000, 27 March 2000, paras 217, 219.

[387] *Ibid.*, para. 219.

[388] ICISS, *Responsibility to Protect* (Ottawa: International Development Research Centre, 2001), 2.

[389] *Ibid.*, 53–5.

[390] GA Res. 60/1 of 24 October 2005, UN Doc. A/RES/60/1, paras 138–9.

[391] See, e.g., SC Res. 1674 of 28 April 2006, UN Doc. S/RES/1674(2006); SC Res. 1706 of 31 August 2006, UN Doc. S/RES/1706(2006).

China's attitude to the R2P may surprise many people. Several months ahead of the 2005 World Summit, in a position paper on UN reform, China expressed its support for the R2P:

> Each state shoulders the primary responsibility to protect its own population . . . No reckless intervention should be allowed. When a massive humanitarian crisis occurs, it is the legitimate concern of the international community to ease and defuse the crisis. Any response to such a crisis should strictly conform to the UN Charter and the opinions of the country and the regional organization concerned should be respected. It falls on the Security Council to make the decision in the frame of UN in light of specific circumstances which should lead to a peaceful solution as far as possible. Wherever it involves enforcement actions, there should be more prudence in the consideration of each case.[392]

According to the position paper, R2P action should be authorised by the Security Council. China did not, however, impose on the R2P the same limitations as the 2005 Outcome does but broadly refers to the 'humanitarian crisis', as in the R2P report.

China later seems to have considered that its position paper went too far: during the 2009 debates on the first General Assembly Resolution on the R2P, China stated that the R2P remained 'a concept' and was not yet 'a norm of international law',[393] and argued that circumstances triggering the R2P should be limited to those provided for in the 2005 Outcome document.[394] In addition, China stressed that the implementation of the R2P should not contravene the principles of state sovereignty and non-intervention in the internal affairs of states, that the R2P should not 'becom[e] a kind of humanitarian intervention', and, in particular, that 'no states must be allowed to unilaterally implement R2P'.[395] In other words, what China supports are R2P actions approved by the Security Council. As Maluwa observes in his chapter in this volume, Brazil, Russia, India, and South Africa – the other four so-called BRICS countries – shared China's position.[396] Furthermore, in China's view, it seems that if the Security Council can be secured as the sole competent institution to approve R2P actions, it is not necessary to seek an alternative. This might explain, as Maluwa observes, why China neither joined the debates on Responsibility while Protecting (RwP)[397] nor gave any

---

[392] China's Position Paper (n. 376), sect. III.1.
[393] *Ibid.*, 24.
[394] *Ibid.*, 23.
[395] *Ibid.*, 23.
[396] Maluwa, 'Between Centralism and Regionalism', Chapter 3 in this volume, section III.B.3.
[397] *Ibid.*

official response to the concept of 'Responsible Protection' that was proposed by an official Chinese think tank.[398]

China's voting on humanitarian crisis situations in the Security Council remains mixed. It has vetoed those initiatives with the stated goal of ending humanitarian crises in states such as Zimbabwe[399] and Syria,[400] but it did vote for those measures against states such as the Sudan. Its voting was clearly based on the R2P.[401] Maluwa notes that China did not veto Resolution 1973, which surprised many observers.[402] This indicates that while China still insists on the principles of non-intervention and the peaceful settlement of international disputes, it has been more open to coercive UN enforcement.

Three major reasons explain China's embrace – albeit reluctant – of the R2P. First, China, as a permanent member of the Security Council, promised and was urged to shoulder more international responsibilities, including to prevent and stop humanitarian crises. Second, as China has become more powerful, it seeks to protect its global interests around the world – especially those in fragile countries. Third, the R2P allows China to give consent to UN actions based on humanitarian considerations without fundamentally compromising its long-standing policies on humanitarian intervention.

3. China as Norm 'Antipreneur'

As the evolution of the international legal order indicates, there is a persistent phenomenon that some states advocate new norms while others seek to resist them. Alan Blomfield and Shirley V. Scott call these latter states 'norm antipreneurs'.[403] This phenomenon is also visible in the Security Council. The 2003 Iraq War and the 2011 Libyan War inspired vocal controversy over whether regime change had emerged as a new international norm; China,

---

[398]   *Ibid.*

[399]   Neil MacFarquhar, '2 Vetoes Quash U.N. Sanctions on Zimbabwe', *The New York Times*, 12 July 2008, available at www.nytimes.com/2008/07/12/world/africa/12zimbabwe.html.

[400]   UN Department of Public Information, 'Security Council Fails to Adopt Draft Resolution Condemning Syria's Crackdown on Anti-Government Protestors, Owing to Veto by Russian Federation, China', 4 October 2011, available at www.un.org/press/en/2011/sc10403.doc.htm.

[401]   See, e.g., SC Res. 1713 of 29 September 2006, UN Doc. S/RES/1713(2006); SC Res. 1755 of 30 April 2007, UN Doc. S/RES/1755(2007); SC Res. 1769 of 31 July 2007, UN Doc. S/RES/1769(2007).

[402]   Maluwa, 'Between Centralism and Regionalism', Chapter 3 in this volume, section III.B.3.

[403]   See generally Alan Blomfield and Shirley V. Scott (eds), *Norm Antipreneurs and the Politics of Resistance to Global Normative Challenge* (London: Routledge, 2017), 1.

together with many other states, resisted the crystallisation of regime change as a new international legal norm.[404]

It has been observed that some measures urged or ordered by the Council have involved political reconstruction in targeted states that may be necessary or helpful in addressing threats to the peace. Nevertheless, the role the Security Council plays in regime change has caused grave concerns among UN members. According to Dire Tladi, two resolutions – namely, Resolution 1973 against Libya and Resolution 1975 against Côte d'Ivoire – are of particular legal significance. These two resolutions largely contributed to the collapse of the Gaddafi and Gbagbo regimes. Tladi suggested that while future development remains to be seen, the two resolutions appeared to authorise regime change through the use of force and for the purpose of protecting civilians.[405]

Given what happened to Côte d'Ivoire and especially Libya, regime change was in the spotlight during debates on several resolutions against Syria. In the debates on draft Resolution 612,[406] which Russia and China vetoed, and on which Brazil, India, Lebanon, and South Africa abstained from voting, Russia stated that it would not 'get involved with legitimising previously adopted unilateral sanctions or attempts at violent regime change'.[407] India argued that the international community should not complicate the situation with 'threats of sanctions, regime change, etc.'.[408] South Africa warned that the 'draft resolution [should] not be part of a hidden agenda aimed at once again instituting regime change'.[409] The four co-sponsors of draft Resolution 612 – namely, France, Germany, Portugal, and the United Kingdom – did not respond directly to the issue of regime change.

---

[404] John Borneman, 'Responsibility after Military Intervention: What is Regime Change?', *Political and Legal Anthropology Review* 26 (2003), 29–42; W. Michael Reisman, 'Why Regime Change is (Almost Always) a Bad Idea', *American Journal of International Law Proceedings* 98 (2004), 289–304; Kevin P. DeMello, 'A Method of Direct Action: The Humanitarian Justification for Regime Change in Iraq', *Suffolk University Law Review* 38 (2005), 789–810; Dire Tladi, 'Security Council, the Use of Force and Regime Change: Libya and Côte d'Ivoire', *South African Yearbook of International Law* 37 (2012), 22–45; Mehrdad Payandeh, 'The United Nations, Military Intervention, and Regime Change in Libya', *Virginia Journal of International Law* 52 (2012), 355–404; Jure Vidmar, 'Democracy and Regime Change in the Post-Cold War International Law', *New Zealand Journal of Public and International Law* 11 (2013), 349–80; Nesam McMillan and David Mickler, 'From Sudan to Syria: Locating Regime Change in R2P and the ICC', *Global Responsibility to Protect* 5 (2013), 283–316; Yasmine Nahlawi, 'The Legality of NATO's Pursuit of Regime Change in Libya', *Journal of the Use of Force and International Law* 5 (2018), 295–323.
[405] Tladi, 'Security Council, the Use of Force and Regime Change' (n. 404), 45.
[406] Draft SC Res. S/2011/62 of 4 October 2011.
[407] UN Doc. S/PV.6627, 4 October 2011, 5.
[408] *Ibid.*, 6.
[409] *Ibid.*, 11.

The issue arose again during debates on draft Resolution 77. This draft resolution garnered the support of 13 Security Council members, but it was vetoed by Russia and China. Russia made the accusation that 'from the very beginning of the Syrian crisis some influential members of the international community, including some sitting at this table, have undermined any possibility of a political settlement, calling for regime change'.[410] South Africa stated that the pursuit of regime change 'would be against the purposes and principles of the United Nations Charter'.[411] Pakistan stressed that 'the offer of no regime change, of plurality, and the promotion of democracy are important aspects of this situation'.[412] Given the grave concerns and fierce criticism, several Western states had to respond directly. France rebutted the relevant accusation as 'patently false' and noted that 'there was no question of imposing a political regime on Syria'.[413] The four co-sponsors explained that draft Resolution 77 did not 'call for' or 'impose' the requirement of regime change, and thus was not 'about' regime change.[414] This did not mean, however, that they had no intention of effecting regime change inside and especially outside of the Security Council. For instance, without naming which states it meant, South Africa noted that regime change 'has been an objective clearly stated' by these states.[415] Indeed, there were some reports in the Western media that NATO's airstrikes against Libya did not aim only to protect civilians but also to weaken the Gaddafi regime, while enabling the rebels.[416] It was even reported that then US President Barack Obama openly demanded that President Assad leave office.[417]

Grave concerns over regime change partly explain why China's voting on the Syrian crisis differed significantly from that on the comparable Libyan crisis. In the Libyan crisis, China abstained from voting on Resolution 1973. However, the United States, the United Kingdom, and France used Resolution 1973 to justify airstrikes against Libya, which led to the collapse of the Gaddafi regime. As a result, China repeatedly exercised the veto power on resolutions against Syria. China firmly opposed 'any externally imposed solution aimed at forcing a regime change'.[418] Specifically, it stressed that

---

[410]   UN Doc. S/PV.6711, 2 April 2012, 9.
[411]   *Ibid.*, 11.
[412]   *Ibid.*, 10.
[413]   *Ibid.*, 4.
[414]   *Ibid.*, 5, 6, 7, 11.
[415]   UN Doc. S/PV.6627, 4 October 2011, 11.
[416]   See Tladi, 'Security Council, the Use of Force and Regime Change' (n. 404), 38–9.
[417]   See, e.g., Scott Wilson and Joby Warrick, 'Assad Must Go, Says Obama', *The Washington Post*, 18 August 2011, available at www.washingtonpost.com/politics/assad-must-go-obama-sa ys/2011/08/18/gIQAelheOJ_story.html.
[418]   UN Doc. S/PV.6826, 30 August 2012, 33.

'there must be no attempt at regime change or involvement in civil war by any party under the guise of protecting civilians'.[419] According to Fung, China sought to 'draw a line demarcating UN Security Council-authorised intervention from imposed regime change'.[420]

In short, China has endeavoured to resist regime change as the norm within or through the Security Council. Notwithstanding, China urged an inclusive political reconstruction in Syria. For instance, in debates on draft Resolution 612, China appealed that the Syrian government should implement commitments to reform and that a Syrian-led inclusive political process be launched as soon as possible, so as to facilitate the early easing of tensions in Syria.[421]

4. China as Norm Entrepreneur?

China has also begun to seek international norm entrepreneurship. Currently, its focus is on economic affairs.[422] China has made some progress by initiating the formation of the Asian Infrastructure Investment Bank (AIIB).[423] However, given the type of threats to the peace and China's global interests, China may expect norm entrepreneurship in the field of peace and security.

Let us look at the role China has played in the development of an international regime for tackling extremism, which, as noted earlier in the chapter, has emerged from the international regulation of counter-terrorism. In the past decade, China has adopted many rigid measures in Xinjiang, a major region where Chinese Uygur Muslims live. Several Western states – especially the United States – thought that China's measures grossly violated the human rights of the Uygur and, more assertively, constituted 'genocide'.[424] As a consequence, the United States adopted sanctions against China.[425] China has firmly disavowed the United States' accusations. China argues that the

---

[419] Statement by H. E. Ambassador Li Baodong, Permanent Representative of China to the United Nations, at the Security Council Open Debate on the Protection of Civilians in Armed Conflict, 10 May 2011, available at http://un.china-mission.gov.cn/eng/chinaandun/securitycouncil/thematicissues/civilians_ac/201105/t20110520_8417469.htm.

[420] Courtney J. Fung, 'Separating Intervention from Regime Change: China's Diplomatic Innovations at the UN Security Council Regarding the Syria Crisis', *The China Quarterly* 235 (2018), 693–712 (705).

[421] UN Doc. S/PV.6627, 4 October 2011, 5.

[422] Yang Wang, 'To Construct Open-Oriented New Economic Regime', *People's Daily*, 22 November 2013 (in Chinese).

[423] Daniel C. K. Chow, 'Why China Established the Asia Infrastructure Investment Bank', *Vanderbilt Journal of Transnational Law* 49 (2016), 1255–98.

[424] See, e.g., US Department of State, *China 2020 Human Rights Report*, available at www.state.gov/wp-content/uploads/2021/03/CHINA-2020-HUMAN-RIGHTS-REPORT.pdf, 1.

[425] See, e.g., US Uyghur Human Rights Policy Act of 2020, Public Law 116–45, 17 June 2020.

relevant measures were taken with the aim of combating terrorism and extremism, and that therefore they do not violate but protect human rights in Xingjian.[426] In particular, according to China's government,[427] the population in Xinjiang, including the Uygur, face grave threats of terrorism and extremism. Here, I do not debate the issue from a factual perspective; instead, I will focus on China's potential for norm entrepreneurship in the realm of counter-extremism.

China is perhaps one of the first states to have endeavoured to develop international laws on counter-extremism. In 2001, the SCO members signed the Convention on Combating Terrorism, Separatism and Extremism, which defines 'extremism' as:

> ... an act aimed at violent seizing or keeping power, and violently changing the constitutional system of a State, as well as a violent encroachment upon public security, including organisation, for the above purposes, of illegal armed formations and participation in them, criminally prosecuted in conformity with the national laws of the Parties.[428]

However, it seems that the 2001 Convention does not distinguish terrorism from extremism. The word 'extremism' appear nowhere other than in the definitions.

In 2017, SCO members signed the Convention of the Shanghai Cooperation Organization on Combating Extremism. The 2017 Convention was the first regional treaty that purported to tackle extremism in implementation of the 2016 UN Global Counter-Terrorism Strategy. It should be noted that the 2017 Convention was initiated by China's President Xi Jinping at the SCO's 14th Meeting of the Council of the Heads of State, held in September 2014.[429]

The 2017 Convention explicitly stated that it was, among other things, 'follow[ing] up the UN Global Counter-Terrorism Strategy, the relevant counter-terrorism resolutions of the UN Security Council, universal counter-terrorism conventions and protocols'.[430] The 2017 Convention defines 'extremism' and the 'extremist act', respectively, as referring to 'ideology and practices

---

[426] State Council Information Office of China, *The Fight against Terrorism* (n. 248), Preamble.
[427] *Ibid.*, Pts II and III.
[428] Art. 1 SCO Convention on Combating Terrorism, Separatism and Extremism of 15 June 2001 (hereinafter 2001 Convention).
[429] Xi Jinping, 'Working Together with Sincerity and Dedication to Take SCO to a New Level', 12 September 2014, available at www.fmprc.gov.cn/mfa_eng/wjdt_665385/zyjh_665391/2014 09/t20140918_678212.html.
[430] Convention of the Shanghai Cooperation Organization on Combating Extremism of 9 June 2017, Preamble.

aimed at resolving political, social, racial, national and religious conflicts through violent and other unlawful actions'[431] – a more concise definition than that in the 2001 Convention. In contrast, the 2001 Convention includes a broader definition of an 'extremist act'.[432] It further requires that SCO members adopt a wide range of legislative, executive, and juridical measures, while enhancing cooperation among them to tackle extremism.[433] It especially stipulates that the SCO members, 'in accordance with their national legislations, may take more stringent measures to combat extremism than those stipulated by this Convention'.[434]

According to China, efforts to combat extremism relied, in addition to relevant SCO conventions, on a new global counter-terrorism strategy.[435] Based on a preventive approach,[436] China took a wide range of measures to combat terrorism and extremism,[437] including by establishing 'education and training centers'[438] – a major measure that was fiercely condemned by some Western states.

In addition to denouncing China's measures aimed to combat extremism in other forums, several Western states brought this issue before the Security Council.[439] Surprisingly, China did not clearly expound in the Security Council norms of counter-extremism based on relevant SCO conventions and its national legal practice. During debates on Resolution 2178, which explicitly linked terrorism and extremism for the first time, China's Foreign Minister Wang Yi stated:

> [W]e must adopt a multipronged approach. The global war on terrorism should be fought in an integrated manner, adopting measures in the political, security, economic, financial, intelligence and ideological fields, inter alia, with a view to addressing both the symptoms and root causes of terrorism, especially removing its root causes and breeding grounds.
>
> [...]
>
> [W]e should promote deradicalization. While taking actions in accordance with law to crack down on and outlaw venues and personnel that are engaged in, advocating and spreading extremist ideology, we should protect

---

431 *Ibid.*, Art. 2(1)(b).
432 *Ibid.*, Art. 2(1)(c).
433 *Ibid.*, Arts 7–25.
434 *Ibid.*, Art. 7(3).
435 State Council Information Office of China, *The Fight against Terrorism* (n. 248), Pt V.
436 *Ibid.*
437 *Ibid.* See also of Xinjiang Uygur Autonomous Region Regulation on De-radicalization, adopted 29 March 2017, chs III–V.
438 State Council Information Office of China, *The Fight against Terrorism* (n. 248), Pt V.
439 See, e.g., Reuters, 'U.S., Germany Slam China' (n. 254).

normal religious activities, promote public awareness and give greater play to the role of local communities, thus injecting more positive energy into society. The United Nations should sum up useful experiences without delay and promote best practices from around the world.[440]

In his speech, Wang condemned the casualties caused by terrorist attacks in Xinjiang.[441] However, he did not say anything further on extremism. In fact, Wang mentioned the word 'extremist' only once and did not mention 'extremism' at all. On this important occasion, China failed to introduce its normative vision on extremism.

Notwithstanding, given that China and other SCO member states have led the way in negotiating conventions on counter-extremism, and that China has acquired significant experience in combating counter-extremism, they may play a considerable role in future international law-making on the subject.

VI. THE FUTURE TRAJECTORY OF SECURITY COUNCIL REFORMS: REVISITING THE UNIVERSAL AND REGIONAL APPROACHES

In the past several decades, states and scholars have never ceased their efforts to enhance the institutional strength of the Security Council itself. These efforts have adopted a universal approach and Van den Herik's chapter in this volume is a part of these efforts. This approach is based on, and in support of, the primary responsibility of the Security Council in the maintenance of international peace, as provided for in the UN Charter. However, there was also a regional approach proposed during the negotiations establishing the United Nations. By examining the partnership between the Security Council and the African Union in his chapter, Maluwa reminds people of the potential of regional arrangements.

Nevertheless, several questions remain open to debate, mainly from the perspective of power politics.

- Why are some legal proposals, while ostensibly persuasive, set aside?
- Are some legal proposals really desirable if they are adopted?
- What legal proposals are feasible and beneficial?
- Are regional arrangements credible and reliable?
- How can regional arrangements make a real difference?

---

[440]   UN Doc. S/PV.7272, 24 September 2014, 17, 18.
[441]   *Ibid.* See also State Council Information Office of China, *The Fight against Terrorism* (n. 248), Pt III, on the most serious terrorist attacks, which happened on 5 July 2009, causing 197 deaths and injuring more than 1,700 people in Urumqi, the capital of Xinjiang.

A. *The Universal Approach*

The universal approach characterises not only the primacy of the Security Council but also the privileges of the great powers. It has been observed that legal proposals are grouped into those aiming to reduce the privileges of the great powers (Group I proposals) and those aiming to improve the workings of the Security Council (Group II proposals).

1. Group I Proposals

Many people assume that the veto power granted to the P5, who often use this privilege in their own interest, is a major source of the Security Council's repeated failures to address the threat to peace. Many legal proposals have therefore been made to constrain the exercise of veto power.[442] The R2P was a major occasion for some states and commentators to suggest that the exercise of the veto power should either be restrained or disallowed. For example, Peters considered the veto on the occasion of the R2P as an 'abuse of right'.[443] Further, in his report on the R2P submitted to the General Assembly in 2009, the then UN Secretary-General urged the P5 to refrain from exercising, or threatening to exercise, the veto in situations of manifest failure to meet obligations relating to the R2P.[444] This recommendation garnered support from 35 UN member states during the General Assembly debates on the R2P.[445] Two significant proposals were later suggested in 2015. France and Mexico submitted a proposal to the General Assembly entitled 'Political Statement on the Suspension of the Veto in Case of Mass Atrocities', calling for UN members to sign it.[446] As of 8 June 2022, 122 UN member states and two observers had

---

[442] For thorough research, see Jennifer Trahan, *Existing Legal Limits to Security Council Veto Power in the Face of Atrocity Crime* (Cambridge: Cambridge University Press, 2020).

[443] Anne Peters, 'The Security Council's Responsibility to Protect', *International Organizations Law Review* 8 (2011), 1–40.

[444] *Implementing the Responsibility to Protect*, Report of the Secretary-General, UN Doc. A/63/677, 12 January 2009.

[445] Global Centre for the Responsibility to Protect, *Implementing the Responsibility to Protect: The 2009 General Assembly Debate – An Assessment*, August 2009, available at www.globalr2p.org/wp-content/uploads/2020/01/2009-UNGA-Debate-Summary.pdf.

[446] Global Centre for the Responsibility to Protect, 'Political Declaration on the Suspension of Veto Powers in Cases of Mass Atrocities', 1 August 2015, available at www.globalr2p.org/resources/political-declaration-on-suspension-of-veto-powers-in-cases-of-mass-atrocities/. See further Jean-Baptiste Jeangène Vilmer, 'The Responsibility not to Veto: A Genealogy', *Global Governance* 24 (2018), 331–49.

done so.[447] The Accountability, Coherence and Transparency (ACT) Group suggested a draft 'Code of Conduct regarding Security Council Action against Genocide, Crimes against Humanity or War Crimes', and called on all of the members of Security Council not to vote against any credible draft resolution intended to prevent or stop mass atrocities.[448] It is of note that while the Code won support from 104 UN members, only two of the P5 – namely, the United Kingdom and France – signed it.[449] Maluwa, while acknowledging the great political significance of these two documents, suggests that they have little normative consequence for the collective security system in that they were not adopted as General Assembly resolutions. He was surprised to find that only 22 African states signed the Code and yet he believes that it is likely to be a focal point for future negotiations on UN reform.[450]

Given the rationale underlying the United Nations' prevention of the 'scourge of war' and 'untold sorrow to mankind',[451] it is justified to consider, as many lawyers have done, some restraints to reduce the undue exercise of the veto power on occasions such as genocide. From a different angle, however, restraint of the veto power is not without risk: while such restraint facilitates the approval of proposed actions in the Security Council, it may also induce some Security Council members – especially the great powers – to rely on voting rather than to seek compromises during debates on proposed actions. In other words, such restraint is likely to bring about some 'tyranny of the majority' within the Security Council. Given that Security Council actions are often initiated as a consequence of the geopolitical calculations among particular great powers, this risk should not be ignored. In other words, while some proposals may constrain the great powers in some aspects, they may also free the great powers in other aspects, thereby creating new risks.

[447] Global Centre for the Responsibility to Protect, 'List of Signatories to the ACT Code of Conduct', 8 June 2022, available at www.globalr2p.org/resources/list-of-signatories-to-the-act-code-of-conduct/.
[448] Annex I to the letter dated 14 December 2015 from the Permanent Representative of Liechtenstein to the United Nations addressed to the Secretary-General, UN Doc. A/70/621–S/2015/978.
[449] Parliamentarians for Global Action, 'Launch of the Code of Conduct regarding Security Council Action against Genocide, Crimes against Humanity or War Crimes', 27 October 2015, available at www.pgaction.org/news/launch-the-code-conduct-regarding-security.html.
[450] Maluwa, 'Between Centralism and Regionalism', Chapter 3 in this volume, section IV.B.
[451] UN Charter, Preamble.

2. Group II Proposals

In contrast with Group I proposals, Group II proposals seek to improve the working – and especially the decision-making – procedures of the Security Council without explicitly reducing the privileges of the great powers.

One of the efforts proposed is improvement of the 'penholder' system.[452] Its major purpose is to give greater voice to elected members of the Security Council. Since the 2000s, on most occasions the P5 – especially the Western 'P3' (i.e., the United States, the United Kingdom, and France) – have prepared the relevant draft resolutions and then circulated them among the other members. Some elected members have complained that the P3-dominated penholder system 'has diminished the opportunity for wider Council engagement, especially by the elected members, and has significantly increased the risk of Council products being crafted in a way that serves only the interests of the permanent members', and hence they have appealed that they should not be precluded from 'offering their drafting ideas for texts'.[453] A compromise was reached only in 2014 with the adoption of a presidential note.[454] That note encouraged:

(i) all Security Council members to act as the penholder(s) in the drafting of documents, including resolutions, presidential statements, and press statements;

(ii) penholders, in the drafting exercise, to exchange information among all Security Council members as early as possible and to engage in timely consultations with all Security Council members; and

(iii) penholders to informally consult with the broader UN membership – in particular, interested members, including countries directly involved or specifically affected, neighbouring states, and countries with particular contributions to make – as well as with regional organisations and informal groups among Security Council members known as Groups of Friends.

Currently, however, the majority of Security Council resolutions are still authored by the Western P3.[455] It is unclear why the elected members have not become major drafters of the Security Council resolutions, although – as Van den Herik argues – the elected members do play a role.

---

[452] Loraine Sievers and Sam Daws, *The Procedure of the UN Security Council* (Oxford: Oxford University Press, 4th edn, 2014), 272–4.

[453] UN Doc. S/PV.7539, 20 October 2015, 8.

[454] Note by the President of the Security Council, UN Doc. S/2014/268, 14 April 2014.

[455] Security Council Report, *The Penholder System*, 21 December 2018, available at www.secur itycouncilreport.org/atf/cf/%7B65BFCF9B-6D27-4E9C-8CD3-CF6E4FF96FF9%7D/Penh olders.pdf, Annex ('Penholder Arrangements as of December 2018').

Since it has been recognised that the use of force cannot totally be prevented, even if it is undertaken by the great powers and approved by the Security Council, people may aim instead to make those who exercise the use of force more accountable for their actions. For this purpose, improvement of the reporting requirement has attracted much attention. In 2011, Mexico and Brazil proposed improvement of the reporting requirements under Article 51 UN Charter.[456] Given that the use of force may on occasion happen without approval from the Security Council, Van den Herik suggests extending the reporting requirements to these occasions.[457] Furthermore, she submits that the relevant facts on the basis of which the Security Council's approval of the use of force is sought should be included in the reporting requirements.[458] Van den Herik notes that there is no universal or collective fact-finding agency[459] – and if there is no impartial mechanism or institution immune from the control of the great powers, it is doubtful that any newly proposed reporting requirements will work well.

The Libyan intervention has demonstrated that the improvement of reporting requirements is of limited help. During their military intervention against Libya, France, the United Kingdom, Italy, and the United States reported to the UN Secretary-General, in accordance with Resolution 1973.[460] According to the United Kingdom, NATO members were 'ensuring carefully that our actions accord with the Security Council resolutions and our other international obligations', and NATO actions were 'designed precisely to protect civilians and to minimise civilian casualties'.[461] Yet Cuba blamed NATO for the 'bombing of cities or populated areas resulting in the death of more innocent civilians' and doubted how such 'indiscriminate bombing' could be justified. Cuba also deplored that the United Nations made no statements regarding the protection of civilian victims from

---

[456] UN Doc. A/75/33, 2 March 2020, 24; UN Doc. A/66/551–S/2011/701, 11 November 2011, 3–4.
[457] Van den Herik, 'A Reflection on Institutional Strength', Chapter 2 in this volume, section II.B.3.
[458] *Ibid.*, section II.B.4.
[459] *Ibid.*
[460] Letter dated 26 April 2011 from the Permanent Representative of the UK to the United Nations addressed to the Secretary-General, UN Doc. S/2011/269; Letter dated 26 April 2011 from the Permanent Representative of Italy to the United Nations addressed to the Secretary-General, UN Doc. S/2011/270; Letter dated 27 April 2011 from the Permanent Representative of France to the United Nations addressed to the Secretary-General, UN Doc. S/2011/274; Letter dated 17 June 2011 from the Permanent Representative of the United States of America to the United Nations addressed to the Secretary-General, UN Doc. S/2011/372; Letter dated 1 July 2011 from the Permanent Representative of France to the United Nations addressed to the Secretary-General, UN Doc. S/2011/402.
[461] UN Doc. S/PV.6531, 10 May 2011, 8.

NATO's military actions.[462] The UN Under-Secretary-General for Humanitarian Affairs and the Emergency Relief Coordinator expressed similar views.[463] Thus, as the Libya case suggests, a crucial issue remains: who can be a reliable party in the evaluation of reporting?

B. *The Regional Approach*

In considering the framework for international peace after World War II, US President Franklin D. Roosevelt initially preferred the regional approach, with no universal organ with great authority.[464] This was partly because there were developed security mechanisms on the American continent. By contrast, then Secretary of State Cordell Hull was a firm advocate of the universal approach. Hull argued that the universal approach would do away with the 'need for sphere of influence, for alliances, for balance of power, or any other special arrangements'.[465] He eventually changed Roosevelt's mind. British Prime Minister Winston Churchill was also a firm advocate of the regional approach, warning that:

> It was only the countries whose interests were directly affected by a dispute who could be expected to apply themselves with sufficient vigour to secure a settlement. If countries remote from a dispute were among those called upon in the first instance to achieve a settlement the result was likely to be merely vapid and academic discussion.[466]

Geopolitical calculations are implicit in the United States' universal approach and the United Kingdom's regional approach. In addition to a high expectation for unity among the great powers,[467] the United States' position as the most powerful state in the 1940s was perhaps a more important factor in leading Roosevelt to change his mind. In other words, it was clear that a universal approach would help the United States to exert its influence. In fact, the UN Charter was 'a 90% American creation'.[468] By contrast, the United Kingdom, which no longer maintained a hegemony as it had in the 19th century, found itself less likely to attain leadership in the United Nations.

---

[462] *Ibid.*, 27.

[463] *Ibid.*, 4.

[464] Bosco, *Five to Rule Them All* (n. 20), 14.

[465] US Department of State, *Foreign Relations of the United States* (Washington, DC: GPO, 1943), sect. I.756.

[466] Citing from Geoffrey L. Goodwin, *Britain and the United Nations* (New York: Manhattan, 1957), 7.

[467] 1943 Declaration of the Three Powers (n. 118).

[468] Paul Kennedy, 'Remarks', *ASIL Proceedings of the 89th Annual Meeting* (1995), 51.

To some extent, this explains Churchill's negative attitude towards the universal approach.

While the universal approach supported by the United States finally prevailed at the San Francisco Conference, the UN Charter included a separate chapter of regional arrangements – namely, Chapter VIII. The relationship between the Security Council and the regional arrangements was, however, not yet fully defined.[469] Over time, the regional arrangements developed some practices that divided the Security Council. Some of them did not have the prior approval of the Security Council, as required by Article 53(1), but were nevertheless gradually accepted.[470]

After the end of the Cold War, the regional approach became more important – especially in Africa. This is largely because, as the Cold War ended, Africa no longer held any strategic interest for the great powers; their interest in maintaining the peace in Africa declined – one reason why the great powers, together with the United Nations, did nothing to stop the genocide in Rwanda. By contrast, in the 2010s, geopolitical considerations influenced policies towards Syria in the opposite direction. Unlike the instance of their inaction in the Rwanda genocide, the Western great powers and Russia spared no effort in their struggle with each other in Syria, because Syria is an 'Archimedean point' of geopolitics in the Middle East. Yet the results of inaction and action were the same: the Security Council failed to stop both humanitarian disasters.

In this context, it is timely to examine – as Maluwa does in his chapter in this volume –how the Security Council and the African Union developed a partnership. A stronger African Union makes the African countries less susceptible to struggles between the great powers in the Security Council. This is particularly significant because such struggles between the great powers have again intensified.

Maluwa evidently supports the African Union's policy of respect for the primacy of the Security Council and regards this policy to be favourable for the maintenance of international peace. In support of this, Maluwa submits two major arguments. First, regional organisations, generally speaking, are not so much a challenge to the authority of the Security Council but a complement to it. Second, regional organisations increase the voice of the periphery, which is less represented in the Security Council.[471] This is true of

---

[469]   Christian Walter, 'Introduction to Chapter VIII', in Simma et al. (eds), *The Charter of the United Nations* 4th ed 2024 (n. 97), MN 19.

[470]   *Ibid.*, MN 21.

[471]   Maluwa, 'Between Centralism and Regionalism', Chapter 3 in this volume, section I.

the African Union. Furthermore, I want to stress that regional organisations are better positioned to develop innovative practices than the Security Council, which is often disabled by the struggles between the great powers. Such practices, over time, are likely to be supported by a large number of states and, eventually, to be accepted by the Security Council.

Maluwa does not, however, mention the negative impact of regional organisations, as evidenced by the NATO interventions in the FRY and Libya, among others, which have significantly damaged the primacy of the Security Council. Such negative impacts should not be ignored. In other words, whether the regional approach works well depends on whether the relevant regional organisations comply with the UN Charter and international law.

Furthermore, according to Maluwa's examination, the African Union does not live up to the expectations of many people in the maintenance of peace in the African continent. A major reason is that the African Union does not have sufficient institutional capability. This seems to be a common difficulty that many other regional organisations face. As a consequence, few regional organisations can play a leading role in the maintenance of peace from where they sit.[472] Unfortunately, Maluwa does not discuss whether and how the African Union might strengthen its institutional capabilities.

Generally speaking, China is in support of regional organisations playing a larger part in the maintenance of international peace. Specifically, China attaches importance to building their capability. For instance, in 2015, China decided to provide a total of US$100 million of free military assistance to the African Union for the establishment of the African Standby Force and the African Capacity for Immediate Response to Crisis.[473] On 8 August 2022, China convened a Security Council meeting to discuss the building of sustainable peace in Africa. A major purpose of the meeting was to explore how the United Nations might help to build the capability of the African Union.[474]

The regional approach also allows China to take a more flexible stance towards proposed actions within the Security Council. Maluwa rightly suggests that the move away from the principle of non-interference, enshrined in Article III(2) of the Organisation of African Unity (OAU) Charter, to the

---

[472] Bosco, *Five to Rule Them All* (n. 20), 253.
[473] Xi Jinping, 'Working Together to Forge a New Partnership of Win–Win Cooperation and Create a Community of Shared Future for Mankind', 28 September 2015, available at www .fmprc.gov.cn/eng/wjdt_665385/zyjh_665391/201510/t20151012_678384.html.
[474] Letter dated 1 August 2022 from the Permanent Representative of China to the United Nations addressed to the Secretary-General, UN Doc. S/2022/592.

principle of non-indifference, provided for in Article 4(h) of the AU Constitutive Act, allows China to engage in African affairs more flexibly.[475]

In this regard, let us examine China's voting in relation to the Haiti crisis in 1993. During the debates on how the Security Council dealt with this matter – whereby the democratically elected government was overthrown by a military coup – China insisted that what happened in Haiti 'is essentially a matter which falls within the internal affairs of that country, and therefore should be dealt with by the Haitian people themselves'.[476] Yet China cast a supportive vote on Resolution 841, imposing sanctions on Haiti.[477] In explaining its voting, China's representative stressed that:

> The Chinese delegation, as its consistent position, does not favour the Security Council's handling matters which are essentially internal affairs of a Member State, nor does it approve of resorting lightly to such mandatory measures as sanctions by the Council. We wish to point out that the favourable vote the Chinese delegation cast just now does not mean any change in that position.[478]

In other words, in China's view, regime change in Haiti was essentially an internal affair.

Nevertheless, China's representative continued:

> As the developments in Haiti have already brought, or will bring, adverse effects on them, the Organization of American States and countries from Latin America and the Caribbean have made similar requests to the Security Council to support the efforts made by the regional Organization. The resolution has also made it very clear that the Council, in dealing with the Haitian crisis, will fully heed and respect the views of the relevant regional Organization and countries in the region, and that any action by the Council should be complementary to, and supportive of, the actions oy the relevant regional Organization.[479]

Clearly, the previous actions of the Organization of American States (OAS), together with relevant requests from other countries in the region, made China deviate from its principled stance and support the adoption of the Resolution, even though such action did not mean China's basic policy had changed. In other words, the OAS's action justified China's voting. Had the

---

[475]   Maluwa, 'Between Centralism and Regionalism', Chapter 3 in this volume, section III.C.
[476]   UN Doc. S/PV.3238, 16 June 1993, 20.
[477]   SC Res. 841 of 16 June 1993, UN Doc. S/RES/841(1993).
[478]   UN Doc. S/PV.3238, 16 June 1993, 21.
[479]   *Ibid.*

OAS not taken that action, then China would likely not have cast its affirmative vote.

Importantly, Resolution 841 took note of the OAS's previous sanctions. While it stated that the Security Council must act in accordance with Chapter VII UN Charter, Resolution 841 included an interesting sentence: it stressed that the Security Council sanctions were consistent with the trade embargo recommended by the OAS and had regard for the view of the OAS's Secretary-General.[480]

VII. CONCLUSIONS

While debates on the precise relationship between law and politics remain unsettled, it has long been recognised that law is a more credible instrument than politics in managing social life. This is true both in domestic society and in international society. Many international legal regimes and institutions were created along these lines in the past centuries. The height of these efforts was the founding of the United Nations, which includes the most powerful organ under current international law, the UN Security Council. Within most sovereign states, advanced legislative, executive, and judicial mechanisms have been established, which ensure the creation and enforcement of law and thus bring politics into the orbit of law. In contrast, states are not capable of developing, and seemingly have no wish to develop, international society as an advanced, sovereign state organism. As a result, the legal process is inevitably deeply embedded in power politics. The functioning of international institutions, including the Security Council, largely depends on the relations between the great powers. People may dislike this phenomenon, but they cannot ignore it.

This does not absolutely mean that the law should and must be subject to power politics. The negative effects of power politics have, again and again, been evidenced by confrontations between states – and especially in the enormous damage and casualties incurred by the two world wars in the 20th century. As a result, in recent decades, people have unceasingly sought to enhance the Security Council and make it more efficient, more accountable, and (especially) less susceptible to the great powers. Mindful of the power politics in which the Security Council is deeply embedded, however, people should not satisfy themselves with advocating ostensibly 'good' legal proposals; they should think further about what these 'good' proposals may bring about, whether they are feasible, and whether they will work as expected.

[480]   SC Res. 841 of 16 June 1993, UN Doc. S/RES/841(1993), 2.

Today, the world seems poised to enter into a 'new Cold War' as the struggles between the great powers intensify, as evidenced by the Ukrainian crisis. From the perspective of power politics, without mutual respect, compromise, and unity among the great powers, the Security Council again risks being marginalised in the maintenance of international peace, as was the case during the original Cold War.

The regional approach represents an alternative to the universal approach and it may be less susceptible to struggles between the great powers in the Security Council. However, it should not be taken for granted that regional organisations will play a prominent role in the maintenance of international peace. They may be so powerful as to disregard the authority of the Security Council and international law, which is evidenced by some NATO actions. They may also lack sufficient institutional capability, so that they cannot operate adequately as partners to the Security Council.

The rise of China opens a new chapter in the book of power politics. There have been growing concerns as to whether a more powerful China will disable the Security Council, as the USSR once did during the Cold War, and what normative role and agenda China will pursue within and through the Council. From the power politics perspective, China, like other great powers, must seek more influence on the Security Council. Specifically, the new landscape of power is expected to influence China's behaviour in the Security Council, some of which will be positive and some of which will be negative. China's normative role in the Security Council has multiple dimensions: it is a norm defender, a norm taker, a norm 'antipreneur', and a norm entrepreneur. Thus no single perspective can help us to fully understand what effects a powerful China will bring about.

2

The UN Security Council: A Reflection on Institutional Strength

Larissa van den Herik

I. INTRODUCTION

The role and position of the United Nations (UN) Security Council, the central organ for peace in the international order, is undergoing change. With a rejuvenating China, a newly assertive and even aggressive Russia, and a United States retreating under former President Donald Trump, the geopolitical landscape has rapidly transformed and power structures are being rebalanced. What are the implications of a refashioning of world order for the UN Security Council? Has the Security Council's failure to agree on action to resolve the February 2022 Russian invasion exposed its obsolescence?

While at the height of US hegemony, the Security Council was perhaps usefully compared to a matryoshka doll that could be unpacked into ever smaller entities – from representing the international community, to 15 members, to the five permanent members (P5), to a single permanent member[1] – this image of a single permanent member constituting the core of the Security Council's being no longer holds. Even though the United States' Biden Administration is re-engaging with the international legal order,[2] China's arrival on the global stage as an awoken superpower has disrupted the status quo. China's unique character and its unwillingness to placidly blend into the US-designed world order is likely to upset

---

[1] W. Michael Reisman, 'The Constitutional Crisis in the United Nations', *American Journal of International Law* 87 (1993), 83–100 (85), cited by Isobel Roele, 'Around Arendt's Table: Bureaucracy and the Non-Permanent Members of the UN Security Council', *Leiden Journal of International Law* 33 (2020), 117–37.

[2] See, for a more general analysis, José Alvarez, 'International Law in a Biden Administration', *Institute for International Law and Justice*, November 2020, available at www.iilj.org/wp-content/uploads/2020/11/Alvarez-Biden-and-IL.pdf.

existing structures and arrangements, the questions being how and to what extent.[3]

Commentators have turned to historical parallels to describe the turn of events that is unfolding. Graham Allison has coined the term 'Thucydides Trap' to underline the structural stress that results from the rise of a new superpower.[4] Yet historical analogies, such as with World War I and the failures of diplomacy to accommodate Germany's rise,[5] or labels as a 'new Cold War' can be considered inadequate, given the intense economic and technological mutual interdependencies of today's globalised world. Indeed, rather than returning to a bipolar world, the international order has effectively become multipolar as a consequence of the 'rise of the rest'.[6] And even if the United States and China were to insist on their current efforts to decouple,[7] the full extent of the existing global interconnectedness will not be easily unravelled. Many of today's threats and challenges simply cannot be disentangled.

Nonetheless, the new power constellations will undoubtedly lead to shifts and the development of new norms, as well as to the modification of practices and normative regimes. China refuses to be a passive rule-taker and is already competing with the European Union as a global business regulator, for example on tech. It aims to supersede – or at least juxtapose – the 'Brussels Effect'[8] with its own 'Beijing Effect'.[9] China will continue to demand more space and respect for its own values and policies, surely including in the realm

---

[3]   Subrahmanyam Jaishankar, 'The Lessons of Awadh: The Dangers of Strategic Complacency', in *The India Way: Strategies for an Uncertain World* (New Delhi: Harper Collins, 2020), ch. 1.

[4]   Graham T. Allison, *Destined for War: Can America and China Escape Thucydides' Trap?* (Boston: Houghton Mifflin Harcourt, 2017), referring to the fear that Athens' rise instilled in Sparta, ultimately leading to the devastating Peloponnesian War.

[5]   Henry Kissinger, 'Epilogue: Does History Repeat Itself?', in *On China* (New York: Penguin, 2011), 514–30.

[6]   Fareed Zakaria, *The Post-American World and the Rise of the Rest, Release 2.0* (New York: Penguin, 2011).

[7]   Even before Trump started raising the prospect of decoupling the US economy from China in 2019, President Xi Jinping had already initiated policy thinking aimed at greater economic self-sufficiency: Podcast with Steve Tsang, 'What China Makes of "New Cold War" with US', *The Rachman Review* [podcast], 20 August 2020, available at https://play.acast.com/s/therachmanreview/whatchinamakesof-newcoldwar-withus.

[8]   Anu Bradford coined the term 'Brussels effect': Anu Bradford, *The Brussels Effect: How the European Union Rules the World* (Oxford: Oxford University Press, 2020). The term refers to the European Union's unilateral ability to regulate global business drawing on market forces. As one of the world's largest and most affluent consumer markets, the European Union is in a position to shape regulation and set standards in diverse areas of data privacy, consumer health and safety, and online hate speech. Corporations tend to extend these EU rules to their global operations to avoid the costs of complying with multiple regulatory regimes.

[9]   Matthew S. Erie and Thomas Streinz, 'The Beijing Effect: China's Digital Silk Road as Transnational Data Governance', *New York University Journal of International Law and Politics*

of collective security.[10] The rebalancing that is ongoing is therefore bound to have direct ramifications for dynamics at the UN Security Council, and for its function and potential within the system of collective security. More fundamentally, even, and intertwined with all of this, the nature of the system of collective security and its core concerns may mutate to more strongly emphasise power and non-interference, and to relegate human rights to a more peripheral role.[11]

Yet there is also resistance to a move away from current structures and liberal values. Germany and France have launched the Alliance for Multilateralism, which insists on strong and agile international organisations.[12] The Alliance presents multilateralism not as an ideology but as a method. It emphasises the importance and effectiveness of evidence-based and rules-based multilateral cooperation as the means of securing peace, stability, and prosperity, and of guaranteeing sovereign equality.[13] Germany has complemented this idea, then Foreign Minister Heiko Maas suggesting a 'Marshall Plan for Democracy'.[14] During the Trump Administration, Ivo Daalder, the former US ambassador to the North Atlantic Treaty Organization (NATO), also called for a Group of Nine (G9) alliance to 'save the liberal world' and to 'maintain the rules-based order'.[15] The alliance would consist of France, Germany, Italy, the United Kingdom, and the European Union, as well as Australia, Japan, South Korea, and Canada, which together represent the largest economic powers with

54 (2021), 1–91. See also Mercy A. Kuo, 'The Brussels Effect and China: Shaping Tech Standards; Insights from Anu Bradford', *The Diplomat*, 7 January 2021, available at https://thediplomat.com/2021/01/the-brussels-effect-and-china-shaping-tech-standards/. See also Tim Rühling, 'China, Europe and the New Power Competition over Technical Standards', *UI Brief* 1 (2021).

[10]   See, e.g., 'Document Number Nine', a document circulated within the Chinese Communist Party in 2013. The status of this document is unclear. See also Rosemary Foot, *China, the UN and Human Protection: Beliefs, Power, Image* (Oxford: Oxford University Press, 2020).

[11]   Tom Ginsburg, 'Authoritarian International Law?', *American Journal of International Law* 114 (2020), 221–60.

[12]   Mirjam Reiter, 'Germany Champions "Alliance for Multilateralism"', *GPIL Blog*, 2 February 2021, available at https://gpil.jura.uni-bonn.de/2021/02/germany-champions-alliance-for-multilateralism/. On informal coalitions outside institutional structures, see also Alejandro Rodiles, *Coalitions of the Willing and International Law: The Interplay between Formality and Informality* (Cambridge: Cambridge University Press, 2018).

[13]   See further www.multilateralism.org. For a critical appraisal, see Reiter, 'Alliance for Multilateralism' (n. 12).

[14]   Daniel Brössler, Matthias Kolband, and Max Muth, 'Maas Fordert Allianz gegen Autokraten', *Süddeutsche Zeitung*, 9 March 2021, available at www.sueddeutsche.de/politik/usa-eu-maas-russland-china-desinformation-microsoft-1.5230094; 'Germany Wants "Marshall Plan for Democracy"', *Deutsche Welle*, 9 January 2021, available at www.dw.com/en/germany-wants-us-eu-to-forge-marshall-plan-for-democracy/a-56181438.

[15]   Ivo Daalder and James Lindsay, 'The Committee to Save the World Order', *Foreign Affairs*, 30 September 2018, available at www.foreignaffairs.com/world/committee-save-world-order.

strong collective military capabilities that would be surpassed only by those of
the United States. Later, in a similar spirit of building a democratic alliance, UK
Prime Minister Boris Johnson invited leaders of Australia, India, South Africa,
and South Korea to the Group of Seven (G7) summit of June 2021, while US
President Joe Biden introduced 'Summits for Democracy'.[16]

China's imprint on the global order and, specifically, on the system of
collective security is analysed in more detail by Congyan Cai in this
volume.[17] In this chapter, I discuss the fallout from the new Security
Council dynamics from an institutionalist perspective. This perspective
emphasises the institutional environment in which the UN Security
Council operates. It is an inclusive perspective that embraces the voice of
middle powers and those more in the periphery, while recognising that those
voices do not necessarily always belong to the same chorus. The aim is not to
harmonise all those voices as such but rather to reinforce others than the P5
and to make those others – in the words of Tiyanjana Maluwa, in his
contribution to this volume – 'effective participants'.[18] As effective participants, those other states can induce and pressure the P5 to act as responsible
great powers, which they will not always be inclined to do of their own
motion. In the extreme case of one of the P5 being the one to threaten or
break the peace, the ten elected members (E10) can play a particularly
crucial role, and hence reinforcing the E10 is in large part about creating
checks and balances on the P5's raw power. I accept Cai's critique that I do
not prove in this chapter in detail how this precisely reduces the 'negative
impacts of power politics'[19] on each occasion. My chapter is based instead on
a general belief in the inherent value of checks and balances for adequate
and proper decision-making.

The institutionalist perspective is thus premised on the idea that, even in the
setting of intense power politics in which the Security Council operates, the
Council is not entirely unbounded; rather, it is governed by its own institutional and procedural framework. After all, the Security Council is not
composed only of the powerful and the permanent, and notions of

---

[16] The first summit was held virtually on 9–10 December 2021 with 111 participants, including
Taiwan, Kosovo, and the European Union. The three main themes were defending against
authoritarianism, fighting corruption, and advancing respect for human rights. A subsequent
summit was held on 28–30 March 2023.

[17] Congyan Cai, 'The UN Security Council: Maintaining Peace during a Global Power Shift',
Chapter 1 in this volume.

[18] Tiyanjana Maluwa, 'The UN Security Council: Between Centralism and Regionalism',
Chapter 3 in this volume, section I (p. 188).

[19] Cai, 'Maintaining Peace during a Global Power Shift', Chapter 1 in this volume, section I (pp.
22–23).

participatory and reasoned decision-making are important in recognising the institutional role of the other members. Moreover, the Security Council forms part of the greater organisation of the United Nations, composed of 193 states, and as such it forms part of an international order that is underpinned by a system of international law. Article 24(1) UN Charter underscores that the Security Council operates *on behalf of* member states and hence not in a vacuum.

As Anne Peters notes, the fact that the UN Security Council is a political organ does not render it an extralegal entity as such.[20] Indeed, this chapter proceeds from the premise that the UN Security Council is bound by the UN Charter and by international law. In contrast to Cai, I submit that the less powerful states do not necessarily need to play a secondary role all of the time – in particular, not if they team up, which is what institutional approaches are all about. This chapter is also guided by the idea that less powerful states, in particular, have an interest in international law guiding international relations as a means of constraining power politics. At its core, and as already stated, the institutionalist perspective taken in this chapter is about checks and balances, as well as about the ways in which the 'others' might make sure their interests are taken into account – those others being those that do not have a permanent seat on the Security Council. This involves the elected members, as well as UN members not on the Security Council at all, and even states that are not fully recognised, such as Taiwan, Palestine, and Kosovo, as well as non-state actors. All these 'others' have their own interests, which can be translated into a need to temper the governance dominance of the powerful and a need for a representative Security Council that serves their interests too. These 'others' can be grouped into regions, which is the third perspective taken in this volume by Maluwa: the regional perspective – more specifically, the African perspective.[21] In the present chapter, I take a more pluriform approach that emphasises the *nature* of the perspective – namely an institutionalist perspective – rather than the *entity* having the perspective.

The institutional perspective that this chapter takes is further discussed in section II. It takes as its starting point the view that the UN Security Council is bound by the UN Charter and by international law, as scholars such as Anne

---

[20] Anne Peters, 'Article 25', in Bruno Simma, Daniel-Erasmus Khan, Georg Nolte, and Andreas Paulus (eds), *The Charter of the United Nations: A Commentary* (Oxford: Oxford University Press, 4th edn, 2024 forthcoming), MN 70–84 (MN 71).

[21] Maluwa, 'Between Centralism and Regionalism', Chapter 3 in this volume.

Peters and Erika de Wet have elaborated.[22] It then turns to the work of the International Law Commission (ILC) on ius cogens to illustrate the dynamics behind continuing contestations surrounding the idea of a governed Security Council. How notions such as ius cogens are used to bolster the Security Council's institutional environment is further discussed in section III, with a discussion on new developments regarding the use of veto. That section also points to other working methods that create space for the non-P5 – specifically, the Arria formula.

Subsequently, the institutionalist perspective is applied to the exercise of distinct Security Council powers pertaining to: the use of force (section IV), UN sanctions (section V), and counter-terrorism legislation (section VI). The exercise of these respective powers raises different institutional questions. In relation to the Security Council's war powers, participatory decision-making and other inclusive principles and processes are particularly important. When it comes to the imposition of sanctions, a crucial question that arises from the move away from UN sanctions to a practice of parallel unilateral sanctions is how dominant and exclusive the UN system is and to what extent it allows at all for this move, which goes beyond the UN Charter. For the UN sanctions that are already in place and will likely remain so for the foreseeable future, a persistent question that continues to hover over those sanctions regimes concerns their compatibility with basic legal principles and guarantees – particularly for sanctions targeting individuals. The Security Council's emerging quasi-legislative activities to counter terrorism are also scrutinised in this chapter, because they evoke fundamental questions about whether the Security Council can and should deal with generic phenomena at all instead of only with concrete threats. This section thus examines how those newly assumed powers fit with or stretch preconceived institutional structures.

Section VII explores future trajectories and it maps how the Security Council deals – or does not deal – with unconventional threats related to health, the environment, and cyber activity. Section VIII concludes the chapter with some reflections on whether the Security Council can and should have a role to play in the remainder of this century – or, at least, in times to come.

While discussing how the institutionalist perspective applies to the exercise of these distinct UN Security Council powers under Chapter VII UN Charter,

---

[22] Peters, 'Article 25' (n. 20); Erika de Wet, *The Chapter VII Powers of the United Nations Security Council* (Oxford: Hart, 2004). For a somewhat more reserved view on legal limits to the Security Council, see Michael Wood and Eran Sthoeger, 'Limits on the Powers of the Security Council', in *The United Nations Security Council and International Law* (Cambridge: Cambridge University Press, 2022), 70–89.

the chapter will particularly examine to what extent those Western states that are very active in professing an attachment to strong institutions (e.g., France, Germany, and the United Kingdom) have been practising what they preach. It will also look at the building blocks that have been put forward by non-Western states – in particular, Latin American states – to contribute to enhanced procedures for the Security Council in the exercise of its powers so as to increase its institutional strength. The discussion in this chapter will focus on situations and practices since the end of the Cold War.

II. AN INSTITUTIONALIST PERSPECTIVE: LIMITS TO THE SECURITY COUNCIL

In his chapter in this volume, Cai underscores that the UN Security Council is a political organ.[23] It has been deliberately tasked with the maintenance and enforcement of *peace*, not law, and it enjoys very wide discretion for doing so. While insisting on the Security Council as a platform for power politics, Cai does not fully dismiss the idea of constraints.[24] Indeed, as an organ of an international organisation, the Council is bound by its constitutive framework, the UN Charter, as also emphasised in Article 25 (decisions must be taken in accordance with the UN Charter) and in Article 24(2), 'the Security Council shall act in accordance with the Purposes and Principles of the United Nations'. It is thus generally agreed – as Maluwa too notes, in his chapter in this volume – that the UN Security Council must act in compliance with the purposes and principles of the UN Charter and with its own procedure.

Building on Peters and De Wet's writings, I regard the purposes and principles of the United Nations, as articulated in Articles 1 and 2 UN Charter, as *substantive* limits to UN Security Council discretion.[25] Even though the purposes and principles are articulated broadly, leaving wide discretion, they are not without meaning – even if their precise legal substance is open to contestation. I also agree with De Wet that the principle of good faith is relevant to the UN Security Council, because it binds states both when acting individually and as an organ of the United Nations.[26] Both Peters and De Wet recognise that there are also legal limits beyond the principles and purposes, particularly in the form of ius cogens, which is what Maluwa too

---

[23] Cai, 'Maintaining Peace during a Global Power Shift', Chapter 1 in this volume, section II.C.
[24] Cai, 'Maintaining Peace during a Global Power Shift', Chapter 1 in this volume, section II.C.
[25] Peters, 'Article 25' (n. 20); Erika de Wet, 'An Overview of the Substantive Limits to the Security Council's Discretion under Articles 40, 41 and 42 of the Charter', in *The Chapter VII Powers* (n. 22), 178–216.
[26] Ibid., 195–8.

points out. How exactly the principles and purposes and ius cogens limit the UN Security Council depends on the precise power being exercised, and these limits may gain new meaning when the UN Security Council expands its powers. But this then touches precisely on the heart of the matter: *who* decides what the contents of the limits are and *how?*

The dynamics behind ongoing controversies over limits on the UN Security Council came very clearly to the fore in the context of the ILC's work on ius cogens. In the text on first reading of its draft conclusions on peremptory norms, the Security Council was mentioned only in the commentaries to conclusion 16 and not in the conclusion itself, as the Special Rapporteur had initially suggested.[27] Conclusion 16 is a provision that deals with conflicts between acts of international organisations and peremptory norms. The reception of this draft conclusion and its commentaries was telling.[28] Quite a few states, including Austria, Belgium, Brazil, Cyprus, Slovenia, South Africa, Spain, Switzerland, and Togo, expressed support for the idea to explicitly recognise that Security Council decisions may not conflict with ius cogens. South Africa and Spain demonstrated special understanding of fears that unilateral allegations that a resolution conflicted with ius cogens could undermine Security Council authority and effectivity; thus they pointed towards the need for procedural guidance. Other states, such as Australia, Germany, Italy, and the Netherlands, did not object to the application of draft conclusion 16 to the Security Council, but they did more squarely emphasise the importance and need for further elaboration of interpretive presumptions and procedural mechanisms, as included in draft conclusions 20 and 21, to avoid unilateral invocation.

The P5, as well as Israel, objected to draft conclusion 16 and particularly to the reference to the Security Council in the commentaries. The core argument that the P5 advanced was that applying draft conclusion 16 to Security Council resolutions – and hence accepting the idea that Security Council decisions would not have binding effect to the extent that they conflicted with a norm of ius cogens – would jeopardise the work of the Security Council and undermine the system of collective security more broadly. Their main concern related to the risk of unilateral abuse. The legal argument that most of the P5 states put forward was that there was insufficient state practice supporting the proposition that states can unilaterally refuse to comply with Security

---

[27] Dire Tladi, Special Rapporteur to the ILC, *Third Report on Peremptory Norms of General International Law (Jus Cogens)*, UN Doc. A/CN.4/714, 12 February 2018, 67.

[28] See particularly UN Doc. A/CN.4/748, 9 March 2022. See also UN Doc. A/C.6/74/SR.23, 13 November 2019; UN Doc. A/C.6/74/SR.24, 11 November 2019; UN Doc. A/C.6/74/SR. 25, 20 November 2019; UN Doc. A/C.6/74/SR.26, 18 November 2019.

Council decisions.[29] That may well be true,[30] but there is considerable practice to support the idea that the Security Council is bound to respect norms of ius cogens in its decision-making.[31] The question of what procedure to follow if a state presents the argument that ius cogens has been violated is a separate question that underscores the need for procedural mechanisms – or, as they are called in draft conclusion 21, dispute settlement provisions.[32]

The concerns of the P5 are valid, as is clear from the fact that other states echoed them. However, this does not necessarily need to lead to silence and to leaving the matter of limits unsettled. There is a need to separate the principle that the Security Council is bound by ius cogens from subsequent questions about processes of invocation and legal consequences. Indeed, ultimately, the ILC did adopt conclusion 16 by consensus, albeit after heated discussion, mentioning the Security Council in the commentaries, but also referring to the importance of conclusion 20 on consistent interpretation and application, and of conclusion 21 on procedural requirements. Thus the trajectory of the ILC instrument and its outcomes illustrate that there is, by now, some shared understanding among all states – even if on occasion reluctant understanding, as subsequent developments in the Sixth Committee have shown[33] – about the existence of limits to the Security Council beyond the Charter. The precise contents of those limits, as well as the process of their invocation, leave room for argument. Yet, space for contestation is precisely what an institutional perspective is about.

[29] The United Kingdom, United States, and Israel put forward this argument. In a similar vein, see Daniel Costelloe, 'Peremptory Norms and Resolutions of the United Nations Security Council', in Dire Tladi (ed.), *Peremptory Norms of General International Law (Jus Cogens): Disquisitions and Disputations* (Leiden: Brill, 2021), 441–68.

[30] But see Antonios Tzanakopoulos, *Disobeying the Security Council; Countermeasures against Wrongful Sanctions* (Oxford: Oxford University Press, 2011).

[31] The Special Rapporteur gave several examples of states expressing the view in Security Council meetings that Security Council decisions could not run counter to norms of ius cogens: see, e.g., UN Doc. S/PV.3370, 27 April 1994; UN Doc. S/PV.5474, 22 June 2006; UN Doc. S/PV.5679, 22 May 2007; and UN Doc. S/PV.5779, 14 November 2007. In addition, there are international judgments supporting this view, most expressly ICTY, *The Prosecutor v. Duško Tadic*, Case No. IT-94-1-A, 15 July 1999, para. 296.

[32] See also Michael Wood, 'The Unilateral Invocation of Jus Cogens Norms', in Dire Tladi (ed.), *Peremptory Norms* (n. 29), 366–85.

[33] The Sixth Committee and the General Assembly postponed consideration of the work of the ILC on peremptory norms: Report of the International Law Commission on the Work of its 73rd Session, UN Doc. A/77/415, 18 November 2022; GA Res. 77/103 of 19 December 2022, UN Doc. A/RES/77/103.

III. BOLSTERING THE SECURITY COUNCIL'S INSTITUTIONAL ENVIRONMENT

Counterbalancing the pushback of the P5 against limits, there are a variety of initiatives to bolster the Security Council's institutional environment. In the context of the debates engendered by the ILC's work on ius cogens, Japan offered a noteworthy observation pertaining to the Security Council: the argument that the obligation to cooperate under draft conclusion 19 – mirroring Article 41 of the Articles on State Responsibility for Internationally Wrongful Acts (ARSIWA)[34] – should include an obligation to refrain from using the veto when a serious breach of ius cogens is at stake.[35] Japan underscored that this suggestion was in tandem with ongoing discussions at the United Nations about restraining the use of veto. Interestingly, France has been a prime mover on this issue. Indeed, in addition to launching the Alliance for Multilateralism, France has been one of the driving forces, alongside Mexico, behind initiatives to restrain the use of veto. Thus while the E10, as well as other member states, are often the driving forces behind efforts aimed at institutional strengthening, permanent members may at times also be engaged.

The initiative of France and Mexico was continued by the Accountability, Coherence and Transparency (ACT) Group, comprising 26 small and middle-sized powers.[36] That work ultimately resulted in a code of conduct that the United Kingdom also supported.[37] As signatories to the ACT Code, UN

---

[34] Article 41(1) ARSIWA reads: 'States shall cooperate to bring to an end through lawful means any serious breach within the meaning of article 40.' Article 40 refers to serious breaches of obligations arising under a peremptory norm of general international law.

[35] UN Doc. A/CN.4/748, 9 March 2022, 87.

[36] For more on this group, see Christian Wenaweser, 'Working from the Outside to Change the Working Methods of the Security Council: Elected Members as a Bridge between the Permanent Members and the Rest of the UN Membership', in Nico Schrijver and Niels Blokker (eds), *Elected Members of the Security Council: Lame Ducks or Key Players?* (Leiden/Boston: Brill Nijhoff, 2020), 279–84.

[37] Letter dated 14 December 2015 from the Permanent Representative of Liechtenstein to the United Nations addressed to the Secretary General, UN Doc. A/70/621–S/2015/978. The list of supporters is published on the website of the Permanent Mission of Liechtenstein to the United Nations. See further Niels Blokker, *Saving Succeeding Generations from the Scourge of War: The United Nations Security Council at 75* (Leiden: Brill Nijhoff, 2020), 47–74. See also Jennifer Trahan, *Existing Legal Limits to Security Council Veto Power in the Face of Atrocity Crimes* (Cambridge: Cambridge University Press, 2020); Jennifer Trahan, 'UNSC Veto Power Symposium: New Perspective for Tackling a Core Challenge to the UN System on the 75th Anniversary of the United Nations', *OpinioJuris*, 30 November 2020, available at https://opiniojuris.org/2020/11/30/unsc-veto-power-symposium-new-perspective-for-tackling-a-core-challenge-to-the-un-system-on-the-75th-anniversary-of-the-united-nations/.

member states 'pledge to support timely and decisive action by the Security Council aimed at preventing or ending the commission of genocide, crimes against humanity or war crimes', and they 'pledge in particular to not vote against a credible draft resolution before the Security Council on timely and decisive action to end the commission of genocide, crimes against humanity or war crimes, or to prevent such crimes'.[38] Such initiatives explicitly aim at constraining the Security Council in the exercise of its powers and they can be seen as a first step in the direction of abolishing the veto power altogether – or, in the words of Cai, a step towards diminishing the gap between the legal privileges and the political promises that come with P5 status.[39] To no one's great surprise, three permanent members resist them: the United States, China, and Russia.

Some scholars have gone beyond the initiative, making the argument that legal limits already exist to the exercise of a veto in a context of atrocity crime.[40] This is not generally accepted, though, with other scholars, including from the Global South, posing some critical questions, such as on the limitation of a veto restraint to only situations of atrocity crimes, or on how to establish a causal link between the use of veto and the commission of atrocity crimes.[41] Indeed, even if one is generally favourable to the idea of constraining the Security Council and even if one regards the veto power as an inappropriate relic of earlier times, one may disagree on the best way forward.

As for the ACT Code, the notions of 'timely and decisive action' and a 'credible draft resolution' are rather subjective. While it is true that the UN Charter itself advocates 'prompt and effective action' in Article 24, there may be genuine discord on timing and on what the most appropriate action is. In his chapter, Cai notes that Western powers have a tendency to urge swift and coercive enforcement measures, and that others may believe that a more temperate approach will sometimes yield better results, especially in the

---

[38] Letter dated 14 December 2015 (n. 37).

[39] Cai, 'Maintaining Peace during a Global Power Shift', Chapter 1 in this volume, section VI (pp. 100–101).

[40] Trahan, *Existing Limits* (n. 37).

[41] These critical remarks were made in a discussion of Trahan's book and not of the ACT-initiative or the Code of Conduct as such: see, e.g., Dire Tladi, 'UNSC Veto Power Symposium: Doing Away with the Veto for Atrocity Crimes? Trimming the Edges of an Illegitimate Institution in Order to Legitimise It', *OpinioJuris*, 1 December 2020, available at https://opiniojuris.org/2020/12/01/unsc-veto-power-symposium-doing-away-with-the-veto-for-atrocity-crimes-trimming-the-edges-of-an-illegitimate-institution-in-order-to-legitimise-it/; Charles Jalloh, 'Are There Jus Cogens Limits to UN Security Council Vetoes in Atrocity Crime Contexts?', *OpinioJuris*, 30 November 2020, available at https://opiniojuris.org/2020/11/30/unsc-veto-power-symposium-are-there-jus-cogens-limits-to-un-security-council-vetoes-in-atrocity-crime-contexts/.

longer run.[42] While opposing, or even vetoing, a useful role for the Security Council can be regarded as highly problematic in some situations, it is also true that the legacy of the West's interventionism does not necessarily always swing the balance in favour of immediate forceful action.

Instead of a focus on the veto or a focus on situations of atrocity crime, therefore, more generalised proposals to improve decision-making might be more in tune with the Security Council's discretion, and the context-specific deliberation and judgement that underlie its decisions and the compromises reached. In this sense, Anna Spain's suggestions for a threefold duty to decide, disclose, and consult[43] – to which Maluwa also positively refers in his chapter in this volume[44] – are noteworthy. They align with the idea that the Security Council acts on behalf of others and is thus accountable to those others in relation to *all* of its decision-making, not only for decisions on atrocity crimes.

A special situation arises, however, when it is one of the P5 that creates a threat or breach of the peace and subsequently uses the veto as shield, as happened when Russia invaded Ukraine in 2022. At the meeting of 25 February 2022 – one day after the invasion – the non-P5 group was particularly large, comprising not only the E10 but also 76 other states, pursuant to Rule 37 of the Security Council's provisional Rules of Procedure. The number of participating states is indicative in itself. The majority of the E10-states (Albania, Gabon, Ghana, Ireland, Kenya, Mexico, and Norway) was very articulate, condemning or deploring the invasion, most labelling it as aggression or otherwise as a breach of Article 2(4) UN Charter and the territorial integrity of Ukraine. India and the United Arab Emirates abstained, while Brazil voted in favour but expressed unease with the use of the word 'aggression', because it felt that word might downplay previous uses of force.[45]

The majority of the E10 states underscored in their statements that Russia's position as a permanent member had particular institutional implications. Ghana expressed deep disappointment. It stated that Russia's actions 'have fallen short of the highest standards expected of those states that are considered to be the enduring guardians of international peace and security. Indeed, for those members of the Security Council with a special privilege, there is also a special responsibility.'[46]

[42] Cai, 'Maintaining Peace during a Global Power Shift', Chapter 1 in this volume, section II.D (pp. 37–38).
[43] Anna Spain, 'The UN Security Council's Duty to Decide', *Harvard National Security Journal* 4 (2013), 320–84.
[44] Maluwa, 'Between Centralism and Regionalism', Chapter 3 in this volume, section IV.C (p. 264).
[45] UN Doc. S/PV.8979, 25 February 2022.
[46] *Ibid.*, 10.

Ghana also voiced dissatisfaction over the fact that the Council was not in a position to act, despite broad agreement, solely because of how the Council is functionally structured. According to Norway, it followed from the spirit of the UN Charter that parties to a dispute should abstain from voting. Norway also held that a veto cast by an aggressor undermined the purposes of the Council.[47] Ireland insisted that the veto would not hinder an adequate response from the international community and expressed support for the comprehensive EU sanctions that had been adopted. Ghana saw the ongoing process in the General Assembly as an alternative opportunity to act and encouraged all states to commit to that process.

The Security Council's predictable dysfunction in relation to the Ukrainian crisis given a permanent member involvement thus created an atmosphere in which the gaze shifted to other organs and organisations. The General Assembly stepped into the limelight, emphasising its potential to 're-unite for peace'.[48] When referring the matter to the General Assembly, given the Security Council deadlock, the E10 once again condemned the use of the veto. Mexico was most forthright in explaining why the use of veto was inappropriate, stating: '[P]ower should not be a privilege. In every situation, it constitutes an enormous and highly sensitive responsibility.'[49]

The 11th Emergency Special Session began on 1 March and resulted in a number of resolutions.[50] Prompted by frustration over the improper use of veto, the General Assembly adopted the veto initiative championed by Liechtenstein during its regular session on 26 April 2022.[51] Resolution ES-11/1, which provides the General Assembly with a standing mandate to convene when a veto is cast in the Security Council, was co-sponsored by 83 states from every UN regional group, including the United States, the United Kingdom, and France. The procedure was triggered quite soon after being created, first in the context of non-proliferation and the Democratic People's Republic of Korea (DPRK) on 8 June 2022, and subsequently on cross-border humanitarian assistance in Syria on 21 July 2022.[52]

---

47 *Ibid.*, 7/8.
48 See also the Valedictory Lecture of Nico Schrijver at Leiden University, 'Re-uniting for Peace through International Law', delivered on 1 July 2022.
49 UN Doc. S/PV.8980, 27 February 2022, 4.
50 GA Res. ES-11/1 of 2 March 2022, UN Doc. A/RES/ES-11/1; GA Res. ES-11/2 of 24 March 2022, UN Doc. A/RES/ES-11/2; GA Res. ES-11/3 of 7 April 2022, UN Doc. A/RES/ES-11/3.
51 GA Res. 76/262 of 26 April 2022, UN Doc. A/RES/76/262.
52 See 'General Assembly Holds Landmark Debate on Security Council's Veto of Draft Text Aimed at Tightening Sanctions against Democratic People's Republic of Korea', UN Doc. GA/ 12423, 8 June 2022, available at https://press.un.org/en/2022/ga12423.doc.htm; 'Speakers Debate Terms, Merits of Cross-Border Aid Operations in Syria's North-West, as General Assembly

Another procedure that allows others – even those not sitting on the Security Council – to inform this body's decision-making and to voice their ideas and/ or concerns is the Arria formula meeting. This type of meeting dates back to 1992, when Venezuelan Ambassador Diego Arria organised an informal meeting in the UN Delegates Lounge to enable a Croatian catholic priest to offer his account of the violence in Bosnia and Herzegovina. Initially organised to allow non-state entities to share their views, in more recent times the formula has also been used to bypass disagreement to hold a formal meeting or as precursor to an Open Debate on a thematic issue.[53] As will be illustrated in this chapter, these meetings provide an opportunity for important conversations about how to improve decision-making and also about future directions for the Security Council in terms of its mandate. In recent years, Arria formula meetings have become increasingly frequent and the variety of states organising them has expanded, which has, in turn, also given rise to claims of a certain politicisation.[54] A significant number of Arria formula meetings have been organised on Ukraine, including on Crimea, by Russia, on the one hand, and by a variety of others states in cooperation with Ukraine, on the other. A considerable number of UN members (some 48 states) have condemned meetings organised by Russia on issues such as alleged violations of humanitarian law committed by Ukraine and on neo-Nazism as abusive and as spreading disinformation.[55]

In sum, the institutional environment has expanded even in dire times. Expansion of the system does not necessarily coincide with its strengthening, as the weaponisation of the Arria formula meetings may illustrate, but it does provide opportunities for other states to participate and to mobilise.

Considers Security Council Text Vetoed by Russian Federation', UN Doc. GA/12436, 21 July 2022, available at https://press.un.org/en/2022/ga12436.doc.htm.

[53] Security Council Report, 'Arria-Formula Meetings', 16 December 2020, available at www.securitycouncilreport.org/un-security-council-working-methods/arria-formula-meetings.php.

[54] Stéphanie Fillion, 'Does the UN Security Council Have an Arria-Formula Problem?', *PassBlue*, 6 July 2021, available at www.passblue.com/2021/07/06/does-the-un-security-council-have-an-arria-formula-problem/. In a similar vein, inviting civil society representatives to speak to the UN Security Council has been politicised recently, as discussed by Stefan Talmon, 'Blocking and Inviting Civil Society Briefers to the UN Security Council', *GPIL Blog*, 22 December 2020, available at https://gpil.jura.uni-bonn.de/2020/12/blocking-and-inviting-civil-society-briefers-to-the-un-security-council/.

[55] See, e.g., Joint Statement following Russia's Arria Formula Meeting on 11 July 2022, available at https://usun.usmission.gov/joint-statement-following-russias-arria-formula-meeting-on-july-11-2022/.

IV. DISPUTED USES OF FORCE AND THE IMPORTANCE OF INCLUSIVE PROCESSES

This section examines the institutional strength of the UN Security Council in relation to its most far-reaching power to maintain peace. The focus of this section is on internal Security Council processes in relation to disputed uses of force. Concrete uses of force, policies, and interpretations that some considered too expansive or even illegal are discussed, with specific attention to the importance of inclusive processes and informed decision-making.

This section discusses, first, the authorised use of force in Libya, based on Resolution 1973, which definitely ended the period of hope and opportunity that had started in the post-1989 moment.[56] Second, it revisits proposals to strengthen use of force discourse in reaction to controversies resulting from the Libya intervention, as well as initiatives of more recent vintage in response to polemics surrounding the exercise of an expanding right to self-defence.

A. *Resolution 1973 and Wavering International Consensus*

Resolution 1973 of 2011 authorised the use of force to protect the civilian population in Libya – especially in Benghazi – excluding foreign occupation forces of any form from any part of Libyan territory. The Resolution was adopted with ten states in favour, none against, and five abstentions – namely, Brazil, China, Germany, India, and Russia. In its immediate aftermath, the ensuing intervention was described by many as successful[57] – but that label very much depends on one's benchmark and may have faded over time. Alex

---

[56] Jochen von Bernstorff, 'The Decay of the International Rule of Law Project (1990–2015)', in Heike Krieger, Georg Nolte, and Andreas Zimmerman (eds), *The International Rule of Law: Rise or Decline* (Oxford: Oxford University Press, 2019), 33–55. According to von Bernstorff, 'the United States and its Western partners arguably missed out on the opportunity to use the "unipolar" moment in modern world history, to eventually realize and entrench a fair rule of law system in international relations': *ibid.*, 34.

[57] Ivo Daalder and James Stavridis, 'NATO's Victory in Libya: The Right Way to Run an Intervention', *Foreign Affairs* 91 (2012), 2–7; Josef Joffé, 'The Libyan War Was a Success. But It Won't Be a Model For Other Wars', *The New Republic*, 24 August 2011, available at https://newrepublic.com/article/94105/joffe-libya-nato-obama-france. For other positive appraisals, See, e.g., Peter Hilpold, 'Intervening in the Name of Humanity: R2P and the Power of Ideas', *Journal of Conflict & Security Law* 17 (2012), 49–79; Alex Bellamy and Paul Williams, 'The New Politics of Protection? Côte d'Ivoire, Libya and the Responsibility to Protect', *International Affairs* 87 (2011), 825–80; Thomas Weiss, 'RtoP Alive and Well after Libya', *Ethics & International Affairs* 25 (2011), 287–92; Gareth Evans, 'The Responsibility to Protect after Libya and Syria' Address to Annual Castan Centre for Human Rights Law Conference, Melbourne, 20 July 2012; Paul D. Williams, 'The Road to Humanitarian War in Libya', *Global Responsibility to Protect* 3 (2011), 248–59.

de Waal was quite quick to nuance the appraisal, submitting that 'the bloodshed of Misrata, the persistent insecurity engendered by armed militias, and the disastrous fallout across the Sahara in Mali are not to be discounted in any final reckoning'.[58] To most international lawyers, the Resolution authorising the 2011 Libya intervention is known especially for its ambiguities and its uncertain precedential value[59] – or even as the nail in the coffin of the Responsibility to Protect (R2P).[60] While the authorisation was clear and explicit in using the 'all necessary means' formula, Resolution 1973 was equivocal as to what measures were authorised exactly. Particular discussion arose, while the operations unfolded,[61] over the question of whether the Resolution also offered a basis for arming opposition groups despite the arms embargo of Resolution 1970 and whether it permitted regime change.

Resolution 1973 must be read in conjunction with Resolution 1970. It was, in fact, the swift adoption of Resolution 1970 that set the stage for the further-reaching Resolution 1973.[62] The adoption of those two resolutions was quite exceptional because of the high speed with which they responded to an unfolding situation (they were adopted, respectively, ten days and three weeks after the uprising started) and because of the consensus that allowed their adoption.[63] Resolution 1970 was even adopted unanimously. It concerned the imposition of an arms embargo, individual sanctions on members of the Gaddafi regime, and a referral to the International Criminal Court (ICC).

Interestingly, the composition of the UN Security Council during the Libya crisis reflected geopolitical power balances optimally, with all BRICS countries (i.e., Brazil, Russia, India, China, and South Africa) having a seat, as well

---

[58]   Alex de Waal, 'African Roles in the Libyan Conflict', *International Affairs* 89 (2013), 365–79 (378).

[59]   Ashley Deeks, 'The NATO Intervention in Libya – 2011', in Tom Ruys, Olivier Corten, and Alexandra Hofer (eds), *The Use of Force in International Law: A Case-Based Approach* (Oxford: Oxford University Press, 2018), 749–59 (749).

[60]   David Berman and Christopher Michaelsen, 'Intervention in Libya: Another Nail in the Coffin for the Responsibility-to-Protect?', *International Community Law Review* 14 (2012), 337–58.

[61]   The military intervention started on 19 March 2011 was named 'Operation Odyssey Dawn' and was conducted by a multilateral coalition led by the United States. Subsequently, NATO stepped in to enforce the no-fly zone and, on 31 March 2011, it took sole command. See 'NATO and Libya (Archived)', last updated November 2015, available at www.nato.int/cps/en/natohq/topics_71652.htm.

[62]   Rebecca Adler-Nissen and Vincent Pouliot, 'Power in Practice: Negotiating the International Intervention in Libya', *European Journal of International Relations* 20 (2014), 889–911.

[63]   Priscilla Hayner, *The Peacemaker's Paradox: Pursuing Justice in the Shadow of Conflict* (London: Routledge, 2018), 181.

as Germany.[64] Notably, all states with permanent seat aspirations were represented. The fact that those states voted positively for an ICC referral can be explained only by a unique set of circumstances coupled with two very determined permanent members (the United Kingdom and France), who wielded their influence astutely.[65] The factor that was arguably decisive was the defection of Libya's deputy permanent representative, and his call for an ICC referral and no-fly zone in a closed Security Council meeting,[66] coupled with the defection of other Libyan ambassadors.[67] In their explanations to the vote, India, South Africa, Nigeria, and Brazil, among others, cited the pleas of the Libyan representatives as influential in their vote.[68] Those states, as well as China, Russia, and Lebanon, also emphasised that, by adopting Resolution 1970, the Security Council supported and complemented demands already made by the Arab League, the Organization of Islamic Cooperation, and the African Union.[69] Russia stated: 'We exhort the Libyan authorities to comply with the demands of the international community, including the League of Arab States and the African Union, which demands have received the support of the Security Council.'[70]

India was even more explicit in admitting that the views and positions of others had directly informed its voting:

> [W]e would have preferred a calibrated and gradual approach. However, we note that several members of the Council, including our colleagues from Africa and the Middle East, believe that referral to the Court would have the effect of an immediate cessation of violence and the restoration of calm and stability. The letter from the Permanent Representative of Libya of 26 February addressed to you, Madame President, has called for such a referral and strengthened this view. We have therefore gone along with the consensus in the Council.[71]

---

[64] Karin Wester, *Intervention in Libya: The Responsibility to Protect in North Africa* (Cambridge: Cambridge University Press, 2020), 124, 126, 131.

[65] On the United Kingdom's and France's negotiation powers, see Adler-Nissen and Pouliot, 'Power in Practice' (n. 62). For a critical appraisal of the penholder practice, see also Cai, 'Maintaining Peace during a Global Power Shift', Chapter 1 in this volume, section II.C.

[66] 'Security Council Press Statement on Libya', UN Doc. SC/10180, 21 February 2011. He was followed by the permanent representative, as well as numerous Libyan ambassadors around the world: Wester, *Intervention in Libya* (n. 64), 108–10.

[67] *Ibid.*

[68] UN Doc. S/PV.6491, 26 February 2011, 2, 3, 7.

[69] *Ibid.*, 4.

[70] *Ibid.*

[71] *Ibid.*, 2.

Broad international consensus was thus a crucial factor behind the unanimous
vote in favour of Resolution 1970. By contrast, Resolution 1973 was adopted in
a much more politically fractured setting. This is clear not only from the voting
record but also – and even more so – from the Resolution's ambivalent construction and the statements made upon its adoption. The Resolution veers between
political and military solution of the conflict. On the one hand, France, the
United Kingdom, the United States, and Lebanon urged swift military action.
France linked the uprising to the broader context of the Arab Spring and warned
of brutal repression: 'The situation in Libya today is more alarming than ever.
[…] We do not have much time left.'[72] The United Kingdom similarly
signalled that Gadaffi's regime was 'now preparing for a violent assault on
a city of 1 million people that has a history dating back 2,500 years. It has
begun air strikes in anticipation of what we expect to be a brutal attack.'[73]

But these premonitions did not gain full traction. India abstained, emphasising
that there was no 'objective analysis of the situation on the ground'.[74] Germany
also abstained, referring to 'the danger of being drawn into a protracted military
conflict that would affect the wider region'.[75] Brazil held a similar view:

> The text of resolution 1973 (2011) contemplates measures that go far beyond
> [the] call [of the League of Arab States for a no-fly zone]. We are not
> convinced that the use of force as provided for in paragraph 4 of the resolution
> will lead to the realization of our common objective – the immediate end to
> violence and the protection of civilians. We are also concerned that such
> measures may have the unintended effect of exacerbating tensions on the
> ground and causing more harm than good to the very same civilians we are
> committed to protecting.[76]

Russia and China equally abstained, cautioning that many questions regarding the use of force had remained unanswered, such as those regarding the
rules of engagements and the limits of the use of force.[77]

The abstaining states attached great importance to the viewpoints and
position of the Arab League and the African Union – in particular, the latter's
efforts towards political reform and a peaceful solution.[78] Nigeria and South

---

[72]   UN Doc. S/PV.6498, 17 March 2011, 2, 3.
[73]   *Ibid.*, 4.
[74]   *Ibid.*, 6.
[75]   *Ibid.*, 5.
[76]   *Ibid.*, 6.
[77]   *Ibid.*, 8.
[78]   The African Union's efforts – and particularly the AU Roadmap – are discussed in more detail
       in Maluwa, 'Between Centralism and Regionalism', Chapter 3 in this volume, section III.B
       (pp. 214–215).

Africa emphasised the language in the resolution that supported a political solution and a role for the Committee established by the African Union.[79] Jointly, these states held the swing vote and so they had a de facto veto power. Nonetheless, despite their preference for a political solution, as proposed by the AU Roadmap, and despite their kingmaker position, the African states greenlit the Security Council resolution authorising force.[80]

The ambiguity that was apparent upon adoption became intractable as the military operations – led first by the United States and then under NATO command – unfolded. The fragile consensus broke almost immediately. As the AU efforts for political solutions were sidelined and those in favour of a military solution formed the Libya Contact Group,[81] South Africa, Russia, and China accused NATO of overreach and mission creep. The interpretive debate over whether Resolution 1973 provided a basis for assistance of the rebels and for regime change was held largely *outside* of the UN Security Council, mainly in newspaper articles and press statements, as well as in the General Assembly dialogue on the R2P.[82] In May 2011, the African Union issued a declaration that rebuked the 'one-sided interpretations of these resolutions', insisting that 'the military and other actions on the ground ... were clearly outside the scope of these resolutions'.[83] It received short shrift and the declaration had little impact.

International law scholars are divided over the interpretive question, with some emphasising the objective articulated in paragraph 4 (to protect civilians and civilian populated areas under threat of attack) as limiting in character and excluding regime change and rebel support,[84] and others suggesting that the use of force against Gaddafi's regime and the assistance of the rebels who were protecting the civilian population were in line with the overall goal and

---

79 UN Doc. S/PV.6498, 17 March 2011, 9.
80 In her book, Karin Wester raises the question of why states that had such misgivings about the resolution did not prevent its adoption. Her interlocutors refer to Libya's pariah status and also the unwillingness of the states concerned to be responsible for a potential massacre: Wester, *Intervention in Libya* (n. 64), 179–80.
81 The Libya Contact Group was established at the initiative of France to guide the operations outside the NATO and the Security Council: Letter dated 29 March 2011 from the Permanent Representative of the United Kingdom of Great Britain and Northern Ireland to the United Nations addressed to the President of the Security Council, UN Doc. S/2011/204, 30 March 2011.
82 Geir Ulfstein and Hege Føsund Christiansen, 'The Legality of the NATO Bombing in Libya', *International and Comparative Law Quarterly* 62 (2011), 159–71.
83 Extraordinary Session of the Assembly of the Union, AU Doc. EXT/ASSEMBLY/AU/DEC/ (01.2011), 25 May 2011, as cited by Christine Gray, *International Law and the Use of Force* (Oxford: Oxford University Press, 4th edn, 2018), 379.
84 Ulfstein and Christiansen, 'The Legality of the NATO Bombing in Libya' (n. 82), 159–71.

spirit of Resolution 1973.[85] Given that Russia, China, and also South Africa voted for a text that clearly included authorising language, and because they were conscious at the time of voting of how others might interpret the Resolution, their claims of illegality seem far-fetched.[86] Indeed, one of the very reasons Russia mentioned, to explain its abstention, was precisely that too many questions remained on what the limits of the use of force would be. It nevertheless chose not to use its veto and left the Resolution intentionally ambiguous.[87] Russia did not insist on an exclusion of regime change, similar to the explicit exclusion of foreign occupation that was included in paragraph 4 of Resolution 1973. In her autobiography, Hilary Clinton recounts her conversation with Russian Foreign Minister Sergey Lavrov ahead of the vote on Resolution 1973, during which she insisted on the possibility of a forceful response against Gaddafi if need be. On his later claims that he and Russia had been misled, Clinton observes, 'that struck me as disingenuous since Lavrov, as a former Ambassador to the UN, knew as well as anyone what "all necessary measures" meant'.[88] The lesson to be learned from Libya, therefore, is not necessarily to veto any subsequent proposal for the use of force, as Russia and China subsequently did in relation to Syria, but rather that the limits to an authorised use of force need to be spelled out in much more detail in the authorising resolution.

Yet even if Resolution 1973 offered a legal basis for the operation, one could still argue that giving so little quarter to African views and concerns during the process of implementation created tensions with the principle of good faith. After all, Africa was the continent where the actions took place and where repercussions were most immediately felt, and hence the way in which Resolution 1973 was implemented does not seem fully in tandem with a broader institutional perspective that emphasises the importance of inclusive processes.

---

[85] Deeks, 'The NATO Intervention in Libya' (n. 59), 749–59; Dire Tladi, 'Security Council, the Use of Force and Regime Change: Libya and Côte d'Ivoire', *South African Yearbook of International Law* 37 (2013), 22–45; Christian Henderson, 'International Measures for the Protection of Civilians in Libya and Côte d'Ivoire', *International and Comparative Law Quarterly* 60 (2012), 767–78; Mehrdad Payandeh, 'The United Nations Military Intervention, and Regime Change in Libya', *Virginia Journal of International Law* 52 (2012), 354–403 (387).

[86] See also, for similar claims, Eric Posner, 'Outside the Law', *Foreign Policy*, 25 October 2011, available at https://foreignpolicy.com/2011/10/25/outside-the-law/.

[87] A point also made by Henderson, 'International Measures' (n. 85), with reference to Michael Byers, 'Agreeing to Disagree: Security Council Resolution 1441 and Intentional Ambiguity', *Global Governance* 10 (2004), 165–86.

[88] Hillary Rodham Clinton, *Hard Choices* (London: Simon & Schuster, 2014), 372, as cited by Wester, *Intervention in Libya* (n. 64), 169.

De Waal submits that the African Union's diagnosis of the conflict was fundamentally correct.[89] The African leaders of Libya's Sahara neighbouring states appreciated the profound differences between the uprisings in Tunisia and Egypt, on the one hand, versus Libya, on the other. Given Libya's history and its institutional void, there was an enormous risk of escalation into fully fledged civil war.[90] Leaders such as Chadian President Idriss Déby Itno were also keenly aware that loosening Gaddafi's grip on transnational armed groups, in combination with the opening of vast arsenals in military bases, planted seeds for great instability across the region.[91] Had the P3 (i.e., the United States, the United Kingdom, and France) joined forces with the African Union, they would have benefited from enhanced African inside knowledge on the ground. And perhaps the AU plan for a negotiated settlement, backed by the P3 threat of force and the threat of implementing the ICC referral, might have resulted in a better managed transition.[92] Instead, African states bore the brunt of the intervention while European states were very unwelcoming to Libyan refugees escaping the turmoil.[93]

Certainly, the African Union itself is partially to blame for these outcomes, because it suffered from internal divisions and took its time to arrive at a clear-cut position. It did not manage to flex its political and diplomatic muscle sufficiently, and it may have deferred too readily to the Arab League under the loose notion of regional subsidiarity, as Maluwa discusses in his chapter in this volume.[94] But it is also true that ignoring Africa to such an extent does not exhibit a spirit of multilateralism and institutionalism. Maluwa highlights lessons that the African Union might learn from the Libya situation in terms of its relationship with the United Nations.[95] Likewise, the UN Security Council – and particularly the P3 – should learn lessons, including that the views of relevant regional organisations must be taken into account more seriously not least because those organisations will often have relevant understanding of events on the ground. This is a lesson very much in the spirit of the 'Ezulwini Consensus', which Maluwa discusses.[96]

---

[89]   De Waal, 'African Roles in the Libyan Conflict' (n. 58), 379.

[90]   See generally, on Libya's trajectory, Dirk Vandewalle, *History of Modern Libya* (Cambridge: Cambridge University Press, 2nd edn, 2012).

[91]   Alex de Waal, '"My Fears, Alas, Were Not Unfounded": Africa's Responses to the Libya Conflict', in Aidan Hehir and Robert Murray (eds), *Libya, the Responsibility to Protect and the Future of Humanitarian Intervention* (Berlin: Springer, 2013), 58–82.

[92]   De Waal, 'African Roles in the Libyan Conflict' (n. 58), 379.

[93]   Wester, *Intervention in Libya* (n. 64), 114–16.

[94]   Maluwa, 'Between Centralism and Regionalism', Chapter 3 in this volume, section III.B (p. 211).

[95]   *Ibid.*, section III.B.2.

[96]   *Ibid.*, section III.A (p. 202).

Remarkably, though, the two countries leading the operation came to very different ex post appreciations regarding their intervention. In a general informative report on Libya of 2015, the French Parliament's Commission of Foreign Affairs concluded that the intervention had unquestionably prevented the announced massacre. As regards the contestation over the implementation of the Resolution, the Commission noted that neither Russia or China nor South Africa had opposed Resolution 1973. The Commission blamed the failure to develop a sound post-intervention plan on the international community as a whole and it singled out Germany for creating 'malaise' in the European position.[97]

In contrast, the Foreign Affairs Committee of the UK House of Commons was much more critical. It held that decision-making regarding the intervention had been 'intelligence-light'. It particularly exposed the failure to identify that 'the threat to civilians was overstated and that the rebels included a significant Islamist element'. The result of the regime change policy, coupled with a lack of strategy for the post-Gaddafi Libya, was 'political and economic collapse, inter-militia and inter-tribal warfare, humanitarian and migrant crises, widespread human rights violations, the spread of Gaddafi regime weapons across the region and the growth of ISIL in North Africa'.[98]

These contrasting parliamentary commentaries are telling in themselves and reflective of the fact that democratic accountability for the use of military force is much more developed in the United Kingdom than in France.[99] The UK account is most aligned with an institutional perspective: the gist of it underscores the imperative of obtaining a good grasp of the situation before going in, which presupposes relying on international consensus and cooperation. The UK account is also more reflective of an ability to engage critically and the United Kingdom thus seems to display a greater willingness to learn lessons. This difference is remarkable, and it evokes the question of whether

---

[97] Assemblée Nationale, *Rapport d'Information sur la Libye*, No. 3259 (2015), 17–24.

[98] House of Commons Foreign Affairs Committee, *Libya: Examination of Intervention and Collapse and the UK's Future Policy Options*, Third Report of Session 2016–17, September 2016, HC 119.

[99] Compare Katja Ziegler, 'The Use of Military Force by the United Kingdom', in Curtis Bradley (ed.), *The Oxford Handbook of Comparative Foreign Relations Law* (Oxford: Oxford University Press, 2019), 771–90, and Mathias Forteau, 'Using Military Force and Engaging in Collective Security: The Case of France', in Bradley (ed.), op. cit., 811–28. See also Veronica Fikfak and Hayley Hooper, *Parliament's Secret War* (London: Hart, 2018); Veronica Fikfak, 'War, International Law and the Rise of Parliament: The Influence of International Law on UK Parliamentary Practice with Respect to the Use of Force', in Helmut Philipp Aust and Thomas Kleinlein (eds), *Encounters between Foreign Relations Law and International Law: Bridges and Boundaries* (Cambridge: Cambridge University Press, 2021), 299–316.

the international law of peace and security should not be more concerned with *domestic* checks and balances and accountability processes (e.g., inquiries) in relation to the resort to war powers.

B. *Proposals to Refine Decision-Making and Discourse on the Use of Force*

As is well known, Russia used the selective interpretation of Resolution 1973 as an argument against meaningful action in Syria.[100] It has been recognised, though, that the 'Libya pretext' does not fully explain the positions of Russia and China, respectively, regarding Syria, because these were mostly guided by the very different geopolitical interests at stake. Russia's position was informed by its close alliance with Assad and its desire to maintain influence in the Middle East.[101] As for China – as Cai also notes in his chapter in this volume[102] – whereas the stakes in Libya were very high[103] and it could not risk blocking the Libya Resolution in isolation,[104] Chinese economic interests in Syria were much less significant and it vetoed in this context consistently in tandem with Russia. In relation to understanding self-interest, Maluwa makes the very important point that this can also include ideological aspects beyond the immediate financial and economic interests of a state, and he points out that, through their attitude in relation to Syria, both China and Russia have underscored and renewed their commitment to the principle of

[100] Explaining its use of veto for a draft resolution on Syria, Russia stated:

> The situation in Syria cannot be considered in the Council separately from the Libyan experience. The international community is alarmed by statements that compliance with Security Council resolutions on Libya in the NATO interpretation is a model for the future actions of NATO in implementing the responsibility to protect. It is easy to see that today's "Unified Protector" model could happen in Syria.

See UN Doc. S/PV.6627, 4 October 2011, 4.

[101] Alex J. Bellamy, 'From Tripoli to Damascus? Lesson Learning and the Implementation of the Responsibility to Protect', *International Politics* 51 (2014), 23–44; Sarah Brockmeier, Oliver Stuenkel, and Marcos Tourinho, 'The Impact of the Libya Intervention Debates on Norms of Protection', *Global Society* 30 (2016), 113–33.

[102] Cai, 'Maintaining Peace during a Global Power Shift', Chapter 1 in this volume, section V.B (p. 80).

[103] While voting in favour of Resolution 1970 (2011) – which included the imposition of UN sanctions – as well as the ICC referral, the Chinese delegation insisted that 'the safety and interests of foreign nationals in Libya must be assured': UN Doc. S/PV.6491, 26 February 2011, 4. China then had approximately 36,000 workers on the ground in Libya working mainly in oil, construction, and telecommunications, and they were evacuated in an unprecedented evacuation operation. See also *ibid.*, cons. 12, 14, which refer to the need to protect foreign nationals and workers, thus taking Chinese concerns in this respect into account.

[104] Yun Sun, 'China's Acquiescence on UNSCR 1973: No Big Deal', *Stimson Center*, 31 March 2011, available at www.stimson.org/2011/china-acquiescence-unscr-1973-no-big-deal/.

non-interference[105] – as well as, it might be added, to a rather absolute and statist understanding of this principle.

Following the disquiet over the Libya controversy, proposals aimed at achieving more structural ambitions of a procedural nature emerged. In essence, these proposals aimed at refining Security Council decision-making on matters related to the use of force. Brazil and, informally, China put forward separate proposals.

1. Responsibility while Protecting and Responsible Protection

Most prominently, Brazil introduced the concept of 'Responsibility while Protecting' (RWP) to complement the R2P.[106] In the wake of the authorised Libya intervention, Brazil's proposal sought to assure that collective security measures meant to implement the R2P would not be abused. It referred to the 'growing perception that the concept of the responsibility to protect might be misused for purposes other than protecting civilians, such as regime change'.[107] Brazil proposed fundamental principles, parameters, and procedures to ensure that the two concepts, R2P and RWP, would evolve hand in hand:

(a) Just as in the medical sciences, prevention is always the best policy; it is the emphasis on preventive diplomacy that reduces the risk of armed conflict and the human costs associated with it;

(b) The international community must be rigorous in its efforts to exhaust all peaceful means available in the protection of civilians under threat of violence, in line with the principles and purposes of the Charter and as embodied in the 2005 World Summit Outcome;

(c) The use of force, including in the exercise of the responsibility to protect, must always be authorized by the Security Council, in accordance with Chapter VII of the Charter, or, in exceptional circumstances, by the General Assembly, in line with its resolution 377 (V);

(d) The authorization for the use of force must be limited in its legal, operational and temporal elements and the scope of military action must abide by the letter and the spirit of the mandate conferred by the Security Council or the General Assembly, and be carried out in strict

---

[105] Maluwa, 'Between Centralism and Regionalism', Chapter 3 in this volume, section III.B (p. 205).

[106] Annex to the letter dated 9 November 2011 from the Permanent Representative of Brazil to the United Nations addressed to the Secretary-General, UN Doc. A/66/551–S/2011/701, 11 November 2011 ('Responsibility while Protecting: Elements for the Development and Promotion of a Concept').

[107] *Ibid.*, para. 10.

conformity with international law, in particular international humanitarian law and the international law of armed conflict;

(e) The use of force must produce as little violence and instability as possible and under no circumstance can it generate more harm than it was authorized to prevent;

(f) In the event that the use of force is contemplated, action must be judicious, proportionate and limited to the objectives established by the Security Council;

(g) These guidelines must be observed throughout the entire length of the authorization, from the adoption of the resolution to the suspension of the authorization by a new resolution;

(h) Enhanced Security Council procedures are needed to monitor and assess the manner in which resolutions are interpreted and implemented to ensure responsibility while protecting;

(i) The Security Council must ensure the accountability of those to whom authority is granted to resort to force.[108]

Brazil's proposal aimed at both improving decision-making in a substantive sense by suggesting concrete criteria and conditions, as well as in an institutional sense by putting forward suggestions for the creation of new procedures, including elements of oversight.

In response to Brazil's proposal and also to justify its position in relation to Syria, China unofficially launched the concept of 'Responsible Protection'.[109] The concept was introduced in a publication by Ruan Zongzhe, vice-president of the China Institute for International Studies (CIIS), which is the official think tank of China's Ministry of Foreign Affairs. The concept proposed six elements: four concerned substantive criteria to guide the UN Security Council in determining the appropriateness of military action for humanitarian purposes; one related to post-intervention responsibilities; and another proposed mechanisms for the monitoring and supervision of any military intervention.[110]

The RWP proposal lost momentum when Brazil's term on the Security Council ended and when it lost the support of its two main champions, President Dilma Roussef and Foreign Minister Antonio Patriota.[111] Neither

---

[108]   *Ibid.*, para. 11.

[109]   See also Cai, 'Maintaining Peace during a Global Power Shift', Chapter 1 in this volume, section V.D (p. 92).

[110]   Andrew Garwood-Gowers, 'China's "Responsible Protection" Concept: Reinterpreting the Responsibility to Protect (R2P) and Military Intervention for Humanitarian Purposes', *Asian Journal of International Law* 6 (2016), 89–118.

[111]   Jeremy Farrell, Marie-Eve Loiselle, Christopher Michaelsen, Jochen Prantl, and Jeni Whalan, 'Elected Member Influence in the United Nations Security Council', *Leiden Journal of International Law* 33 (2020), 101–15 (107). See also Andrés Serbin and Andrei Serbin

did China formally adopt the concept of Responsible Protection or advocate it otherwise. Both proposals to refine use-of-force decision-making post Libya were discontinued.

2. Article 51 Reporting as a Means of Enhancing Decision-Making and Discourse on the Use of Force

Other states not (permanently) on the UN Security Council have, more recently, revived the call for improved use-of-force decision-making. These new calls concern the exercise of the right to self-defence, and they zero in on greater transparency and on increasing the conversation on the law governing the use of force.

While originally in tandem with Brazil, Mexico is currently taking the lead. Its call aims to create possibilities for more inclusive debates. Mexico's concern around this topic emerged from its discontent with the 'unable and unwilling' doctrine, which then incumbent US President Trump had also referred to in a tweet regarding the movement of migrants from Central America, exclaiming that 'Mexican soldiers hurt, were unable, or unwilling to stop Caravan'.[112] Being a US neighbour, Mexico thus had special interests in circumscribing a doctrine that was developed in the context of other situations. Yet while its proposals originated from anxiety over the 'unable and unwilling' doctrine in the context of self-defence justifications, Mexico framed its questions in a more generic way pertaining to self-defence and Article 51 reporting more broadly. Mexico's concern has thus expanded into a broader commitment to creating more space at the Security Council for proper discourse on the law of peace and war.

In the Special Committee on the Charter of the United Nations and on the Strengthening of the Role of the Organization, Mexico noted the increase of Article 51 communications, and it introduced a fully fledged proposal that sought to create space for discussion by all UN member states on Article 51 UN Chapter and its interrelationship with Article 2(4). Mexico's concrete aim was

---

Pont, 'Brazil's Responsibility while Protecting: A Failed Attempt of Global South Norm Innovation?', *Pensamiento Proprio* 20 (2015), 171–92; Kai Michael Kenkel and Cristina G. Stefan, 'Brazil and the Responsibility while Protecting Initiative: Norms and the Timing of Diplomatic Support', *Global Governance* 22 (2016), 41–58.

[112] Pablo Arrocha Olabuenaga, 'An Insider's View on the Life-Cycle of Self-Defense Reports by UN Member States: Challenges Posed to the International Order', *Just Security*, 2 April 2019, available at www.justsecurity.org/63415/an-insiders-view-of-the-life-cycle-of-self-defense-reports-by-u-n-member-states/.

to provide more clarity as to the implementation of Article 51's reporting requirement and it subdivided the relevant questions into three groups:

(a) **Substantive issues:** Given that under Article 51 the right to self-defence may only be invoked if there has been an armed attack:

    (i) What must be included in reports submitted to the Security Council under Article 51?

    (ii) What level of detail is required in reports under Article 51 as a precondition for the invocation of self-defence?

    (iii) How should Article 51 be interpreted with regard to attacks perpetrated by non-State actors, in particular, but not exclusively, terrorist attacks?

    (iv) Under Article 51 of the Charter, can self-defence be invoked in respect of another State when that State is considered to lack the capacity or the will to address an armed attack?

(b) **Procedural issues:** Given that the inherent right to self-defence may be exercised, under Article 51, 'until the Security Council has taken measures necessary to maintain international peace and security', and that 'measures taken by Members in the exercise of this right of self-defence shall be immediately reported to the Security Council':

    (i) What is a reasonable time frame for the submission of a report under Article 51 following an armed attack?

    (ii) Must a report under Article 51 be submitted before the use of force in self-defence, or can it be submitted afterwards?

    (iii) Is it desirable and necessary for the Security Council to discuss, examine and consider reports submitted to it under Article 51?

    (iv) Is it necessary for the Security Council to take measures necessary to maintain international peace and security after a State has invoked its right to self-defence?

    (v) How can a lack of action by the Security Council following receipt of a report under Article 51 be interpreted, in particular with regard to recurring reports concerning the same situation?

(c) **Transparency and publicity issues:** Since reporting under Article 51 is an obligation under the Charter and is directly related to issues of international peace and security, it serves the interests of all Member States. In this regard:

    (i) How can the transparency and publicity of reports submitted under Article 51 be improved?

   (ii) What can be done to facilitate the access of Member States to
         these reports?
  (iii) What can be done to facilitate the access of Member States to any
         responses and reactions to these reports?
   (iv) What can be done to improve access to information, taking into
         account the delay in the publication of the Repertoire of the
         Practice of the Security Council?
    (v) How can the lack of responses from Member States to reports
         submitted under Article 51 be interpreted, taking into account the
         current lack of transparency and publicity?[113]

Within the General Assembly's Charter Committee, however, there was no
consensus to transpose this item from the category of new proposals to the
main agenda. One of the arguments barring consensus was that it was for the
Security Council to deal with those matters. As a non-permanent member
elected to sit on the Security Council in 2021–22, Mexico then pursued its
quest at that level and expressed its ambition to address 'the opacity with which
the Security Council has been handling situations on which States have
invoked their right to self-defence in accordance with Article 51 of the UN
Charter'.[114] It effectively organised an Arria formula meeting to this effect on
24 February 2021, which is discussed below.[115]

   3. Substantiating the Reporting Requirement: The Importance of Facts

The first question that Mexico raised was: what must be included in reports
submitted to the Security Council under Article 51? One element of this
question regards factual substantiation: to what extent are states required to
release information substantiating their legal claims? As a starting point, one
may argue that the prohibition on the use of force is a cornerstone of the
international legal order and non-authorised use of force is the exception. This
starting point implies that states using force – and thus violating a central
norm – should provide appropriate justification not only in legal terms but also

[113] Annex to the Report of the Special Committee on the Charter of the United Nations and on
       the Strengthening of the Role of the Organisation, UN Doc. A/76/33, 25 February 2021,
       para. 14.
[114] Pablo Arrocha Olabuenga and Ambassador H.E. Juan Ramón de la Fuente, 'Mexico's
       Priorities as an Elected Member to the Security Council for 2021–2022', *Just Security*,
       7 July 2020, available at www.justsecurity.org/71241/mexicos-priorities-as-an-elected-mem
       ber-to-the-security-council-for-2021-2022/.
[115] See 'Upholding the Collective Security System of the UN Charter: Security Council Open
       Arria Formula Meeting, 24 February 2021', 16 March 2021, available at www.unmultimedia.org/
       avlibrary/asset/2604/2604457/.

with facts supporting their legal claims. Specifically in the context of self-defence against non-state actors, the Leiden Policy Recommendations on Counterterrorism and International Law, which offer expert perspectives aimed at clarifying the law and which highlight areas in which greater consensus needs to be pursued, underscore this obligation of states to justify their actions and insist that states using force in self-defence bear the burden of making their case:

> Self-defence may also be necessary if the armed attack cannot be repelled or averted by the territorial State. States relying on self-defence *must therefore show* that the territorial State's action is not effective in countering the terrorist threat.
>
> As the application of [the principle of necessity and proportionality] is heavily fact-dependent, States using force in self-defence should be prepared to make publicly available information and data that will support the necessity and proportionality of their conduct. International law does not prevent third States from scrutinizing the necessity and proportionality of self-defence operations from requesting further evidence.
>
> Any use of force in anticipatory self-defence should be justified publicly by reference to the evidence available to the State concerned; the facts do not speak for themselves, and the State should explain, as fully as it is able to do, the nature of the threat and the necessity for anticipatory military action.[116]

The Chatham House Principles of International Law on the Use of Force by States in Self-Defence also emphasise the eminence of facts, including in cases of anticipatory self-defence.[117] Principle 4 states that 'force may be used only on a proper factual basis and after a good faith assessment of the facts', and it elaborates thus:

> Each case will necessarily turn on its own facts.
>
> [...]
>
> The determination of 'imminence' is in the first place for the relevant state to make, but it must be made in good faith and on grounds which are capable of objective assessment. Insofar as this can reasonably be achieved, the

[116] Larissa van den Herik and Nico Schrijver, 'Leiden Policy Recommendations on Counterterrorism and International Law', *Netherlands International Law Review* 57 (2010), 531–50 (paras 42, 44, 48, respectively) (emphasis added).
[117] Elizabeth Windhurst, 'The Chatham House Principles on the Use of Force in Self-Defence', *International and Comparative Law Quarterly* 55 (2006), 963–72. Positively referenced too by, e.g., the Australian Attorney-General Senator the Hon. George Brandis QC, in his lecture 'The Right to Self-Defence against Imminent Armed Attack in International Law', *EJIL: Talk!*, 25 March 2017, available at www.ejiltalk.org/the-right-of-self-defence-against-imminent-armed-attack-in-international-law/.

evidence should be publicly demonstrable. Some kinds of evidence cannot be reasonably produced, whether because of the nature or source, or because it is the product of interpretation of many small pieces of information. But evidence is fundamental to accountability, and accountability to the rule of law. The more far-reaching, and the more irreversible its external actions, the more a state should accept (internally as well as externally) the burden of showing that its actions were justifiable on the facts. And there should be proper internal procedures for the assessment of intelligence and appropriate procedural safeguards.[118]

Whatever one's opinion on the permissibility of self-defence against non-state actors, the 'unable and unwilling' doctrine, or anticipatory self-defence, the general idea that states invoking an exception must make their case in a legal sense supported by facts is not extravagant. In fact, it is precisely the obligation to provide a substantiated legal justification to the entire international community that positions other states to react and offer their views on legality and permissibility.

Yet, at the Mexico Arria formula meeting of February 2021, states expressed very different views on this matter. Liechtenstein upheld the idea that states invoking self-defence owe the international community of UN members a 'thorough and convincing' justification that, at a minimum, includes evidence of proportionality and necessity – and imminence, if applicable.[119] Austria too emphasised that Article 51 letters should not only report measures but also include relevant background information so as to enable assessments of proportionality, necessity, and imminence.[120] The United States, in sharp contrast, insisted that Article 51 did not prescribe what should be included in reporting letters other than a description of measures taken. It noted that state practice varies and that these letters may include a detailed legal justification but that this is not required. The purpose of the letters, according to the United States, was only to put the Security Council on notice.[121] With fewer words, France took the same position,[122] and the United Kingdom echoed that the UN Charter does not impose a specific form. The United Kingdom observed that even oral notification was allowed.[123] These positions are not easily

---

[118]   Windhurst, 'The Chatham House Principles' (n. 117), 968.
[119]   Letter dated 8 March 2021 from the Permanent Representative of Mexico to the United Nations addressed to the Secretary-General and the President of the Security Council, UN Doc. S/2021/247, 16 March 2021, 47. See also n. 115 for the full statement.
[120]   *Ibid.*, 14.
[121]   *Ibid.*, 30–1.
[122]   *Ibid.*, 35. The Netherlands also plainly noted that 'the Charter does not specify how to notify or what to include in a notification under Article 51': *ibid.*, 55.
[123]   *Ibid.*, 64.

aligned with the calls by these very same states for strong institutions and multilateralism. In particular, the position of France that Article 51 does not impose formalism, and hence does not call for evidence-based reporting, stands in quite some contrast with France's call for agile organisation as part of the Alliance for Multilateralism. The same is true of Germany's absence in the debate.

In the specific context of cyber operations, too, the question of whether there is a legal obligation to release underlying evidence has been openly disputed. On the one hand, the 2015 UN Group of Experts noted that 'accusations of organizing and implementing wrongful acts brought against States should be substantiated'.[124] Yet, in contrast, US Legal Adviser Brian J. Egan stated in 2016 that:

> [T]here is no legal obligation to reveal evidence on which attribution is based prior to taking appropriate action. There may, of course, be political pressure to do so, and States may choose to reveal such evidence to convince other States to join them in condemnation, for example. But this is a policy choice – it is not compelled by international law.[125]

British legal adviser Jeremy Wright articulated similar views: 'There is no legal obligation requiring a state to publicly disclose the underlying information on which its decision to attribute hostile activity is based, or to publicly attribute hostile cyber activity that it has suffered in all circumstances.'[126] These views, however, particularly concern cyber operations below the use-of-force threshold. They are informed by the classified nature that specifically surrounds the cyber capabilities and vulnerabilities of states, and especially the interests of accusing states not to disclose the sources and methods used by their law enforcement and intelligence agencies. In addition to the United States and the United Kingdom, other Western states and allies, such as France and the Netherlands, have also insisted that there is no legal obligation to disclose evidence in the context of cyber accusations.[127] Russia and China,

---

[124] Report of the Group of Governmental Experts on Developments in the Field of Information and Telecommunications in the Context of International Security, UN Doc. A/70/174, 22 July 2015 (hereinafter UNGGE Report), para. 28(f); GA Res. 70/237 of 30 December 2015, UN Doc. A/RES/70/237.

[125] Brian J. Egan, 'International Law and Stability in Cyberspace', *Berkeley Journal of International Law* 35 (2017), 169–80.

[126] Jeremy Wright QC MP, 'Cyber and International Law in the 21st Century', 23 May 2018, available at www.gov.uk/government/speeches/cyber-and-international-law-in-the-21st-century.

[127] French Ministry of the Armies, *Droit International Appliqué aux Opérations dans le Cyberspace* [*International Law Applicable to Operations in Cyberspace*], September 2019;

in contrast, have instead pushed for a requirement to substantiate.[128] This is easily explained by the fact that these latter two states are generally on the receiving end of such accusations, which they tend to deny.[129] These two states also take the position that attribution is almost impossible – a view also taken by Cai in his chapter in this volume[130] – which would mean that a requirement to substantiate would effectively create an insurmountable burden.

The divergence of views on the obligation to substantiate has been recognised in the Tallinn Manual 2.0.[131] Kristen Eichensehr has made compelling arguments against the Western positions that block the development of evidentiary standards for cyber accusations. She underscores that clarity on facts can ultimately contribute to clarity about what is permissible state behaviour.[132] Martha Finnemore and Duncan Hollis have also predicted that demands for documentations will rise as public cyber accusations become more common, which will then likely result in efforts to normalise and streamline informational practices.[133] In its position paper of March 2021 on the application of international law to cyberspace, Germany paves the way for such a future development:

> Germany agrees that there is no general obligation under international law as it currently stands to publicize a decision on attribution and to provide or to submit for public scrutiny detailed evidence on which an attribution is based. This generally applies also if response measures are taken. Any such publication in a particular case is generally based on political considerations and does not create legal obligations for the State under international law. Also, it is within the political discretion of a State to decide on the timing of a public act of attribution. Nevertheless, Germany supports the UN Group of Governmental Experts' position in its 2015 report that accusations of cyber-related misconduct against a State *should* be substantiated. States should

---

Letter dated 5 July 2019 from the Minister of Foreign Affairs to the President of the House of Representatives on the international legal order in cyberspace, available at www.government.nl/documents/parliamentary-documents/2019/09/26/letter-to-the-parliament-on-the-international-legal-order-in-cyberspace.

[128] See, e.g., Draft GA Res. A/C.1/73/L.27 of 22 October 2018 on developments in the field of information and telecommunications in the context of international security, para. 10.

[129] Kristen E. Eichensehr, 'The Law and Politics of Cyberattack Attribution', *UCLA Law Review* 67 (2020), 520–98.

[130] Cai, 'Maintaining Peace during a Global Power Shift', Chapter 1 in this volume, section IV.C (p. 72).

[131] Michael N. Schmitt and Liis Vihul (eds), *Tallinn Manual 2.0 on the International Law Applicable to Cyber Operations* (Cambridge: Cambridge University Press, 2nd edn, 2017), 83.

[132] Eichensehr, 'Cyberattack Attribution' (n. 129).

[133] Martha Finnemore and Duncan B. Hollis, 'Beyond Naming and Shaming: Accusations and International Law in Cybersecurity', *European Journal of International Law* 31 (2020), 969–1003.

provide information and reasoning and – if circumstances permit – attempt to communicate and cooperate with the State in question to clarify the allegations raised. This may bolster the transparency, legitimacy and general acceptance of decisions on attribution and any response measures taken.[134]

Similarly, even if less expressly, Italy stressed the importance of transparency, and maintained that attribution of wrongful cyber activities should be reasonable and credibly based on factual elements related to relevant circumstances of the case, even if there is no general international requirement for this.[135] In the same vein, the report of the UN on Developments in the Field of Information and Telecommunications in the Context of International Security also stated in its 2021 report that accusations should be substantiated.[136]

While the law on attribution and substantiation in the context of cyber operations below the use-of-force threshold is as yet rather immature and cannot be extrapolated to more generic settings nor to the broader law on peace and war, it is still notable that core ideas on substantiation are ever more present in this still very unsettled cyber context. Interestingly, in the same position paper, Germany took a firm position on the reporting requirement in the context of self-defence actions against malicious cyber-attacks. It held that the determination of whether a certain malicious cyber operation was comparable to a traditional armed attack in scale and effects, thereby justifying resort to the use self-defence, was not a decision left to the discretion of the victim state. Instead, according to Germany's position, such a determination 'needs to be comprehensively reported to the international community, i.e., the UN Security Council, according to art. 51 UN Charter'.[137]

Proceeding on this premise that the obligation to release some evidence is inherent in the exceptional nature of non-authorised use of force and thus

---

[134] The Federal Government, *On the Application of International Law in Cyberspace* [Position Paper], March 2021, available at https://documents.unoda.org/wp-content/uploads/2021/12/Germany-Position-Paper-On-the-Application-of-International-Law-in-Cyberspace.pdf, 12 (footnotes omitted). No specific position was taken on this point in the Final Substantive Report of the Open-Ended Working Group on Developments in the Field of Information and Telecommunications in the Context of International Security, UN Doc. A/AC. 290/2021/CRP.2, 10 March 2021.

[135] Italy, *On International Law and Cyberspace* [Position Paper], 4 November 2021, available at www.esteri.it/mae/resource/doc/2021/11/italian_position_paper_on_international_law_and_cyberspace.pdf. See also Switzerland, *On the Application of International Law in Cyberspace* [Position Paper], 27 May 2021, available at www.eda.admin.ch/dam/eda/en/documents/aussenpolitik/voelkerrecht/20210527-Schweiz-Annex-UN-GGE-Cybersecurity-2019-2021_EN.pdf, para. 6.1.

[136] UNGGE Report (n. 124), para. 71(g).

[137] *Ibid.*, 15.

indirectly flows from Article 2(4)'s cornerstone status, as well as that it is also
consistent an institutional perspective, the next question that emerges is: what
exactly needs to be shown? Obviously, this depends on the legal basis used to
justify the use of force and the precise claims made.[138] The evidentiary
requirement may even differ among claims based on the same overall legal
ground. For instance, Article 51 provides the legal basis for a host of very
different claims, ranging from traditional inter-state self-defence to anticipatory self-defence, and from self-defence against non-state actors to the protection of own nationals. What the application of legal principles of, for example,
necessity and proportionality precisely entail in these different situations
remains contested, but those different scenarios of self-defence may clearly
call for different types of necessity and proportionality test. The question how
these different tests can be met in practice also remains unclear, but the
differentiation in legal tests does presuppose varied factual assessments.[139]
Thus the type of legal ground invoked to justify a use of force entails its own
informational requirements.

In practice, though, most states' reporting on the use of force are very elusive
and, regardless of the precise legal claim, they offer little factual detail. States
tend to make rather generic statements.[140] The practice of not substantiating
legal claims and of greatly varying assessments of the same situation is clearly
not limited to use-of-force situations involving self-defence. Even use of force
authorised by the Security Council can (subsequently) be deemed improper
on the basis that the underlying situation was assessed inadequately. Indeed, as
noted elsewhere in this chapter, the UK Foreign Affairs Committee came to
harsh conclusions on the Security Council's authorisation of the Libya intervention. It found that 'the scale of the threat to civilians was presented with
unjustified certainty'.[141] The Committee also stated:

> We have seen no evidence that the UK Government carried out a proper
> analysis of the nature of the rebellion in Libya. It may be that the UK

---

[138]   For a more theoretical analysis of why legal justifications are made at all, see Dino Kritsiotis,
        'Theorizing International Law on Force and Intervention', in Anne Orford and
        Florian Hoffmann (eds), *The Oxford Handbook of the Theory of International Law* (Oxford:
        Oxford University Press, 2016), 655–83.

[139]   See, more elaborately, Larissa van den Herik, 'Article 51's Reporting Requirement as a Space
        for Legal Argument and Factfulness', in Claus Kress and Robert Lawless (eds), *Necessity and
        Proportionality in International Peace and Security Law (Lieber Studies)* (Oxford: Oxford
        University Press, 2020), 221–44.

[140]   James A. Green, 'The Article 51 Reporting Requirement for Self-Defense Actions', *Virginia
        Journal of International Law* 55 (2015), 563–624 (604). See also Van den Herik, 'Article 51's
        Reporting Requirement' (n. 139).

[141]   House of Commons Foreign Affairs Committee, *Libya* (n. 98) para. 37.

Government was unable to analyse the nature of the rebellion in Libya due to incomplete intelligence and insufficient institutional insight and that it was caught up in events as they developed. It could not verify the actual threat to civilians posed by the Gaddafi regime; it selectively took elements of Muammar Gaddafi's rhetoric at face value; and it failed to identify the militant Islamist extremist element in the rebellion. UK strategy was founded on erroneous assumptions and an incomplete understanding of the evidence.[142]

The Committee further held that insufficient attention had been paid to the possibility that militant groups would benefit from the rebellion[143] and that political ways of dealing with the crisis had been insufficiently explored.[144]

Processes to scrutinise or expose facts, assessments, and reason-giving for a certain use of force that later appeared not to match the situation on the ground, such as the UK parliamentary process or other types of domestic inquiry, are not a given at Security Council level. Indeed, the centralisation of the power to maintain international peace and security in the Council has not been accompanied by the establishment of a universal or collective fact-finding agency to find facts ex ante or to make an assessment ex post.[145] The absence of such a body has, at times, undermined the credibility, authority, and stability of the whole collective security system, whose proper functioning hinges on the establishment of accurate factual information and a shared appreciation and evaluation of facts. On several occasions, the Security Council has also been presented with or acted upon the basis of misinformation, such as the claims regarding the presence of weapons of mass destruction in Iraq in 2003[146] and the attribution of the Madrid terrorist attacks to Basque separatist group ETA in 2004.[147] Yet while the speech of Colin Powell is still the most referred-to example of misleading the Security Council, exaggerated claims, counterfactuals, and denials continue to be presented in Council

---

[142]   *Ibid.*, para. 38.
[143]   *Ibid.*, para. 28.
[144]   *Ibid.*, para. 57.
[145]   There are, of course, ad hoc examples of inquiries, such as the UN Secretary-General's Inquiry regarding the Fall of Srebrenica (Report of the Secretary-General pursuant to General Assembly Res. 53/35, UN Doc. A/54/549, 15 November 1999) and on the United Nations' failure to prevent the genocide in Rwanda (Report of the Independent Inquiry into the Actions of the United Nations during the 1994 Genocide in Rwanda, UN Doc. S/1999/1257, 16 December 1999). See, more generally, Catherine Harwood and Larissa van den Herik, 'Commissions of Inquiry and *Jus ad Bellum*', in Leila Nadya Sadat (ed.), *Seeking Accountability for the Unlawful Use of Force* (Cambridge: Cambridge University Press, 2018), 171–93.
[146]   UN Doc. S/PV.4701, 5 February 2003.
[147]   SC Res. 1530 of 11 March 2004, UN Doc. S/RES/1530(2004).

debates without much repercussion, including Russia's denials of international crimes being committed by its forces in Ukraine[148] and its unsubstantiated genocide claims against Ukraine.[149] The question of whether there is a right not to be subjected to false claims is currently being litigated before the International Court of Justice (ICJ) and, if granted, this could – in theory, at least – have some sanitising effect on Security Council debates.[150]

Because the legality of a use of force often hinges on the establishment and appreciation of facts as much as, or even more than, the precise legal claim that is being made, there is merit in rethinking structures and processes that build in some more structural (semi-)independent elements in fact-finding and threat appreciation at Security Council level rather than only outsourcing this to states or using ad hoc fact-finding missions. Other international organisations can play enhanced roles for fact-finding, such as the International Atomic Energy Agency and the Organisation for the Prohibition of Chemical Weapons (OPCW).[151] Moreover, and by way of comparison, it may be noted that all UN sanctions regimes do have – on paper – independent elements in the form of panels of experts. These

---

[148]   For example, the denial of responsibility for killed civilians in Bucha: UN Doc. S/PV.9011, 5 April 2022, 16. The Independent International Commission of Inquiry on Ukraine came to contrasting findings in its report of 18 October 2022 to the UN General Assembly: UN Doc. A/77/533, paras 65–74.

[149]   UN Doc. S/2022/154, 24 February 2022. For earlier examples in relation to a different conflict, see also Russia's intervention on hostilities in Georgia in August 2008, referring to the death of 2,000 innocent civilians and asking whether this counted as genocide ('How many people, how many civilians must die before we describe it as genocide?'): UN Doc. S/PV.5953, 10 August 2008, 8. The Independent International Fact-Finding Mission on the Conflict in Georgia, established by the Council of the European Union later stated:

> The number of casualties among the Ossetian civilian population turned out to be much lower than claimed at the beginning. Russian officials stated initially that about 2000 civilians had been killed in South Ossetia by the Georgian forces, but later on the number of overall South Ossetian civilian losses of the August 2008 conflict was reduced to 162.

See Report of the Independent International Fact-Finding Mission on the Conflict in Georgia, vol. I, September 2009, 21.

[150]   ICJ, *Allegations of Genocide under the Convention on the Prevention and Punishment of the Crime of Genocide* (Ukraine v. Russian Federation), order of 16 March 2022. Particularly relevant is the separate opinion of Judge Robinson, who points out that there is nothing in practice or doctrine that would preclude the Court from making a finding that a breach has not been committed: *ibid.*, para. 16.

[151]   See, e.g., on fact-finding processes regarding the use of chemical weapons in Syria and particularly also the question of individual attribution, Gregory D. Koblentz, 'Chemical-Weapon Use in Syria: Atrocities, Attribution, and Accountability', *The Nonproliferation Review* 26 (2019), 575–98.

experts are appointed by the Secretary-General after consultation with the relevant sanctions committee. Typically, the experts assist the committee in carrying out its mandate, including by providing information relevant to the potential designation of individuals and entities, and they also assist the committee in refining and updating information on the list of individuals subject to the assets freeze, travel ban, and targeted arms embargo, including by providing identifying information and additional information for the publicly available narrative summary of reasons for listing. The experts thus have a strong fact-finding mandate, and they are tasked with gathering, examining, and analysing information from states, relevant UN bodies, regional organisations, and other interested parties regarding the implementation of the sanctions.

It is already the case that information gathered by sanctions panels of experts may have ius ad bellum relevance. For example, the panel of experts for Yemen has reported on the relationship between Iran and the Houthis – a factor of relevance to assessments in the context of the consent-based use of force by the Gulf Coalition Forces.[152] And the panel of experts for Libya reported critically on arms deliveries by third states in contravention of the arms embargo imposed by Resolution 1970.[153] The panel of experts for the Central African Republic (CAR) reported on violations of international humanitarian law by Russian military instructors operating in CAR with the consent of the CAR government.[154] And, finally, the panel of experts for

[152] See, e.g., several findings of the Panel of Experts on Yemen of the UN sanctions regime regarding the allegations of linkages between the Houthi rebels and Iran and Iranian shipments of missiles and rockets: Letter dated 20 February 2015 from the Panel of Experts on Yemen established pursuant to Security Council Resolution 2140 (2014) addressed to the President of the Security Council, UN Doc. S/2015/125, Annex (Final Report); Letter dated 22 January 2016 from the Panel of Experts on Yemen established pursuant to Security Council Resolution 2140 (2014) addressed to the President of the Security Council, UN Doc. S/2018/192, Annex (Final Report) (formerly issued as UN Doc. S/2016/73); Letter dated 27 January 2017 from the Panel of Experts on Yemen addressed to the President of the Security Council, UN Doc. S/2018/193, Annex (Final Report) (formerly issued as UN Doc. S/2017/81). Most recently, on alleged Iranian supplies, see Letter dated 22 January 2021 from the Panel of Experts on Yemen addressed to the President of the Security Council, UN Doc. S/2021/79, 25 January 2021, Annex (Final Report), para. 21. See also Benjamin Nußberger, 'Military Strikes in Yemen in 2015: Intervention by Invitation and Self-Defence in the Course of Yemen's "Model Transitional Process"', *Journal on the Use of Force and International Law* 4 (2017), 110–60 (139).

[153] The Panel of Experts concluded that the arms embargo was totally ineffective: Letter dated 8 March 2021 from the Panel of Experts on Libya established pursuant to Resolution 1973 (2011) addressed to the President of the Security Council, UN Doc. S/2021/229.

[154] Final Report of the Panel of Experts on the Central African Republic extended pursuant to Security Council Resolution 2536 (2020), UN Doc. S/2021/569, 25 June 2021, paras 83–96. For more on the operation of Russian private military contractors, including the Wagner Group

the Democratic Republic of Congo (DRC) spelled out in quite some detail Rwanda's support for M23 rebels – even finding substantial evidence of the Rwandan Defence Force intervening directly on DRC territory to reinforce M23 or to conduct military operations against the Forces démocratiques de libération du Rwanda (FDLR).[155]

In his chapter in this volume, Cai questions whether reporting requirements can have any meaning in the absence of objective mechanisms or 'institution immune from great powers'.[156] This is, of course, a valid query. But it is also an invitation to recognise the potential of panels of experts as building blocks for an independent and objective fact-finding mechanism, as well as an encouragement to ensure that their institutional independence is secured and further strengthened, especially to resist interference by the great power. Moreover, the very fact that states must report opens the possibility for anyone, including civil society actors, to scrutinise states and hold states to account, as the *New York Times'* investigation of the erroneous drone strike in Afghanistan of 29 August 2021 illustrates.[157] This does presuppose a free press, though.

Obviously, the legal framework governing UN sanctions is very different from the rules on ius ad bellum. UN sanctions have come to be more focused on individuals, which has been one of the incentives for the push towards proceduralisation, as will be discussed in the next section. Nonetheless, some of the elements of the UN sanctions architecture may still be useful as a very general blueprint for thinking about ways of designing an enabling and 'factful' environment for use-of-force discourse.[158]

---

    in the CAR and other African states, see Maluwa, 'Between Centralism and Regionalism', Chapter 3 in this volume, section III.D.

[155] Letter dated 16 December 2022 from the Group of Experts on the Democratic Republic of the Congo addressed to the President of the Security Council, UN Doc. S/2022/967, Annex (Midterm Report).

[156] Cai, 'Maintaining Peace during a Global Power Shift', Chapter 1 in this volume, section IV.A. (p. 102).

[157] Eric Schmitt and Helene Cooper, 'Pentagon Acknowledges Aug. 29 Drone Strike in Afghanistan Was a Tragic Mistake that Killed 10 Civilians', *New York Times*, 16 October 2021, available at www.nytimes.com/2021/09/17/us/politics/pentagon-drone-strike-afghanistan.html.

[158] The word 'factful' is inspired by the book of Hans Rosling, which highlights contrasts between worldly understandings informed by instincts, preconceptions, and biases with those based on data acquired through statistics, graphs, and questionnaires: Hans Rosling, Anna Rosling Rönnlund, and Ola Rosling, *Factfulness: Ten Reasons We're Wrong about the World and Why Things are Better than You Think* (London: Sceptre, 2018).

4. Broadening the Reporting Requirement to Other Uses of Force[159]

Mexico's proposal was tethered to Article 51's reporting requirement, which is expressly written down in the UN Charter. Yet use-of-force reporting does not need to be intrinsically limited to cases of self-defence. Brazil's RWP proposals suggested enhanced Security Council procedures to monitor and assess the manner in which authorising resolutions are interpreted and implemented. These proposals correspond with earlier arguments made by Niels Blokker and Erika de Wet in favour of reporting on authorised use of force to ensure the validity of the authorisation.[160] Indeed, during their Libya intervention, France, the United Kingdom, Italy, and the United States reported to the UN Secretary-General in line with paragraph 4 of Resolution 1973.[161] As noted, the panel of experts of the Libya sanctions regime also informed the UN Security Council of actions by third states relating to the delivery of arms and other military material.[162]

Unlike self-defence and Security Council authorisation, intervention by invitation is not anchored in the UN Charter. The requirements governing this legal basis to use force thus cannot be derived from a concrete provision and there is no treaty obligation to report similar to Article 51, second sentence. One may, however, still consider a parallel reporting requirement for consent-based use of force – or at least reflect on how a practice of reporting on consent-based use of force could be stimulated.

The initial rationale of Article 51's reporting requirement was to alert the Security Council that force had been used in self-defence and to place the

---

[159] Note that this and the following sections of this chapter draw on the present author's earlier publications – namely, Van den Herik, 'Article 51's Reporting Requirement' (n. 139) and Larissa van den Herik, 'Replicating Article 51: A Reporting Requirement for Consent-Based Use of Force', *Heidelberg Journal of International Law* 79 (2019), 707–11.

[160] Niels M. Blokker, 'Is the Authorization Authorized? Powers and Practice of the UN Security Council to Authorize the Use of Force by "Coalitions of the Able and Willing"', *European Journal of International Law* 11 (2000), 541–68; De Wet, *The Chapter VII Powers* (n. 22), 270.

[161] The UN Secretary-General was notified by the following general letters: Letter dated 26 April 2011 from the Permanent Representative of the UK to the United Nations addressed to the Secretary-General, UN Doc. S/2011/269; Letter dated 26 April 2011 from the Permanent Representative of Italy to the United Nations addressed to the Secretary-General, UN Doc. S/2011/270; Letter dated 27 April 2011 from the Permanent Representative of France to the United Nations addressed to the Secretary-General, UN Doc. S/2011/274; Letter dated 17 June 2011 from the Permanent Representative of the United States of America to the United Nations addressed to the Secretary-General, UN Doc. S/2011/372; Letter dated 1 July 2011 from the Permanent Representative of France to the United Nations addressed to the Secretary-General, UN Doc. S/2011/402.

[162] See also Letter dated 15 February 2013 from the Panel of Experts on Libya established pursuant to Resolution 1973 (2011) addressed to the President of the Security Council, UN Doc. S/2013/99, 9 March 2013.

matter on the international agenda, with a view to enabling the Council to exercise its primary responsibility to maintain peace and security.[163] As the system of collective security becomes more decentralised, and as the Security Council adopts a new role whereby it condones and/or blesses non-authorised uses of force rather than authorising use of force itself,[164] the reporting requirement is taking on new meaning. In such a constellation, the purpose of the reporting requirement is not mainly to notify or alert so that the Council can take over but rather to report in the ordinary sense – namely, to offer information and to account for the action, such that the Security Council and the international community at large can discuss whether the use of force was in accordance with the applicable rules and requirements.

The use of force by invitation also often occurs in situations in which the Security Council refrains from authorising use of force itself. Instead, the Council may appraise the circumstances surrounding the formulation of the invitation, thereby endorsing the consent. Whether the Security Council makes such appraisal in concrete situations depends, among other things, on whether the use of force is reported and whether the matter is placed on the Security Council's agenda. This raises the question of whether reporting on consent-based use of force is or should be mandatory.

Since the UN Charter is silent on intervention by invitation, any legally binding reporting requirement would have to be construed under customary international law. Scholarly arguments have been made in this respect, proposing that Article 51's reporting requirement should be applied mutatis mutandis to consent-based use of force.[165] In its resolution on military assistance on request, the Institut de Droit International also stated that 'any request that is followed by military assistance shall be notified to the Secretary-General of the United Nations'.[166] Suggesting the UN Secretary-General as recipient of notifications rather than the Security Council might be explained by political sensitivities and the reluctance of states to accept any hard-core reporting

---

[163] Green, 'The Article 51 Reporting Requirement' (n. 140), 568.
[164] As also discussed by Monica Hakimi, 'The Jus Ad Bellum's Regulatory Form', *American Journal of International Law* 112 (2018), 151–90.
[165] Karine Bannelier and Théodore Christakis, 'Under the UN Security Council's Watchful Eyes: Military Intervention by Invitation in the Malian Conflict', *Leiden Journal of International Law* 26 (2013), 855–74 (870). See also, more tentatively, Olivier Corten, 'Intervention by Invitation: The Expanding Role of the UN Security Council', in Dino Kritsiotis, Olivier Corten, and Gregory H. Fox, *Armed Intervention and Consent*, Max Planck Trialogues on the Law of Peace and War (Anne Peters and Christian Marksen, series eds), vol. 4 (Cambridge: Cambridge University Press, 2023), 101–78.
[166] IDI, *Present Problems of the Use of Force in International Law, Sub-Group C – Military Assistance on Request*, Rhodes, 2011 (Rapporteur: Gerhard Hafner).

obligation. In this vein, the following US statement may be noted when reporting on missile strikes in Houthi-controlled territory in Yemen in 2016:

> These actions were taken with the consent of the Government of Yemen. Although the United States therefore does not believe notification pursuant to Article 51 of the Charter of the United Nations is necessary in these circumstances, the United States nevertheless wishes to inform the Council that these actions were taken consistent with international law.[167]

This can be read as implying that no reporting requirement exists at all or that Article 51 cannot serve as a legal basis for a reporting requirement on consent-based use of force.

It is, in any event, not self-evident that a legally binding reporting requirement for consent-based use of force can be construed under customary international law. Even if there is a certain practice of informing the Security Council of forceful action taken pursuant to an invitation,[168] there are also clear examples of non-reporting.[169] Reporting on consent-based use of force may be particularly sensitive when the consent is not public. In considering a reporting requirement for consent-based use of force, specifically, other complex questions also arise on timing and modalities, as well as on when and how consent-based use of force that is very temporary or which involves a one-off action must be reported, and on what exactly must be reported under this heading – that is, whether a reporting requirement would also cover pure aiding. These questions mirror the questions raised by Mexico, slightly altered to a consent setting.

To construe a customary reporting rule for consent-based use of force, there needs to be opinio iuris, which does not seem to clearly exist (yet). States outside the Security Council, as well as non-permanent members, could

---

[167] Letter dated 15 October 2016 from the Permanent Representative of the United States of America to the United Nations addressed to the President of the Security Council, UN Doc. S/2016/869, 17 October 2016.

[168] For example, Saudi Arabia in Yemen, the United States in Iraq, Russia in Syria, France in Mali, and Senegal in The Gambia.

[169] See Ashley Deeks, 'A Call for Article 51 Letters', *Lawfare*, 25 June 2014, available at www.lawfaremedia.org/article/call-article-51-letters. On the United States' non-reporting of its drone strikes and other operations in Yemen, Somalia, and Pakistan, see Columbia Law School Human Rights Clinic and Sana'a Center for Strategic Studies, *Out of the Shadows: Recommendations to Advance Transparency in the Use of Lethal Force*, June 2017, available at https://hri.law.columbia.edu/sites/default/files/publications/out_of_the_shadows.pdf, 54; James Cavallaro, Stephan Sonnenberg, and Sarah Knuckey, *Living under Drones: Death, Injury and Trauma to Civilians from US Drone Practices in Pakistan* (Stanford, New York: International Human Rights and Conflict Resolution Clinic, Stanford Law School; NYU School of Law, Global Justice Clinic, 2012), 123. See also David L. Bosco, 'Letters from the Front Lines: State Communications to the U.N. Security Council During Conflict', *Columbia Journal of International Law* 54 (2016), 341–81.

perhaps play a role in contributing to the expression and formation of such
opinio iuris. In this regard, Brazil's statements in 2018 in the Sixth Committee
are noteworthy. It insisted on a more meaningful reporting requirement for
Article 51,[170] as well on the need for periodic reporting on military operations
pursuant to Article 42 UN Charter,[171] thus suggesting a more holistic reporting
requirement that disregards the exact legal basis upon which force is used.
Overall, the aim of such proposals and thinking is to broaden use-of-force
discourse and to enable wider participation on the contents and application of
rules that are of concern to the entire international community.

5. The Potential Backlash against Insisting on Reporting

Despite the absence of a fully fledged institutional environment and of a clear
requirement to report on consent-based use of force thus far, states nonetheless
tend to report to the Security Council, and they often rely on multiple
justifications, including consent. Given this existing practice, the issue
whether a perceived duty to explain translates into a hard legal obligation to
report and whether this obligation extends to consent-based use of force in
addition to self-defence is perhaps not the most pressing one. Even absent
overall agreement that reporting on all uses of force is legally required, states
have in fact reported beyond Article 51's requirement – or at least they are, at
times, still inclined to make statements that are meant to be explanatory. The
problem is therefore not necessarily absence of reporting[172] – although, with
the rise of low-intensity conflicts, the question of what to report, as well as
when and how, often does become more pressing.[173] In any event, this is not

---

[170] Statement by Brazil in the UN General Assembly (Sixth Committee) debate on the Report of
the Special Committee on the Charter on the United Nations, 15 October 2018, available at
http://statements.unmeetings.org/media2/20303642/brazil-85.pdf.
[171] Statement by H.E. Ambassador Mauro Vieira in the UN Security Council open debate on
upholding international law within the context of the maintenance of international peace and
security: UN Doc. S/PV.8262, 17 May 2018, at 44–5. On effective monitoring and accountability, see also Letter dated 9 November 2011 from the Permanent Representative of Brazil to
the United Nations addressed to the Secretary-General, with an Annex on Responsibility
while Protecting: Elements for the Development and Promotion of a Concept, UN Doc.
A/66/551–S/2011/701, 11 November 2011, para. 11(h) and (i).
[172] But see Report of Special Rapporteur Agnes Callamard on extrajudicial, summary or arbitrary
executions, UN Doc. A/HRC/44/38, 29 June 2020, paras 65–82.
[173] For a description of key developments in 2019 of the low-intensity conflict between the United
States and Iran, see Miloš Hrnjaz, *The War Report: The United States of America and the
Islamic Republic of Iran – An International Armed Conflict of Low Intensity*, Geneva
Academy, December 2019, available at www.geneva-academy.ch/joomlatools-files/docman-
files/The%20United%20States%20Of%20America%20And%20Islamic%20Republic%20Of%
20Iran%20An%20International%20Armed%20Conflict%20Of%20Low%20Intensity.pdf.

the only problem: a perhaps bigger problem lies in the absence of central publication of reports. As Mexico's legal adviser has noted, reporting letters are not standardly circulated to all UN member states and they are difficult to find without the official document symbol, which the Repertoire of the Practice of the Security Council is incomplete, omitting reactions, and has a huge backlog.[174] These are mundane and basic, yet very real, shortcomings. Private actors may try to remedy and plug the gap. The Harvard catalogue of Article 51 Communications serves as an excellent example,[175] but this still leaves responding practice disorganised and it lacks formality. As a result, letters reporting the use of force with excessive and/or elusive legal claims often remain largely uncontested, apart from the victim state's response. An encouragement to report without an enabling structure for other states to react might thus ricochet, since reporting states will have a tendency to broaden possibilities to use force.

Indeed, the Community of Latin American and Caribbean States has expressed concern over 'the increase in the number of letters to the Security Council under Article 51 of the Charter submitted by some States in order to have recourse to the use of force in the context of counter-terrorism, most of the times "ex post facto"'.[176] The Non-Aligned Movement has underlined that 'Article 51 of the UN Charter is restrictive and should not be re-written or re-interpreted'.[177] One-sided Article 51 letters can indeed have the effect of rewriting the exception of self-defence. Many of the states participating in Mexico's Arria formula debate recognised the proliferation of Article 51 letters and underscored the need to improve accessibility, with a view to ensuring an inclusive and transparent dialogue. A variety of states, including Austria,

---

[174] Arrocha Olabuenaga, 'An Insider's View' (n. 112).

[175] The catalogue is presented in Dustin A. Lewis, Naz K. Modirzadeh, and Gabriella Blum, *Quantum of Silence: Inaction and* Jus ad Bellum, Harvard Law School Program on International Law and Armed Conflict, 2019, available at https://pilac.law.harvard.edu/quantum-of-silence, as introduced in Dustin A. Lewis, Naz K. Modirzadeh, and Gabriella Blum, 'Silence and the Use of Force in International Law', *EJIL:Talk!*, 18 July 2019, available at www.ejiltalk.org/silence-and-the-use-of-force-with-a-new-catalogue-of-article-51-communicationsl/. For compilations of reactions on concrete operations, see, e.g., Mehrnusch Anssari and Benjamin Nussberger, 'Compilation of States' Reactions to US and Iranian Uses of Force in Iraq in January 2020', *Just Security*, 22 January 2020, available at www.justsecurity.org/68173/compilation-of-states-reactions-to-u-s-and-iranian-uses-of-force-in-iraq-in-january-2020/.

[176] Measures to Eliminate International Terrorism: Statement by the Permanent Mission of El Salvador to the United Nations on Behalf of the Community of Latin American and Caribbean States (CELAC), 2 October 2017, available at https://enaun.cancilleria.gob.ar/en/measures-eliminate-international-terrorism.

[177] Final Document of the 17th Summit of Heads of State and Government of the Non-Aligned Movement (NAM), Doc. NAM 2016/CoB/DOC.1.Corr.1, 17–18 September 2016, para. 25.2.

Liechtenstein, the United Kingdom, and Russia, emphasised that lack of
reaction or follow-up to a letter either by the Security Council or by other
states did not lead to legality or the formation of a new norm.[178] Austria even
stated that silence had to be 'unequivocally intentioned' to have legal meaning
and not simply occur.[179] These comments build on the work of the ILC on
customary international law and subsequent practice – particularly views
expressed in that context on how to weigh silence.

Often, third states – and especially those not on the Security Council nor
otherwise directly implicated, for example as a regional actor – may (choose
to) remain silent on a certain issue because they have no diplomatic or
political interest or imperative to speak out in the situation at hand. While,
logically, silence is best regarded as an absence of confirming practice, it has
often rather been implicitly equated with support.[180] In the ius contra bellum
setting, the questions of how to weigh lack of protest and what the legitimising
effects of silence are have been particularly relevant in the context of discussions on drones and targeted killing,[181] as well as regarding the scope of the
right to self-defence more generally and specifically the status of the 'unable
and unwilling' test.[182]

In a generic sense, the question of silence's relevance for the formation of
customary international law was discussed by ILC Special Rapporteur Sir
Michael Wood in his third report, under the heading 'Inaction as practice and/
or evidence of acceptance as law'.[183] Given the politics and methodological
challenges involved (how does one prove silence?), the Special Rapporteur
indicated that only 'qualified silence' could have meaning and that inaction
(or passive practice) had to be determined in relative terms.[184] Relative factors

---

[178] UN Doc. S/2021/247 (n. 118), 14, 48, 64, and 68.
[179] See n. 115 for the full statement.
[180] Gray, *International Law and the Use of Force* (n. 83), 11.
[181] Anthony Dworkin, 'Drones and Targeted Killing: Defining a European Position', European
       Council on Foreign Relations Policy Brief, July 2013, available at https://ecfr.eu/wp-content/
       uploads/ECFR84_DRONES_BRIEF.pdf; Jessica Dorsey and Christophe Paulussen,
       'Towards a European Position on Armed Drones and Targeted Killing: Surveying EU
       Counterterrorism Perspectives', ICCT Research Paper, April 2015, available at www.icct.nl/
       publication/towards-european-position-armed-drones-and-targeted-killing-surveying-eu-coun
       ter. See also Elisabeth Schweiger, 'The Risks of Remaining Silent: International Law
       Formation and the EU Silence on Drone Killings', *Global Affairs* 1 (2015), 269–75.
[182] Olivier Corten, 'The "Unwilling or Unable" Test: Has it Been, and Could it Be, Accepted?',
       Leiden Journal of International Law 29 (2016), 777–99; Jutta Brunnée and Stephen J. Toope,
       'Self-Defence against Non-State Actors: Are Powerful States Willing but Unable to Change
       International Law?', *International and Comparative Law Quarterly* 67 (2018), 263–86.
[183] UN Doc. A/CN.4/682, 27 March 2015, paras 19–26.
[184] *Ibid.*, para. 22.

whereby a given inaction might be found legally meaningful included the questions of whether a response was called for in the circumstances, whether the silent state was aware of the underlying practice to which it was silent, and whether the silence or inaction was sustained over a sufficient period of time.[185]

Ultimately, draft conclusion 6, paragraph 1, of the ILC's Draft Conclusions on the Identification of Customary International Law state that '[p]ractice may take a wide range of forms. It includes both physical and verbal acts. It may, under certain circumstances, include inaction.'[186]

The commentary specifies that:

> Paragraph 1 . . . makes clear that inaction may count as practice. The words 'under certain circumstances' seek to caution, however, that only deliberate abstention from acting may serve such a role: the State in question needs to be conscious of refraining from acting in a given situation, and it cannot simply be assumed that abstention from acting is deliberate. [187]

In relation to establishing opinio iuris, the ILC Draft Conclusions also set out that '[f]ailure to react over time to a practice may serve as evidence of acceptance as law (*opinio juris*), provided that States were in a position to react and the circumstances called for some reaction'.[188]

Some scholars have reflected on the meaning of silence specifically in an ius contra bellum context. They have argued – in tandem with the ILC provisions and the remarks by states during the Arria formula meeting referred to above – that silence should not so easily be considered as acquiescence and as generating in itself 'norm-evolutionary effects'.[189] Silence may have some legal value only if a third state could have legitimately been expected to take a position and did not.[190] A legitimate expectation, Paulina Starski argues, arises only if certain strict conditions apply that relate to the nature, clarity, and

---

[185] *Ibid.*, paras 23–5.
[186] ILC, *Draft Conclusions on the Identification of Customary International Law*, Report on the Work of its 70th Session, UN Doc. A/73/10(2018).
[187] *Ibid.*, draft concl. 6, commentary para. 3.
[188] *Ibid.*, draft concl. 10, para. 3; Similarly, para. 2 reads:

> 2. The number of parties that must actively engage in subsequent practice in order to establish an agreement under article 31, para. 3 (b), may vary. Silence on the part of one or more parties may constitute acceptance of the subsequent practice when the circumstances call for some reaction.

[189] Paulina Starski, 'Silence within the Process of Normative Change and Evolution of the Prohibition on the Use of Force: Normative Volatility and Legislative Responsibility', *Journal on the Use of Force and International Law* 14 (2017), 14–65.
[190] *Ibid.*

specific circumstances of the legal claim made by the state using force and of
the reactions of other states, as well as the capacity of the silent state to act, and
on timing.[191] Elisabeth Schweiger, in turn, develops the following four con-
textual parameters to determine the communicative value of silence: the
presence of a prompt; the perceived deliberateness of silence; the assumed
relevance of the unsaid; and the expectation of speech by those who interpret
silence.[192] It has also been suggested that the acquiescence of specially affected
states or a large number of states is more meaningful than the silence of a third
state that is only remotely linked to the situation,[193] but even then it is not
always easy to determine what exactly to infer from the silence or inaction of
those states. Indeed, in her work, Schweiger draws attention to the politics
involved in attributing meaning to silence, and to the one-sidedness and
potential subjectivity of making a claim that there actually is silence.[194] In
particular, when operations are covert and/or justified by ambiguous and
inconsistent legal claims, the subsequent silence may remain without 'legal
quality'.[195] Moreover, states may be selectively silent and, to illustrate this
point, Schweiger contrasts the great number of states that have protested
within the Security Council against Israeli targeted killing practices[196] with
the absence of discussion of US targeted killing in that same arena. This
absence shifted the debate into the Human Rights Council instead.[197]

It remains altogether unclear what properly counts as silence and what the
legal value is in a concrete setting of alleged silence. For that reason, it is

[191] *Ibid.*
[192] Elisabeth Schweiger, 'Listen Closely: What Silence Can Tell us about Legal Knowledge
       Production', *London Review of International Law* 6 (2020), 293–411 (398).
[193] Tom Ruys, *'Armed Attack' and Article 51 of the UN Charter: Evolutions in Customary Law and
       Practice* (Cambridge: Cambridge University Press, 2010), 38.
[194] See, e.g., Schweiger, 'Listen Closely' (n. 192), 398; Elisabeth Schweiger, '"Targeted Killing"
       and the Lack of Acquiescence', *Leiden Journal of International Law* 32 (2019), 741–57.
[195] Schweiger, 'Targeted Killing' (n. 194), 742.
[196] See, e.g., UN Doc. S/PV.4929, 23 March 2004, in response to the killing of Sheik Ahmed
       Yassin; UN Doc. S/PV.4945, 19 April 2004, in response to the killing of Abdel Aziz Al-Rantisi,
       as cited by Schweiger, 'Targeted Killing' (n. 194). This still leaves a very high number of other
       Israeli targeted killings out of the loop, as detailed in Roonen Bergman, *Rise and Kill First:
       The Secret History of Israel's Targeted Assassinations* (New York: Random House, 2018).
[197] See, e.g., Report of the Special Rapporteur on the Promotion and Protection of Human
       Rights and Fundamental Freedoms while Countering Terrorism, Ben Emmerson, submitted
       in accordance with General Assembly Resolution 66/171 and Human Rights Council
       Resolution 15/15, UN Doc. A/68/389, 18 September 2013. On targeted killing and the co-
       applicability of international humanitarian law and human rights, see also Helen Duffy,
       'Trial and Tribulations: Co-applicability of IHL and Human Rights in an Age of
       Adjudication', in Ziv Bohrer, Janina Dill, and Helen Duffy, *Law Applicable to Armed
       Conflict*, Max Planck Trialogues on the Law of Peace and War (Anne Peters and
       Christian Marxsen, series eds), vol. 2 (Cambridge: Cambridge University Press, 2020), 15–105.

imperative that transparency on reporting go hand in hand with the development of more overarching procedures. If circulation of Article 51 letters is enhanced, Liechtenstein's observation that procedures must be developed so that states can provide a reaction also becomes more important to break the silence.

Whether Mexico, on its own, will be able to pursue this matter successfully remains to be seen. Effectively, Mexico's proposal aims to overturn the norm of secrecy in the ius contra bellum and replace it with the norm of transparency. Yet, as Orna Ben-Naftali and Roy Peled astutely observe, '[t]elling truth to power is a tall order. Demanding power to tell the truth is taller.'[198] These scholars have equally pointed out that '[i]njecting transparency into the normative framework of war is, therefore, likely to be resisted and, in the short run, may well generate less compliance'.[199] Thus even if Mexico were to succeed and structures facilitating use of force discourse were implemented, there are significant follow-up questions on the table. It is, for example, of great importance to recognise that the new structures could also entail that the silence of states and failure to react to excessive reporting might be more heavily weighted. The more formal structures exist at Security Council level to engage in use-of-force discourse, the more states are 'in a position to react', and hence the sooner failure to react can be regarded as 'qualified silence' indicating some acceptance.[200] Mexico's proposal thus presupposes continued engagement from all states, not only to materialise the proposals as such but also for substantive follow-up.

V. SANCTIONS OUTSIDE AND INSIDE THE UN INSTITUTIONAL FRAMEWORK

Proposals for improved decision-making and better procedures have also been put forward in the context of the exercise of a different Chapter VII power – namely, the imposition of UN sanctions. In this context, Western European states were generally in the lead and not Latin American states, which might be explained by the reservations of these latter states towards the tool of sanctions as such. In this section, I first examine the reticence of non-Western states towards the tool of sanctions: specifically, the question of whether the imposition of sanctions is within the exclusive domain of the

---

[198] Orna Ben-Naftali and Roy Peled, 'How Much Secrecy Does Warfare Need?', in Andrea Bianchi and Anne Peters (eds), *Transparency in International Law* (Cambridge: Cambridge University Press, 2013), 321–64 (363).

[199] *Ibid.*, 363.

[200] UN Doc. A/CN.4/682, 27 March 2015, paras 19–26, esp. para. 22.

United Nations and whether non-UN sanctions should be regarded as
a challenge to the system – particularly to the UN Security Council. I then
turn to UN sanctions and discuss the sanctions reform efforts of the past three
decades, mapping the development of better procedures for the imposition of
UN sanctions, including persistent shortcomings.

A. *Non-UN Sanctions as a Challenge to the Security Council's Prerogative?*

Not all states embrace the tool of sanctions as a legitimate instrument. Many
states of the Global South remain aloof, if not outright opposed to it. In
contrast, states of the Global North can be described as quite sanctions-eager
and they regard it as one of their most compelling foreign policy tools. Given
the Security Council's inability to act, non-UN sanctions constituted the core
of the Western response to the aggression against Ukraine, together with
military assistance.

The centrality of sanctions in the reaction of the West to Russia's aggression
against Ukraine in 2022 underscored three moves in relation to sanctions that
had already been ongoing – namely:

   (i) a move *towards* sanctions as a key instrument to address international
      crises;
   (ii) a move *away* from UN Security Council sanctions; and
   (iii) a move *back* to more comprehensive sanctions.

States on the receiving end of sanctions and states from the Global South more
generally have, in the past decades, advanced arguments against sanctions,
labelling them unilateral coercive measures and therefore contrary to international law. As of 1996, the UN General Assembly has annually adopted
resolutions explicitly stating that unilateral coercive measures are contrary to
international law.[201] In those resolutions, the General Assembly urges states
not to adopt unilateral measures that are not in accordance with the UN
Charter – in particular, coercive measures.[202] These serial resolutions do not

---

[201] More recently, the Human Rights Council (HRC) has started adopting resolutions with
a similar bearing. See e.g., HRC, *The Negative Impact of Unilateral Coercive Measures on the
Enjoyment of Human Rights*, UN Doc. A/HRC/RES/49/6, 12 April 2022, as well as the work of
the UN Special Rapporteurs on this matter. See also the Declaration of the Russian
Federation and the People's Republic of China on the Promotion of International Law,
25 June 2016, para. 6.

[202] See, e.g., GA Res. 75/181 of 16 December 2020, UN Doc. A/RES/75/181; GA Res. 74/154 of
18 December 2019, UN Doc. A/RES/74/154; GA Res. 73/167 of 17 December 2019, UN Doc.
A/RES/73/167. For the first of the series, see GA Res. 51/103 of 12 December 1996, UN Doc.
A/RES/51/103.

specify what type of unilateral measure is not in accordance with the UN Charter, however, or when a measure can be considered coercive.

In 2019, then Special Rapporteur on Unilateral Coercive Measures Idriss Jazairy held that, as a basic principle, the Security Council should be recognised as having the *exclusive* power to impose financial, economic, and other non-forcible measures.[203] Yet, in a more recent report, new Special Rapporteur Alena Douhan – albeit referring to the Security Council's unique powers – did recognise that states are free to decide with whom to entertain economic relations, and she also appreciated the legality of retorsions and proportional countermeasures taken by directly affected states.[204] According to this latter view – which is in line with mainstream understandings of international law and, specifically, the law on state responsibility – non-UN sanctions are not illegal as such and should not be regarded as a challenge to the UN Security Council or the UN Charter. The UN Charter does not explicitly prohibit economic pressure in the same way as it prohibits the use of force. This does not mean that any type of sanction is allowed, of course, and core concerns related to their humanitarian impact may evoke serious questions of proportionality (depending on the violation of international law to which they react) and other international law principles. Moreover, the question of the legality of third-party countermeasures has not been fully settled.

In the discussions during the General Assembly's 11th Emergency Special Session on the Russian invasion of Ukraine, those states that are generally weary of non-UN sanctions drew attention to their core concerns. Brazil, for example, emphasised that Resolution ES-11/1 should not be seen as permitting the *indiscriminate* application of sanctions.[205] Likewise, Egypt rejected sanctions adopted outside a multilateral framework *because of* the dire humanitarian consequences and suffering for civilians.[206] States also expressed concern over the consequences of sanctions for the global economy. As Maluwa also notes in his chapter in this volume, African states were particularly worried about the collateral impact of the sanctions on their populations.[207] Such concerns relate more to the form and scope of the sanctions than to the legality of the sanctions instrument as such.

Interestingly, Colombia put forward the view that the General Assembly should recommend that all member states impose sanctions simultaneously

---

[203] UN Doc. A/HRC/42/46/Add.1, 29 August 2019, para. 5.
[204] UN Doc. A/HRC/48/59, 18 July 2021, paras 71–3.
[205] UN Doc. A/ES-11/PV.5, 2 March 2022, 17.
[206] *Ibid.*, 25.
[207] Maluwa, 'Between Centralism and Regionalism', Chapter 3 in this volume, section IV.B (p. 263).

and comprehensively, possibly pursuant to the obligation to cooperate to bring to an end, using lawful means, Russia's serious breach of ius cogens.[208] This suggestion aims at reviving the General Assembly's historic practice of recommending sanctions, as it did against Apartheid South Africa. That earlier practice stands in sharp contrast with the Assembly's more recent series of resolutions against unilateral sanctions just referred to.[209] A role for the General Assembly in recommending sanctions would fit with the new balance that is being struck between the Security Council and the General Assembly by the resumed resort to the 'Uniting for Peace' procedure.

Specifically in relation to the sanctions imposed on Russia, I generally agree with Maluwa's observations on their legality and legitimacy as a response to a particularly serious breach of ius cogens by a permanent member. Without making a detailed assessment of each sanctions measure, it can be noted that many of those measures qualified as retorsions. For those that should be justified as countermeasures, it is unfortunate that the ILC has, on repeated occasions, not pronounced on the legality of third-party countermeasures as a response to serious violations of ius cogens despite prevalent state practice.[210] As a consequence, these measures remain largely unregulated. Recognising that third-party countermeasures are legal under customary international law given the existing state practice would open the door to further regulation and a more detailed understanding of how Articles 49–53 of the Articles of State Responsibility apply. Such regulation of third-party countermeasures could also make room for rules about their relationship with the UN system. Suggestions have been made for a reporting requirement to the UN General Assembly analogous to Article 51;[211] one might also conceive of a role for the

---

[208]   UN Doc. A/ES-11/PV.3, 1 March 2022, 2.

[209]   As discussed by Rebecca Barber, 'An Exploration of the General Assembly's Troubled Relationship with Unilateral Sanctions', *International & Comparative Law Quarterly* 70 (2021), 343–78.

[210]   Linos-Alexander Sicilianos, 'The Classification of Obligations and the Multilateral Dimension of the Relations of International Responsibility', *European Journal of International Law* 13 (2002), 1127–45. The ILC ignored a Dutch call to revisit its 2001 position, as maintained in 2011 for the Articles on the Responsibility of International Organizations: Dutch Advisory Committee on International Law, *Advisory Report on the Draft Conclusions of the International Law Commission on Peremptory Norms of General International Law*, 27 July 2020. In a subsequent report, the Dutch Advisory Committee expressly discussed the legality of third-party countermeasures: Dutch Advisory Committee on International Law, *Legal Consequences of a Serious Breach of a Peremptory Norm: The International Rights and Duties of States in Relation to a Breach of the Prohibition of Aggression*, 17 November 2022. Both reports are available at www .advisorycommitteeinternationallaw.nl/. The author is chair of the Committee.

[211]   Tom Ruys, 'Sanctions, Retortions and Countermeasures: Concepts and International Legal Framework', in Larissa van den Herik (ed.), *Research Handbook on UN Sanctions and International Law* (Cheltenham: Edward Elgar, 2017), 19–51.

General Assembly in impact assessment. Additionally, the General Assembly could act as a forum in which states can exercise their right to consult when confronted with special economic problems arising from the sanctions, analogous to Article 50 UN Charter.

Whatever may come of such suggestions, unilateral sanctions, whether recommended by the General Assembly or not, should not be regarded as a challenge to the UN Security Council but rather as a correction in the event of inactivity (i.e., dysfunction)[212] or perhaps as complementary. They are an inevitable consequence of Security Council deadlock.

B. UN Sanctions and the Development of Procedures and Remedies

Even if it may not be exclusive, the power of the UN Security Council to impose sanctions, as well as its primacy in this regard, is undisputed. Article 41 creates a basis on which the UN Security Council can maintain international peace and security by means of measures short of the use of force. Such measures may include the interruption of economic relations in the form of UN sanctions.[213] Post-1990, UN sanctions have become the instrument of choice for maintaining peace, with typically between 10 and 15 UN sanctions regimes in operation at any given moment.[214] However, since the sanctions relating to the situation in Mali in 2017,[215] no new UN sanctions regimes were created until October 2022, when the Haiti sanctions regime was established.[216] Instead, as noted, there has been a move towards coordinated unilateral sanctions facilitated, inter alia, by the emergence of multiple Magnitsky-style sanctions regimes in different Western jurisdictions.[217] Most recently, both China and Russia have adapted the US approach of using

---

[212] Address by New Zealand Prime Minister Jacinda Ardern, *A Pacific Springboard to Engage the World: New Zealand's Independent Foreign Policy*, Lowy Institute, Sydney, 7 July 2022, available at www.lowyinstitute.org/publications/address-new-zealand-prime-minister-jacinda-ardern.

[213] See, on terminology and conceptualisation of UN sanctions, Ruys, 'Sanctions, Retortions and Countermeasures' (n. 211).

[214] Erika de Wet, 'Article 41', in Simma et al. (eds), *The Charter of the United Nations* (n. 20), MN 15–25.

[215] SC Res. 2374 of 5 September 2017, UN Doc. S/RES/2374(2017).

[216] Through SC Res. 2653 of 21 October 2022, UN Doc. S/RES/2653(2022), the Security Council created the Haiti sanctions regime for individuals, armed groups, and criminal networks engaged in criminal activities and violence.

[217] In addition to the United States, Canada, the United Kingdom, and the European Union have all adopted Magnitsky-style sanctions regimes for the potential designation of individuals for violating human rights norms.

individualised asset freezes and travel bans to target foreign nationals in retaliation for sanctions on their own nationals.[218]

One could argue that this decentralisation of sanctions decreases the importance of reform processes at UN level. Yet this section is premised on precisely the opposite view. It presents an argument for further UN sanctions reform despite the recent decline in the adoption of new UN sanctions regimes. In fact, precisely because the future of targeted sanctions may be (partly) unilateral, the general principle that all sanctions imposed on persons should be governed by fair and clear procedures, regardless of the exact political and jurisdictional context in which they are adopted, becomes even more imperative.[219] The United Nations has an important role to play in setting the global standards for appropriate listing criteria and due process, and for facilitating the emergence of general norms regarding fair and clear procedures for individuals who have been subjected to sanctions.

1. Three Types of UN Sanctions Regime and the Move from Comprehensive to Targeted Sanctions – and Back

At the UN level, a distinction can be made between three types of UN sanctions regime, depending on the kind of threat they aim to address – that is, (i) counter-terrorism sanctions, (ii) counter-proliferation sanctions, and (iii) conflict resolution or armed conflict sanctions. As Maluwa also notes, this third type of sanction was often imposed in African internal conflicts.[220]

The three types of regime vary in many respects, including political sensitivity, and the appetite to impose new sanctions in contexts of internal conflict particularly may be in decline. A quintessential difference among the three types concerns the origin of the primary threat. Counter-terrorism sanctions, such as the so-called Islamic State of Iraq and the Levant (ISIL, also known as Da'esh) and Al-Qaeda sanctions regime, aim to curb a threat that emanates

---

[218] See, e.g., Federal Law of the Russian Federation on Coercive Measures for Individuals Violating Fundamental Human Rights and Freedoms of the Citizens of the Russian Federation, Russian Federation Collection of Legislation, 2012, No. 53, Item 7597; Amendments to Federal Law on Measures against Individuals Complicit in Violation of Fundamental Human Rights and Freedoms of the Citizens of the Russian Federation, and to Article 27 of the Federal Law on the Procedure to Exit and Enter the Russian Federation of 4 March 2022.

[219] For the argument that the individualisation of sanctions, i.e., the targeting of individuals rather than states, requires a greater formalisation and proceduralisation, see Larissa van den Herik, 'The Individualization and Formalization of UN Sanctions', in Van den Herik (ed.), *UN Sanctions* (n. 211), 1–16.

[220] Maluwa, 'Between Centralism and Regionalism', Chapter 3 in this volume, section III.C (pp. 237–238).

from a non-state actor, and this regime has been territorially delinked over time, thus gaining a universal focus. In contrast, the counter-proliferation sanctions regimes are still very much state-focused because the threat that they confront stems principally from a state. Yet even the counter-proliferation regimes are individualised in their design and they list individuals closer or further removed from the state apparatus – albeit that a return to more comprehensive sanctions has taken place in recent years.[221]

As is well known, the comprehensive sanctions that were imposed twice during the Cold War and reused in situations regarding Iraq, Haiti, and the former Yugoslavia post-1990, were criticised for their disproportional humanitarian consequences for the civilian population. In reaction, the model of targeted sanctions emerged, focused on individual decision-makers and other principal actors, as well as their supporters.[222] Switzerland, Germany, and Sweden have been the main drivers of the evolution from comprehensive to targeted sanctions. They sponsored three sanctions reform processes, the Interlaken, Bonn-Berlin, and Stockholm processes, to discuss the design and implementation of targeted sanctions.[223]

2. The Procedural Deficit of Targeted Sanctions

The transition from comprehensive to targeted sanctions was thus justified by reference to legitimacy concerns over broad Security Council measures and the strong public backlash. However, the individualised targeted sanctions came with their own legitimacy deficit. The state-oriented institutional framework within which the Security Council operates was architecturally unprepared to accommodate the individual as a new target of sanctions. While Rule 37 of the Council's provisional Rules of Procedure makes sure that a state whose interests are affected by a matter discussed in the Council is invited to present its view and Article 50 of the UN Charter grants third states that are confronted with special economic problems arising from the sanctions a right to consult, targeted individuals initially had no access to the Security Council whatsoever. It took some time before it came to be understood that the shift towards targeting individuals also presupposes a broader refashioning of

---

[221] This recomprehensivation of UN sanctions can occur through a series of rounds, eventually culminating in unprecedented tough and comprehensive sanction packages, or because UN sanctions are complemented by further-reaching unilateral sanctions, e.g., by the United States and the European Union: see Sue Eckert, 'The Evolution and Effectiveness of UN Targeted Sanctions', in Van den Herik (ed.), *UN Sanctions* (n. 211), 52–71 (67).

[222] Van den Herik, 'Individualization and Formalization' (n. 219).

[223] As also discussed in Eckert, 'Evolution and Effectiveness' (n. 221).

procedures and accountability mechanisms – an understanding that may still be resisted in some quarters.

Famously, the issue became particularly pressing in the context of the 1267 sanctions regime. The regime was established in 1999 as a regular sanctions regime. Similar to other regimes, it imposed sanctions on elite decision-makers exercising de facto control in Afghanistan – namely, the Taliban. After the events of 11 September 2001 (i.e., 9/11), Resolution 1390 reinvigorated the 1267 regime and extended it to address the threat posed by Al-Qaeda. Effectively, Resolution 1390 severed the regime's geographical ties and turned it into a thematic sanctions regime with global reach.[224] This development was facilitated by the Security Council's generic determination of terrorism as a threat to international peace. In the immediate post-9/11 moment, the list was flooded with names in a quest to respond decisively.[225] This resulted in many flawed designations lacking adequate documentation to support the listing, which exposed the institutional shortcomings of the targeted sanctions machinery.

The excessive and flawed listings, in turn, generated worldwide litigation, with the *Kadi* case in the Court of Justice of the European Union (CJEU) at the apex.[226] The threat of non-compliance with UN sanctions by all EU states propelled institutional and procedural reform at Security Council level. The Watson reports of Thomas Biersteker and Sue Eckert, sponsored by Switzerland, Germany, and Sweden, made great contributions towards realising reform by putting forward concrete proposals.[227] Biersteker and Eckert highlighted the key elements of a proper listing process – namely, proper

---

[224] This move towards global sanctions was modelled on the US sanctions framework, as observed by Lisa Ginsborg, 'UN Sanctions and Counter-Terrorism Strategies: Moving towards Thematic Sanctions against Individuals?', in Van den Herik (ed.), *UN Sanctions* (n. 211), 73–104.

[225] For more on why the Bush Administration did this, see Thomas Biersteker and Sue Eckert, '(Mis)Measuring Success in the Financial "War" on Terrorism', in Peter Andreas and Kelly M. Greenhill (eds), *Sex, Drugs, and Body Counts: The Politics of Numbers in Global Crime and Punishment* (Ithaca: Cornell University Press, 2010), 247–65.

[226] As discussed, e.g., in Larissa van den Herik, 'Peripheral Hegemony in the Quest to Ensure Security Council Accountability for its Individualized UN Sanctions Regimes', *Journal of Conflict and Security Law* 19 (2014), 427–49.

[227] Thomas Biersteker and Sue Eckert, *Strengthening Targeted Sanctions Through Fair and Clear Procedures*, 30 March 2006 (the Watson Report), available at www.files.ethz.ch/isn/27 118/Strengthening_Targeted_Sanctions.pdf and as official UN Doc. A/60/887–S/2006/331; Thomas Biersteker and Sue Eckert, *Addressing Challenges to Targeted Sanctions: An Update of the 'Watson Report'*, October 2009, available at www.files.ethz.ch/isn/111057/2009 _10_FB09_sanctionsreport.pdf; Thomas Biersteker and Sue Eckert, *Due Process and Targeted Sanctions: An Update of the 'Watson Report'*, December 2012. The present author drafted the legal chapters of these reports.

designation criteria, a requirement for a narrative summary or a statement of reasons for listing, evidentiary standards, notification, and periodic review. The key elements for the delisting process that they emphasised concerned specification of delisting criteria, access to independent and impartial review mechanisms, a hearing, access to counsel, impartial review of an evidentiary base on which designations are made and maintained, independent review, and a binding decision. In their 2006 report, Biersteker and Eckert offered a roster of institutional options to ensure review in accordance with those elements, ranging from increased roles for the monitoring team and the panel of experts to judicial review proper. While the first two options were considered insufficiently independent, the latter was too intrusive for the Security Council setting to be acceptable, particularly for the P5.

Drawing on Scandinavian experiences, one suggestion concerned an ombudsperson. The ombudsperson would be independent and directly accessible to listed individuals, yet not able to render binding decisions; for that reason, it would be more palatable for certain states. As it became clear that some reform was inevitable given the litigation, the outcry, and the many reports, the work of like-minded and committed states ultimately led to the creation of the Ombudsperson (first as the 'Ombudsman') in December 2009 through Resolution 1904, as well as to other procedural improvements concerning listing and periodic review.[228] While the other sanctions regimes have gradually 'copied and pasted' many of the procedural improvements, the Ombudsperson's mandate remains confined to the 1267 regime. In this regime only, listed individuals can turn to the Ombudsperson with a petition to be delisted. Upon receiving such a request, the Ombudsperson gathers information and enters into dialogue with the relevant actors, including the petitioner and relevant states, and presents a report of its observations and arguments concerning the delisting request.

Within a decade, the combined threat that the Taliban and Al-Qaeda posed in 2001 gradually morphed. The distinction between the two groups became more predominant than their mutual connections, which made their grouping into one sanctions regime less obvious. Furthermore, with a view to promoting the comprehensive peace process in Afghanistan, the Afghan government requested a more flexible and expedient approach to delisting requests for those Taliban members engaged in reconciliation efforts who had severed their ties with Al-Qaeda. In light of these developments, the Security

---

[228] The Group of Like-Minded States for Targeted Sanctions comprised Austria, Belgium, Chile, Costa Rica, Denmark, Finland, Germany, Liechtenstein, the Netherlands, Norway, Sweden, and Switzerland.

Council split the 1267 regime into two separate regimes – one targeting the Taliban as a national movement (the sanctions regime established by Resolution 1988); another targeting Al-Qaeda as a global actor (the sanctions regime established pursuant to Resolution 1989) – with a reinforced role for the Ombudsperson (but only for the regime targeting Al-Qaeda). Within the Taliban regime, the Afghan government was given greater ownership, as requested, and Resolution 1988 explicitly stipulated that due regard had to be given to its delisting requests as part of the reconciliation process.

The separation of these two regimes emphasised the different nature and rationale that guide counter-terrorism and armed conflict sanctions regimes, respectively. While the view is tenable that differences between types of sanctions regime should have consequences for the manner in which delisting and review is organised in each type, the decision to fully exclude a role for the Ombudsperson for the Taliban sanctions is mostly indicative of the aversion of some Security Council members towards independent review as such.

3. Additional Flaws in the UN Sanctions Regimes

Recent developments have also brought another flaw to light. With the fall of the Afghan government in August 2021 and the Taliban takeover, questions arose about the extent of the UN sanctions regime – particularly what the implications were of the fact that key officials in the Taliban Administration had long been listed under UN and unilateral sanctions regimes. The argument has been made that individual sanctions against persons who become a minister do not extend to the ministry as such and hence that payments to the ministry can continue to be made.[229] In this respect, it is to be noted that, in contrast to the United States and in contrast to the Haqqani Network, the UN sanctions regime did not list the Taliban as an entity. Nonetheless, the confusion that arose on this matter specifically, and on the extent of the UN and other sanctions more generally, put payments on hold and has had immense chilling effect.[230] This has been exacerbated by the prolonged unwillingness of Security Council members to create a general carve-out for humanitarian action, as existed in the 751 sanctions regime for Somalia and as was finally created for the 1988 regime for Afghanistan with Resolution 2615 of

---

[229] Emanuela-Chiara Gillard, 'Learnings Must Become Practice as the Taliban Return', *Chatham House*, 7 September 2021, available at www.chathamhouse.org/2021/09/learnings-must-become-practice-taliban-return.

[230] Sue Eckert, 'Afghanistan's Future: Assessing the National Security, Humanitarian and Economic Implications of the Taliban Takeover', Testimony before the US Senate Committee on Banking, Housing and Urban Affairs, 5 October 2021.

December 2021, as well as for the Haiti sanctions regime in Resolution 2653 of October 2022. Thus, in these three cases, the matter was addressed on an ad hoc basis for one specific sanctions regime only.

Meanwhile, the Al-Qaeda sanctions regime had taken its own route. Another major turning point for this sanctions regime came with Resolution 2253 in 2015, which expanded the regime further to cover ISIL/Da'esh. The regime was renamed the '1267/1989/2253 ISIL (Da'esh) and Al-Qaeda' sanctions regime. The regime thus targeted quite different groups, including groups that actually opposed each other, and its targeting loop included those that were relatively loosely associated with them, such as the organisation of Al-Qaida in the Islamic Maghreb, as well as others operating in Mali and the Sahel region.[231] It has been observed that 'the current 1267 regime has evolved into the realm of the permanent exception'.[232] This permanence may be in tune with the ongoing terrorist threat as an enduring reality, with expanding scope and geographical reach. It is, however, more difficult to shoehorn it into Chapter VII's exceptional emergency status. For this reason, it has been suggested that a separate body (and not a sanctions committee) might be more appropriate to address this threat.[233] With the situation in the Middle East evolving, it remains to be seen what will ultimately happen to the 1267 regime. Given that the Ombudsperson is exclusively linked to the 1267/1989/2253 sanctions regime, the fact is that – as things stand now – once, if ever, this regime ceases to exist, the institution of the Ombudsperson will fade with it.

The Ombudsperson for the ISIL/Al-Qaeda sanctions regime is thus unique in many ways: unique in the sense of exclusive, because it reviews listings for only one regime, but also unique in the sense of unprecedented and extraordinary, because it is the first time that the Security Council openly and explicitly agreed to constrain itself and to be reviewed. Many international lawyers tend to underline the fact that, ultimately, the Ombudsperson cannot make binding decisions, but this emphasis underappreciates the unparalleled nature and potential of the Ombudsperson – in theory. Moreover, while scholars and litigators have challenged the sufficiency of the Ombudsperson's role as a non-judicial process, they have so far largely ignored the restrictions on its scope and particularly the fact that the review it does provide is connected to one sanctions regime only. Yet the weak institutional embedding of the Ombudsperson within the greater UN bureaucracy and its very limited mandate for a single sanctions regime are fundamentally problematic. The third person to fulfil the role of

---

[231] SC Res. 2295 of 29 June 2016, UN Doc. S/RES/2295(2016).
[232] Eckert, 'Evolution and Effectiveness' (n. 221).
[233] *Ibid.*

Ombudsperson, Daniël Kipfer Fasciati, gave notice of his resignation mid-2021 because of the lack of institutional independence of his office.[234] In addition to the institutional weaknesses, the political decision to limit the Ombudsperson mandate to the ISIL/Al-Qaeda regime only is plainly at odds with the underlying principle established through litigation that any listed individual should have a remedy and a meaningful opportunity to challenge their listing. Several attempts have been made by the like-minded states to expand the mandate of the Ombudsperson to other UN sanctions regimes, but so far to no avail.[235]

4. Improving the UN Sanctions Architecture: Attempts and Accomplishments

In this context of a stalemate, new avenues are being explored. In 2018, the UN University Centre for Policy Research published a report commissioned by the Swiss Federal Department of Foreign Affairs' Directorate of International Law. This report was entitled *Fairly Clear Risks: Protecting UN Sanctions' Legitimacy and Effectiveness through Fair and Clear Procedures*.[236] One of its proposals was a different type of review mechanism, which it called a context-sensitive non-judicial review arrangement. The main idea was that different types of UN sanctions regime – that is, the counter-terrorism regimes, the armed conflict regimes, and the non-proliferation regimes – operated in different political and informational contexts, which also warranted a different review setting. The idea pursued a suggestion made during the Australia-led assessment of the High-Level Review – namely, 'to focus on the expansion of the Ombudsperson's *functions* to non-counter-terrorism sanctions regimes, rather than seek immediate agreement on an expanded Ombudsperson mandate'.[237]

---

[234] UN Doc. S/2021/676, 23 July 2021. See also Colum Lynch, 'How a Dream Job Became a Bureaucratic Nightmare for a Top U.N. Lawyer', *Foreign Policy*, 27 July 2021, available at https://foreignpolicy.com/2021/07/27/un-terrorism-lawyer-resigning-ombudsperson-bureaucracy/.

[235] See, e.g., Statement delivered by Ambassador Olof Skoog of Sweden on behalf of the Group of Like-Minded States on Targeted Sanctions at the UN Security Council Open Debate on Working Methods of the Security Council, 6 June 2019. See also High-Level Review of United Nations Sanctions, UN Doc. A/69/941–S/2015/432, 12 June 2015, 32, recommendation no. 24.

[236] James Cockayne, Rebecca Brubaker, and Nadesha Jayakody, *Fairly Clear Risks: Protecting UN Sanctions' Legitimacy and Effectiveness Through Fair and Clear Procedures* (New York: United Nations University, 2018).

[237] Identical letters dated 21 June 2017 from the Permanent Representative of Australia to the United Nations addressed to the Secretary-General and the President of the Security

The publication of the report illustrates that the like-minded states remain committed to the idea of integrating a rule-of-law dimension into all UN sanctions regimes and to keeping the matter on the agenda. Indeed, in June 2021, the like-minded states (namely, Austria, Belgium, Chile, Costa Rica, Denmark, Finland, Germany, Ireland, Liechtenstein, Netherlands, Norway, Sweden, and Switzerland) submitted a letter to the Security Council promoting the idea of a context-sensitive review mechanism for the other sanctions regimes.[238] Ultimately, their efforts led to renewed appreciation of the Ombudsperson, so as not to overcomplicate the system. Notably, Resolution 2653 establishing a Haiti sanctions regime explicitly stated, in its 20th preambular paragraph, that it 'Recogniz[ed] the need to ensure that fair and clear procedures exist for delisting individuals, groups, undertakings, and entities designated pursuant to this resolution and expressing its intent to consider authorizing the Ombudsperson to receive such delisting requests'. The persistent efforts of states such as Switzerland seem to have paid off with this noteworthy openness to the idea of a broader role for the Ombudsperson.

The *Fairly Clear Risks* report also made some other suggestions. One of them that is, at the very least, of equal importance concerned strengthening groups or panels of experts.[239] As already noted, panels of experts are typically established for each UN sanctions regime to gather information and to monitor implementation of the sanctions.[240] They have an independent fact-finding mandate, and thus they play an important role in establishing the facts that are pertinent for the design and the evolution of the sanctions regime at stake. As such, these panels have the potential to contribute considerably to the institutional strength of the UN sanctions machinery and, as suggested in the previous section, they could also be considered a blueprint for a more fact-based environment for use-of-force discourse. Yet the legal and institutional situation of experts has always been precarious, especially when compared with other UN officials and consultants. Despite their perilous work terrain, they do not enjoy the privileges of medical evacuation insurance or health care

---

Council, UN Doc. A/71/943-S/2017/534, 23 June 2017, Annex, 11, Recommendation 5, as cited in Cockayne et al., *Fairly Clear Risks* (n. 236), 30 (emphasis added).

[238]   UN Doc. S/2021/567, 14 June 2021.

[239]   Cockayne et al., *Fairly Clear Risks* (n. 236), 28.

[240]   The first panel of experts was created as part of the Angola sanctions regime under SC Res. 1237 of 7 May 1999, UN Doc. S/RES/1237(1999), pursuant to a recommendation by Canadian Ambassador to the United Nations Robert Fowler. See, more generally on innovations in UN sanctions architecture, Joanna Weschler, 'The Evolution of Security Council Innovations in Sanctions', *International Journal: Canada's Journal of Global Policy Analysis* 65 (2010), 31–43.

nor do they carry an official UN passport.[241] Moreover, their resources may be curtailed by the UN budget committees.[242]

Panels of experts affiliated with different sanctions regimes each operate on the basis of their own differing procedural guidelines. Some panels of experts have been exceptionally bold in publicly naming individuals, even including photographs in their reports. Such steps emphasise the need for fair procedures as part of investigation and listing, not only for delisting. Indeed, in the context of commissions of inquiry, there have been calls for caution regarding the practice of 'naming names' as a short-track accountability measure.[243] Reforms regarding listing processes currently occur on an ad hoc basis within regimes, depending on which state chairs the sanctions committee.

The question of procedural reform regarding delisting, the strengthening of panels of experts, and the need to include some type of independent review mechanism for sanctions regimes other than the 1267/1989/2253 regime does not, at present, enjoy the spotlight. Even if there is litigation at the EU courts rather similar to the *Kadi* case, as the *Fairly Clear Risks* report describes (particularly the *Aisha Qadaffi* case[244]), the issue is not squarely on the radar and states do not feel pressed to engage in further reform. The pace and level of reforms in this respect therefore largely depend on the stamina of the like-minded states and other actors, and their ability to create and expand alliances.

Reform is possible, though. An initiative very successfully led by Ireland – jointly with the United States, and advocated by special rapporteurs and humanitarian organisations – resulted in Resolution 2664 of 9 December 2022. The Resolution created a standing humanitarian exception applicable to all existing UN financial sanctions and those yet to be established. Paragraph 1 of Resolution 2664 states that:

> [T]he provision, processing or payment of funds, other financial assets, or economic resources, or the provision of goods and services necessary to

---

[241] Colum Lynch, '"The Worst Bloody Job in the World"', *Foreign Policy*, 20 October 2021, available at https://foreignpolicy.com/2021/10/20/sanctions-enforcers-united-nations-panel-experts/.

[242] Colum Lynch, 'Sunset for UN Sanctions?', *Foreign Policy*, 14 October 2021, available at https://foreignpolicy.com/2021/10/14/sanctions-united-nations-expert-panels-russia-china-africa-western-countries/.

[243] Carsten Stahn and Catherine Harwood, 'What's the Point of "Naming Names" in International Inquiry? Counseling Caution in the Turn towards Individual Responsibility', *EJIL:Talk!*, 11 November 2016, available at www.ejiltalk.org/whats-the-point-of-naming-names-in-international-inquiry-counseling-caution-in-the-turn-towards-individual-responsibility/.

[244] CJEU, *Aisha Muammer Mohamed El-Qaddafi v. Council of the European Union*, Case T-322/19, 21 April 2021.

ensure the timely delivery of humanitarian assistance or to support other activities that support basic human needs ... are permitted and are not a violation of the asset freezes.

This breakthrough is all the more remarkable given the Security Council's overall malfunction after the Ukraine aggression. The Resolution was co-sponsored by 53 states from different regions and adopted with P5 consensus and 14 votes in favour. India was the only state to abstain. It recorded its reservations referring to the risk of terrorist groups taking advantage of the humanitarian carve-out.[245]

Thus like-minded states mostly from Europe are taking the lead on reform issues for UN sanctions regimes. The fear that their initiatives could be hampered by the international community's divide over the sanctions tool as such has not proven well founded. This divide particularly relates to unilateral sanctions: a policy tool mostly used by the West.[246] Perhaps the turn to unilateral sanctions in response to the Russian aggression has prompted states to take UN sanctions reform more seriously. Indeed, UN sanctions that are governed by fair and clear procedures could also – in theory, at least – undercut the turn to unilateralism in this domain; if not, they could serve as a model. Clearly, from a perspective of institutional strength, a centralised sanctions machinery premised on independent fact-finding capacity is to be preferred over unilateral measures.

VI. SECURITY COUNCIL ACTION ON TERRORISM AND EXTREMISM: STRETCHING PREROGATIVES BEYOND BREAKING POINT?

The Security Council's sanctions against ISIL and Al-Qaeda can be regarded as part of the broader UN sanctions machinery that developed post Cold War. Yet they are also an indelible component of the counter-terrorism architecture that the Security Council constructed in the immediate aftermath of 9/11. Indeed, while the UN General Assembly had, up until that moment, been the motor of the UN's counter-terrorism efforts through its resolutions and pro-motion of treaties, 9/11 was a game-changer in many ways.[247] Specifically regarding the UN's counter-terrorism work, it was the moment when the

---

[245] UN Doc. S/PV.9214, 9 December 2022, 8.

[246] See, e.g., Alexandra Hofer, 'The Developed/Developing Divide on Unilateral Coercive Measures: Legitimate Enforcement or Illegitimate Intervention?', *Chinese Journal of International Law* 16 (2017), 175–214.

[247] Sebastian von Einsiedel, 'Assessing the UN's Efforts to Counter Terrorism', Occasional Paper 8, United Nations University Centre for Policy Research, October 2016, available at https://collections.unu.edu/eserv/UNU:6053/AssessingtheUNsEffortstoCounterterrorism.pdf.

UN Security Council took the driver's seat. In response to 9/11, the UN Security Council accepted the idea of a counter-terrorist right to self-defence[248] and it universalised the existing 1267 sanctions regime, disconnecting it from a particular conflict. While these were all bold moves, the most groundbreaking step was undoubtedly the adoption of Resolution 1373. With this Resolution, the UN Security Council started legislating, and it imposed generic and temporally unlimited counter-terrorist obligations on states.[249] It also developed an organic institutional structure to monitor the implementation of those obligations, the Counter-Terrorism Committee (CTC), which was later joined by the Counter-Terrorism Committee Executive Directorate (CTED).[250] Over time, the formal structures were complemented with informal platforms and taskforces – most notably, the Financial Action Task Force, which entertained an opaque and unregulated relationship with the UN Security Council.[251]

Hinojosa-Martínez distinguishes between three sets of obligations in Resolution 1373.[252] First, and most innovatively, the Resolution contained obligations that were transposed from the UN Convention for the Suppression of the Financing of Terrorism, which had been adopted by the General Assembly without a vote but had not yet entered into force. These obligations concerned asset freezing and the criminalisation of funding terrorism.[253] Secondly, there was an amalgam of other binding obligations concerning denial of safe haven and prevention of movement, but also obliging states to criminalise terrorism as a *serious* crime with punishment duly reflecting its seriousness.[254] Thirdly, Resolution 1373 stipulated a set of measures that states were called upon to perform, such as ratifying treaties and intensifying cooperation, but also aiming to prevent them offering refugee status to terrorism suspects.[255] In its

---

[248] See, for a discussion, Mary Ellen O'Connell, Christian J. Tams, and Dire Tladi, *Self-Defence against Non-State Actors*, Max Planck Trialogues on the Law of Peace and War (Anne Peters and Christian Marxsen, series eds), vol. 1 (Cambridge: Cambridge University Press, 2019).

[249] As welcomed by Paul Szasz, 'The Security Council Starts Legislating', *American Journal of International Law* 96 (2002), 901–05. For an appraisal of the Council's legislative activity and its limits, see also Stefan Talmon, 'The Security Council as World Legislature', *American Journal of International Law* 99 (2005), 175–93.

[250] Luis M. Hinojosa-Martínez, 'Security Council Resolution 1373: The Cumbersome Implementation of Legislative Acts', in Ben Saul (ed.), *Research Handbook on International Law and Terrorism* (Cheltenham: Edward Elgar, 2020), 564–87.

[251] Alejandro Rodiles, 'The Design of UN Sanctions Through the Interplay with Informal Arrangements', in Van den Herik (ed.), *UN Sanctions* (n. 211), 177–93.

[252] Hinojosa-Martínez, 'Security Council Resolution 1373' (n. 250), 564.

[253] SC Res. 1373 of 28 September 2001, UN Doc. S/RES/1373(2001), para. 1.

[254] *Ibid.*, para. 2.

[255] *Ibid.*, para. 3.

supervision, the CTC did not clearly distinguish between these three types and hence it blurred the legal distinctions among them in practice.[256]

Resolution 1373 was unique and unprecedented at its adoption, but it did not remain so. It was followed by a string of resolutions imposing on states ever bolder obligations to address terrorism and associated activity. Unlike Resolution 1373, these resolutions did not originate from a consensually adopted General Assembly document. Most notably, in 2005, Resolution 1628 called upon states to prohibit incitement of terrorism; in 2014, Resolution 2178 imposed obligations on states to respond to the threat of foreign fighters – obligations further elaborated on in 2017, in Resolution 2396, including an obligation to create global watch lists and databases of suspected terrorists. In 2019, Resolution 2462 built on Resolution 1373 by requiring states to enact domestic laws to counter terrorism financing.

Objections to the Security Council's exercise of quasi-legislative powers as ultra vires that were raised upon the adoption of Resolution 1373[257] have been muted by this sustained subsequent practice.[258] Notably, Resolution 2178 was adopted at summit meeting level and co-sponsored by 103 states. Yet widespread criticism against the substance of the resolutions, such as that expressed by special rapporteurs, has remained steadfast ever since Resolution 1373 was adopted.[259] The definitional deficit and the expansive approach to criminal law are considered ill at ease with the core principle of legality.[260] By obliging – on the basis of its Chapter VII powers – states to adopt legislation criminalising

---

[256]   Hinojosa-Martínez, 'Security Council Resolution 1373' (n. 250), 564–65.

[257]   See, e.g., Happold, who argued that, based on the structure of the UN Charter and previous practice, the Security Council could respond only to a particular situation or conduct: Matthew Happold, 'Security Council Resolution 1373 and the Constitution of the United Nations', *Leiden Journal of International Law* 16 (2003), 593–610. See also Derek W. Bowett, 'Judicial and Political Functions of the Security Council and the International Court of Justice', in Hazel Fox (ed.), *The Changing Constitution of the United Nations* (London: British Institute for International and Comparative Law, 1997), 79–80; Björn Elberling, 'The Ultra Vires Character of Legislative Action by the Security Council', *International Organizations Law Review* 2 (2005), 337–60.

[258]   Luis M. Hinojosa-Martínez, 'The Legislative Role of the Security Council in its Fight against Terrorism: Legal, Political and Practical Limits', *International and Comparative Law Quarterly* 47 (2008), 333–59; Bart S. Duijzentkunst, 'Interpretation of Legislative Security Council Resolutions', *Utrecht Law Review* 4 (2008), 188–209.

[259]   See, e.g., Helen Duffy and Larissa van den Herik, 'Terrorism and the Security Council', in Robin Geiß and Nils Melzer (eds), *The Oxford Handbook of the International Law of Global Security* (Oxford: Oxford University Press, 2021), 193–212. See also Arianna Vedaschi and Kim Lane Scheppele (eds), *9/11 and the Rise of Global Anti-Terrorism Law: How the UN Security Council Rules the World* (Cambridge: Cambridge University Press, 2021).

[260]   Martin Scheinin, 'A Proposal for a Kantian Definition of Terrorism: Leading the World Requires Cosmopolitan Ethos', in Vedaschi and Scheppele (eds), *9/11* (n. 259), 15–33; Lisa Ginsborg, 'Moving toward the Criminalization of "Pre-crime": The UN Security Council's

all types of behaviour, some of which might be quite tenuously related to a terrorist act (which, as already noted, has been left undefined), the Security Council allows – arguably even encourages – states to bypass regular parliamentarian discussion and other domestic checks and balances that aim to put theories of criminal law and its limits into practice. The question of to what extent the criminalisation of pre-crime behaviour creates tension with fundamental principles of criminal law is then left undebated. Under the guise of a Security Council mandate, states have engaged in intense normative activity resulting in the labelling of political dissent, artistic or journalistic expression, humanitarian assistance, and environmental activity, among other actions, as terrorist in nature; the Security Council's resolutions have also generated far-reaching administrative measures, such as stripping of citizenship.[261] In his chapter in this volume, Maluwa adds that the participation of Russia and China in UN efforts to fight terrorism affords them 'a cover of legitimacy for their own campaigns against alleged terrorist groups at home (for China) or in the so-called near abroad (for Russia)'.[262]

In a 2019 report, the Special Rapporteur on the Promotion and Protection of Human Rights and Fundamental Freedoms while Countering Terrorism linked the shrinking of space for civil society directly with the proliferation of security measures prompted by the Security Council, and she offered numerous examples of how the Security Council's counter-terrorism resolutions have provided states with extraordinary latitude and have effectively been misused to suppress dissent.[263] The Special Rapporteur expressed her concern about using Security Council resolutions as a 'legal super highway'.[264] Operating as 'supranational legal dictates', these legislative resolutions pay

Recent Legislative Action on Counterterrorism', in Vedaschi and Scheppele (eds), 9/11 (n. 259), 133–54.

[261] Christophe Paulussen, 'Countering Terrorism Through the Stripping of Citizenship: Ineffective and Counterproductive', 17 October 2018, available at www.icct.nl/publication/countering-terrorism-through-stripping-citizenship-ineffective-and-counterproductive. See also Dana Burchardt and Rishi Gulati, 'International Counter-terrorism Regulation and Citizenship-Stripping Laws: Reinforcing Legal Exceptionalism', *Journal of Conflict and Security Law* 23 (2018), 203–28.

[262] Maluwa, 'Between Centralism and Regionalism', Chapter 3 in this volume, section III.C (p. 236).

[263] Impact of Measures to Address Terrorism and Violent Extremism on Civic Space and the Rights of Civil Society Actors and Human Rights Defenders: Report of the Special Rapporteur on the Promotion and Protection of Human Rights and Fundamental Freedoms while Countering Terrorism, UN Doc. A/HRC/40/52, 1 March 2019.

[264] Report of the Special Rapporteur on the Promotion and Protection of Human Rights and Fundamental Freedoms while Countering Terrorism on the human rights challenge of states of emergency in the context of countering terrorism, UN Doc. A/HRC/37/52, 1 March 2018, para. 63.

insufficient attention to rule-of-law requirements within domestic systems.[265] The Special Rapporteur also submitted that the quasi-legislative character of the resolution presupposes broad consultation rather than fast-track adoption through closed procedures. She has recommended an a priori human rights review or some other internal procedural mechanism to ensure that core concerns regarding legitimacy, legality, and proportionality are addressed.[266]

Despite these grave concerns that the Security Council intrudes on a healthy state–society relationship and participatory decision-making at the domestic level,[267] the passing of 20 years since landmark Resolution 1373 was marked by a presidential statement reaffirming its significance.[268] In the ensuing videoconference meeting, certain states shared some of their distress over Resolution 1373, while others sturdily rebutted any alarm. The great majority of states underscored the importance of abiding by human rights law in the fight against terrorism and they warned that counter-terrorism measures should not be misused to silence or to prevent legitimate humanitarian action. The United Kingdom explicitly mentioned the detention of 1 million people in Xinjiang. In contrast, India and China insisted that no distinction should be made between good and bad terrorists. Russia boldly stated that 'the use of human rights as a pretext to refuse cooperation with foreign partners is not acceptable' and that 'the Security Council pays too much attention to the human rights aspects of counter-terrorism, to the detriment of ensuring security'.[269]

Within the panoply of viewpoints and approaches over time, the term 'violent extremism' emerged as some kind of twin notion of terrorism. The concept of 'Countering Violent Extremism' was initially developed under the administration of US President Barack Obama as a counterweight to the earlier militarised approach and it was included in Resolution 2178, mentioned earlier in this discussion. The Resolution was adopted by the Security Council during its US presidency at a session chaired by President Obama

[265] *Ibid.*, para. 20.
[266] Report of the Special Rapporteur on the Promotion and Protection of Human Rights and Fundamental Freedoms while Countering Terrorism, UN Doc. A/73/45453, 3 September 2018, para. 50(e).
[267] On the crucial relevance of a proper balance between state and society, see Daron Acemoglu and James A. Robinson, *The Narrow Corridor: States, Societies, and the Fate of Liberty* (New York: Penguin, 2019).
[268] UN Doc. S/PRST/2021/1, 12 January 2021.
[269] '20 Years after Adopting Landmark Anti-Terrorism Resolution, Security Council Resolves to Strengthen International Response against Heinous Acts, in Presidential Statement', UN Doc. SC/14408, 12 January 2021.

himself.[270] Secretary-General Ban Ki-moon lauded the turn towards more emphasis on prevention and adopted the Plan of Action for Preventing Violent Extremism.[271] This plan dovetailed with the United Nations' long-standing emphasis on prevention, yet it met with intense resistance from many sides. Overall, the plan was seen to risk the securitisation of development and the politicisation of the humanitarian space.[272] The plan's most prominent failure was – again – the absence of a definition of 'violent extremism'.

In 2020, the Special Rapporteur on the Promotion and Protection of Human Rights and Fundamental Freedoms while Countering Terrorism presented a report specifically dealing with violent extremism. She underlined that the target population for measures concerning the prevention of extremism was much broader than that of counter-terrorism measures. The Special Rapporteur noted how the discourse of countering (violent) extremism had increasingly become part and parcel of the post-9/11 globalised security regime. She expressed particular concern over the opaque nature of the notion of violent extremism and indicated that it was highly contested. The Special Rapporteur underlined that the absence of a definition became even more problematic if the term were used without the adjective of 'violent' in policy and legal terrains with purposes other than prevention. Referring, for example, to the use of the term in the Shanghai Convention – a cooperation convention of 2001, updated in 2017[273] – the Special Rapporteur emphasised that, if operative as a criminal legal category, the term 'extremism' is incompatible with the principle of legal certainty, which requires that criminal behaviour be proscribed clearly and foreseeably.

The outsized role of a non-democratic and non-representative Security Council on counter-terrorism and its engagement in detailed standard-setting has thus been subject of intense criticism, and it has also, in some sense, been counter-productive, deepening grievances rather than truly addressing them.[274] The Security Council's activity on counter-terrorism

---

[270]   David H. Ucko, 'Preventing Violent Extremism Through the United Nations: The Rise and Fall of a Good Idea', *International Affairs* 95 (2018), 251–70.

[271]   UN Doc. A/70/764, 24 December 2015.

[272]   Ucko, 'Preventing Violent Extremism' (n. 270), 251–70. See also Naz Modirzadeh, 'If it's Broke, Don't Make it Worse: A Critique of the UN Secretary-General's Plan of Action to Prevent Violent Extremism', *Lawfare*, 23 January 2016, available at www.lawfaremedia.org/article/if-its-broke-dont-make-it-worse-critique-un-secretary-generals-plan-action-prevent-violent-extremism.

[273]   For an appraisal of this convention from a human rights perspective, see OSCE, Note on the Shanghai Convention on Combating Terrorism, Separatism and Extremism, Warsaw, 21 September 2020.

[274]   Recommendations to 'right-size' the Security Council's approach were offered by the Securing the Future Initiative: Eric Rosand, Alistair Millar, and Naureen Chowdhury Fink, *Counterterrorism and the United Nations Security Council since 9/11: Moving beyond*

could be regarded as the product of a strong and united institution, but it is actually deeply problematic from a human rights perspective. It is in tension with the very purposes and principles of the UN Charter that are meant to guide the Council. The sweeping obligations on states to criminalise all kinds of non-violent conduct, such as travelling and supportive behaviour, has encouraged states to assume repressive modes and it has given a pretext to already repressive states to further suppress dissent. From an institutionalist perspective, the Security Council might well have overstepped its mandate, and the way forward should therefore be a gradual turn away from the use of comprehensive and detailed Chapter VII resolutions as quasi-legislation for counter-terrorism purposes. This is indeed quite the opposite view from Cai's suggestions in his chapter in this volume for more Chinese norm entrepreneurship on counter-extremism.[275]

VII. FUTURE TRAJECTORIES AND UNCONVENTIONAL GLOBAL THREATS

In addition to terrorism, the Security Council has labelled other global phenomena as threats to peace. An early example of a non-traditional threat on the Security Council's agenda was HIV/AIDS. In 2000, in the unanimously adopted Resolution 1308, the Security Council stressed 'that the HIV/AIDS pandemic, if unchecked, may pose a risk to stability and security'.[276] It did not label HIV/AIDS as a threat to peace as such, but it did make some recommendations bearing in mind its primary responsibility. It particularly recognised the potential damaging impact of HIV/AIDS on peacekeeping personnel, thus linking back to concerns that came within its more traditional purview. The UN Security Council came back to the issue in 2022, in Resolution 1983.[277] In 2014, in Resolution 2177, and again in 2018, in Resolution 2439, the Council considered Ebola.[278] Resolution 2439 concerned the armed conflict in the DRC and was thus intrinsically linked to a more traditional military threat, but Resolution 2177 zeroed in on the outbreak of Ebola in West Africa as such, the Security Council determining

---

the 2001 Paradigm – Findings and Recommendations, September 2022, available at https://sfi-ct.org/wp-content/uploads/2022/09/SFI-Report_Summary.pdf.

[275] Cai, 'Maintaining Peace during a Global Power Shift', Chapter 1 in this volume, section V.D.4. Such a leading role by China might, in fact, be quite alarming from a rule-of-law perspective and given the fierce criticisms voiced by, among others, 51 UN Special Rapporteurs against the (then still draft) Hong Kong National Security Law of 26 May 2020.

[276] SC Res. 1308 of 17 July 2000, UN Doc. S/RES/1308(2000).

[277] SC Res. 2177 of 18 September 2014, UN Doc. S/RES/2177(2014).

[278] SC Res. 2439 of 30 October 2018, UN Doc. S/RES/2439(2018).

that the 'unprecedented extent of the Ebola outbreak in Africa constituted a threat to international peace and security'.[279]

It was against this background that Resolution 2532 was adopted in 2020 on COVID-19.[280] While this Resolution was also adopted unanimously, it was considerably more hard-won, with US–China contestations over the origins and name of the virus seeping into the negotiations, as well as the by-then-politicised question of a reference to the role of the World Health Organization (WHO).[281] Because it concerned a pandemic, the Resolution was global in scope and not regionally limited, as had been Resolution 2177. In other respects, the COVID 19-Resolution was more modest in its approach in comparison with the Ebola resolutions. Resolution 2532 considered that 'the unprecedented extent of the COVID-19 pandemic is likely to endanger the maintenance of international peace and security' – a more careful framing than in Resolution 2177. It focused on one core demand concerning a cessation of hostilities. A caveat was included for military operations against ISIL, Al-Qaeda, and Al Nusra, and affiliated individuals and entities, as well as other terrorist groups designated by the Security Council, thus implicitly construing a hierarchy of threats.

Western states have been important drivers of the inclusion of unconventional global threats on the Security Council's agenda. Besides global health, the Security Council has also considered the climate crisis. In contrast to the resolutions concerning transnational health crises, though, the Security Council's engagement with the climate crisis has been much more contested. In 2007, the Security Council held its first ministerial-level open debate – organised by the United Kingdom – on the relationship between energy, security, and climate. A great number of states expressed discomfort with the Security Council's mission creep, fearing that it would undermine other bodies of the UN system. Speaking on behalf of the Group of 77 (G77) and China, Pakistan stated:

> The issues of energy and climate change are vital for sustainable development. Responsibilities in the field of sustainable development belong to the General Assembly, the Economic and Social Council, their relevant subsidiary bodies, including the Commission on Sustainable Development, and

---

[279]   SC Res. 2177 of 18 September 2014, UN Doc. S/RES/2177(2014), cons. 5.
[280]   SC Res. 2352 of 1 July 2020, UN Doc. S/RES/2352(2020). See also Erin Pobjie, 'COVID-19 and the Scope of the UN Security Council's Mandate to Address Non-Traditional Threats to International Peace and Security', *Heidelberg Journal of International Law* 1 (2021), 117–46.
[281]   Security Council Report, 'Security Council Resolution on COVID-19', 30 June 2020, available at www.securitycouncilreport.org/whatsinblue/2020/06/security-council-resolution-on-c ovid-19.php.

the United Nations Environment Programme. Climate change is the subject of a binding multilateral agreement – the United Nations Framework Convention on Climate Change – and a supportive protocol – the Kyoto Protocol. No role was envisaged for the Security Council.[282]

Speaking on behalf of the African Group, Sudan added:

> The Group also stresses that the increasing and alarming encroachment of the Security Council on the mandates of other United Nations bodies – which the Security Council tries to justify by linking all issues to the question of security – compromises the principles and purposes of the United Nations Charter and is also undermining the relevant bodies.[283]

While part of the G77, the small Pacific islands of Fiji, Nauru, Micronesia, Marshall Islands, Palau, Samoa, Solomon Islands, Tonga, Tuvalu, Vanuatu, and Papua New Guinea took an autonomous position linking the climate crisis to the R2P. On their behalf, Papua New Guinea stated:

> The Security Council, charged with protecting human rights and the integrity and security of States, is the paramount international forum available to us. We do not expect the Security Council to get involved in the details of discussions in the Framework Convention on Climate Change, but we do expect the Security Council to keep the matter under continuous review so as to ensure that all countries contribute to solving the climate change problem and that their efforts are commensurate with their resources and capacities. We also expect that the Security Council will review particularly sensitive issues, such as implications to sovereignty and to international legal rights from the loss of land, resources and people.[284]

A 2011 debate on climate change gave rise to similar oppositions.[285] Brazil stated: 'Security tools are appropriate to deal with concrete threats to international peace and security, but they are inadequate to address complex and multidimensional issues such as climate change.'[286]

In reaction to these concerns, states wishing to discuss the climate crisis at Security Council level have changed strategy and Arria formula meetings have assumed a greater role. In addition, open debates on climate security risks have continued to take place in the Security Council. The issue of Security Council mandate and overlap or interference with the work of other bodies was still

---

[282] UN Doc. S/PV.5663, 17 April 2007, 24.
[283] *Ibid.*, 12.
[284] *Ibid.*, 29.
[285] UN Doc. S/PV. 6587, 20 July 2011.
[286] *Ibid.*, 8.

discussed, and contested most vigorously by Russia, but more states acceded that the Security Council had also a role to play.[287] During the High-Level Open Debate on Climate and Security, chaired by Ireland on 23 September 2021,[288] and the Arria Formula Meeting on Sea-Level Rise, organised by Viet Nam, Ireland, Saint Vincent and the Grenadines, and Tunisia. and co-sponsored by several non-Council members on 18 October 2021, only Russia, China. and India continued to hold the view that the Security Council should not engage with this issue on a thematic level.[289]

The 2019 debate notably introduced the notion of 'threat multiplier' to describe the impacts of the climate crisis on global security, in the form of extreme weather events, warming temperatures, and rising sea levels.[290] Resolution 2349 of 2017, on the Lake Chad basin, also illustrates that the Security Council is not entirely agnostic to the theme and that there is a willingness to consider the security implications of the climate crisis in concrete situations.[291] In that Resolution, the Security Council explicitly recognised 'the adverse effects of climate change and ecological changes among other factors on the stability of the Region, including through water scarcity, drought, desertification, land degradation, and food insecurity'.[292]

Language on the climate crisis is now increasingly included in Security Council outcomes and the number of signature events on this topic has risen remarkably since mid-2020.[293] This development may be further encouraged by the United States' change of stance on this matter. If so, particular attention should be paid to the views and input of African states on this issue, given that they suffer its consequences keenly despite not having contributed to it most, as Maluwa also suggests in his chapter in this volume.[294]

---

[287]   UN Doc. S/PV.8307, 11 July 2018.
[288]   UN Doc. S/PV.8864, 23 September 2021.
[289]   Russia vetoed Draft SC Res. S/2021/990 of 13 December 2023 on climate change and security for this reason. India also voted against, while China abstained.
[290]   UN Doc. S/PV.8451, 25 January 2019. See also Valentine Bourghelle, 'Climate Change in the Security Council: On the Road to Qualifying Climate Change as "Threat Multiplier"', *Völkerrechtsblog*, 9 December 2019, available at https://voelkerrechtsblog.org/climate-chang e-in-the-security-council/.
[291]   SC Res. 2349 of 31 March 2017, UN Doc. S/RES/2349(2017). See also Somalia: SC Res. 2408 of 27 March 2018, UN Doc. S/RES/2408(2018); West Africa and the Sahel: UN Doc. S/PRST/2018/3 of 30 January 2018; Mali: SC Res. 2423 of 28 June 2018, UN Doc. S/RES/2423(2018); and Darfur: SC Res. 2429 of 13 July 2018, UN Doc. S/RES/2429(2018).
[292]   SC Res. 2349 of 31 March 2017, UN Doc. S/RES/2349(2017), para. 26.
[293]   Security Council Report, 'Resolution on COVID-19' (n. 281).
[294]   Maluwa, 'Between Centralism and Regionalism', Chapter 3 in this volume, section IV.D (pp. 268–274).

Despite this greater openness to considering the climate crisis in the setting of the Security Council, it is still important to recognise that noting linkages between environmental or health factors and insecurity in concrete situations that have been characterised as a threat to peace on other grounds is one thing; making generic determinations that the climate crisis or pandemics in themselves constitute a threat to peace to be addressed by the Security Council is quite another. Generic determinations potentially open the door to equally generic and thus far-reaching measures, such as measures aimed at ensuring equitable global access to vaccines and medical technology.[295] While the COVID-19 pandemic has underlined the need for such measures, the discussion on legislative resolutions has also indicated that the Security Council is not necessarily able to produce comprehensive and generic resolutions that are balanced, adequate, and in the interests of all states, as well as all the societies they represent.[296]

Arguments against the securitisation of health and climate crises have also been advanced, and they are not without merit. In response to the Ebola resolutions, WHO legal counsel Gian Luca Burci indicated that Security Council engagement on global health is premised on a direct link between infectious diseases and political instability, which has in fact been disproved by scholars on the basis of historical examples. Panicked or coercive government reactions to diseases may present a danger in themselves, but framing a disease as a national security issue may also stimulate such reactions rather than create a conducive political environment in which to address the disease.[297] While Burci appreciates the increase in political profile, political commitment, and financial resources that Security Council attention may entail, he also cautions that the risks of securitising public health should not be ignored.[298]

One new 21st-century threat that the Security Council has addressed only marginally is cyber-security. At the 2017 annual workshop for newly elected members, the UN Secretary-General urged the Security Council to

---

[295] Erin Pobjie, 'COVID-19 as a Threat to International Peace and Security: The Role of the UN Security Council in Addressing the Pandemic', *EJIL:Talk!*, 27 July 2020, available at www.ejiltalk.org/covid-19-as-a-threat-to-international-peace-and-security-the-role-of-the-un-security-council-in-addressing-the-pandemic/.

[296] See also Jordan Street, 'Bringing Climate and Terrorism Together at the UN Security Council: Proceed with Caution', *Just Security*, 6 December 2021, available at www.justsecurity.org/79443/bringing-climate-and-terrorism-together-at-the-un-security-council-proceed-with-caution/. On the risks of the climate security narrative, see particularly Eliana Cusato, 'Of Violence and (In)Visibility: The Securitisation of Climate Change in International Law', *London Review of International Law* 10 (2022), 203–42.

[297] Gian Luca Burci, 'Ebola, the Security Council and the Securitization of Public Health', *Questions of International Law* 10 (2014), 27–39.

[298] *Ibid.*

conceptualise its role in dealing with the issue.[299] The matter has been discussed in five Arria formula meetings, with Estonia and Ukraine being particularly active players.[300] Compared to global health and climate crises, cyber-security has more in common with traditional threats. Despite these clear linkages to its primary responsibility, however, the Security Council has largely remained inactive. This is easily explained by the fact that the P5 are among the most prominent cyber-actors and hence their veto power generally prevents the Security Council's consideration of the matter unless unconventional approaches are taken. This happened, for example, when Georgia notified the Security Council of a large-scale cyber-attack on 28 October 2019 against the websites, servers, and other operating systems of the Administration of the President of Georgia, courts, various municipal assemblies, state bodies, and the private sector.[301] In May 2020, when Estonia chaired the Security Council as an elected member, it – together with the United States and the United Kingdom – raised this matter under the standing agenda item 'Any Other Business',[302] and it attributed the attacks to Russia's military intelligence service, the GRU. The three states held that 'these cyber-attacks are part of Russia's long-running campaign of hostile and destabilizing activity against Georgia and are part of a wider pattern of malign activity'.[303] This action formed part of a coordination approach to publicly attribute the attack to and accuse Russia.[304]

Such surprise moves aside, it is far from likely that the Security Council will develop a leading role in this domain, for the obvious reasons just mentioned.

---

[299] Annex to the letter dated 30 April 2018 from the Permanent Representative of Finland to the United Nations addressed to the President of the Security Council, UN Doc. S/2018/404, 3 May 2018 ('"Hitting the Ground Running": Fifteenth Annual Workshop for Newly Elected Members of the Security Council, 2 and 3 November 2017, Greentree Foundation, New York').

[300] The five Arria formula meetings were organised, respectively, by: Senegal and Spain on cybersecurity and international peace and security, and specifically on the protection of critical infrastructure against terrorist attacks by Ukraine, both in 2016; Ukraine on hybrid wars as a threat to international peace and security also organised in 2017; and Estonia on cyber-stability, conflict prevention and capacity building, and Indonesia, in cooperation with Belgium, Estonia, Viet Nam, and the International Committee of the Red Cross (ICRC), on cyber-attacks against critical infrastructure, both in 2018.

[301] Letter dated 21 February 2020 from the Permanent Representative of Georgia to the United Nations addressed to the Secretary-General and the President of the Security Council, UN Doc. A/74/714–S/2020/135, 24 February 2020.

[302] Security Council Report, 'In Hindsight: Making Effective Use of "Any Other Business"', 1 April 2016, available at www.securitycouncilreport.org/monthly-forecast/2016-04/in_hind sight_making_effective_use_of_any_other_business_1.php.

[303] Joint Press Statement by Estonia, the United Kingdom, and the United States on Russian Cyberattacks in Georgia, 5 May 2020.

[304] Eichensehr, 'Cyberattack Attribution' (n. 129).

There have been calls for establishment of a centralised international agency to focus on cyber operations outside the Security Council. Some of the earlier proposals, such as the 2016 Microsoft proposal, still advocated a role for the P5 in such an institution, but later proposals focused more on technical fact-finding somewhat similar to the OPCW technical secretariat and perhaps legal attribution.[305] If established, the Security Council could draw on such findings for follow-up action, which would be in line with other suggestions regarding better fact-finding structures for the Security Council.

VIII. CONCLUDING REFLECTIONS

What is a proper role and function for the UN Security Council in an accelerated 21st-century world that is leaning eastwards?[306] Can the Council preserve peace while a deeply interconnected world is turning at warp speed and tilts towards permanent instability?[307] Will a less US-dominated era witness fewer unnecessary wars and less overseas interventionism[308] – ventures so closely linked to the continued post-colonial hegemony of the West after World War II?[309] Will an Eastphalian world, instead, inevitably be more authoritarian and marked by internal repression?[310] In short: what will the

---

[305] See, on the Microsoft proposal, Kristen E. Eichensehr, 'Digital Switzerlands', *University of Pennsylvania Law Review* 167 (2019), 665–732. For a more recent proposal, see Michael N. Schmitt and Yuval Shany, 'An International Attribution Mechanism for Hostile Cyber Operations?', *International Law Studies* 96 (2020), 196–222.

[306] See also the analysis of Gideon Rachman, *Easternisation: War and Peace in the Asian Century* (London: Penguin, 2016).

[307] See, for the suggestion that an open and fast world is by definition unstable, Fareed Zakaria, 'Buckle Up', in *Ten Lessons for a Post-Pandemic World* (New York: WW Norton & Co., 2020), 13–28.

[308] The term 'unnecessary war' in relation to Iraq comes from John J. Mearsheimer and Stephen Walt, 'An Unnecessary War', *Foreign Policy* 134 (2003), 51–9. On the United States' militarised efforts to remake the world more generally, see John J. Mearsheimer, *The Great Delusion: Liberal Dreams and International Realities* (New Haven: Yale University Press, 2018).

[309] For an account of the birth of the US quest for global supremacy, see Stephen Wertheim, *Tomorrow, the World: The Birth of US Global Supremacy* (Cambridge: Harvard University Press, 2020).

[310] On the features of an Eastphalian world, see Tom Ginsburg, 'Eastphalia as the Perfection of Westphalia', *Indiana Journal of Global Legal Studies* 17 (2010), 27–45, suggesting that a China-centred world would be more peaceful, in the sense of reduced chances for international conflict, but also more violent as a result of lesser emphasis on individual protection. For the role of international law in an authoritarian world, see also Ginsburg, 'Authoritarian International Law?'(n. 11), 221–60.

world look like in the remainder of this century and what are the main insecurities that the UN Security Council should be concerned with in the future?

This chapter did not seek to provide a definitive answer to these daedal questions. It merely suggests that a spiralling world needs structure more than anything else and it presented a perspective in favour of further institutionalisation for the near future – precisely because it is so unclear what the world will look like 50, or even 25, years from now. The main premise of this chapter is that an inclusive and deliberative environment based on and guided by international law is required to safeguard somewhat controlled next steps that are to the benefit of all. This is quite the opposite of what is proposed in the recent Joint Statement by the Foreign Ministers of China and Russia on Certain Aspects of Global Governance in Modern Conditions, which is aimed at releasing the P5 from its institutional setting and which proposes to deliberate on platforms rather than through fully fledged international organisations.[311] Likewise, the repeated invocations of a rules-based order by Western states may, inadvertently, open the door to a pick-and-choose approach that deviates from the idea of the Security Council operating within a broader and universal system of international law.[312]

As the technology and wealth gap between East and West shrinks and US influence wanes, it is clear that some states, particularly in the West, have to reposition to accommodate the rise of China, as well as the 'rise of the rest'. New power constellations have led French President Macron to observe that 'the United Nations Security Council no longer produces useful solutions today'.[313] But calls for multilateralism also recognise that the way forward is still to reinvigorate and to strive for greater

---

[311] Joint Statement by the Foreign Ministers of China and Russia on Certain Aspects of Global Governance in Modern Conditions, 23 March 2021, paras 3 and 4. See, for a critical appraisal, Achilles Skordas, 'Authoritarian Global Governance? The Russian-Chinese Joint Statement of March 2021', *Heidelberg Journal for International Law* 81 (2021), 293–302.

[312] *Cf.* John Dugard, 'The Choice before Us: International Law or "Rules-Based Order"?', Lecture delivered at the University of Minas Gerais in Brazil, XVIII Edition of Brazilian International Law Winter Program, 19 July 2022, published in the *Leiden Journal of International Law* 36 (2023), 223–32. See also Stefan Talmon, 'Rules-Based Order v. International Law?', *GPIL Blog*, 20 January 2019, available at https://gpil.jura.uni-bonn.de/2019/01/rules-based-order-v-international-law/.

[313] Le Grand Continent, 'La doctrine Macron: une conversation avec le Président français', 16 November 2020, available at https://legrandcontinent.eu/fr/2020/11/16/macron/.

institutionalisation with a view to securing 'a historic balance between human civilisations'.[314]

In this chapter, I have discussed the Security Council's institutional strength by looking at the Security Council's exercise of its distinct powers from an institutional perspective, acknowledging that the Council operates in an ever-more-uncertain and restless world. Recognising that the world is becoming increasingly antagonistic and that it is repolarising, I first discussed the authorised Libya intervention, which, in hindsight, became a turning point for the Security Council. It is submitted that, while the use of force was not clearly illegal, neither was the operation the product of enlightened multilateralism. In response to Libya, as well as to controversial exercises of the right to self-defence, proposals have been presented to enhance use-of-force discourse and to embed such discourse better institutionally. These proposals could most certainly enhance the Council's inclusiveness and they may also help to avoid a world in overdrive spinning out of control. States calling for multilateralism and an evidence-based legal order would do well to seriously engage with such proposals, including with ideas for a centralised cyber fact-finding agency.

In the sanctions domain, greater procedural reforms have been implemented over time – most notably, the panels of experts and the Ombudsperson. Sanctions reform tends to be performed in a very ad hoc and also arbitrary fashion, but states might feel a need to up their game within the United Nations to regain ground from the unilateral sanctions that are increasingly used as the alternative. Sanctions reform is therefore a work in progress, at best, and while some important steps have been made in recent years, the risk of backsliding remains. Further institutionalisation in this domain is certainly warranted. Here, again, states advocating democracy, the rule of law, and multilateralism in the abstract – including, at the time of writing, the United States – should ensure that: proper remedies exist at the UN level in the form of a truly independent office of the Ombudsperson – not someone who is sidelined through precarious contracts and a consultancy status only; and that adequate remedies exist for UN sanctions regimes across the board. In addition, they should further provide humanitarian exceptions that reach beyond financial sanctions;[315] they

---

[314] The suggestion that the world is returning to something like a historic balance among different human civilisations comes from Kishore Mahbubani, 'Introduction', in *Has China Won? The Chinese Challenge to American Primacy* (New York: Hachette, 2020), 1–24.

[315] Emanuela-Chiara Gillard, 'Humanitarian Exceptions: A Turning Point in UN Sanctions', *Chatham House*, 20 December 2022, available at www.chathamhouse.org/2022/12/humanitarian-exceptions-turning-point-un-sanctions.

should also reinforce the mandates of panels of experts with a view to guaranteeing, and underscoring the importance of, independent fact-finding as a basis for decision-making.

The most worrisome developments since the end of the Cold War, from an institutionalist perspective, are the Security Council's pervasive counter-terrorism activities. These practices go well beyond preconceived institutional structures, and they create significant tensions with the principle of legal certainty and the domestic rule of law. More generally, the Council's securitisation measures have allowed – perhaps even incentivised – states to pursue immensely repressive strategies, which is hardly compatible with the United Nations' purposes and principles.

The Security Council's still-prevalent consensus on terrorism as a threat stands in sharp contrast with the Council's near-inability to tackle new challenges – in particular, those related to cyber activity and new technologies. Yet as societies digitalise and with malicious state-sponsored cyber operations on the rise, traditional distinctions between the notion of peace and war erode. An organ entrusted with the primary responsibility to maintain peace and security that is incapable of broaching the greatest threats risks becoming incredible. This is not to say that the Security Council should be the central organ for cyber operation fact-finding or attribution; this is indeed better left to a specialised mechanism. But, on the basis of such independently established facts, the Security Council should be able to discuss massive, concrete, hostile cyber-attacks if they occur and it is clear that these need to be discussed in an inclusive setting if deliberations are to be balanced deliberations. It is also clear that the veto issue and its propriety is at stake here as well.

The suggestions for institutional strengthening and reorientation that are made in this chapter reveal a certain expectation that the Security Council will remain the world's primary organ for peace in the near future and that it is worthwhile investing in it. Yet recent events have once again underscored the Security Council's imperfection. That does not necessarily have to lead to the conclusion that the Security Council has already become *permanently* and *fully* dysfunctional, bearing in mind that such a view risks playing into the hands of those states that prefer to take an extra-institutional turn. An institutional perspective implies that further strengthening is desirable for Security Council activity in those areas in which it is still possible, requiring a continued commitment to working on checks and balances and holding space for the non-permanents. Yet whenever the Security Council fails to exercise its primary function – and those instances are becoming more prevalent – the gaze will shift elsewhere. A future-oriented institutional perspective will thus also be about opening up and about finding a new balance between the UN Security Council and the UN General Assembly, as well as between the UN Security Council and other international organisations, including those at the regional level.

3

The UN Security Council: Between Centralism and Regionalism

Tiyanjana Maluwa

I. INTRODUCTION

The view that the UN Security Council is the linchpin of the United Nations' collective security system may seem straightforward and incontrovertible. Under Article 24 UN Charter, UN member states have conferred on the Security Council the primary responsibility for the maintenance of international peace and security. One of the issues that arise from this, which lies at the centre of the Max Planck Trialogues on the Law of Peace and War book series, relates to the Security Council's contribution to the law of peace and war. Discussions in previous contributions to the Trialogues and the preceding chapters in this volume have dealt with various aspects of this question. This chapter examines the practice of the Security Council in its interactions with regional organisations in the context of collaborative peace operations. The discussion does not cover all of the regional organisations that the Security Council has collaborated with, which might have the advantage of a broad sweep but the disadvantage of a shallow and fragmented focus.[1] Instead, I focus on one regional organisation, the African Union, to offer a specific yet illustrative perspective.

In discharging its responsibility for the maintenance of international peace and security, the Security Council plays a critical role in two respects. First, using its powers under Chapter VII UN Charter, it determines the existence of security threats and the required responses, authorises the establishment of UN missions to deal with the threats, and oversees their operation. Secondly, it determines the role, if any, of regional organisations and authorises the action

---

[1] These include the Economic Community of West African States (ECOWAS), the European Union, the League of Arab States (LAS), the North Atlantic Treaty Organization (NATO), the Organization of American States (OAS), and the Organization for Security and Co-operation in Europe (OSCE).

they can take to address threats to peace in their regions in partnership with the United Nations or on their own, within the terms of Chapter XIII. Although political and diplomatic power rests with the states that serve on the Security Council – especially the five permanent members (P5) who hold the veto – in the changing international political landscape of the post-Cold-War world, other powers have begun to challenge their influence. These include the elected non-permanent members (E10) and other formal and informal coalitions within this group, such as the three African members (A3), who are increasingly asserting their voices and interests, along with other UN members outside the Security Council. This suggests, to borrow Larissa van den Herik's words in this volume, 'an inclusive perspective that embraces the voice of middle powers and those more in the periphery, while recognising that those voices do not necessarily always belong to the same chorus'.[2] The contestations between them in their various permutations – say, P5 vs E10, P5 vs A3, or France, United Kingdom, and United States (P3) vs China and Russia (P2) – revolve around the power to set the agenda and determine global policy and action under the formal UN mandate.

Since its founding, the United Nations has carried out numerous missions in collaboration with several regional organisations or has authorised operations by these organisations. Largely because of the prevalence of intra-state conflicts in the continent, Africa has hosted the largest number of UN peace missions. Africa provides not only the site for the type of conflicts that have necessitated the establishment of UN peace operations but also hosts a regional organisation that has engaged the most with the United Nations in the maintenance of international peace and security. The African Union is thus an appropriate regional body whose partnership with the world body forms a framework within which to address the Security Council's continuing primacy, vis-à-vis regional organisations, in the collective security system of the post-Cold-War era.

In his chapter in this volume, Congyan Cai explores the changing power dynamics in the Security Council in the wake of the rise of China both as a global economic and political power and as a more assertive (or 'reawakened') P5 member. In a broad sense, he presents the unique perspectives of this new global power over the vanishing unipolar hegemony of the immediate post-Cold-War period. The present chapter shares the multilateralist perspective that Van den Herik advances in her own, but through a specific regional lens. To be sure, the objective of this chapter is not to

---

[2] Larissa van den Herik, 'The UN Security Council: A Reflection on Institutional Strength', Chapter 2 in this volume, section I.

present specifically African or AU perspectives on *every* aspect of Security
Council decisions and actions relating to peace and security issues in Africa,
nor is this a general discussion of UN peacekeeping as such. I agree with Van
den Herik's general submission that the less powerful states do not need to play
a secondary role all the time. That sentiment lies behind the increasing efforts
of African states to make themselves heard more loudly in the United Nations
and other global forums. Yet, as I aim to demonstrate in this chapter, regional
organisations – or at least the African Union – recognise and reaffirm the
primacy of the Security Council, insofar as peacekeeping and other partnerships for the maintenance of international peace and security are concerned.
The African Union's perspectives are themselves collective positions forged
from the multilateralist perspectives of its member states. Examples discussed
in this chapter include the common positions of the African states on issues
such as the right of humanitarian intervention, counter-terrorism, Security
Council reform, and climate-related security risks.

I argue that, as a general matter, the concern of regional organisations and
their members is not so much to challenge the supremacy of the United
Nations or the primacy of the Security Council by establishing their own
competing norms and institutions but to complement the role of the Council.
Further, and more importantly, they seek to become more effective participants in the Security Council's decision-making on the issues of peace and war
that affect them and their regions, and to push for necessary normative and
institutional reforms. My overarching argument is that, notwithstanding the
disruptions and changes in the international political landscape of the post-
Cold-War period, as witnessed by the rise of other voices from the periphery,
the status of the Security Council as custodian of the collective security system
has not been diminished.

At the same time, however, the responsibility of the Security Council for the
maintenance of international peace and security has been tested on several
occasions since the end of the Cold War, the most recent being the Russian
invasion of Ukraine in 2022. The Security Council's failure to agree on
measures to bring the war to a speedy end has renewed questions about its
efficacy and continuing relevance as custodian of the collective security
system. I discuss aspects of the war as they relate to some of the issues covered
in this chapter.

This chapter has a double objective. First, it seeks to examine the role of the
Security Council in managing collective security in the post-Cold-War era
through the prism of its peacekeeping collaborations with the African Union.
As already stated, this is not a discussion on peacekeeping in general or of every
aspect of UN peace operations in Africa. Secondly, it aims to highlight the

extent to which the Security Council's practice, as manifested through both the adoption of resolutions and its substantive actions, has contributed, or not, to the confirmation and further development of the international law as it relates to collective security. Both objectives aim to reinforce the view that recent practice has reaffirmed the centrality and primacy of the Security Council.

One way of understanding the decision-making process of the Security Council is to study the debates and voting patterns of the members. As a rule, among the P5, the three Western powers, the P3, tend to stand on one side from the non-Western powers, the P2. While the P3 generally represent the Global North, which claims to set great store by its commitment to the rule of law and human rights, the P2 seek to prioritise solidarity with the Global South, emphasising the principles of the primacy of state sovereignty and non-interference in domestic affairs of states. Cai makes the same points in his discussion of the 'new Cold War' and the influence of China's international legal policies on its behaviour in the Security Council.[3] Interestingly, both sides claim to base their positions on the provisions of the UN Charter and norms of international law to provide legitimacy to their voting decisions. Thus international legal norms are invoked to explain and justify political choices and decisions that may simply reflect national and coalition interests.

Understanding the national and coalition interests at play lends context to the decision-making processes in respect of individual UN peace operations established or authorised by the Security Council. Methodologically, I adopt a positivist approach to unpack Security Council decision-making by examining not only the texts of resolutions but also records of Security Council meetings and, where relevant, individual statements that the members may give to provide insight into their voting decisions on a resolution – especially on negative votes or abstentions.

I proceed as follows. In section II, following this introduction, I briefly review the historical debates of regionalism versus centralism as they played out at the San Francisco Conference leading to the adoption of the UN Charter. The Charter confirmed centralism as the paradigm underpinning the new post-war era until the end of the Cold War around 1990, when the United Nations adopted the concept of partnership peacekeeping as a matter of policy and in practice. Partnership peacekeeping represents a return to regionalism. In addition, I discuss an issue relevant to the centralism and primacy of the Security Council – namely, the concept of the 'international rule of law'.

---

[3]　Congyan Cai, 'The UN Security Council: Maintaining Peace during a Global Power Shift', Chapter 1 in this volume, sections III.C and V.C.

In section III, I turn to the post-Cold-War phase of partnership peace operations involving the United Nations and the African Union. This is not a discussion about UN peacekeeping or peace operations in general; rather, I have limited myself to three case studies: Libya, Mali, and Somalia. These cases provide lenses through which to focus on some normative and policy issues arising from UN–AU peace operations.

First, why Libya? The conflict of 2011 implicated the right of intervention incorporated in the African Union's constituent instrument and its implications for the primacy of the Security Council over the regional organisation. Furthermore, the principle of the Responsibility to Protect (R2P) loomed large in the debates surrounding the Security Council's authorisation of the intervention in Libya, creating the most significant challenge that the African Union had faced since its establishment. I discuss the African Union's response, as the regional body most directly connected to the Libyan crisis, and the post-intervention ramifications not only for AU member states, but also for the policy positions of other members of the Security Council.

Secondly, I have selected Mali and Somalia as case studies to explore another set of related issues also at the heart of the collaborations between the United Nations and the African Union: peacekeeping and the fight against terrorism and violent extremism in these countries. In temporal terms, Somalia represents the oldest UN–AU peacekeeping collaboration, while Mali is the most recent. In this respect, I examine some normative and policy developments in the fight against international terrorism in more detail than the other issues. Counter-terrorism is a shared objective between the African Union and the United Nations, which has been a significant factor in Security Council decisions to authorise certain peace operations in Africa. I also discuss China's role in African peacekeeping to highlight China's changing perspective on collective security, as examined by Cai, and its engagement with Africa.[4] While China has not played a role in the AU peace operation in Somalia, it was involved in the UN-led mission in Mali.

Section IV turns to three issues that exemplify current challenges and future trajectories, and which are also relevant for the unfinished business of UN reform: the quest for a permanent African seat on the Security Council; the problem of Security Council inaction; and climate as a new, unconventional threat to global security. I also discuss the Russian invasion of Ukraine in this section.

Section V concludes the discussion.

---

[4] *Ibid.*, sections V.C.3 and VI.B.

II. THE UNITED NATIONS AND REGIONAL ORGANISATIONS:
PARTNERING FOR THE MAINTENANCE OF PEACE

The role played by the Security Council in the various instances in which it has collaborated with regional organisations draws out two overarching issues that underlie this discussion. The first is the dichotomy between law and politics – that is, how law and politics play out in the Security Council's decision-making on collective security operations; the second is the tension between the centre (the Security Council) and the periphery (the regional organisations). These two issues sometimes come to the fore when regional organisations claim to be better interpreters and arbiters of regional disputes or threats to the peace than the Security Council, notwithstanding its primary responsibility for dealing with such issues. The Security Council has often authorised operations by regional organisations (and/or, in some cases, member states acting individually or within the framework of a regional organisation) acting under Chapter VII, and not under Article 53, of the UN Charter.[5]

A. *Historical Debates of Centralism versus Regionalism*

The arrangement set out in Articles 52–54 of the Charter represents an international consensus reached, although not fully worked out, at the Dumbarton Oaks Conference in late 1944 and at the San Francisco Conference that adopted the Charter in June the following year. Anthony Arend's summary of the early debates about a 'new world order' that preceded the establishment of the United Nations is instructive – particularly on the evolution of the thinking on the part of the major powers at the time on the role of regional organisations in conflict management.[6] There were two opposing views. One, championed by British Prime Minister Winston Churchill, advocated the idea of both a centralised organisation and a series of 'regional councils', but with the regional councils assuming primary responsibility for the maintenance of international peace and security in their regions and the centralised organisation playing a supporting role. The other view, favoured by US Secretary of State Cordell Hull, was for a strong global

---

[5]   See Christian Walter, 'Regional Arrangements, Article 53', in Bruno Simma, Daniel Erasmus-Khan, Georg Nolte, and Andreas Paulus (eds), *The Charter of the United Nations: A Commentary* (Oxford: Oxford University Press, 4th edn, 2024 forthcoming), MN 33.

[6]   Anthony C. Arend, 'The United Nations, Regional Organizations, and Military Operations: The Past and the Present', *Duke Journal of Comparative & International Law* 7 (1996), 3–33 (5–8).

organisation that would play the primary role in conflict management, while 'regional agencies' could play a part in addressing local conflicts, but in a clearly subordinate role and consistent with the authority of the global body.

At the Dumbarton Oaks Conference, which prepared the first draft of the UN Charter, the four powers that subsequently became permanent members of the Security Council – namely, China, the United Kingdom, the United States, and the Union of Soviet Socialist Republics (USSR) – adopted Hull's vision in its totality.[7] They did so despite concerns from Latin American states, which advocated for the incorporation of a provision requiring states to submit regional disputes to regional organisations *before* submitting them to the United Nations and which were opposed to the proposal that regional organisations should undertake enforcement action *only with the authorisation* of the Security Council.[8]

B. *Partnership Peacekeeping as a Return of Regionalism*

The four powers thus opted for a model that accorded the proposed Security Council primary responsibility over the management of conflicts and the maintenance of international peace and security, and which granted regional organisations a *subordinate* role. They privileged the centre at the expense of the periphery, thereby ordaining centralism as the paradigm for the management of the post-war order. Leaving aside the concessions to regionalism, the UN Charter vested the key organ of the newly established global organisation with unprecedented authority and paramountcy over the management of conflicts.

Since the creation of the United Nations, the Security Council has authorised the establishment of 71 peacekeeping operations as part of its function of maintaining international peace and security. Just over half of these operations (36) have been authorised in the period since 1995.[9] There are two main explanations, both reflecting a changing politics, for this explosion in UN peacekeeping operations. First is the change of power dynamics in the Security Council following the end of the Cold War. For roughly the next two decades, this change unblocked the political impasse between the two

---

[7]   See generally 'Dumbarton Oaks Conversations on World Organization', reprinted in Royal Institute of International Affairs, *United Nations Documents 1941–1945* (London: Royal Institute of International Affairs, 1946), 92–101.

[8]   *Ibid.*, 98–9.

[9]   See UN Department of Peace Operations (DPO), 'List of Peacekeeping Operations, 1948– 2017', available at https://peacekeeping.un.org/sites/default/files/unpeacekeeping-operation list_1.pdf.

superpowers that had made it difficult for the veto-carrying permanent members to agree on major decisions affecting international peace and security. Second is the rise in complex conflicts around the world, including intra-state civil conflicts, crying out for attention and action from the reinvigorated and activist Security Council.

The change of power dynamics in the Security Council resulted, first and foremost, in the disappearance of the old East–West ideological rivalries led by the USSR and the United States, respectively. Another consequence was the increasing assertiveness of a hitherto fairly inactive permanent member, China, as well as the non-permanent members of the Security Council, discussed by Cai and Van den Herik in their chapters in this volume. I return to this later. In the realm of peace operations, these developments enabled the emergence of the notion of partnership peacekeeping, which involves two models:

(i)   the 'subcontracting' model, whereby the United Nations outsources peace operations to regional agencies; and

(ii) the 'collaborative' model, whereby the United Nations and regional organisations deploy peace operations jointly and, among other things, share planning, personnel, and resources.

In a sense, partnership peacekeeping represents a return to regionalism – although not a diminution of the centrality of the Security Council in the maintenance of international peace and security as such. The pivotal development was the adoption of General Assembly Resolution 49/57, the Declaration on the Enhancement of Cooperation between the United Nations and Regional Arrangements or Agencies in the Maintenance of International Peace and Security.[10] The Declaration was adopted based on the conviction that it would help to strengthen the role and enhance the effectiveness of both the United Nations and regional arrangements or agencies in the maintenance of international peace and security.

The adoption of Resolution 49/57 was a logical follow-up to the proposals laid out by UN Secretary-General Boutros Boutros-Ghali in his report *An Agenda for Peace: Preventive Diplomacy, Peacemaking and Peacekeeping* in 1992.[11] Among other things, *Agenda for Peace* recognised that part of the solution to the problems faced by the United Nations in its post-Cold-War management of conflicts lay in reconsidering how regional organisations

[10]   GA Res. 49/57 of 9 December 1994, UN Doc. A/RES.49/57.
[11]   *An Agenda for Peace: Preventive Diplomacy, Peacemaking and Peacekeeping*, Report of the Secretary-General, UN Doc. A/47/277/S/24111, 17 June 1992.

interacted with the global organisation, including in matters relating to the
maintenance of international peace and security.

C. *Relevance of the International Rule of Law in the Security Council's Operations and Decision-Making Processes*

Before turning in section III to the Security Council's practice in selected
partnership operations with the African Union, a related question for preliminary consideration concerns the relevance and application of the 'international rule of law' in the operations of the Security Council. This
question is significant because the ability of the Security Council to impose
its authority and primacy on regional organisations such as the African Union
may – at a political level, at least – be influenced by perceptions of the
legitimacy of its actions and decision-making processes. Legitimacy is
a relevant factor for understanding the meaning of the 'international rule of
law', especially in the context of international institutions.

I do not propose to offer a detailed analysis of this question in this limited
discussion. Suffice it to say that the issue has recently received some attention
in the legal literature, and it has been invoked by member states in their
statements both in the Security Council and General Assembly.[12] At the
national level, the rule of law requires a government of laws, the supremacy
of the law, and equality before the law – that is, the idea that both the governors
and the governed are subject to regulation by the same law. Yet this is only
a shorthand description: there are differences in how, at the domestic level, the
rule of law is understood in common law and civil law systems, as well as in
other legal traditions.

When applied to the international system, the rule of law may be understood as the application of some, although not all, of the principles of the
domestic concept of the rule of law to relations between states and other
subjects of international law.[13] This, too, is a sweeping description that does
not precisely define the term. Adopting a very specific meaning for the
purposes of their discussion, Heike Krieger and Georg Nolte acknowledge
the difficulty of defining 'the international rule of law' thus: 'We are aware that
the term "the international rule of law" has been given many meanings, just

---

[12] See generally Sherif Elgebelly, *The Rule of Law in the United Nations Security Council
      Decision-Making Process: Turning the Focus Inwards* (London: Routledge, 2017). See also
      Clemens Feinäugle (ed.), *The Rule of Law and Its Application to the United Nations* (Oxford/
      Baden-Baden: Hart/Nomos, 2016).
[13] Simon Chesterman, 'An International Rule of Law?', *The American Journal of Comparative
      Law* 56 (2008), 331–61 (355).

like the term "rule of law" itself."[14] Needless to say that the understanding of the international rule of law I have noted above, which I share, is adequate only for the purposes of this chapter.

While the domestic model arose as a response to the dangers of centralised authority by the state, the international rule of law arose as an institutional solution to the opposite problem of decentralised authority. Under the latter, numerous independent, legally equal, and sovereign states interact and produce decisions separately or through institutions that they have collectively established and endowed with certain powers.[15] The most significant and powerful such institution is the Security Council, which is empowered by the UN Charter to decide if a given situation constitutes a threat to peace and security, and if so, what action to take to address such a threat. In this sense, the Security Council enjoys an unassailable status in the international system, sitting atop an international legal hierarchy. Yet this does not mean that it is unconstrained by international law when exercising its powers. Although there has been a long-running debate on how far the Security Council is bound by international law, there seems to be agreement on two basic propositions: first, that the powers of the Security Council are constrained by the Charter; and secondly, that, at the very least, it is also bound by rules of international law that have the status of ius cogens. This is a cautious position, which recognises that the Charter itself does not, as such, spell out the relationship between the Security Council and international law more generally.[16] I agree with this position.

Although the General Assembly adopted a declaration calling for the rule of law to be applied internally to the United Nations in 2012, the Security Council is yet to establish a rule-of-law framework to govern its decision-making process.[17] Some commentators have proposed a set of specific criteria for determining the international rule of law in the context of Security Council decision-making, drawing from some of the elements of the domestic model.[18] A common thread running through these discussions is the notion of

[14] Heike Krieger and Georg Nolte, 'The International Rule of Law: Rise or Decline? Approaching Current Foundational Challenges', in Heike Krieger, Georg Nolte, and Andreas Zimmermann (eds), *The International Rule of Law: Rise or Decline?* (Oxford: Oxford University Press, 2019), 3–30 (6 and fn. 16).

[15] Ian Hurd, 'The UN Security Council and the International Rule of Law', *The Chinese Journal of International Politics* 7 (2014), 1–19 (16).

[16] *Ibid.*, 13. See also Michael Wood and Eran Sthoeger, *The Security Council and International Law* (Cambridge: Cambridge University Press, 2022), 70–89.

[17] GA Res. 67/1 of 30 November 2012, UN Doc. A/RES/67/1 (Declaration of the High-Level Meeting of the General Assembly on the Rule of Law at the National and International Levels).

[18] See Elgebelly, *Rule of Law in the United Nations* (n. 12).

legitimacy: the argument that satisfaction of these elements ensures legitimacy and enhances acceptance of the Security Council's decisions, in the same way as perceptions of compliance with the rule of law in domestic systems increases the chances of obedience to the law.

Legitimacy is an elusive concept. In the context of institutions, such as the Security Council, it has more to do with how certain audiences perceive the acceptability of the institution's particular acts or decisions, sometimes from a purely political point of view, than about their normative goodness or moral rightness. Despite this subjectivity, I would argue that perceptions of legitimacy should matter as a core defining feature of the international rule of law for the Security Council. As Ian Hurd puts it:

> The power of the UN Security Council is a function of both its legal and its political settings. The first is derived from the Charter, and the second from the political interests of powerful states and the legitimacy that the institution commands in the international system. [This] legal authority comes into action only when the permanent members of the Council are sufficiently in agreement to allow it to happen, *and only when the broader audience for Council resolutions sees the action as legitimate.*[19]

The broader audience for the Security Council resolutions for whom the question of compliance with the international rule of law potentially matters is the entire UN membership. A substantive part of my discussion in the next section is on Resolution 1973, which authorised intervention in Libya.[20] The paradox of this Resolution is that it was at once one of the most consequential decisions ever adopted by the Security Council in the context of UN–AU relations and the most contested in terms of its legitimacy and, by implication, its compliance with some of the presumed international rule-of-law requirements among the most affected audience for the Resolution – namely, the African states.

III. THE SECURITY COUNCIL'S PRACTICE IN SELECTED PARTNERSHIP PEACE OPERATIONS WITH THE AFRICAN UNION

The evolution of the Security Council's policy on partnership peacekeeping with regional organisations since the end of the Cold War has focused on Africa. Under Resolution 1631, adopted on 17 October 2005, the Security Council specifically expressed its determination 'to take appropriate steps to

---

[19]   Hurd, 'The UN Security Council' (n. 15), 18–19 (emphasis added).
[20]   SC Res. 1973 of 17 March 2011, UN Doc. S/RES/1973(2011).

the further development of cooperation between the United Nations and regional and subregional organisations in maintaining international peace and security, consistent with Chapter VIII of the [UN Charter]'.[21] Although the Resolution addressed cooperation between the United Nations and regional organisations broadly, it also put a particular focus on strengthening the capacity of '[African] regional and subregional organisations in conflict prevention and crisis management, and post-conflict [stabilisation]'.[22]

On 12 January 2012, the Security Council held an open debate on the partnership between the United Nations and the African Union. Resolution 2033, adopted after the debate, welcomed more regular and meaningful meetings and interactions between the UN Secretariat and the AU Commission, and it supported a stronger working relationship between the Security Council and the AU Peace and Security Council (PSC), which was established in 2002 and is responsible for the regional organisation's peace operations.[23]

These two resolutions, which are only select examples, speak to the multi-faceted aspects of the role of the UN peacekeeping operations and the role that regional and subregional organisations can play. This role goes beyond the specific function of peacekeeping to embrace the entire gamut of conflict prevention and management, peacemaking, peacekeeping, peace enforcement, and peacebuilding. In Libya, Mali, and Somalia, this has involved engaging with the post-conflict political processes.

A. *Article 4(h) of the Constitutive Act of the African Union and the Primacy of the Security Council*

On 11 July 2000, members of the Organisation of African Unity (OAU) – the African Union's predecessor – adopted the Constitutive Act of the African Union in Lomé, Togo.[24] Article 4(h) AU Constitutive Act provides for 'the right of the Union to intervene in a Member State pursuant to a decision of the Assembly in respect of grave circumstances, namely: war crimes, genocide and crimes against humanity'. Further, Article 4(j) provides for 'the right of Member States to request intervention from the Union in order to restore

---

[21] SC Res. 1631 of 17 October 2005, UN Doc. S/RES/1631(2005), para. 1.

[22] *Ibid.*, para. 2.

[23] Protocol Relating to the Establishment of the Peace and Security Council, adopted on 9 July 2002, entered into force on 26 December 2003, available at https://au.int/en/treaties/protocol-relating-establishment-peace-and-security-council-african-union (hereinafter Peace and Security Protocol).

[24] Constitutive Act of the African Union of 11 July 2000, 2158 UNTS 3.

peace and security'. The incorporation of the right to intervention in Article 4(h) was partly a response to African states' disappointment over the failure of the Security Council to deal with the most traumatic event to have occurred on African soil since the end of the Cold War: the Rwanda genocide of 1994.

By incorporating the right to intervene in Article 4(h), African states sought to move beyond the OAU era, when adherence to the principle of non-interference in the internal affairs of member states precluded intervention, and the shadow of the Rwanda genocide. While the debate over the status of the right of humanitarian intervention continues, Article 4(h) nevertheless represents a substantial legal innovation. Although it is phrased as a 'right to intervene', in essence it should be construed as a 'right of *humanitarian* intervention'. The provision has crystallised into a treaty norm a diffuse set of ideas and concepts that are similar to, and form the basis of, the related R2P principle, but it is not an expression of that principle as such. I return to the R2P in the next section.

I have previously argued that, in an era in which post-independence Africa had witnessed the horrors of genocide and ethnic cleansing on its own soil and against its own kind, with memories of the Rwanda genocide still fresh, it would have been absolutely remiss for the AU Constitutive Act to remain silent on the question of the right to intervene in respect of grave circum-stances such as genocide, war crimes, and crimes against humanity.[25] Before discussing the implications of Article 4(h) for the relationship between the Security Council and the African Union in the maintenance of international peace and security, it is worth recalling the two interventions carried out by the Economic Community of West African States (ECOWAS) without prior Security Council authorisation. ECOWAS intervened in Liberia and Sierra Leone in 1990 and 1998, respectively.[26] These interventions undoubtedly contravened Article 53(1) UN Charter, which provides in part: 'The Security Council shall, where appropriate, utilise such regional arrangements or agen-cies for enforcement action under its authority. But no enforcement action shall be taken under regional arrangements or by regional agencies without the authorisation of the Security [Council].' Nevertheless, the Security

---

[25] Tiyanjana Maluwa, 'Reimagining African Unity: Some Preliminary Reflections on the Constitutive Act of the African Union', *African Yearbook of International Law* 9 (2001), 3–38 (28–9).

[26] Cyril Obi, 'Economic Community of West African States on the Ground: Comparing Peacekeeping in Liberia, Sierra Leone, Guinea Bissau, and Côte d'Ivoire', *African Security* 2 (2009), 119–35 (122–6).

Council neither condemned them nor, significantly, did it expressly grant them ex post facto authorisation.[27]

The question of whether the Security Council, having failed to act, subsequently helped to legitimise ECOWAS's interventions in Liberia and Sierra Leone has been the subject of debate. Some scholars have suggested that, by means of this action, African states were the first to force the pendulum to swing towards a 'regional' doctrine of intervention that overrides state sovereignty to protect human rights and democracy. Jeremy Levitt has argued that the Security Council placed a *'retroactive de jure seal* on the ECOWAS intervention'.[28] Ben Kioko shares this interpretation and has asserted that 'the UN Security Council has never complained about its powers being usurped, [apparently] because the interventions were in support of popular causes and were carried out partly because the Security Council had not taken action or was unlikely to do so at the time'.[29] Ademola Abass and Mashood Baderin have gone further to assert that the absence of protest by the Security Council and members of the regional organisation, in the case of such a 'quasi-Article 39' of the UN Charter determination, 'must be accepted as a development of new norms of State practice'.[30] Abass and Baderin are referring to practice purporting to support a new norm of intervention by regional organisations without Security Council authorisation. Like Levitt and Kioko, they conclude that the absence of condemnation by the Security Council implies that it effectively endorsed the practice. I do not share this view. If the Security Council had wanted to endorse these interventions ex post facto, it would have done so by way of an explicit decision, instead of letting such a consequential conclusion be inferred from its silence.

I would also argue that the proposition that there is now a regional norm permitting the African Union to use force for humanitarian intervention *without* Security Council authorisation, based on either Article 4(h) AU Constitutive Act or new state practice, rests on a faulty premise. It suggests that a regional treaty norm can usurp the UN Charter, which would

---

[27] SC Res. 788 of 19 November 1992, UN Doc. S/RES/788(1992); SC Res. 1162 of 17 April 1998, UN Doc. S/RES/1162(1998).

[28] Jeremy Levitt, 'Humanitarian Intervention by Regional Actors in Internal Conflicts: The Cases of ECOWAS in Liberia and Sierra Leone', *Temple International and Comparative Law Journal* 12 (1998), 333–76 (347) (emphasis original).

[29] Ben Kioko, 'The Right of Intervention under the African Union's Constitutive Act: From Non-Interference to Non-Intervention', *International Review of the Red Cross* 85 (2003), 807–25 (821).

[30] Ademola Abass and Mashood Baderin, 'Towards Effective Collective Security and Human Rights Protection in Africa: An Assessment of the Constitutive Act of the African Union', *Netherlands International Law Review* 49 (2002), 1–38 (22–3).

contravene its Article 103. Alternatively, it suggests that the Charter prohibition of the use of force in Article 2(4) – generally characterised as a rule of ius
cogens or a peremptory norm of international law – can be superseded by
a new customary rule permitting humanitarian intervention based on changes
in state practice. As a legal matter, a peremptory norm can be changed only by
another peremptory norm. There is no agreement that the right of humanitarian intervention has attained that status.

In my view, Article 4(h) AU Constitutive Act purports to establish a right of
humanitarian intervention of an auto-determinative nature. Unsurprisingly,
following its adoption, there was concern that a regional organisation was
attempting to usurp the authority of the Security Council and that this did not
accord with the view that regional arrangements can never, under any circumstances, override the primacy of the Security Council, in terms of Article 53(1)
UN Charter.[31] As it happens, in the two decades since the adoption of its
Constitutive Act, the African Union has not actually invoked Article 4(h)
intervention *involving the use of force* in any situation, despite the existence
of at least four occasions on which it could arguably have done so. For a host of
different reasons in each of these cases, the African Union did not find it either
expedient or pertinent to invoke Article 4(h) and intervene unilaterally without Security Council authorisation.[32] The fear that it would usurp the authority of the Security Council has not materialised, and I argue that this is
unlikely ever to happen and that such action would violate the UN Charter.[33]

To appreciate the potential ramifications of Article 4(h) on the AU–UN
relationship, and my prediction that the African Union is not likely to usurp
the authority of the Security Council, it is necessary to examine the Protocol
Relating to the Establishment of the Peace and Security Council of the
African Union.[34] The Peace and Security Protocol was adopted in 2002 to
establish the operational structure to implement effectively the decisions
taken by the AU Assembly pursuant to the authority conferred upon it by

[31] See Jean Allain, 'The True Challenge to the United Nations System of the Use of Force: The
Failures of Kosovo and Iraq and the Emergence of the African Union', *Max Planck Yearbook of
United Nations Law* 8 (2004), 237–89 (264–87); Martin Kunschak, 'The African Union and the
Right to Intervention: Is There a Need for UN Security Council Authorisation?', *South African
Yearbook of International Law* 31 (2006), 195–208; Gabriel Amvane, 'Intervention Pursuant to
Article 4(h) of the Constitutive Act of the African Union without United Nations Security
Council Authorisation', *African Human Rights Law Journal* 15 (2015), 282–98.
[32] Tiyanjana Maluwa, 'Reassessing Aspects of the Contribution of African States to the
Development of International Law through African Regional Multilateral Treaties',
Michigan Journal of International Law 41 (2020), 327–415 (391–3, fns 284–9).
[33] See Walter, 'Regional Arrangements' (n. 5), MN 66.
[34] Peace and Security Protocol (n. 23).

Article 9(1)(g) AU Constitutive Act regarding the 'management of conflicts, war and other emergencies and the restoration of peace'.[35]

Under Article 17(1) Peace and Security Protocol, AU member states pledge that, in fulfilment of the African Union's mandate to promote and maintain peace and security in Africa, the PSC 'shall cooperate and work closely with the United Nations Security Council, which has the primary responsibility for the maintenance of international peace and security'.[36] However, in his reading of the subsequent clauses of Article 17, Jean Allain concludes that the relationship envisaged between the PSC and the Security Council is neither on an equal footing nor one that places the latter over the former.[37] Furthermore, he asserts that, for the PSC, the Security Council is simply one of many UN bodies that it is supposed to work with closely, and that its interaction is meant to be first and foremost of a logistical nature.[38] To the latter point, he notes that, in fact, Article 17(2) does not speak of the need to seek Security Council authorisation to use force; rather, it calls on the United Nations to provide assistance.[39] Allain sees a diffusion and dilution of the primacy of the Security Council, vis-à-vis the PSC, in the wording of Article 17(3) and (4), whose essence is that the role of the Security Council is to assist the PSC and not vice versa.[40] He concludes categorically:

> As a result of the fact that the Protocol, while paying lip-service to the primacy of the UN Security Council, seeks, at every turn, to dissipate its pre-eminence makes clear that intervention as envisioned by the Constitutive Act of the African Union usurps the ultimate control vested in the United Nations System over the use of force.[41]

I disagree with Allain. As a practical matter, it is inconceivable that if the African Union were to invoke Article 17(1) Peace and Security Protocol, the United Nations would be satisfied with its role being limited merely to that of providing financial, logistical, and military support without allowing the Security Council to address the issue of authorisation of the use of force. The argument that, by enshrining Article 4(h) in its Constitutive Act, the African Union has subverted the primacy of the Security Council rests on an interpretation of two seemingly

[35] Art. 3(a)–(c) *ibid.*
[36] Art. 17(1) *ibid.*
[37] Allain, 'The True Challenge' (n. 31), 286.
[38] *Ibid.*
[39] Art. 17(2) provides, in part: 'Where necessary, recourse will be made to the United Nations to provide the necessary financial, logistical and military support for the African Union's activities in the promotion and maintenance of peace, security and stability [in Africa].'
[40] See Allain, 'The True Challenge' (n. 31), 286.
[41] *Ibid.*, 287.

irreconcilable provisions. While Article 17(1) recognises the primacy of the
Security Council in the maintenance of international peace and security,
Article 16(1) provides that the African Union 'has the primary responsibility for
promoting peace, security and stability in Africa'. From this, Christian Wyse,
like Allain, has concluded that, despite the AU Peace and Security Protocol's
repeated references to cooperation with the United Nations, it never actually
states that the African Union should seek the approval of the Security Council
prior to intervention and it fails to clarify how the latter is viewed.[42] Wyse
reached this conclusion despite the fact that the African Union had clarified
the issue in 2005, when it adopted 'The Common African Position on the
Proposed Reform of the United Nations: "The Ezulwini Consensus"'.[43]

The 'Ezulwini Consensus' was endorsed by a decision of the AU Assembly
three years later as a common policy position addressing various issues, including, principally, Security Council reform.[44] In this context, it addresses the issue
of collective security and the use of force. In terms of this common policy, the
African Union reaffirmed the primacy of the Security Council in matters of
collective security, including the R2P and the legality of the use of force.

Three points in the 'Ezulwini Consensus' deserve emphasis. First, the AU
Executive Council agreed that, since the General Assembly and the Security
Council are often far from the scenes of conflicts and may not be in a position
to undertake effectively a proper appreciation of the nature and development
of conflict situations, it is imperative that regional organisations, in areas of
proximity to conflicts, are empowered to take actions in this regard. Secondly,
the AU Executive Council also agreed that intervention by regional organisations should take place only with the approval of the Security Council. At the
same time, however, it recognised that, in some situations and in circumstances requiring urgent action, the Security Council could grant its approval
ex post. Thirdly, it acknowledged the potential tension between the R2P
principle and state sovereignty by reiterating the obligation of states to protect
their citizens but not use this principle as a pretext to undermine the sovereignty, independence, and territorial integrity of states.[45] In sum, the
'Ezulwini Consensus' reaffirmed the UN Charter's provisions on collective
security, the circumstances circumscribing the use of force, the primacy of the

---

[42]   Christian Wyse, 'The African Union's Right of Humanitarian Intervention as Collective Self-
      Defense', *Chicago Journal of International Law* 19 (2018), 295–332 (311).
[43]   The Common African Position on the Proposed Reform of the United Nations, AU Doc.
      Ext/EX.CL/2 (VII), 8 March 2005 (hereinafter Ezulwini Consensus).
[44]   Decision on Reform of the United Nations Security Council, AU Doc. Assembly/AU/Dec.184
      (X), 2 February 2008.
[45]   *Ibid.*, para. B(i).

Security Council in the maintenance of international peace and security, and the obligation incumbent upon the African Union to seek the Council's approval before invoking Article 4(h).

The AU Assembly endorsed the Executive Council's recommendations at its summit in July 2005, thus making the 'Ezulwini Consensus' a formal AU policy decision.[46] I argue that this policy framework provides the broader context for understanding Article 4(h) AU Constitutive Act, and I do not share the view that 'the statements about intervention therein are no more than either political manoeuvring or a statement of what would be true if the UNSC were actually effective'.[47]

B. *The Security Council, the African Union, and the Libyan Conflict of 2011*

1. Resolution 1973 and the NATO Intervention: The Responsibility to Protect?

On 17 March 2011, as Colonel Muammar Gaddafi's forces closed in on the eastern city of Benghazi in response to the rebel uprising against his regime, the Security Council adopted Resolution 1973.[48] The Resolution authorised member states that had informed the UN Secretary-General and the Secretary-General of the League of Arab States (LAS), acting alone or through regional organisations, to 'take all necessary measures [to] protect civilians and civilian populated areas under threat of [attack]'.[49] It also requested that member states notify them of all necessary measures taken to implement the Resolution.[50] Critically, Resolution 1973 established a no-fly zone over Libya, which the LAS had requested five days prior to its adoption.[51] Within two days

---

[46] Decision on the Expansion of the Follow-up Mechanism on the Reform of the United Nations, AU Doc. Assembly/AU/Dec.87 (V), 5 July 2005.

[47] Wyse, 'The African Union's Right of Humanitarian Intervention' (n. 42), 312.

[48] SC Res. 1973 of 17 March 2011, UN Doc. S/RES/1973(2011).

[49] *Ibid.*, para. 4.

[50] *Ibid.*, para. 11.

[51] See Arab League Statement on Libya, No. 7360, Cairo, 12 March 2011 ('The outcome of the Council of the League of Arab States meeting at Ministerial level in its extraordinary session on the implications of the current events in Libya and the Arab position'). Opening para. 1 reads:

> [Decides] *To call on* the Security Council to bear its responsibilities towards the deteriorating situation in Libya, and to take the necessary measures to impose immediately a no-fly-zone on Libyan military aviation, and to establish safe areas in places exposed to shelling as a precautionary measure that allows the protection of the Libyan people and foreign nationals residing in Libya, while respecting the sovereignty and territorial integrity of neighbouring States.

of the adoption of Resolution 1973, British and French military forces – later joined by forces from Canada, the United States, and other allies – launched aerial bombing raids against Gaddafi's military and intelligence forces and resources. On 31 March 2011, the North Atlantic Treaty Organization (NATO) formally took command of the operation, which ended on 31 October 2011 after seven months of almost non-stop daily bombings. By the end of the NATO operation, Gaddafi's regime had fallen; he had been killed by a group of insurgents on 20 October 2011.

Resolution 1973 followed Resolution 1970, adopted on 26 February 2011. The earlier resolution had condemned the Gaddafi government's use of violence against civilian populations and imposed sanctions on Libya.[52] Both resolutions signified the Security Council's new approach to civilian protection, bringing together the two still-evolving norms of the R2P and protection of civilians in the same peace operation. The Security Council's resolutions and actions on Libya – in particular, Resolution 1973 – raised some questions, including the role of politics in Security Council decision-making and the ability of powerful members to manipulate the decision-making to advance their national interests under the guise of advancing the common good, and so on.[53]

All three chapters in this book discuss Resolution 1973 from each author's perspective and in varying degrees of detail. Cai focuses attention on China's role, in the context of its rising power and re-engagement in the Security Council. Van den Herik examines the adoption of the Resolution in the face of wavering international consensus. I discuss at greater length the position of the African Union, as a regional body, the role of the A3, and the implications of the implementation of the Resolution and NATO's involvement for the AU–UN collaborative relationship in the management of threats to peace and security in Africa. I think it is fair to say that, in general, we agree on the narrative accounts and analyses of Resolution 1973. Differences of interpretation are more a matter of emphasis and nuance than substance. I briefly address some of these.

Cai and I share the view that the adoption of Resolution 1973 demonstrated starkly that the behaviour of states and the decisions they take as members of the Security Council are inevitably driven by their national interests. The power dynamics and balance of power matter. Sometimes, these interests

---

[52]   SC Res. 1970 of 26 February 2011, UN Doc. S/RES/1970(2011).
[53]   See Tom Keating, 'The UN Security Council on Libya: Legitimation or Dissimulation?', in Aidan Hehir and Robert Murray (eds), *Libya, the Responsibility to Protect and the Future of Humanitarian Intervention* (London: Palgrave Macmillan, 2013), 162–90 (163).

converge, in which case the Security Council can adopt decisions unanimously or without any of the P5 casting their veto. But even where they do not converge, states may nevertheless calculate that the outcome of a particular decision will not adversely affect their differing national interests or concerns. I believe the latter explains why some members of the Security Council either supported Resolution 1973 or elected not to veto it even though their national interests diverged from those of the three Western powers that pushed for its adoption and, moreover, even though they may have had misgivings about the decision. Cai has described Resolution 1973 as representing a turning point for China's voting in the Security Council from the perspective of power politics and identified two lessons that China has learned from this episode: first, that despite its growing power, Western powers such as the United States still pay little regard to China's interests; and secondly, that China's global interests are more likely to be affected by the workings of the Security Council.[54] I agree that China's experience concerning Libya has had a direct impact on its behaviour in the Security Council regarding Syria. As I point out below, this was also the case with other key actors, such as Russia and South Africa. Beyond Syria, this has had an impact on subsequent disagreements in the Security Council over the crises in Myanmar and Yemen.

Interestingly, in staking out its opposition to draft resolutions aimed at authorising intervention in Syria, China has repeatedly proclaimed that it has 'no self-interest' in addressing the Syrian crisis. Cai appears to accept this disavowal at face value, while also accepting that, unlike China, Russia has strategic interests in Syria. It seems to me that part of the problem in examining these issues lies in our understanding of how states define or perceive their 'national interests'. China's national interests circumscribing its support for Security Council actions, for example, on Mali, Sudan (Darfur), and South Sudan, and its opposition to action on Syria and Myanmar, are largely understood in terms of its economic, trading, and financial interests in these countries. Yet a broader definition of 'self-interest' or 'national interest' might include a state's belief in, and promotion of, certain normative values and principles that underpin its commitment to the international rule of law. To the extent that China proclaims, as both Cai and I accept, commitment to the principles of state sovereignty and non-interference as core pillars of its foreign policy, I would argue that China *does* have a 'self-interest' in upholding its position on Syria. Part of this is its avowed opposition to foreign-imposed regime change – a key interest it formally shares with Russia and other allies.

---

[54] Cai, 'Maintaining Peace during a Global Power Shift', Chapter 1 in this volume, section V.B.

In her discussion of Resolution 1973, Van den Herik also provides a brief discussion of Resolution 1970, which preceded the former. She offers two interesting insights in this regard. The first is the observation that, at the time of the Libyan crisis and the adoption of Resolution 1970, the composition of the Security Council reflected an optimal geopolitical balance, including as it did all the BRICS countries and Germany, all of which have permanent seat aspirations.[55] There is an implied suggestion that the ease with which the Security Council agreed to impose sanctions on Libya and refer the situation to the International Criminal Court (ICC) was, at least in part, due to the eagerness of these countries to demonstrate responsible leadership in the Security Council. Yet this consideration does not seem to have held up when these same members came to vote on Resolution 1973 barely a month later. Not all of them supported the Resolution.

The second issue that Van den Herik points to is the role played by the then Libyan deputy permanent representative to the United Nations, Ibrahim Dabbashi, who defected from the Gaddafi regime. On 21 February 2011, Ambassador Dabbashi, backed by other Libyan diplomats, supported the proposal to impose a no-fly zone over Libya, an investigation into human rights violations, and a referral of the situation to the ICC.[56] This might suggest the value of personal dynamics in diplomatic calculations in decision-making even by a body with such formalised authority and procedures as the Security Council. Van den Herik is right to characterise Dabbashi's defection, and his call for an ICC referral and a no-fly zone, as 'the factor that was arguably decisive' in the Security Council meeting.[57] Individual personality and character clearly matter in diplomacy, and Ambassador Dabbashi's move galvanised other Libyan diplomats, both at the United Nations and in various missions around the world, to abandon the Gaddafi regime. Yet I would not overplay this factor. I think it equally important here that the African Union, which had rallied around President Omar Al-Bashir of Sudan in 2005 to oppose his referral to the ICC over the crimes committed in Darfur, did not raise collective opposition against the Libyan referral. In the end, this accounted for the fact that the three African members of the Security Council, Gabon, Nigeria, and South Africa, supported the referral, despite ongoing tensions between African states and the ICC over the Court's Darfur

---

[55] The BRICS grouping was founded by Brazil, Russia, India, and China in 2006 as an informal association of major emerging national economies, with South Africa joining in 2010.
[56] See Colin Moynihan, 'Libya's U.N. Diplomats Break with Gaddafi', *New York Times*, 21 February 2011, available at www.nytimes.com/2011/02/22/world/africa/22nations.html.
[57] Van den Herik, 'A Reflection on Institutional Strength', Chapter 2 in this volume, section IV.A.

and Kenyan investigations, as well as lingering resentment over the fact that three of the P5 members voting for the referral were not even parties to the Rome Statute of the ICC.

This last point ties in with another observation that Van den Herik makes: 'Nonetheless, despite their preference for a political solution, as proposed by the AU Roadmap, and despite their kingmaker position, the African states greenlit the Security Council resolution authorising force.'[58] I partly address this issue in my discussion of the African Union's response to the Security Council decision and action on Libya later in this section. A relevant point to make here is that the African Union had also accepted that there was a major difference between the Libyan situation and the earlier uprisings in Tunisia and Egypt: the authorities in those countries did not respond to the protestors with the kind of force that Gaddafi's regime unleashed on its population, with the declared aim of exterminating the protestors, thus triggering a full-scale civil war and possible violations of Article 4(h) AU Constitutive Act.

In the section that follows, I turn to two other questions that I consider particularly relevant to the objectives of this chapter. The first concerns the roles that the Security Council and the African Union played in responding to the Libyan crisis and discharging their responsibilities under the UN Charter and the AU Constitutive Act, respectively. This question goes to the legal and political dynamics of the relationship between the United Nations and the African Union – to the relationship between the centre and the periphery – as it relates to collaborative action for the maintenance of international peace and security.

The second question – going to the overarching theme of this book series – is whether, in adopting and implementing Resolution 1973, the Security Council contributed to the advancement of the R2P norm, which would be an aspect of the advancement of the law of peace and war. In addressing this second question, it is important to recall that although the Security Council has subsequently referred to the R2P in the context of certain peace-keeping operations, in the case of Libya in 2011 it authorised military action to protect civilians *without* explicit reference to the R2P. It made only passing reference to it in the Preamble to the Resolution, reiterating 'the responsibility of the Libyan authorities to protect the Libyan population'.[59]

Some commentators have nevertheless argued that the desire to implement the R2P principle provided the underlying rationale for Resolution 1973.[60]

---

[58] *Ibid.*, section IV.A.
[59] SC Res. 1973 of 17 March 2017, UN Doc. S/RES/1973(2017), cons. 4.
[60] See Paul R. Williams and Colleen Popken, 'Security Council Resolution 1973 on Libya: A Moment of Legal and Moral Clarity', *Case Western Reserve Journal of International Law* 44 (2011), 225–50 (227, fn. 7). See also Pierre Thielbörger, 'The Status and Future of International

Indeed, following its adoption, UN Secretary-General Ban Ki-Moon also emphasised the historic dimension of the Resolution, as 'affirm[ing], clearly and unequivocally, the international community's determination to fulfil its responsibility to protect civilians from violence perpetrated upon them by their own government'.[61]

An analysis of the debates surrounding the adoption of Resolution 1973 and the NATO intervention in Libya, and the questions set out above, serves to remind us of the legal realist's claim that law happens in a context and that this context is circumscribed by politics. Another way of framing this claim is to ask: does international law, in certain respects, constrain international political discourse and decision-making (e.g., by the Security Council), or does the existence of an international political consensus on a proposed course of action trigger a push to legitimise that action through the formulation of suitable international law? This calls for a better understanding of the relationship between international law (as expressed in the emerging, but contested, R2P norm) and international politics (as evidenced in the decisions and actions of the Security Council). Put differently, how did international politics on Libya influence the interpretation and application of international law?

A recap of the voting pattern on Resolution 1973 provides a useful context and departure point. The Resolution was adopted with the affirmative vote of ten members of the Security Council: the P3 and seven non-permanent members, comprising the A3 (i.e., Gabon, Nigeria, and South Africa) plus Bosnia-Herzegovina, Colombia, Lebanon, and Portugal. These countries believed that the Resolution was necessary to prevent Gaddafi's forces carrying out further attacks against the Libyan opposition and considered it an appropriate response to the Gaddafi regime's disregard of Resolution 1970. While no member voted against the Resolution, five abstained: Brazil, Germany, and India, along with the two remaining permanent members, China and Russia. Collectively, these states abstained for a variety of reasons, including fears of a protracted military conflict that could involve the broader region, the risk of massive loss of civilian life, uncertainty about the methods and mechanisms for enforcing the no-fly zone, the need to protect Libya's territorial integrity and unity, and lack of unanimity among the members on the appropriateness of invoking – even if only impliedly – the R2P principle in this situation.

Law after the Libya Intervention', *Goettingen Journal of International Law* 4 (2012), 11–28 (23–6), noting the Security Council's ambivalence in invoking the doctrine.

[61] 'Secretary-General Says Security Council Action on Libya Affirms International Community's Determination to Protect Civilians from Own Government's Violence', UN Docs SG/SM 13454, SC/10201, AFR/2144, 17 March 2011.

Specifically, Germany felt that it was necessary to tighten the international sanctions imposed by the previous resolution, and it was concerned that implementation of Resolution 1973 would result in large-scale loss of life and 'protracted military conflict'.[62] Brazil was concerned that the Resolution contemplated measures that went beyond the minimum needed to protect the civilian population, and it believed that humanitarian intervention would exacerbate the situation in Libya, 'causing more harm than good [to] civilians'.[63] China, India, and Russia preferred more political dialogue and processes to secure a ceasefire and resolve the conflict peacefully. In addition, Russia warned against 'unpredicted consequences', and it expressed concerns about who would enforce the no-fly zone and how they would do so.[64] Similarly, India was concerned about the implementation of the Resolution and its unintended consequences, calling for full respect for the sovereignty, unity, and territorial integrity of Libya.[65] China was generally opposed to the Resolution for authorising force before all peaceful means had been exhausted, recalling that it '[has] always emphasised that, in its relevant actions, the Security Council should follow the UN Charter and the norms governing international law, respect the sovereignty, independence, unity and territorial integrity of Libya and resolve the current crisis through peaceful means'.[66]

Two observations may be made. First, as major or rising economic powers, some of the abstaining states appear to have made a calculation based on their respective economic or special interests in the Libyan energy industry. They were therefore more inclined to avoid direct confrontation with the Libyan government, unlike the A3. Secondly, they were at the same time mindful that once the international community – including the relevant regional organisations, the African Union and the LAS – agreed that there was a need to intervene on humanitarian grounds, it would be unconscionable to vote against the Resolution. In the end, members of the Security Council either voted for the Resolution or abstained on the basis of national political interests, in some cases influenced by their existing or potential trade and economic interests in Libya.[67] This much was made clear when India's representative noted that:

---

[62] UN Doc. S/PV.6498, 17 March 2011, 4–5.
[63] *Ibid.*, 6.
[64] *Ibid.*, 8.
[65] *Ibid.*, 5–6.
[66] *Ibid.*, 10.
[67] For example, during the period January–November 2010, Germany and China accounted for 10 per cent and 11 per cent, respectively, of Libya's oil exports by destination. See US Energy Information Administration, 'Today in Energy', 21 March 2011, available at www.eia.gov/tod ayinenergy/detail.php?id=590#. See also Christopher Davidson, 'Why Was Muammar Qadhafi Really Removed?', *Middle East Policy* 24 (2017), 91–116, (110–11).

[The] financial measures that are proposed in the resolution could impact directly or through indirect routes the ongoing trade and investment activities of a number of Member States, thereby affecting the economic interests of the Libyan people and others dependent on these trade and economic ties.[68]

The NATO intervention in Libya became the subject of controversy almost as soon as it started and has remained so since. Much of this discussion has revolved around NATO's role in implementing Resolution 1973. Although NATO was not explicitly mentioned anywhere in the Resolution, it soon became apparent that it had anticipated its involvement. On 22 March 2011, five days after the adoption of Resolution 1973, NATO Secretary-General Anders Fogh Rasmussen announced: '[NATO] has completed plans to enforce the no-fly zone – to bring our contribution, if needed, in a clearly defined manner, to the broad international effort to protect the people of Libya from violence of the Gaddafi regime.'[69] Meanwhile, the British-French-US coalition had initiated the bombing on 19/20 March.[70] The subsequent decision that NATO would become formally involved and take full command of the Libya operation on 31 March 2011 was thus hardly a surprise. The counterpoint to NATO's involvement was the marginalisation of the African Union and total disregard by the P3 of its efforts to mediate among the Libyan protagonists with a view to resolving the conflict peacefully and securing a democratic transition.[71]

When the PSC first discussed the Libyan conflict at its meeting on 23 February 2011, it did not recommend intervention on humanitarian grounds. On paper, the crisis in Libya offered the African Union a legal basis to invoke Article 4(h) AU Constitutive Act. The PSC strongly condemned the indiscriminate and excessive use of force and lethal weapons in violation of human rights and international humanitarian law, and it acknowledged the loss of human life.[72] Yet it did not determine that these violations amounted to any of the crimes enumerated in Article 4(h). Indeed, there is nothing on the record to suggest that the PSC addressed this possibility. One commentator, however, has

---

[68]   UN Doc. S/PV.6498, 17 March 2011, 6.
[69]   'Statement by the NATO Secretary-General on Libya Arms Embargo', 22 March 2011, available at www.nato.int/cps/en/natolive/news_71689.htm.
[70]   Patrick Terry, 'The Libya Intervention (2011): Neither Lawful nor Successful', *Comparative and International Law Journal of Southern Africa* 48 (2015), 162–82 (165–6).
[71]   See generally Sandy Africa and Rantia Pretorius, 'South Africa, the African Union and the Responsibility to Protect: The Case of Libya', *African Journal of Human Rights* 12 (2012), 394–416; Alex de Waal, 'African Roles in the Libyan Conflict', *International Affairs* 89 (2013), 365–79; Geir Ulfstein and Hege Christiansen, 'The Legality of the NATO Bombing in Libya', *International and Comparatively Law Quarterly* 62 (2013), 159–71.
[72]   AU Peace and Security Council, Communiqué of 261st Meeting, AU Doc. PSC/PR/COMM. (CCLXI), 23 February 2011.

posited that Gaddafi's government had not, at that point, committed any of these crimes.[73] It is reasonable to conclude that the PSC made the same assumption. Having thus decided not to invoke its right to intervene, the African Union embarked on its ultimately unsuccessful search for a peaceful solution to the crisis. Despite the criticism levelled against it for failing to use military force to intervene against the Gaddafi regime, the African Union believed that it proceeded correctly to protect human lives and broker a peaceful and democratic transition among the warring parties in Libya.

In my view, another political consideration that drove the PSC's decision – albeit one not articulated openly – was the possibility of the African Union finding itself on the opposite side from the LAS within the Libyan crisis. For most of the years of his rule and particularly in his last two decades, Gaddafi had pivoted away for a variety of reasons from the LAS in favour of the African Union. Yet Libya remained nominally a member of the LAS, even if Gaddafi was shunned by most of his fellow Arab leaders. When the conflict broke out, the African Union and the LAS had an equal interest in its speedy resolution, both being concerned that the conflict should not engulf the broader region. This was the context in which the PSC let the LAS take the lead in coordinating with the Security Council, based on a loose notion of regional subsidiarity: that the LAS was closer to the problem and better placed to address it. More importantly, however, both organisations agreed that there should be no external military occupation of Libya – a demand that was incorporated in Resolution 1973.[74] With the prospect of the LAS opposing any intervention by the African Union based on Article 4(h) AU Constitutive Act, the PSC had no choice politically but to opt for a peaceful and diplomatic solution to the crisis.

Finally, there is another reason why the African Union did not – indeed, could not – sidestep the Security Council and unilaterally launch a military intervention in Libya. In assessing the AU response, one should also not overlook the policy that guided the organisation: the 'Ezulwini Consensus'. As discussed earlier, under this policy, the African Union acknowledged the primacy of the Security Council in matters of international peace and security, even as it reaffirmed its role as a regional organisation under Article 53 UN Charter and pursuant to the powers established under Article 4(h) AU Constitutive Act. The African Union could not have usurped the role of the Security Council by unilaterally invoking Article 4(h) to intervene in Libya

---

[73] Ademola Abass, 'The African Union's Response to the Libyan Crisis: A Plea for Objectivity', *African Journal of Legal Studies* 7 (2014), 123–47 (128, 132–3).

[74] SC Res. 1973 of 17 March 2011, UN Doc. S/RES/1973(2011), para. 4.

even if it had wished to do so, and even if it had the requisite political will and resources needed to implement such a decision.

All of this answers the question of why the African Union did not invoke the norm of intervention that it has uniquely established in Article 4(h) AU Constitutive Act. My argument is that, leaving aside the factual question of whether the violations in Libya had reached the threshold set out in Article 4(h), the African Union's ability to invoke its own normative instrument was constrained by the realpolitik of the AU–LAS relationship and the political desire not to upset intra-regional cooperation between the two organisations. The African Union achieved this with a diplomatic sleight of hand, characterising the violations in Libya as not amounting to the prescribed crimes justifying Article 4(h) intervention.

Some commentators have offered different perspectives on this question. For example, Ademola Abass suggests that the disagreement between the African Union and its critics on its handling of the Libyan crisis highlights the doctrinal uncertainty about the nature of the international responsibility to protect a people when their governments have failed in their primary responsibility to do so.[75] Another commentator has argued that the African Union's response simply reflected the tendency of African organisations to prioritise politics over human lives, peer solidarity over effective action, and unwillingness to hold one of the organisation's main funders to account for the egregious international crimes committed by his own government.[76]

These arguments may be legitimate – but only up to a point. I think they oversimplify the African Union's position on the Libyan crisis in some respects. The argument that the African Union was simply protecting one of the organisation's main funders might seem tendentious. Gaddafi was notorious for spreading his financial largesse among those African leaders whose loyalty he sought to cultivate; he also funded impecunious rulers – notably, when they urgently needed to pay their dues to the African Union, so that they could vote at summit meetings on issues in which he had a particular interest. The claim that some commentators make, that he was the African Union's principal benefactor, sometimes conflates his financial backing of individual 'client states' with his supposed funding of the organisation. Libya never funded the African Union beyond its assessed budget contributions.[77]

---

[75] Abass, 'The African Union's Response' (n. 73), 138.

[76] See generally Eki Yemisi Omorogbe, 'The African Union, the Responsibility to Protect and the Libyan Crisis', *Netherlands International Law Review* 59 (2012), 141–63.

[77] In 2011, Libya was only one of five top contributors to the African Union's regular budget (accounting for 60 per cent of the budget) – along with Algeria, Egypt, Nigeria, and South Africa – based on the Union's scale of assessment for member states' contributions.

In mandating the intervention in Libya, the Security Council acted wholly within its Chapter VII powers and authority under the UN Charter, as the UN organ with primary responsibility for the international community's collective security. The possibility that the P3 and their NATO allies went beyond the intended objective of Resolution 1973 in carrying out the enforcement action could not as such have delegitimised the authority of the Security Council in adopting the Resolution. But this is separate from the questions regarding the P3's good faith and the supposed unlawfulness of the NATO action.[78] In my view, the African Union acted properly by not invoking Article 4(h) to intervene in Libya without Security Council authorisation, because that would have been a usurpation of the Council's authority and a violation of Article 53 UN Charter.

I do not address the argument that the NATO intervention in Libya was altogether unlawful in any detail here. While it is true that Resolution 1973 did not mention NATO by name, it authorised national governments 'acting alone or through regional organisations'. This provided the basis for France, the United Kingdom, and the United States to involve NATO, as a regional organisation, in the Libyan crisis. There was nothing in Resolution 1973 to suggest that the reference to 'regional organisations' was limited to the African Union or the LAS. I thus disagree with the view that characterises NATO's involvement in the Libyan intervention as illegal as such. There was a legal basis for the use of force to the extent that it was properly authorised by the Security Council acting within its Chapter VII powers. Nonetheless, one can argue that the abuse of that authorisation by NATO subsequently rendered its intervention illegal. Although the matter has been much debated by scholars and politicians alike, there is no consensus on whether NATO went beyond what Resolution 1973 permitted. I believe this to be the case – but, for reasons of scope and space, I do not reprise this debate here.[79]

2. The African Union's Response to the Security Council's Decision and Action on Libya

When the PSC first met to discuss the uprising in Libya, it decided not to invoke Article 4(h) AU Constitutive Act; rather, it focused on the repression of demonstrations by the Libyan authorities and Gaddafi's threats against the

---

[78] See, e.g., Terry, 'The Libyan Intervention' (n. 70).

[79] See Tiyanjana Maluwa, 'Stalling a Norm's Trajectory? Revisiting U.N. Security Council Resolution 1973 on Libya and Its Ramifications for the Principle of the Responsibility to Protect', *California Western International Law Journal* 53 (2022), 69–114 (81–94).

opposition.[80] There was also no question of invoking Article 4(j) AU Constitutive Act. Unlike Article 4(h), this provision grants AU member states the right to request intervention from the African Union to restore peace and security. Gaddafi's government, which was still the legitimate authority in Libya, had not requested any such intervention.

On 10 March 2011, the PSC met again, at the level of heads of state and government, to forge the African Union's response to the growing crisis. This meeting developed a four-point plan, which became known as the 'AU Roadmap'. The elements of the plan were:

(i) the immediate cessation of all hostilities;
(ii) the cooperation of the competent Libyan authorities to facilitate the timely delivery of humanitarian assistance to the needy populations;
(iii) the protection of foreign nationals, including the African migrants living in Libya; and
(iv) the adoption and implementation of the political reforms necessary for the elimination of the causes of the crisis.[81]

The PSC expressed deep concern that the situation in Libya posed a serious threat to peace and security in that country and in the region. While it once again strongly and unequivocally condemned the indiscriminate use of force and lethal weapons, and it deplored the loss of human life, it also reaffirmed the African Union's strong commitment to the respect of the unity and territorial integrity of Libya, as well as its rejection of any foreign military intervention, whatever its form.[82]

The African Union established an ad hoc High-Level Committee on Libya, chaired by President Jacob Zuma of South Africa. The Committee's mandate was to 'engage with all the parties in Libya and continuously assess the evolution of the situation on the ground', to 'facilitate an inclusive dialogue among the Libyan parties on the appropriate reforms', and to 'engage AU's partners, in particular the League of Arab States, the Organisation of the Islamic Conference, the European Union and the United Nations to facilitate coordination of efforts and seek their support for the early resolution of the crisis'.[83]

---

[80] AU Peace and Security Council, Communiqué of 261st Meeting, AU Doc. PSC/PR/COMM. (CCLXI), 23 February 2011, para. 2.

[81] AU Peace and Security Council, Communiqué of 261st Meeting, AU Doc. PSC/PR/COMM.2 (CCLXV), 10 March 2011, para. 7.

[82] *Ibid.*, paras 5–6.

[83] *Ibid.*, para. 8. See also Report of the Chairperson of the Commission on the Activities of the AU High-Level Ad Hoc Committee on the Situation in Libya, AU Doc. PSCPR/2 (CCLXXV), 26 April 2011.

Several attempts at shuttle diplomacy by the ad hoc Committee – which involved meetings with the major actors in the Libyan conflict, including Gaddafi – failed to persuade any of the parties to the conflict, as well as the P3 and their allies in the Security Council, to accept the 'AU Roadmap'. As these failed efforts went on, the Transitional National Council (TNC) of Libya, established by the anti-Gaddafi forces as an alternative government, began to gain support among many states. But it was not before mid-August 2011 that some major powers, including the United States, recognised it as the de facto government, with China and the African Union following suit in late September.

In my view, the African Union's response to the Libya crisis was doomed to fail. In one sense, throughout the crisis, the African Union was responding to the initiatives of the Security Council, on the one hand, while simultaneously trying to mediate the opposing postures of some of its own leading members, on the other. As chair of the ad hoc Committee, South Africa was caught in the middle, but generally inclined towards supporting Gaddafi for reasons largely to do with his previous support for the anti-Apartheid struggle. For South Africa, the situation was complicated by the fact that, like Nigeria, it had supported Resolution 1973. Disagreement between two of the African Union's leading members over their preferred outcomes and the associated divisions that they created within the organisation served not only to exacerbate already-fragile political loyalties but also to weaken the African Union's negotiating hand vis-à-vis interested external actors – especially the P3, who were most invested in the success of the NATO operation.

Within the Security Council and subsequently in the General Assembly, the debate on Libya turned on the different understandings of the permission given to UN member states under Resolution 1973 to use 'all measures necessary'. In the Security Council, the A3 accused the P3 of deliberately misinterpreting the Resolution to carry out a predetermined NATO agenda of regime change in Libya. There was no disguising what many African states came to view as NATO's conceited posturing. At the start of its military operation in March 2011, NATO expressed its position thus: 'NATO is not engaged in Libya to decide the future of the Libyan people. That is up to the Libyans themselves.'[84] Three months later, in a change of tone, NATO was proclaiming: '[The] game is over for Gaddafi. He should realise sooner than later that there is no future for him or his regime.'[85] US President Barack

---

[84] 'Joint Press Briefing on Libya', 31 March 2011, available at www.nato.int/cps/en/natolive/news_71907.htm.

[85] Statement attributed to NATO Secretary-General Anders Fogh Rasmussen, cited in Alberto Arce, 'NATO Says Gaddafi's Time is Up', *The Sydney Morning Herald*, 9 May 2011, available at www.smh.com.au/world/nato-says-gaddafis-time-is-up-20110509-1eeit.html.

Obama had made a similar statement a month earlier, when he insisted that only after regime change in Libya could 'a genuine transition from dictatorship to an inclusive constitutional process [really] begin' and that, 'in order for that transition to succeed, Colonel Gaddafi must go, and go for good'.[86]

Alex de Waal and Tom Keating have argued that the subsequent actions of the P3 indicated that their disavowal of regime change 'was an exercise in dissimulation'.[87] Similarly, Dire Tladi argues that the implementation of Resolution 1973 and Resolution 1975[88] (also adopted in March 2011, authorising intervention in Côte d'Ivoire) led to the collapse of the Muammar Gaddafi and Laurent Gbagbo regimes, respectively, and suggests that these resolutions appeared to authorise regime change through the use of force for the purposes of protecting civilians.[89] I agree with these writers' readings and characterisation of the resolutions. The outcomes in these two instances, intended or not, validated the concerns that China and Russia had expressed – namely, that humanitarian intervention should not be manipulated to achieve ulterior ends. Further Security Council practice in this direction can only erode the trust and confidence of the less powerful states in the system of collective security of which it is the custodian.

From their perspective, African leaders felt aggrieved that the P3 and other Western governments thwarted and misrepresented the African response to the Libyan conflict. The anger against the P3's perceived deception and selective interpretation of Resolution 1973 was widely shared among AU member states other than the A3. In his report to the AU Executive Council in June 2011, the AU Commission's chairperson to this issue, charging that it was becoming increasingly clear that the pursuit of the military operations would not only undermine the very purpose for which Resolution 1970 and Resolution 1973 were adopted – that is, the protection of civilians – but also compound any transition to democratic institutions. He also argued that the military campaign was 'significantly expanding beyond the objectives for which it was in the first place authorised, raising questions about the legality

---

[86] See op-ed article co-authored by the US President Barack H. Obama, French President Nicholas Sarkozy, and the British Prime Minister David Cameron, 'Libya's Pathway to Peace', *New York Times*, 14 April 2011, available at www.nytimes.com/2011/04/15/opinion/15iht-edlibya15.html.

[87] De Waal, 'African Roles' (n. 71), 368. See also generally Keating, 'The UN Security Council on Libya' (n. 53).

[88] SC Res. 1975 of 30 March 2011, UN Doc. S/RES/1975(2011).

[89] Dire Tladi, 'Security Council, the Use of Force and Regime Change: Libya and Côte d'Ivoire', *South African Yearbook of International Law* 37 (2012), 22–45 (45); cf. Mehrdad Payandeh, 'The United Nations, Military Intervention, and Regime Change in Libya', *Virginia Journal of International Law* 52 (2012), 355–403 (387–9).

and legitimacy of some of the actions being carried out and the agenda being pursued'.[90]

In fact, prior to this report, South Africa's president had been criticised for voting in favour of the Resolution apparently despite counsel from his own advisers that 'all measures necessary' was open to very flexible interpretation and thus threatened to negate the AU initiative for a peaceful resolution of the conflict that he had led.[91] South Africa justified its affirmative vote for Resolution 1973 in the context of the discourse on UN peacekeeping reform, which emphasised the principle of civilian protection. It also pointed out that it supported the Resolution after ensuring that its operative paragraphs precluded any foreign occupation and unilateral external military action, which was consistent with the position adopted earlier by the African Union.[92] We can reasonably speculate that, because of its regional superpower status, had South Africa led the other African members on the Security Council to abstain or vote against it, Resolution 1973 might never have been adopted. As already noted, although South Africa carried along its fellow African non-permanent members, all of its BRICS partners – Brazil, China, India, and Russia – abstained. I return to the BRICS position in the Security Council and on the R2P in the next section.

Resolution 1973 has been described as 'spongy' and 'vague', and as employing 'very broad language' in its wording, which revealed 'a mismatch of the intervention's rationale expressed in the text of the resolution as opposed to the one which shone through its execution'.[93] Thielbörger has noted, first, that the Security Council determined – as it had done in respect of previous resolutions – that the situation in Libya constituted a 'threat to international peace and security' without providing explanations of why the situation in Libya had an international dimension. Secondly, he also notes that, in authorising 'all necessary measures to [protect] civilians and civilian populated areas under threat of attack', the Resolution was very indistinct and extraordinarily wide in determining which actions it permitted, while explicitly ruling out

---

[90] African Union Executive Council, Report of the Chairperson to the Executive Council, 19th Ordinary Session of 23–28 June 2011, para. 11.

[91] See de Waal, 'African Roles' (n. 71), 371, citing Eusebius McKaiser, 'Looking an International Relations Gift Horse in the Mouth: [South Africa's] Response to the Libyan Crisis', 2011 Ruth First Memorial Lecture, Johannesburg, 17 August 2011. See also Sean Christie, '[South Africa] at the UN: Do They Jump or Are They Pushed?', *Mail & Guardian*, 6 May 2011, available at https://mg.co.za/article/2011-05-06-do-they-jump-or-are-pushed/.

[92] Statement by Spokesperson of the South African Department of International Relations and Cooperation, Pretoria, 18 March 2011, quoted in Garth Abraham, 'South Africa and R2P', in Doutje Lettinga and Lars van Troost (eds), *Shifting Power and Human Rights Diplomacy* (Amsterdam: Amnesty International Netherlands, 2016), 69–78 (72).

[93] Thielbörger, 'Status and Future' (n. 60), 18.

only one thing in absolute terms – namely, 'any foreign occupation force of any kind'.[94] This diplomatic 'fudging', which Van den Herik also discusses in her chapter, is hardly surprising:[95] the Security Council, as Thielbörger and other legal scholars recognise, operates as a political body and does not engage in a legal analysis or clarification as might be the case in judgments by international courts. The vague wording of Resolution 1973 gave rise to several questions that elicited much debate and diverse commentary. Did Resolution 1973, for example, permit, or even enable, the NATO allies to supply rebels with weapons, as France explicitly assumed[96] and others rejected?[97] Could NATO deploy ground forces to train or assist the rebels, or protect civilians, as long as they did not turn into occupation forces?[98] And were targeted attacks on senior Libyan officials, including the assassination of Gaddafi, justified if such attacks were necessary to protect civilians?[99] I agree with Van den Herik's observation about the 'ambivalent construction' of the Resolution, and that it veered between political and military solution of the conflict.

---

[94]   *Ibid.*, 19–20.
[95]   The ambiguity and vagueness of the language resulted from the desire to reach a compromise between the members of the Security Council – especially France and the United Kingdom, who advocated for robust military action, and China and Russia, who would have used their veto had the resolution authorised measures that were not constrained by at least explicitly precluding foreign occupation forces. See *ibid.*, 22. See also Van den Herik, 'A Reflection on Institutional Strength', Chapter 2 in this volume, section IV.A (pp. 124, 127–28).
[96]   See David Jolly and Kareem Fahim, 'France Says it Gave Arms to the Rebels in Libya', *New York Times*, 29 June 2011, available at www.nytimes.com/2011/06/30/world/europe/30fra nce.html. For the view that the NATO coalition's military support for the rebels was legal within the terms of Resolution 1973, see Dapo Akande, 'Does SC Resolution 1973 Permit Coalition Military Support for the Libyan Rebels?', *EJIL:Talk!*, 31 March 2011, available at www.ejiltalk.org/does-sc-resolution-1973-permit-coalition-military-support-for-the-libyan-rebe ls/. Contra this view, see Olivier Corten and Vaios Koutroulis, 'The Illegality of Military Support to the Rebels in the Libyan War: Aspects of *Jus contra Bellum* and *Jus in Bello*', *Journal of Conflict and Security Law* 18 (2013), 59–93 (66–77).
[97]   Russian Foreign Minister Sergey Lavrov criticised the French military support for Libyan rebels as 'a very crude violation of UN Security Council Resolution 1970': 'Russia Decries French Arms Drop to Libya Rebels', *BBC News*, 30 June 2011, available at www.bbc.co.uk/ news/world-europe-13979632.
[98]   For example, a group of British international law scholars and experts was convened by a British newspaper on 21 March 2011 to analyse the UK government's Note on the Legal Basis for Deployment of UK Forces and Military Assets. Professors Ryszard Piotrowicz, Malcom Shaw, and Nick Grief, and Mr Anthony Aust generally agreed that although Resolution 1973 did not permit a foreign occupation force, it did not exclude the use of ground forces to protect civilians: see 'Our Panel of Experts Discuss UK's Basis for Military Action in Libya', *The Guardian*, 21 March 2011, available at www.guardian.co.uk/law/2011/m ar/21/international-law-panel-libya-military.
[99]   *Ibid.* Professors Shaw and Piotrowicz supported this position.

There is little doubt that NATO's involvement in the Libyan conflict displeased the African Union. I take the view that the African Union was, in large measure, the author of its own displeasure. Principally, this was because of the inability of its members to speak with one voice and to coalesce around its new security structure and the R2P norm implied in Article 4(h) AU Constitutive Act. The PSC made no effort to verify with specificity any violation of the crimes under Article 4(h), even as it acknowledged ongoing violations of human rights and international humanitarian law in the conflict. A determination that the Libyan government was in violation of Article 4(h) would, at the very least, have opened the door to the *possibility* of the African Union invoking its right to intervene, subject to the necessary consultations with the Security Council, consistent with the 'Ezulwini Consensus' and the requirements of Article 53 UN Charter.

From this, one can draw the conclusion that the African Union could act neither as a legitimate peace-broker nor as a capable peace-enforcer in Libya. Related to this, the disagreements over the interpretation and implementation of Resolution 1973 revealed that there was a need to agree on a set of principles aimed at clarifying the UN–AU relationship, which should revolve around support for African ownership, and the division of labour and sharing of responsibilities in the collaborative peace operations involving the two organisations. This was no doubt the motivation for South Africa's decision to convene a meeting of the Security Council during its rotating presidency in January 2012 – namely, to discuss ways of strengthening the cooperation and partnership between the two. The United Nations did not disagree with this thinking. Indeed, in his statement, UN Secretary-General Ban Ki-Moon agreed that cooperation between the African Union and the United Nations demands 'common strategic objectives and a clear division of responsibilities, based on shared assessments and concerted decisions of the two organisations'.[100]

Still, it is by no means certain that the efforts made by both sides since then, consisting of mostly non-institutionalised consultations between the Security Council and the PSC, have achieved the aspirations expressed by Secretary-General Ban Ki-Moon. A recent empirical study by the International Crisis Group (ICG) on the relationship between the Security Council and the PSC has addressed the issue of mistrust between the two organs. It concludes that, although the leadership of both organisations has made the deepening of the AU–UN partnership a priority, the two bodies often fail to coordinate their positions during major crises threatening peace and security for a combination

---

[100] SC Res. 2033 of 12 January 2012, UN Doc. S/RES/2033(2012).

of political and procedural reasons, and that continuing tensions between the A3 and P5 have exacerbated the differences.[101] The ICG's report captures the crux of the matter succinctly:

> Proposals to improve PSC and A3 diplomacy are unlikely to make much difference unless Security Council members pay the AU's views greater heed. Discussions of problems between the two councils frequently circle back to PSC members' frustration that their counterparts do not treat their views with respect. PSC members often scan Security Council resolutions to see if they echo the language of AU decisions at all, but seldom find traces of their views.[102]

This diagnosis is correct. But it is also important to underscore that disagreements and tensions between the two sides have not impacted *every* instance of Security Council decision-making in relation to Libya since 2011. As Table 1 shows, the A3, P3, and P2 have voted in support of all key resolutions since the P3 and the P2 abstained on Resolution 1973. The P2 have abstained on two subsequent resolutions only: Resolution 2441 of 2018, extending by a year the mandate of the Panel of Experts assisting the 1970 Libya Sanctions Committee; and Resolution 2542 of 2020, which extended for a year the United Nations Support Mission in Libya (UNSMIL). Russia alone abstained on Resolution 2509 of 2020, also extending the mandate of the Panel of Experts. These abstentions reflect opposition to a prolonged UN presence in Libya.

Undoubtedly, the NATO intervention in Libya, based on a skewed interpretation of Resolution 1973 by the P3, has lessons for the African Union in its relations with the Security Council. Understanding the respective roles of the African Union and the Security Council in the Libyan conflict is important for framing the limits of the possibilities for the collaborative relationship between the United Nations and the African Union in the maintenance of international peace and security. The shared objectives of the P3 members

---

[101] International Crisis Group, 'A Tale of Two Councils: Strengthening AU–UN Cooperation', Africa Report No. 279, 25 June 2019, available at www.crisisgroup.org/africa/279-tale-two-councils-strengthening-au-un-cooperation, 2.

[102] *Ibid.*, 22. To this point, after the unanimous adoption of Resolution 2568 on 12 March 2021, reauthorising the African Union Mission in Somalia, Niger nevertheless complained on behalf of the African members (Kenya, Niger, and Tunisia) and Saint Vincent and the Grenadines – known informally as the A3+1 – that their views had been rejected without explanation. He implored the Security Council to listen more to the African Union, and he criticised the penholder system as outmoded and at odds with managing peace and security. See 'Security Council Reauthorizes African Union Mission in Somalia, Unanimously Adopting Resolution 2568 (2021)', UN Doc. SC/14467, 12 March 2021.

TABLE 1 *Key Resolutions and Votes on Libya, 2011–21*

SC Resolution	Security Council Action/Decision	Votes Y (Yes); A (Abstention)			
		A3	China	Russia	P3
Res. 1970 (2011)	Imposes sanctions; calls for humanitarian aid; refers case to ICC	YYY	Y	Y	YYY
Res. 1973 (2011)	Establishes no-fly zone; imposes more sanctions	YYY	A	A	YYY
Res. 2009 (2011)	Acts to stop proliferation of portable surface-to-air missiles and other arms	YYY	Y	Y	YYY
Res. 2146 (2014)	Bans illicit export of crude oil from Libya	YYY	Y	Y	YYY
Res. 2298 (2016)	Authorises member states to destroy Libya's chemical weapons	YYY	Y	Y	YYY
Res. 2357 (2017)	Renews measures on arms embargo for a year	YYY	Y	Y	YYY
Res. 2441 (2018)	Extends mandate of experts panel on measures on illicit export of crude oil from Libya until 15 February 2020	YYY	A	A	YYY
Res. 2509 (2020)	Extends mandate of experts panel on measures on illicit export of crude oil from Libya until 30 April 2020	YYY	Y	A	YYY
Res. 2542 (2020)	Extends mandate of mission in Libya until 15 September 2021	YYY	A	A	YYY
Res. 2546 (2020)	Renews for a year authorisation for member states to inspect vessels on high seas off coast of Libya suspected of migrant smuggling	YYY	Y	Y	YYY
Res. 2570 (2021)	Strongly urges member states to withdraw all foreign forces and mercenaries without delay	YYY	Y	Y	YYY
Res. 2571 (2021)	Renews ban on illicit export of crude oil from Libya and extends mandate of experts panel until 15 August 2022	YYY	Y	Y	YYY

also coincided with the relative lack of strategic interest of the P2 in Libya, thus facilitating the NATO military action. Moreover, for the African Union, the Libyan crisis revealed the limitations of its still-evolving mechanisms for managing peace and security, collectively termed the African Peace and Security Architecture (APSA), established pursuant to the Peace and Security Protocol. The African Union could not invoke its own new normative guidelines, let alone trigger its nascent APSA mechanisms in probably the most significant crisis it has faced to date.

If Libya was intended to be the crucible in which the international community hoped to test the R2P principle, the outcome was far from a success. This has had catastrophic consequences for the ability of the Security Council to achieve consensus, especially among the P5, on how to address subsequent conflicts. The reluctance of four of the five BRICS countries to support Resolution 1973 foreshadowed a suspicion towards Western humanitarian intervention; this has led to normative resistance and become a barrier to the implementation of the R2P elsewhere.

After the Libyan intervention, all of the BRICS countries opposed the adoption of strong Security Council resolutions against Syria. The representative of Russia, speaking in a Security Council meeting on Syria on 4 October 2011, stated that the Syrian situation could not be considered separately from the Libyan experience, and worried that the NATO interpretation of Resolutions 1970 and 1973 could be a model for NATO actions in implementing the R2P principle in Syria.[103] The representative of South Africa also objected to the proposed Syrian resolutions on the basis that recent Security Council resolutions had been abused and that their implementation had gone beyond what was intended.[104] Unsurprisingly, on three occasions, China and Russia successively vetoed draft resolutions on Syria in the aftermath of the Libya campaign: on 4 October 2011,[105] 4 February 2012,[106] and 19 July 2012.[107] There is some agreement among commentators that perceptions of NATO's military overreach and overstepping of the UN mandate in Libya doomed the R2P, and that this may turn out to have been both the first and last use of the principle.[108] As I noted earlier, there is no consensus on the charge that NATO overstepped the UN mandate. I do think, however, that, from the perspective of international politics, perceptions of NATO's abuse of the authorisation are as important as the reality, and it is arguable that, besides Syria, the situations in Myanmar and Yemen might have invited R2P intervention but for Libya.

---

[103] UN Doc. S/PV.6627, 4 October 2011, 4.
[104] *Ibid.*, 11.
[105] *Ibid.*
[106] UN Doc. S/PV.6711, 4 February 2012.
[107] UN Doc. S/PV.6810, 19 July 2012.
[108] Ulfstein and Christiansen, 'The Legality of the NATO Bombing' (n. 71), 171.

The Security Council action on Libya has proved to be a setback in its role as a promoter of normative developments. The future trajectory of the R2P remains to be seen, but it is fair to say that it currently stands on a perilous porch. In the next section, I discuss the short-lived efforts made by two of the BRICS countries to advance their own alternative visions of the R2P following the Libya intervention: in the one case, as an official proposal; and in the other case, semi-officially. For the African Union, Libya did not prove to be a ready ground for testing its norm entrepreneurship either, as the promoter of the right of humanitarian intervention. Article 4(h) AU Constitutive Act had been hailed as evidence that the African Union could be a norm-creator and not just a norm-taker. Libya exposed the African Union's limitations in enforcing its own norms.

3. The BRICS Countries and the Responsibility to Protect Post-Libya

With the relative decline of the influence of the United States in the international realm over the last decade, new coalitions of states, dubbed 'rising powers', have emerged. The BRICS countries form one such coalition. Over the period since its first annual summit in 2009, the group has been viewed as progressing economically and strengthening the members' network of political influence, with the potential to establish new forms of security cooperation in line with their own normative perspectives. The rise of the BRICS has attracted the attention of international law scholars too. Some have asked questions such as whether the BRICS countries, as a set of rising powers, can contribute to the development of international law, and what their influence would entail for the conceptualisation and development of international law in the future.[109] In this context, attention has focused on the voting patterns of the BRICS countries in the United Nations as a way of empirically assessing their convergences and consensus in international norm-creation and policy-making. I pay attention to the BRICS in this discussion because they represent an alliance comprising the P2, who share views and voting patterns on many issues concerning Africa, and three states that are frontrunners among those aspiring to permanent seats on a reformed Security Council. Their collective positions, where appropriate, matter. As Aniruddha Rajput puts it: '[The] impact of BRICS countries on the future development of international law can be analysed on the basis of their participation and positions in existing

---

[109] See, e.g., Aniruddha Rajput, 'The BRICS as "Rising Powers" and the Development of International Law', in Krieger et al., *The International Rule of Law* (n. 14), 105–24 (105).

institutions and participation in norm-creation, along with the articulation of their vision of these institutions and norms."[110]

As already noted, although Resolution 1973 made only a passing reference to the R2P, the common view is that the Resolution was in effect an operationalisation of it. Below, I briefly recap the positions that the BRICS countries adopted on the R2P and the limited efforts to reconceptualise it since the Libya intervention.

The 2005 World Summit Outcome, which sets out the R2P framework negotiated by states since 2001, was adopted unanimously.[111] As endorsed by world leaders at the General Assembly in 2005, the R2P consists of three mutually reinforcing pillars.

- 'Pillar One' states that each state has a responsibility to protect its population from mass atrocity crimes (i.e., genocide, war crimes, crimes against humanity, and ethnic cleansing).
- 'Pillar Two' stipulates that the international community should encourage and assist states failing in their 'Pillar One' obligations.
- 'Pillar Three' provides that if a state is manifestly failing to protect its populations, the international community is prepared to take timely and decisive collective action on a case-by-case basis, in accordance with the UN Charter.[112]

Cai has noted that China's position on the R2P has evolved. He points out that, in its position paper issued in June 2005, China generally expressed its support for the R2P while requiring that any R2P action be authorised by the Security Council.[113]

Although China supported the 2005 World Summit Outcome, China stated in the first General Assembly debate on the R2P in 2009 that its implementation should be limited to the circumstances provided for in the World Summit Outcome, and should not contravene the principles of state sovereignty and non-interference in internal affairs of states. China stated categorically: 'No state must be allowed to unilaterally implement R2P.'[114] From its point of view, '[the]

[110] *Ibid.*, 111.
[111] 2005 World Summit Outcome, GA Res. 60/1 of 24 October 2005, UN Doc. A/RES/60/1.2005.
[112] *Ibid.*, paras 138–40.
[113] Cai, 'Maintaining Peace during a Global Power Shift', Chapter 1 in this volume, section V.D.2. See People's Republic of China, Position Paper on the United Nations Reforms, 7 June 2005, available at www.china.org.cn/english/government/131308.htm, sect. III.1. See also Rosemary Foot, 'The Responsibility to Protect (R2P) and its Evolution: Beijing's Influence in Norm Creation in Humanitarian Areas', *St. Antony's International Review* 6 (2011), 47–66 (49–50).
[114] UN Doc. A/63/PV.98, 24 July 2009, 23.

responsibility to protect remains a concept and does not constitute a norm of international law'.[115] China's position on the R2P has been consistent: it has time and again rejected it as a legal rule. China's unwillingness to embrace the R2P as an international legal norm is consistent with its espousal of the principles of state sovereignty and non-interference in the internal affairs of states, and with its preference for diplomatic and peaceful solutions to conflicts that threaten international peace and security. Thus, while not positively obstructing the development of this concept as such, China broadly and reluctantly endorsed the idea of invoking the concept only in certain exceptional circumstances to respond to gross human rights violations. Furthermore, China emphasised the capacity-building functions of the R2P and the need to ensure its limited application and differentiation from humanitarian intervention.

Russia, like China, formally espouses the position that maintaining the sovereignty of existing states is the most fundamental principle of diplomacy in the modern world. Thus while Russia also generally supported the R2P in both 2005 and 2009, it expressed concern about its implications on state sovereignty, noting that the development and implementation of the principle 'could significantly shape key trends that will determine the entire system of international relations and the international rule of law'.[116] It also warned 'against taking rash and hasty steps to apply that idea arbitrarily to specific countries and interpreting it too broadly'.[117] Russia shares with China its preference for diplomacy as the best route for resolving civil conflicts and crises, and insists that humanitarian intervention should only ever be sanctioned through the Security Council.[118]

As with China, Russia also favours the involvement of relevant regional organisations when making decisions on whether a particular situation really does represent a threat to international peace and security – or at least ensuring that the regional organisation legitimises them. This explains why Russia (along with China and South Africa) opposed a Security Council draft resolution on Myanmar in 2007,[119] which one regional organisation – namely, the Association of Southeast Asian Nations (ASEAN) – opposed, but abstained

---

[115] *Ibid.*, 24.
[116] UN Doc. A/63/PV.10, 28 July 2009, 12.
[117] *Ibid.*
[118] This claim was contradicted by Russia's behaviour when it justified its brief war with Georgia in 2008 as an act of humanitarian intervention to prevent mass killings in the disputed region of South Ossetia. The action was not authorised by the Security Council. See generally Gareth Evans, 'Russia, Georgia and the Responsibility to Protect', *Amsterdam Law Forum* 1 (2009), 25–8.
[119] 'Security Council Fails to Adopt Draft Resolution on Myanmar, Owing to Negative Votes by China and Russian Federation', UN Doc. SC/8939, 12 January 2007.

on Resolution 1973, which had the support of the two relevant regional
organisations (i.e., the African Union and the LAS). Despite their initial
hesitancy towards the R2P, Russia and China have come to formally embrace
it, but they both remain wary of Western intervention in internal conflicts after
the Cold War and are critical of armed intervention for humanitarian purposes. They are hesitant about supporting the third pillar of the R2P.

Of the remaining BRICS countries, India shares Russia's and China's
positions in insisting that the R2P should not be used as a pretext to weaken
the sovereignty of states and the principle of non-interference. Brazil and
South Africa also signed up to the 2005 consensus despite their misgivings
but have continued to insist that implementation of the concept should not
exceed the framework agreed at the World Summit.[120] As members of the
Security Council in 2011, the BRICS countries were therefore united both in
their formal support for the R2P and in their misgivings about the potential for
its abuse by powerful states intent on pursing a regime change agenda mas-
querading as humanitarian intervention. For the four BRICS countries that
abstained from the vote, the eventual removal of the Gaddafi regime confirmed their worst fears. In the immediate aftermath of the adoption of
Resolution 1973, India issued a statement expressing its strong belief that 'the
Security Council had passed a resolution authorising far-reaching measures
under Chapter VII of the Charter, with relatively little credible information on
the situation on the ground in Libya'.[121] As noted earlier, after its affirmative
vote, South Africa subsequently expressed concern about the way in which the
Resolution had been implemented.[122] Brazil and China responded in ways
that may yet impact the ongoing debate on the R2P.

Apart from the fact that the post-Libya backlash against the R2P was partly
responsible for the deadlock in the Security Council over Syria, as I suggest,
another consequence was that it reignited a debate about the strengths and
weaknesses of the third pillar of the R2P norm. In November 2011, Brazil
presented an initiative proposing a series of decision-making criteria and
monitoring mechanisms to guide the implementation of the R2P's coercive
measures under the third pillar.[123] Brazil's proposed alternative principle, the

---

[120] UN Doc. A/63/PV.10, 28 July 2009, 16–17.
[121] UN Doc. S/PV.6498, 17 March 2011, 6.
[122] UN Doc. S/PV.6627, 4 October 2011, 11.
[123] On 9 November 2011, the Brazilian permanent representative to the United Nations,
       Ambassador Maria Luisa Viotti, presented a letter with a concept note titled 'Responsibility
       while Protecting: Elements for the Development and Promotion of a Concept' during the
       12th Security Council Debate on the Protection of Civilians in Armed Conflict. See Letter
       dated 9 November 2011 from the Permanent Representative of Brazil to the United Nations
       addressed to the Secretary-General, with an Annex on Responsibility while Protecting:

'Responsibility while Protecting' (RwP), was regarded as a conceptual advancement on the R2P and was welcomed as a norm innovation from the Global South. However, Brazil's attempt at norm entrepreneurship did not last long, because of a combination of factors, including rejection by Western powers, different priorities and interests among the major Global South players, and, ironically, lack of follow-up by Brazil itself. Brazil effectively abandoned its advocacy of the RwP when its term on the Security Council ended and it lost its two main champions, Brazilian President Dilma Rousseff and Foreign Minister Antonio Patriota. Nevertheless, I agree with Van den Herik in characterising the RwP as an example of efforts by a non-permanent member of the Security Council to refine use-of-force decision-making and contribute to norm-making.[124]

The RwP was an attempt to articulate the need for responsible means of protection when military force is used in the name of collective security and humanitarianism. Part of the explanation for its short life and failure to generate sustained interest is scepticism on the part of some analysts, politicians, and policy-makers who questioned whether it represented an attempt to challenge or substitute the R2P, or was an addendum or complementary contribution to the R2P.[125] While most states welcomed it, the P3 were initially critical of it, seeing it as a direct criticism of the R2P and a challenge to the narrative that NATO's operation was a success.[126]

Although RwP as a political project is no longer on the United Nations' radar, its discursive influence can be seen in the General Assembly debate on the R2P in 2012, at which numerous states spoke favourably of the proposal as an advance on the R2P. Moreover, the UN Secretary-General explicitly addressed the Brazilian initiative and the concept in his report.[127] The limited

---

Elements for the Development and Promotion of a Concept, UN Doc. A/66/551–S/2011/701, 11 November 2011.

[124] Van den Herik, 'A Reflection on Institutional Strength', Chapter 2 in this volume, section IV.B.1 (p. 132). See generally Andrew Garwood-Gowers, 'The BRICS and the Responsibility to Protect in Libya and Syria', in Rowena Maguire, Bridget Lewis, and Charles Sampford (eds), *Shifting Global Powers and International Law: Challenges and Opportunities* (London: Routledge, 2013), 81–99.

[125] For a comprehensive analysis of RwP, see Andrés Serbin and Andrei Serbin Pont, 'Brazil's Responsibility while Protecting: A Failed Attempt of Global South Innovation?', *Pensamento Propio* 41 (2015), 171–92; Alyse Prawde, 'The Contribution of Brazil's "Responsibility while Protecting" Proposal to the "Responsibility to Protect" Doctrine', *Maryland Journal of International Law* 29 (2014), 184–209 (200–8).

[126] See Marcos Tourinho, Oliver Stuenkel, and Sarah Brockmeier, '"Responsibility while Protecting": Reforming R2P Implementation', *Global Society* 30 (2016), 134–50 (140).

[127] *Responsibility to Protect: Timely and Decisive Response*, Report of the Secretary-General, UN Doc. A/66/874-S/2012/578, 25 July 2012, paras 49–58.

academic commentary on the proposal suggests that, although short-lived, the RwP has helped to broaden and deepen policy debates about the R2P.[128] Some have suggested that it is the most significant recent development in the evolution of the R2P doctrine,[129] describing Brazil as an example of those non-Western agents whose contributions usually go overlooked, yet which are the most likely to address the legitimacy deficits of norms like the R2P.[130] Brazil's proposal may have suffered from the fact that, as some commentators argue, '[the] idea of responsibility while protecting remained largely abstract and was never sufficiently developed to materialise into specific proposals that could address the problems of collective security and human protection in practice'.[131] This assessment is correct: the constituent elements of RwP remained to be fleshed out from the abstract to the concrete, to distinguish it more clearly from the R2P.

China's decision not to veto Resolution 1973 came as something of a surprise to many observers, given its insistence on the primacy of the principles of sovereignty and non-intervention, and on the primacy of the first and second pillars of the R2P. I have argued already why the P2 found it unconscionable to veto the Resolution once it had the support of the A3. Unlike Brazil, post-Libya, China did not officially articulate an alternative principle to the R2P. However, at about the same time as Brazil's proposal was losing steam, in mid-2012, the official think tank of China's Ministry of Foreign Affairs floated a proposal titled 'Responsible Protection' (RP).[132] To date, China has not explicitly adopted the concept as its formal policy statement on the R2P. Nevertheless, there seems to be little doubt that, because of the official status of the think tank, China has endorsed it implicitly. The RP proposal is thus, to all intents and purposes, a 'semi-official' initiative of the Chinese government.[133] As a 'semi-official' initiative that China has not

---

[128]   See, e.g., Tourinho et al., '"Responsibility while Protecting"' (n. 126).

[129]   Derek McDougall, 'Responsibility while Protecting', *Global Responsibility to Protect* 6 (2014), 64–87.

[130]   Cristina Stefan, 'On Non-Western Norm Shapers: Brazil and the Responsibility while Protecting', *European Journal of International Security* 2 (2017), 88–110.

[131]   Tourinho et al., '"Responsibility while Protecting"' (n. 126), 149.

[132]   The originator of this proposal was Ruan Zongze, vice president of the China Institute for International Studies. He first published this as an op-ed article: Ruan Zongze, 'Responsible Protection', *China Daily News*, 15 March 2012, available at www.chinadaily.com.cn/opinion/2012-03/15/content_14838467.htm. He expanded and republished it as Ruan Zongze, 'Responsible Protection: Building a Safer World', *China International Studies* 34 (2012), 19–41.

[133]   For an overview of the origins and analysis of the RP concept, see generally Andrew Garwood-Gowers, 'China's "Responsible Protection" Concept: Reinterpreting the Responsibility to

formally advanced, the RP has been the subject of only limited public discussion and scholarly commentary.

Van den Herik and Cai both discuss this initiative in their contributions. One of the points on which we all converge is the characterisation of the rising China as a norm entrepreneur, even if we do not all use the specific term. One example that we all mention to varying degrees of detail is the RP proposal. Analysis of this putative doctrine by non-Chinese scholars is very limited, at least in the English language. This is an issue that might have benefited from a more expansive discussion in Cai's chapter in this volume, drawing upon his insights as a Chinese international law scholar and his familiarity with relevant Chinese-language sources, both official and unofficial. But it is also plausible that, given that the Chinese government did not deem it necessary to advance the proposal formally, there is not much else to excavate or opine about. This might explain the limited scholarly interest in or discussion of the RP concept: engagement with the issue might seem like a purely speculative exercise for the sake of continuing scholarly debate.

I would add only that the RP proposal is primarily concerned with the R2P's third pillar. Specifically, it provides a set of guidelines to constrain the implementation of non-consensual, coercive measures comprising six principles mostly drawn from, inter alia, just war theory, earlier R2P proposals, and Brazil's RwP. Not surprisingly, some have described the RP proposal as a repackaging of previous ideas, rather than an entirely original initiative, which seeks to narrow the circumstances in which non-consensual use of force can be applied for humanitarian purposes.[134] Since the Libya intervention, China has continued to engage with other states on the R2P instead of advancing its own proposal.

I conclude that the BRICS countries have not advanced a coordinated initiative on the R2P in the period since the Libyan conflict. They supported the RwP in the informal interactive discussions on the R2P in the General Assembly not only as members of the BRICS group but also as members of other alliances constituted for the purposes of advocating for common interests on global issues in the United Nations, such as the 'G77 and China'. Notwithstanding the demise of the RwP initiative and the absence of an officially sanctioned RP proposal, the elements advanced in these initiatives will remain relevant to future debates on the R2P. China's RP and Brazil's RwP demonstrate the growing assertiveness of rising, non-Western powers,

---

Protect (R2P) and Military Intervention for Humanitarian Purposes', *Asian Journal of International Law* 6 (2016), 89–118.

[134] See generally *ibid.*

such as the BRICS countries, in the post-Cold War international order and
their readiness to advance their own normative choices and preferences on
issues relating to collective security, sovereignty, and intervention.

I have not discussed the issue of regime change in any detail in this chapter.
And certainly not in as much detail as Cai discusses it in relation to the
implementation of Resolution 1973, the R2P principle, and the subsequent
Security Council debates over the failed draft resolutions on Syria.
Nevertheless, I am intrigued by two things in Cai's discussion: first, the choice
of the descriptive label he attaches to China as a 'norm "antipreneur"'; and
secondly, the suggestion that the Security Council might have served as a site
for the creation of a new norm of regime change, which China resisted. As he
puts it: 'In short, China has endeavoured to resist regime change as the norm
within or through the Security Council.'[135] As a metaphor, the notion of 'norm
"antipreneur"' is quite novel, but it is not clear to me if it means anything more
than the more familiar notion of 'persistent objector' in customary international law. Substantively, the argument that, in this specific instance,
China has acted to disrupt an emerging norm suggests that the Western
powers that pursued regime change in Libya – and presumably sought to do
the same in Syria – based their position on the assertion of the existence of
such a norm or a conscious disposition to establish it as a new norm.

I have argued that although the Libyan NATO intervention ended in
regime change with the fall of Gaddafi's regime, it was not designed as
such – at least in terms of Resolution 1973. This is not to dispute the fact
that, subsequently, political leaders of the P3 powers did not disguise their
preference for Gaddafi's departure nor that it was unreasonable to impute
regime change motives from their statements.[136] One would be hard put to
deny that, whatever its original motivation, the NATO operation quickly
descended into a project for regime change once Gaddafi's vulnerability and
the possibility of his being dislodged by the rebels became obvious. But none
of these states made statements on the record in the formal deliberations in the
Security Council proclaiming this objective. After Libya, China, Russia, and
South Africa were justified in being wary of the P3's motives in Syria.

The conclusion that China wants to resist the emergence of a new norm of
regime change in or through the Security Council implicates a broader
question about the legislative role of the Security Council in creating international law. The authority of the Security Council to adopt decisions with

---

[135]   Cai, 'Maintaining Peace during a Global Power Shift', Chapter 1 in this volume,
        section V.D.3 (p. 95).
[136]   See Obama et al., 'Libya's Pathway to Peace' (n. 86).

binding effect on the UN member states pursuant to Article 25 UN Charter is not in doubt. But, as Vera Gowland-Debbas opines, the Security Council's resolutions are not generally legislative in the sense of applying outside the framework of particular cases of restoration of international peace and security; moreover, unlike General Assembly resolutions, they cannot be said to reflect an emerging opinion or generality of the requisite state practice for the formation of customary international law.[137] It is simply inconceivable that the Security Council could ever use its powers under this provision to impose a new norm of regime change, for that would necessarily result in the violation of one or more principles of the Charter. The principles of non-intervention and the prohibition of the use of force clearly preclude the forcible removal of a government of a state by other states, unless the action is authorised by the Security Council as a case of self-defence against the concerned state, consistent with Article 51 UN Charter.

In my reading, China was not so much acting as a norm 'antipreneur' by opposing the proposed Security Council decisions on Syria but as a 'defender' of *existing* norms of international law, which purportedly underpin its foreign policy, including the principles of state sovereignty and non-intervention. China shares its formal commitment to these principles with Russia and its allies in the developing world – a point both Cai and I articulate in our discussions of the apparent partnership between the P2 members.[138]

C. *China's Position in the Security Council Regarding UN Peacekeeping in Africa*

Cai has examined China's expanding power and global interests, and its growing engagement within the Security Council. He has argued that, since the 2010s, China has exhibited a new image in the Security Council as evidenced by, among other things, its growing financial and personnel contributions to UN peacekeeping operations,[139] as well as its more frequent use of the veto.[140] I propose to build on these insights specifically with reference to the role that China currently plays in the Security Council with regard to the

---

[137] Vera Gowland-Debbas, 'The Limits of Unilateral Enforcement of Community Objectives in the Framework of UN Peace Maintenance', *European Journal of International Law* 11 (2000), 361–83 (377).

[138] See Cai, 'Maintaining Peace during a Global Power Shift', Chapter 1 in this volume, sections III.B (pp. 48–9, 56–8) and II.C.

[139] *Ibid.*, section V.A (p. 78–9).

[140] *Ibid.*, pp. 77–8

AU–UN partnership and peacekeeping operations in Africa in the post-Cold-War era.

As a P5 member, China has traditionally taken a reactive position on issues relating to peace and security in Africa, with the result that it has not been able to set the agenda let alone take up the role of penholder in the Security Council. Nevertheless, because of its advocacy and support for African causes, and its growing economic and strategic interests in Africa, the P3 often do consider China's (along with Russia's) positions to ensure smooth passage of proposed resolutions on situations in Africa. As Cai has noted, for the first decade of its membership of the Security Council – from 1971, when it replaced the Republic of China, until 1980 – China was largely a passive member, sitting on the fence when it came to peacekeeping issues. It usually abstained from voting on peacekeeping resolutions and did not contribute funds or personnel to UN missions. For some scholars, this stance of neutrality sometimes translated into inactivity, if not outright hostility to UN peace operations.[141] This changed in 1980, with Deng Xiaoping's policy of opening up to the West.[142] China launched this new policy with its first contribution to the United Nations's assessed funds for peacekeeping in 1982.

Since the end of the Cold War, China has increasingly deployed units to participate in UN peace operations. Beginning in 2000, China has contributed enabler units, such as engineering, logistics and medical personnel, to various UN missions around the world.[143] More recently, it has also deployed force protection units and troops, mostly in Africa, even as it has reiterated repeatedly its strict interpretation of the twin principles of respect for state sovereignty and non-interference in the internal affairs of states. While the numbers are relatively modest compared to those of other traditional troop-contributing countries, China's contributions to UN peace operations today surpass those of Russia, as well as the P3 members, who prefer to contribute funds, equipment, and logistics rather than military personnel. China's deployments in Africa have included UN missions in the Central African Republic (the Multidimensional Integrated Stabilization Mission in the Central African Republic, or MINUSCA), the Democratic Republic of the Congo (the Organization Stabilization Mission in the Democratic Republic

---

[141] See generally Zhengyu Wu and Ian Taylor, 'From Refusal to Engagement: Chinese Contributions to Peacekeeping in Africa', *Journal of Contemporary African Studies* 29 (2011), 137–54.

[142] Marissa Mastronianni, 'Growing Numbers of Chinese Blue Helmets: China's Changing Role within the Security Council', *Florida Journal of International Law* 27 (2015), 121–59 (128–9).

[143] Courtney Richardson, 'A Responsible Power? China and the U.N. Peacekeeping Regime', *International Peacekeeping* 18 (2011), 286–97 (288).

of the Congo, or its French acronym MONUSCO), Mali (the Multidimensional Integrated Stabilization Mission in Mali, or MINUSMA), Sudan (the UN–AU Mission in Darfur, or UNAMID), South Sudan (the United Nations Mission in South Sudan, or UNMISS), and Western Sahara (United Nations Mission for the Referendum in Western Sahara, or its French acronym MINURSO). As of 31 May 2021, the total personnel contributions of the P5 to UN peace missions worldwide stood at: China, 2,471; France, 622; United Kingdom, 550; Russia, 71; and United States, 31. The P2 powers have tended to adopt a common approach to African causes and to support the positions of the A3, and the African Union, in the Security Council. Yet China's participation in peacekeeping operations in Africa is well ahead that of Russia. Table 2 offers a snapshot of this comparison in six current or recent UN peace operations in Africa (the UNAMID mission ended on 31 December 2020).[144]

I should note that, outside the UN framework, China's support for the African Union in security matters is also manifested in the financial and logistical assistance it has given to AU peacekeeping missions, for example in Sudan and Somalia. Moreover, starting with a US$100 million pledge in 2015, China is committed to supporting the African Standby Force, which the African Union has been developing since 2004 as a key part of its APSA.[145]

TABLE 2 *China and Russia in African UN Peace Operations: Personnel Contributions as at 31 May 2021*

UN Mission	Police and Staff		Military Experts on Mission		Troops	
	China	Russia	China	Russia	China	Russia
MINUSCA	2	10	0	3	0	0
MINUSMA	9	0	0	0	413	0
MINURSO	0	0	15	10	9	0
MONUSCO	0	8	13	7	221	0
UNAMID	0	0	0	0	370	0
UNMISS	23	10	5	2	1031	0

[144] UN Peacekeeping, 'Troop and Police Contributors as at 31 May 2021', available at https://peacekeeping.un.org/en/troop-and-police-contributors.

[145] Symbolically, Chinese President Xi Jinping made the pledge for the contribution to AU peacekeeping at a Leaders' Summit on Peacekeeping at the United Nations, alongside other pledges to contribute to a UN peace and development fund. See 'President Xi Jinping Pledges at UN Show that China Can Meet its Global Responsibilities', *South China Morning Post*, 1 October 2015, available at www.scmp.com/comment/insight-opinion/article/1863079/president-xi-jinpings-pledges-un-show-china-can-meet-its/.

I think four factors explain China's change of policy and attitude towards engagement with UN peacekeeping in Africa. First, in the same year that the African states adopted the AU Constitutive Act establishing the African Union in 2000, China initiated the Forum on China–Africa Cooperation (FOCAC) as part of its new drive for economic cooperation with the African continent.[146] In his opening speech to the first ministerial FOCAC meeting on 10 October 2000, President Jiang Zeming reaffirmed the two principles of state sovereignty and non-interference as among the guiding principles of its relations with African states.[147] At the same time, one of the most significant normative changes brought about by establishment of the African Union was the move away from the principle of non-interference, which had been enshrined in Article III(2) OAU Charter, to the principle of non-indifference articulated in Article 4(h) AU Constitutive Act. This normative shift allowed China to adopt a more flexible approach towards the question of non-interference and primacy of state sovereignty, and it removed the pretext for China's reluctance to get involved in peace operations in Africa as a violation of these principles.

The second factor is China's growing economic power and its extensive economic, investment, and trading relations across Africa – especially over the two decades since FOCAC's inception.[148] China has been the African continent's largest trading partner and source of direct foreign investment since 2000.[149] By 2016, for example, China's exports to and imports from Africa stood in real terms at 15 per cent and 20 per cent of Chinese global trade estimates, respectively; roughly this translated to US$82.9 billion, while imports from the continent were valued at US$54.3 billion.

The need to protect its economic interests in some of the fragile states in Africa that face security challenges is driving China's increasing participation in, and contributions to, peacekeeping in Africa. To this point, in 2011 a non-governmental organisation noted:

> [In] some more general ways, peacekeepers do serve China's economic interests: they promote peace in countries where Chinese banks and

---

[146] Garth Shelton and Farhana Paruk, *The Forum on China–Africa Cooperation: A Strategic Opportunity*, ISS Monograph No. 156 (Pretoria: Institute of Security Studies, 2008), available at www.files.ethz.ch/isn/103618/mono156full.pdf, 74.

[147] Jiang Zemin, 'China and Africa Usher in the Century Together', Opening speech to Forum on China-Africa Cooperation, First Ministerial Conference, Beijing, 10 October 2000, available at www.focac.org/chn/ljhy/dyjbzjhy/hyqk12009/.

[148] See generally Ian Taylor, *The Forum on China-Africa Cooperation (FOCAC)* (London: Routledge, 2012).

[149] Wenjie Chen, David Dollar, and Heiwai Tang, 'Why is China Investing in Africa? Evidence from the Firm Level', *The World Bank Economic Review* 32 (2018), 610–32.

commercial actors have made significant investments and have an interest in restoring stability. They also improve bilateral relations with governments that have given their consent to peace-keeping missions.[150]

Three years after publication of this commentary, unconfirmed reports emerged in 2014 to the effect that China had sought to deploy UN peace-keepers to protect its oil instalments in South Sudan following allegations that Chinese workers had suffered terrorist attacks there.[151]

Thirdly, China's growing support for, and participation in, peacekeeping in Africa can be seen as an aspect of its ideological positioning and self-identification as a leader of the Global South and a champion of South–South cooperation. Its new assertiveness as a P5 member has not, however, diminished its preference for diplomatic and peaceful solutions in inter-state and intra-state conflicts in Africa or its traditional support for the principle of 'African solutions to African problems'. By maintaining this position, China can demonstrate not only that its national economic interests in Africa are not the sole determining factor in its decision-making, but also that it is a responsible power invested in African development and security. Furthermore, unlike some of the P5 powers that have been accused of impos-ing paternalistic solutions in Africa, China is more inclined to take its cue from African states when addressing peace and security issues there. It is thus more willing to participate in peace operations that have unmistakable buy-in and support from the A3 and the African Union, recognising the central role of the African states themselves. Significantly, China has never used its veto to block a resolution on peace and security issues or peacekeeping in Africa. My discussion here reinforces Cai's analysis of China's growing assertiveness in the Security Council, as evidenced in its increasing participation in voting on resolutions and contributions to UN peacekeeping missions in terms of budget and personnel.[152]

Fourthly, China's concerns about security in some states in Africa go beyond the protection of its economic interests and investments. For example,

---

[150] Saferworld, *China's Growing Role in African Peace and Security*, January 2011, available at www.saferworld.org.uk/resources/publications/500-chinas-growing-role-in-african-peace-an d-security.

[151] This led to domestic pressure on the government to protect its citizens abroad. See Nicholas Bariyo, 'China Deploys Troops in South Sudan to Defend Oil Fields, Workers', *Wall Street Journal*, 9 September 2014, available at www.wsj.com/articles/china-deploys-troops-in-south-sudan-to-defend-oil-fields-workers-1410275041; Alice Su, 'China's Business and Politics in South Sudan', *Foreign Affairs*, 6 June 2016, available at www.foreignaffairs.com/articles/sout h-sudan/2016-06-06/chinas-business-and-politics-south-sudan.

[152] See Cai, 'Maintaining Peace during a Global Power Shift', Chapter 1 in this volume, section V.A.

one can explain its participation in the operation in Mali (MINUSMA) in terms of another phenomenon: the global fight against terrorism. It is trite that the events of 11 September 2001 (i.e., 9/11) galvanised an international consensus on the fight against terrorism. Some commentators have observed that the 2001 terrorist attacks helped to forge a more united front between the P2 and P3 in peace operations on the African continent, especially when the conflicts in question have an element of international terrorism.[153] To this, I would add that China's support for such operations becomes more certain when African states themselves request the involvement of the Security Council to authorise action to help them deal with terrorist threats or attacks in their territories.

I also believe that, for China, as for Russia, participation in UN-led efforts to fight terrorism in Africa and elsewhere affords a cover of legitimacy for their own campaigns against alleged terrorist groups at home (for China) or in the so-called near-abroad (for Russia). The P2 supported all of the resolutions on Mali and the somewhat controversial re-hatting of AU peacekeepers to establish MINUSMA. Like the other members of the Security Council, they viewed the crisis as arising not only from a failure of governance that lay the conditions for a coup d'état but also, and more importantly, because of a terrorist insurgence mounted by three groups operating in northern Mali and across the Sahel region. They understood that the insurgency by Al-Qaeda in the Islamic Maghreb (AQIM), the Movement for Unity and Jihad in West Africa (MUJWA), and Ansar Dine posed a serious threat to the peace and security of the broader region, and they supported the ECOWAS and AU plans for political negotiations, as well as, later, the Security Council proposal for a robust mission.[154] To be sure, both had concerns with some aspects of the mission – in particular, the African Union was not altogether happy with the timing and process of handing over an AU peace operation to the United Nations. Yet neither China nor Russia considered abstaining from, let alone vetoing, the re-hatting resolution.[155] Moreover, neither raised their usual concerns about interventionist action that ignored state sovereignty. In any case, any objection on that ground would have been untenable because the

---

[153] Not all conflicts that have an element of international terrorism in Africa have led to the establishment of UN peace operations. An example is the jihadist terrorist group so-called Islamic State in West Africa (commonly known as Boko Haram), which has been operating for two decades in north-eastern Nigeria and, intermittently, in Chad, Niger, and Cameroon. In addition to Boko Haram, terrorist organisations operating in the Sahel region include Al-Qaeda in the Islamic Maghreb, Al-Mourabitoun, and Movement for Unity and Jihad in West Africa.

[154] SC Res. 2100 of 25 April 2013, UN Doc. S/RES/2100(2013).

[155] SC Res. 2295 of 29 June 2016, UN Doc. S/RES/2295(2016).

beleaguered Mali government had requested the intervention by the United Nations and France.[156]

In conclusion, I submit that the new Chinese assertiveness in the Security Council that Cai has comprehensively discussed has not been detrimental to the African Union's efforts to forge an institutionalised and more effective strategic partnership with the United Nations. On the contrary, China has been among the foremost advocates in the Security Council for strengthening this partnership and for the notion of connecting the centre to the periphery in matters pertaining to the maintenance of international peace and security – perhaps more so than any other P5 member. With the pivot to the principle of non-indifference by African states under the AU Constitutive Act, China has increasingly adopted a more flexible position regarding the principle of state sovereignty and become more tolerant of African peace operations, including robust peacekeeping mandated by the Security Council. The outcome of the convergence of China's economic and strategic interests in Africa and its rise as a global power and a more assertive P5 member has been the elevation of issues and positions advocated by the African Union, the A3, and key African actors to the Security Council for debates. These debates do not always yield the desired outcomes – but they do open the door for China and the A3, along with other like-minded members, to act collectively as agenda-setters and norm-shapers, rather than simply as norm-takers following an agenda and resolutions crafted by others as penholders.

The other chapters in this volume also both comprehensively address the issue of sanctions, albeit from different perspectives. Cai has offered a comprehensive history of China's participation in the adoption of sanctions resolutions by the Security Council and its general opposition to the imposition of sanctions. Van den Herik has noted that there is a divide regarding unilateral sanctions, which she describes as a tool mostly used by the West.[157] African states have tended to join China in opposing unilateral sanctions, especially, viewing the trend as encouraging a turn to unilateralism.

The reticence of African states towards some UN sanctions must be understood in its proper context. In the post-Cold-War era, the highest number of

---

[156] This element makes the Mali operation, in part, a case of intervention by invitation. See Olivier Corten, 'Intervention by Invitation: The Expanding Role of the Security Council', in Dino Kritsiotis, Olivier Corten, and Gregory H. Fox, *Armed Intervention and Consent*, Max Planck Trialogues on the Law of Peace and War (Anne Peters and Christian Marksen, series eds), vol. 4 (Cambridge: Cambridge University Press, 2023), 101–78 (146–60).

[157] Cai, 'Maintaining Peace during a Global Power Shift', Chapter 1 in this volume, sections V.A and V.C.4; Van den Herik, 'A Reflection on Institutional Strength', Chapter 2 in this volume, section V.B.4.

UN sanctions have targeted African states, entities, groups of people, and individuals. A recent study found that, of the 63 UN targeted sanctions imposed in the first decade after the Cold War, between 1991 and 2013, 43 (68 per cent) were applied against African states.[158] The data also reveals that UN sanctions in Africa are characterised by features that set them apart from other UN sanctions regimes and practice. In particular, whereas non-African sanctions pursue a variety of goals, UN sanctions in Africa are imposed to support the Security Council's primary objective of addressing threats to international peace and security in the form of internal armed conflicts, mostly in the context of UN peace support operations.[159]

I agree with Van den Herik that unilateral sanctions are likely to remain a divisive issue in the United Nations. African members of the Security Council may continue to oppose or abstain on sanctions resolutions (as South Africa did on Resolution 1706 on Darfur and on a draft resolution on Myanmar, which China and Russia vetoed in 2007). The exceptions are situations in which the AU member states themselves have requested the sanctions, for example to deal with rebel and terrorist groups, such as Al-Shabab in Somalia, as part of the African Union's peace operations supported or authorised by the United Nations.

D. *Russia's Rising Presence in Africa*

I have noted above that China and Russia share a self-image as advocates and supporters of Africa's causes in the Security Council. In their relations with Africa, both seek to present themselves as an alternative to the West, while playing down accusations that they wish to recreate Cold-War-era proxy state clientelism or to initiate a neo-colonial partition. As the world's second biggest economy and superpower, China has a clear advantage over Russia in its quest for influence. Given that, in the decade between 2005 and 2015, its trade and investment in Africa witnessed a growth of 185 per cent, however, the phenomenon of Russia's rising presence in Africa cannot be doubted.[160]

This rise can be examined from three perspectives: economic/trade (the entry of Russian companies in the extractive industries); diplomatic/political (engagement between Russia and African countries bilaterally and multilaterally

---

[158]   See generally Thomas Biersteker, Sue Eckert, Marcos Tourinho, and Zuzana Hudáková, 'UN Targeted Sanctions Datasets (1991–2013)', *Journal of Peace Research* 55 (2018), 404–12.

[159]   See Andrea Charron and Clara Portela, 'The UN, Regional Sanctions and Africa', *International Affairs* 91 (2015), 1369–85 (1371–4).

[160]   Ronak Gopaldas, 'Russia and Africa Meet Again', *ISS Today*, 13 March 2018, available at https://issafrica.org/iss-today/russia-and-africa-meet-again/.

through the Russia–Africa summit format); and military/security (direct involvement by the state and through state-linked private military contractors). These engagements enable Russia to pursue three goals: projecting power on the global stage, accessing raw materials and natural resources, and increasing its arms exports and security footprint. These interests are intertwined, but since the focus of this chapter is on issues of peace and security, in this section I will limit my brief comments to Russia's involvement in the military and security sectors.

In October 2019, Russia hosted the inaugural Russia–Africa Summit in Sochi, which was attended by 43 heads of state or government. In hosting the summit, Russia was following the template of organising and institutionalising Africa summits set by other powers who seek to increase their engagement on the African continent, such as the European Union, China, France, India, Japan, and Turkey. According to Russian sources, the summit spawned $12.5 billion business deals, largely in arms and grains.[161] Despite half of the AU membership voting to condemn its invasion of Ukraine at the United Nations,[162] Russia still sees Africa as a powerful voting bloc that can strengthen the Kremlin's image on the international stage. Unsurprisingly, even as the war in Ukraine was ongoing, Russia hosted the second Russia–Africa Summit, initially scheduled for October 2022, in St. Petersburg on 27 and 28 July 2023.[163]

Since 2015, Russia has been the most dominant supplier of arms to Africa, accounting for 49 per cent in sales to at least 21 countries.[164] In terms of its military presence through participation in UN peacekeeping missions in Africa, Russia lags way behind China, as Table 2 shows. But even its relatively modest personnel contributions to UN peacekeeping worldwide, which stood at 71 as at 31 May 2021, is more than that of the United States, at 31. More than

---

[161] Danielle Paquette, 'As the U.S. Looks Elsewhere, Russia Seeks a Closer Relationship with Africa', *Washington Post*, 25 October 2019, available at www.washingtonpost.com/world/afri ca/as-the-us-looks-elsewhere-russia-seeks-a-closer-relationship-with-africa/2019/10/25/7e329124 -f69e-11e9-b2d2-1f37c9d82dbb_story.html.

[162] See below, section IV.B.

[163] In what was seen by some commentators as evidence of Russia's waning influence and the political fallout from the war in Ukraine, the second Russia–Africa Summit was attended by only 17 African heads of state (out of 49 delegations) – a significant drop from the 43 who attended the 2019 Summit. See, e.g., Vadim Zaytsev, 'Second Russia–Africa Summit Lays Bare Russia's Waning Influence', *Carnegie Politika*, 31 July 2023, available at https://carne gieendowment.org/politika/90294.

[164] See Mark Episkopos, 'How Russia Became Africa's Dominant Arms Dealer', *The National Interest*, 23 February 2021, available at https://nationalinterest.org/blog/buzz/how-russia-beca me-africa%E2%80%99s-dominant-arms-dealer-178656.

half of these personnel are deployed in Africa.[165] As regards the presence of Russian private military contractors, the Wagner Group has become the vanguard of a major Russian push into Africa and is currently operating in several states, including Central African Republic (CAR), Libya, Madagascar, Mali, Mozambique, and Sudan. The Wagner Group's operations were said to be funded by a company owned by the late Yevgeny Prigozhin, a Kremlin-linked oligarch and former close confidant of Russian President Vladimir Putin. Prigozhin died in a plane crash on 23 August 2023. The company's involvement in the mining, gas, and oil industries in CAR, Libya, Mali, and Sudan helps to finance its operations.[166] It is possible to draw the general conclusion that Russia's resurgence in Africa has benefited largely from the rise of Islamist terrorism in parts of the continent, from the Sahel in the west to Mozambique in the east. Russia has taken advantage of fragile states and ongoing conflicts to secure arms deals and concessions, formally through negotiating military agreements with governments and informally through deals negotiated by private military contractors – principally, the Wagner Group.[167]

The presence of private military contractors in these countries raises certain questions from an international law perspective and presents political problems for Russia, the concerned African states, and international community. First, legally speaking, private military contractors are not mercenaries, provided that they are properly registered as business entities under the relevant laws of the concerned states. The Wagner Group, which operates as a network of companies and individuals, does not officially exist because it is not registered in Russia or anywhere else. Yet it is common cause that, as a paramilitary group, it operates in support of Russian interests or foreign policy and has close links to the Russian government. Consequently, it is generally regarded by the outside world as a network of Russian-backed mercenaries.

Howsoever one views the Wagner Group, its operations raise questions under international law, including its status as a non-state actor involvement in armed conflict, its responsibility for violations of international humanitarian law and international human rights law, and the prohibition of

---

[165] See above, n. 143.

[166] See Kimberly Marten, 'Russia's Use of Semi-State Security Forces: The Case of the Wagner Group', *Post-Soviet Affairs* 35 (2019), 181–204 (196–8); Declan Walsh, 'How Russia's Wagner Group is Expanding in Africa', *New York Times*, 31 May 2022, available at www.nytimes.com/2022/05/31/world/africa/wagner-group-africa.html.

[167] Marten, 'Russia's Use of Semi-State Security Forces' (n. 166). See generally Ahmed Albassoussy, 'The Growing Russian Role in Sub-Saharan Africa: Interests, Opportunities and Limitations', *Journal of Humanities and Applied Social Sciences* 4 (2021), 251–70.

mercenarism under relevant UN[168] and AU[169] treaties. The Wagner Group has been accused of human rights violations, including extrajudicial killings and torture, and civilian massacres in the CAR and Mali, by other governments and UN human rights experts.[170] Russia's use of Wagner Group mercenaries creates an enabling environment in which countries that are parties to the UN convention (Libya) and the OAU convention (Libya, Madagascar, and Sudan) can violate their treaty obligations.

Secondly, there are political problems arising from alleged contacts and interactions between private military contractors and UN peacekeepers, which the host governments encourage. In both the CAR and Mali, UN human rights experts have been alarmed by the 'proximity and interoperability' between the contractors and the UN peacekeepers.[171] The United States and the European Union have also complained about their presence and activities, leading them to impose sanctions against the Group.[172]

Overall, from the perspective of African states, Russia's increasing presence in Africa is beneficial. For many, Russia is a partner they are familiar with from their anti-colonial struggles. For some, Russia allows them to diversify their sources of foreign investment to avoid becoming too dependent on their Western partners or China, India, and others. For others still, an even more attractive aspect of these engagements is that, unlike Western governments, Moscow does not offer them its economic and military support with political conditionalities requiring them to respect democracy, human rights, and the rule of law. On the contrary, Russia mostly seems to target countries with abysmal records of democracy and good governance.

---

[168] International Convention against the Recruitment, Use, Financing and Training of Mercenaries, 4 December 1989, 2163 UNTS 75.

[169] OAU Convention for the Elimination of Mercenarism in Africa, 3 July 1977, 1490 UNTS 95.

[170] See Jason Burke and Emmanuel Akinwotu, 'Russian Mercenaries Linked to Civilian Massacres in Mali', *The Guardian*, 4 May 2022, available at www.theguardian.com/world/2022/may/04/russian-mercenaries-wagner-group-linked-to-civilian-massacres-in-mali. See also Stephanie Nebehay and Aaron Ross, 'U.N. Experts Alarmed by Russian Security Contractors' "Abuses" in Central Africa', *Reuters*, 31 March 2021, available at www.reuters.com/article/us-centralafrica-security-russia/u-n-experts-alarmed-by-russian-security-contractors-abuses-in-ce ntral-africa-idUSKBN2BN288.

[171] UN Office of the High Commissioner for Human Rights, 'CAR: Experts Alarmed by Government Use of "Russian Trainers", Close Contacts with UN Peacekeepers', 31 March 2021, available at www.ohchr.org/en/press-releases/2021/03/car-experts-alarmed-gov ernments-use-russian-trainers-close-contacts-un.

[172] Robin Emmott, 'EU Hits Russian Mercenary Group Wagner with Sanctions', *Reuters*, 13 December 2021, available at www.reuters.com/world/europe/eu-hits-russian-mercenary-gr oup-wagner-with-sanctions-2021-12-13/.

E. *AU–UN Collaboration in Fighting International Terrorism through Peace Operations*

1. The OAU Convention on the Prevention and Combating of Terrorism

The OAU, the African Union's predecessor, began addressing the threat of international terrorism about a decade prior to the 9/11 terrorist attacks in the United States. The outbreak of the Algerian civil war in late 1991 awakened other African countries to the potential threat posed by religious fundamentalism and extremism to peace and security within their territories and regions. In response to this, the OAU adopted two instruments: first, the Resolution on the Strengthening of Cooperation and Coordination among African States, adopted on 1 July 1992;[173] and secondly, the Declaration on a Code of Conduct for Inter-African Relations of 15 June 1994.[174] Although non-binding, both instruments called upon the OAU member states to increase their cooperation and coordination to combat terrorism, and both condemned those states that were sponsoring terrorism.[175]

On 7 August 1998, terrorist bombings targeting American embassies in Nairobi and Dar es Salaam went off within minutes of each other, killing many people. These attacks prompted a debate within the OAU on the need to elaborate a legally binding instrument to promote international cooperation on all aspects of counter-terrorism. The following year, at its summit in Algiers, the OAU adopted the OAU Convention on the Prevention and Combating of Terrorism.[176]

Under the OAU Terrorism Convention, states parties undertake to enact national legislation and establish as criminal offences certain acts as required. The OAU Terrorism Convention is significant, especially because it seeks to codify counter-terrorism norms and to consolidate common standards for the fight against terrorism in Africa. The Algiers summit also adopted the Algiers Declaration, which, among other things, acknowledged that terrorism is a '[flagrant] violation of human rights and fundamental freedoms' and '[poses] serious threats to the stability of [states] as well as to international peace and security'.[177]

The OAU Terrorism Convention entered into force on 6 December 2002 – six months after the inauguration of the African Union. The African Union thus

---

[173] OAU Doc. AHG/Res. 213 (XXVIII), 1 July 1992.
[174] OAU Doc. AHG/Decl. 2 (XXX), 15 June 1992.
[175] *Ibid.*, para. 10.
[176] Adopted 14 July 1999, entered into force 6 December 2002.
[177] OAU Doc. AHG/Decl. 1 (XXXV), 14 July 1999.

inherited the legacy of the OAU in addressing terrorism and the challenge of implementing the normative framework set out in the Convention. A glaring omission, however, was that the treaty did not provide for a monitoring mechanism to track states' compliance with it. Two different instruments subsequently remedied this omission. The first was the Peace and Security Protocol, adopted in 2002, which designated the PSC as the monitoring mechanism.[178] This decision followed logically from the African Union's characterisation of the fight against terrorism as an aspect of the maintenance of regional peace and security (thus following the approach of the United Nations, where responsibility for dealing with terrorism matters rests with the Security Council).

Following the adoption of the Peace and Security Protocol, and in anticipation of the ratification of the OAU Terrorism Convention, the African Union adopted a Plan of Action of the African Union for the Prevention and Combating of Terrorism in Algiers on 14 August 2002. The Plan of Action addresses some key provisions of Security Council Resolution 1373,[179] and it establishes a network of cooperation and exchange of information among AU member states on various aspects of counter-terrorism activities. Alongside the adoption of the Plan of Action, the meeting also considered a proposal to establish the African Centre for the Study and Research on Terrorism (ACSRT).[180]

In 2004, the African Union adopted the second binding instrument, the Protocol to the OAU Convention for the Prevention and Combating of Terrorism.[181] The Protocol on Terrorism reaffirmed the role of the PSC as the mechanism for monitoring the implementation of the OAU Terrorism Convention and established the ACSRT. The ACSRT's mandate includes conducting assessment missions to various AU member states, to ascertain their counter-terrorism capacity and compliance with the OAU Terrorism Convention and other international legal instruments, and providing advice on necessary action. One of the international pre-eminent partners that the ACRST has engaged with since its establishment is the UN Office of Counter-Terrorism.[182]

---

[178]   Art. 7(1)(i) Peace and Security Protocol (n. 23).

[179]   SC Res. 1373 of 28 September 2001, UN Doc. S/RES/1373(2001).

[180]   The African Centre for the Study and Research on Terrorism (ACSRT) was established under section H, paras 19–21 of the AU Plan of Action and pursuant to relevant decisions adopted by the AU Assembly and Executive Council: AU Doc. Assembly/AU/Dec.15 (II); AU Doc. EX.CL/Dec.13 (II); AU Doc. EX.CL/Dec.82 (IV); and AU Doc. EX.CL/Dec.126 (V). It was inaugurated on 14 October 2004.

[181]   Protocol to the OAU Convention for the Prevention and Combating of Terrorism; adopted 2 July 2004, entered into force 26 February 2014, 3269 UNTS.

[182]   The most recent engagement between the two bodies was the joint Online Workshop on Protecting Vulnerable Targets against Terrorist Attacks, 12–13 December 2022. See 'UNOCT and ACSRT Convene African Union Member States to Strengthen Resilience of Vulnerable

The African Union's policy to combat terrorism rests on three assumptions. The first is that the fight to prevent, and eventually eradicate, terrorism in Africa requires cooperation at every level and in every respect. The second premise is that the United Nations has the primary responsibility for leading the fight for the prevention and combatting of terrorism globally. Thirdly and relatedly, as a regional body, the African Union must prosecute its fight against terrorism on the continent in coordination with the international community, as part of the global anti-terrorism regimes led by the United Nations. Consequently, the African Union's actions and initiatives in counter-terrorism are influenced not only by the realities within African states but also by the global realities and the policies and actions of the United Nations, as decided and mandated by the Security Council.

To my mind, the peacekeeping operations in Mali and Somalia provide the most appropriate illustration of the cooperation between the African Union and the United Nations in responding to threats to peace and security arising wholly or partly from transnational terrorism in Africa. But I should qualify this with recognition that the 2015 Report of the UN Secretary-General's High-Level Independent Panel on Peace Operations explicitly recommended that UN peacekeeping forces not be mandated to conduct counter-terrorism operations and that, where a UN mission operates in parallel with counter-terrorism forces, the respective roles of each presence be clearly delineated.[183] UN Secretary-General António Guterres subsequently echoed this, noting: '[We] need to understand that UN peacekeeping has limits. We face more and more situations where we need peace enforcement and counter-terrorism operations that can only be carried out by our partners – namely, the African Union and various subregional configurations.'[184] The Secretary-General was right to point out that UN peacekeeping has limits. The question is: should it be left to the African Union and subregional organisations to lead counter-terrorism operations?

An analysis of AU peace operations shows that, from the first deployment in Burundi in 2003 until 2010, all AU missions deployed by the African Union – other than the African Union Mission in Somalia (AMISOM) – were similar to traditional UN peacekeeping, with no counter-terrorism mandates. As Jide

---

Targets against Terrorist Attacks', available at www.un.org/counterterrorism/events/unoct-a nd-acsrt-convene-african-union-member-states-strengthen-resilience-vulnerable-targets.

[183] *Uniting Our Strengths for Peace: Politics, Partnership and People*, Report of the High-Level Independent Panel on United Nations Peace Operations, UN Doc. A/70/95-S/2015/446, 16 June 2015, 47–8.

[184] Statement of Secretary-General on Strengthening Peacekeeping Operations in Africa, UN Doc. S/PV.8407, 20 November 2018, 4.

Okeke has noted, the African Union increasingly began authorising counter-terrorism operations in 2011; by 2015, it was authorising more counter-terrorism operations than traditional peacekeeping missions.[185] But authorising such missions is not necessarily the same thing as leading them or carrying out the counter-terrorism operations. Quite apart from the issue of resources and capabilities, I think it is wrong for the African Union to assume that responsibility. The AU peacekeepers should no more be leading counter-terrorism operations than should UN peacekeepers. The human and financial costs associated with such operations in Africa – as the African Union learned during its AMISOM operations – are simply beyond the organisation's means and are unsustainable in terms of its envisaged role under its own counter-terrorism regime.

Returning to the question I posed above, it is my view that the PSC and the Security Council should work collaboratively to authorise counter-terrorism operations when required in AU-led peace operations. Authorising an operation is necessary to give it political legitimacy, to facilitate more enablers and supporters for the operation, but the authorising organ does not assume full responsibility for or command and control of the operation and resources. The African Union's responsibility should be to provide support to states rather than to take full command and control of counter-terrorism operations. By complementing the host state's own military and security institutions, instead of substituting for them, the AU peacekeeping operations would be consistent with the objectives and policy of the AU counter-terrorism strategy set out in its normative instruments. That said, it should be possible, within the framework of AU–UN collaboration, for the two organisations to share the role of mandating authority, understanding that UN peacekeeping has its limits.

Although they do not engage in counter-terrorism operations as such, in carrying out their mandate of protection of civilians against imminent attacks and enabling national militaries to defend their populations against armed terrorist attacks, UN peacekeepers in effect contribute to the counter-terrorism fight, broadly speaking. This has been the case with the UN peace operation in Mali and the UN-authorised AU mission in Somalia. The transitioning of an AU-led mission to a UN-led operation in Mali demonstrates both the possibilities and challenges of collaboration between the periphery, the African Union, and the centre, the Security Council, in the shared objective of the maintenance of international peace and security.

---

[185]   Jide Okeke, *Policy Brief: Repositioning the AU's Role in Counter-Terrorism Operations* (Pretoria: Institute for Security Studies, 2019), 4.

2. AU and UN Peace Operations as Responses to Threats of International Terrorism in Africa

A) THE MULTIDIMENSIONAL INTEGRATED STABILISATION MISSION IN MALI (MINUSMA). In early January 2012, a Tuareg separatist movement that had emerged in November 2011, Mouvement national de libération de l'Azawad (MNLA), started attacking and capturing villages and localities in northern Mali amidst an emerging political and security crisis in the country. The crisis resulted from unhappiness among the military with a faltering civilian government. The MNLA proclaimed an 'independent state of Azawad' on 6 April 2012.[186] The declaration of the separatist state came on the heels of a military coup that overthrew President Amadou Toumani Touré's government on 21 March.

With the African Union's backing, ECOWAS initiated negotiations to put in place a military plan to deal with the crisis. The Security Council initially supported the ECOWAS and AU efforts, encouraging them to coordinate with the transitional authorities of Mali for the restoration of constitutional order.[187] Subsequently, it adopted a resolution endorsing UN military support for the ECOWAS mission, and it requested the Secretary-General to provide military and security planners to assist ECOWAS and the African Union, in close consultation with Mali's neighbours, interested bilateral partners, and international organisations.[188] Later, in December 2012, the Security Council authorised the deployment of the African-led International Support Mission in Mali (AFISMA), which subsumed the ECOWAS mission, with a mandate to support the national military forces.[189] Between July 2012 and June 2020, the Security Council adopted ten resolutions on Mali unanimously, with no expressions of concern by any of the Security Council members regarding their content or language.

The unanimity over the Mali resolutions can be explained in several ways. First of all, the resolutions were approving or endorsing intervention requested by the host government, which therefore met one of the basic principles of UN peacekeeping – namely, consent by the host state.[190] The legitimacy of the new authorities in Bamako to request assistance from the Security Council and the international community, although initially questioned by some states, was accepted by the Security Council as providing a provisional basis

---

[186] See Baz Lecocq and Georg Klute, 'Tuareg Separatism in Mali', *International Journal* 68 (2013), 424–34 (430).
[187] SC Res. 2056 of 5 July 2012, UN Doc. S/RES/2056(2012), para. 1.
[188] SC Res. 2071 of 12 October 2012, UN Doc. S/RES/2071(2012).
[189] SC Res. 2085 of 20 December 2012, UN Doc. S/RES/2085(2012).
[190] Corten, 'Intervention by Invitation' (n. 156).

for the military operation. Members of the Security Council – in particular, the P2, who had traditionally been loath to support interventions or peace-keeping operations that they viewed as a violation of the principles of non-interference and state sovereignty – were assuaged by this.

Secondly, the support of the A3 and both ECOWAS and the African Union for the proposals was critical. Indeed, it helped that the A3 states, Morocco, South Africa, and Togo, partnered with other Security Council members, including the traditional penholders, France, the United Kingdom, and the United States, in drafting the resolutions.[191]

Thirdly, and most importantly, the United Nations and the African regional and subregional organisations, as well as other major actors, all regarded the Mali operation as a necessary collective fight against transnational terrorism with a potential to destabilise the greater Sahara–Sahel region. As noted earlier, the P2 states have been as keen to join the post-9/11 international consensus on the fight against terrorism as the African states. China contributed staff and troops to MINUSMA. Although it did not contribute troops to the mission or supported it financially, Russia supported the establishment of MINUSMA because of – to paraphrase the words of its representative – the gravity of the complex situation, the consent of the host state, and the involvement of relevant regional organisations.[192]

Despite this convergence of opinion on the level of the threat to regional peace and security posed by the Mali crisis, the African Union's peace enforcement mission stalled because of limited operational capacity. This prompted France – which was concerned about the risk of the AQIM-linked terrorist groups, such as the MNLA, overwhelming the Mali government – to launch its own military operation, 'Operation Serval'. Officially, France did not characterise its intervention as aimed at suppressing the Azawad secession but as a force to assist the Malian authorities to fight against international terrorism. France notified both the UN Secretary-General and the President of the Security Council as follows:

> France has responded to a request for assistance from the Interim President of the Republic of Mali, Mr. Dioncounda Traoré. Mali is facing terrorist elements from the north, which are currently threatening the territorial integrity and very existence of the State and the security of its population.[193]

[191] UN Doc. S/PV.6846, 12 October 2012; UN Doc. S/PV.6898, 20 December 2012.
[192] UN Doc. S/PV.6952, 25 April 2013, 2.
[193] Identical letters dated 11 January 2013 from the Permanent Representative of France to the United Nations addressed to the Secretary-General and the President of the Security Council, UN Doc. S/1013/17.

Because of the focus France placed on the fight against terrorism as the justification for its positive response to Mali's request for assistance, both ECOWAS and the AU Assembly endorsed it.[194]

The Security Council set aside questions regarding the legitimacy of the new government in Bamako and its authority to grant host state consent to the intervention. The Security Council confirmed its support in Resolution 2085 thus:

> [9.] *Decides* to authorise the deployment of an African-led Support Mission in Mali (AFISMA) for an initial period of one year [to carry out the following tasks]:
>
> [(b)] To support the Malian authorities in recovering the areas in the north of its territory under the control of terrorists, extremist and armed groups and in reducing the threat posed by terrorist organisations, including AQIM, MUJWA and associated extremist groups, while taking appropriate measures to reduce the impact of military action upon the civilian population.[195]

In a statement issued just before France launched Operation Serval, the Security Council reiterated its call to UN member states to assist the Malian military and security forces to reduce the threat posed by terrorist organisations and associated groups.[196] At the end of Operation Serval, the Security Council welcomed the swift action by the French forces in stopping the terrorist offensive, denounced terrorist groups, and called on rebel groups to cease hostilities.[197]

I earlier noted that although the United Nations refrains from undertaking counter-terrorism operations itself, where there is need for peace enforcement and counter-terrorism operations to go hand in hand, the United Nations supports its partners, such as the African Union and various subregional configurations or third states, to carry these out. The Mali situation confirms this approach, evidenced in some of the Security Council's resolutions. In Resolution 2391, the Security Council noted that 'the activities of terrorist organisations, including those benefiting from transnational organised crime, in the Sahel region constitute a threat to international peace and security', and it pledged UN support to the G5 Sahel (G5S) countries. Also referred to as the FC-G5S, the G5S is a grouping of five countries – Burkina Faso, Chad, Mali, Mauritania, and Niger – coordinating with France to strengthen development

---

[194] Statement of ECOWAS Authority of Heads of State and Government, 42nd Ordinary Session, 27–28 February 2013, para. 25. See also AU Doc. Assembly/AU/Decl.3 (XX), 2, para. 5.
[195] SC Res. 2085 of 20 December 2012, UN Doc. S/RES/2085(2012).
[196] 'Security Council Press Statement on Mali', UN Doc. SC/10878-AFR/2505, 10 January 2013.
[197] SC Res. 2100 of 25 April 2013, UN Doc. S/RES/2100(2013).

and security, and to combat the threat of jihadist organisations in the Sahel region. The Security Council:

> [12]. *Stresses* that the efforts of the FC-G5S to counter the activities of terrorist groups and other organised criminal groups will contribute to create a more secure environment in the Sahel region, and thus facilitate the fulfilment by MINUSMA of its mandate to stabilise Mali, and *further stresses* that operational and logistical support from MINUSMA [has] the potential to allow the FC-G5S, given its current level of capacities, to enhance its ability to deliver on its mandate.[198]

In Resolution 2531, which extended the mandate of MINUSMA to 30 June 2021, the Security Council reiterated its support for other security presences in Mali and the Sahel region, and it requested the UN Secretary-General '[to] ensure adequate coordination, exchange of information and, where applicable, support within their respective mandates and through exiting mechanisms between MINUSMA, the MDSF, the FC-G5S, the French Forces and the European Union missions [in Mali]'.[199]

The shared objective of fighting international terrorism expressed in the various resolutions and statements by the Security Council, the African Union, and ECOWAS reveals a strong consensus at international, regional, and subregional institutional levels that facilitated the multidimensional peace operation in Mali and sustained it until its termination in 2023.

The risk posed by transnational terrorist groups in Mali and the Sahel region remains, and sustained international cooperation is indispensable in the fight against this scourge. This requires cooperation and unity of purpose among the members of the Security Council. Such cooperation must involve all of the P5, other key players such as the A3 and the ten elected members (E10), who are asserting their voices ever more strongly in the Security Council, and the various national, subregional, regional, and international actors invested in the fight against terrorism.

---

[198] SC Res. 2391 of 8 December 2017, UN Doc. S/RES/2391(2017).
[199] SC Res. 2531 of 29 June 2020, UN Doc. S/RES/2531(2020), para. 30. MINUSMA's mandate was extended for another one year on 30 June 2021: see SC. Res. 2584 of 30 June 2021, UN Doc. S/RES/2584(2021). On 15 May 2022, Mali announced its withdrawal from the FC-G5S. Despite this, the Security Council once again renewed the mandate for one year, until 30 June 2023: see SC Res. 2640 of 29 June 2022, UN Doc. S/RES/2640(2022). On 30 June 2023, at the request of the Malian authorities, the Security Council unanimously approved the termination of MINUSMA's mandate and requested MINUSMA to immediately commence, on 1 July 2023, the cessation of its operations, to be phased over a six-month period: see SC Res. 2690 of 30 June 2023, UN Doc. S/RES/2690(2023).

B) THE AU MISSION IN SOMALIA (AMISOM) Following consultations with the Security Council, in January 2007, the PSC decided to establish AMISOM as a peace support operation with a broad threefold mandate:

(i) to facilitate dialogue and reconciliation;
(ii) to provide humanitarian assistance; and
(iii) to create conducive conditions for long-term stabilisation, reconstruction, and development in the country.[200]

The Security Council authorised the AU member states to establish the operation for a period of six months.[201]

In recent years, reauthorisations of the mission have expanded its mandate to include targeted operations against Al-Shabaab and other groups. Although, as we have seen, the Security Council refrains from mandating counter-terrorism actions in UN peace operations, it authorised AMISOM to '[reduce] the threat posed by Al-Shabaab and the other armed opposition groups'.[202]

AMISOM was a perfect example of what the UN Secretary-General has called 'partnership peacekeeping': the type of peacekeeping that involves several international organisations, individual states, local authorities, and other actors. For the African Union, AMISOM was its longest lasting, largest, most expensive, and deadliest peace operation; for the United Nations, AMISOM remains its most profound experiment with providing logistical support to a regional organisation in a conflict zone and collaborating on the political front, and it is the only AU-led operation with counter-terrorism objectives mandated by the Security Council.[203]

The African Union did not conceive of or deploy AMISOM as a unilateral intervention to respond to the occurrence of the crimes stipulated in Article 4(h) AU Constitutive Act, as one commentator has it.[204] The Transitional Federal Government of Somalia requested the African Union to intervene with a 'strong peace-making force', not a traditional peacekeeping

---

[200]   AU Peace and Security Council, Communiqué of 69th Meeting, AU Doc. PSC/PR/COMM. (LXIX), 19 January 2007, para. 8.
[201]   SC Res. 1744 of 20 February 2007, UN Doc. S/RES/1744(2007).
[202]   SC Res. 2372 of 30 August 2017, UN Doc. S/RES/2372(2017). Subsequent resolutions modified the language of this provision to read: '[Reduce] the threat posed by Al-Shabaab and the other armed opposition groups, including through mitigating the threat posed by improvised explosive devices.' See SC Res. 2431 of 30 July 2018, UN Doc. S/RES/2431(2018).
[203]   Paul D. Williams, *Lessons for 'Partnership Peacekeeping' from the African Union Mission in Somalia* (New York: International Peace Institute, 2019), 1–2.
[204]   See Abou Jeng, *Peace Building in the African Union: Law, Philosophy and Practice* (Cambridge: Cambridge University Press, 2012), 261.

or peace enforcement force, to help to restore peace and order.[205] Formally, the African Union deployed AMISOM as an 'intervention by invitation' by the internationally recognised government of Somalia, consistent with Article 4(j) AU Constitutive Act.

AMISOM's mandate evolved significantly in its 15-year existence to include the fight against Al-Shabaab, which both the African Union and the United Nations regard as a terrorist organisation that poses a threat not only in Somalia but also to the broader region.[206] The Security Council validated this shift in all of its resolutions renewing AMISOM. In similar language, Resolutions 2371,[207] 2341,[208] 2472,[209] and 2520[210] authorised the mission to 'reduce the threat posed by Al-Shabaab and other armed opposition groups, including through mitigating the threat posed by improvised explosive devices'.

As Okeke has rightly observed, 'reduction of threats posed by specific terrorist groups' has progressively been included since 2008 in political mandates by the African Union or United Nations when authorised in Africa's peace support operations.[211] The AMISOM operation, however, met with limited success, at a relatively substantial financial and human cost. When the PSC first requested the Security Council to authorise the deployment of AMISOM in 2007, it also urged the Council to consider authorising a UN operation that would take over from AMISOM at the expiration of its proposed six-month mandate.[212] The Security Council did not consider the request and this remained the case for the next 15 years. In May 2020, the Security Council decided – and the African Union concurred – to renew AMISOM with a scheduled termination date and handover of security to Somalia's security forces by the end of 2021.[213] In renewing the mandate, the Security Council

[205] Report of the Chairperson of the Commission on Conflict Situations in Africa to the Seventh Ordinary Session of the Executive Council, AU Doc. EX.CL/191 (VII), 28 June–2 July 2005, para. 13.
[206] On 12 April 2010, the Security Council's Committee established pursuant to Resolution 751 (1992) concerning Somalia placed Al-Shabaab on its '1844 Sanctions List' as a terrorist entity, in accordance with para. 8 of Resolution 1844 of 20 November 2008.
[207] SC Res. 2372 of 30 August 2017, UN Doc. S/RES/2372(2017).
[208] SC Res. 2431 of 30 July 2018, UN Doc. S/RES/2431(2018).
[209] SC Res. 2472 of 31 May 2019, UN Doc. S/RES/2472(2019).
[210] SC Res. 2520 of 29 May 2020, UN Doc. S/RES/2520(2020).
[211] Okeke, *Repositioning the AU's Role* (n. 185), 5.
[212] SC Res. 2520 of 29 May 2020, UN Doc. S/RES/2520(2020), para. 14.
[213] *Ibid.*, paras 5, 9. The Security Council reauthorised AMISOM with the same end date on 12 March 2021. See SC. Res. 2568 of 12 March 2021, UN Doc. S/RES/2568(2021); 'Security Council Reauthorizes African Union Mission in Somalia, Unanimously Adopting Resolution 2568 (2012)', UN Doc. SC/14467, 12 March 2021.

reiterated that Al-Shabaab posed a serious threat to the stability of Somalia and its neighbours and condemned its terrorist attacks.

As was the case in Mali, the United Nations' endorsement of the fight against terrorism complements its support for a political process aimed at bringing the Federal Government of Somalia (FGS), the Federal Member States (FMS), and Somali political factions to an inclusive political settlement to end the country's decades-long political crisis. In Resolution 2520, the Security Council:

> *Reiterates* that Al-Shabaab and other armed groups will not be defeated by military means alone, and in this regard, *calls on* the FGS, FMS, AMISOM, the UN and international partners to work closer together to take a comprehensive approach to security which is collaborative, gender-responsive and stabilising, and *calls on* international partners to provide support to the FGS to counter Al-Shabaab's finance, procurement and propaganda efforts.[214]

Clearly, the African Union's approach to counter-terrorism differs from the United Nations'. While the United Nations has been careful to distinguish peace support operations from counter-terrorism and counter-insurgency, the African Union has not been as discerning. Furthermore, as has been noted, the United Nations has not authorised UN-led operations with mandates to undertake counter-terrorism and counter-insurgency operations as such, beyond providing support to national security institutions involved in such activities. AMISOM, however, morphed into just such an operation, evolving from a passive to an active recognition of terrorism-related threats as part of its mandate.

AMISOM was replaced by the AU Transition Mission in Somalia (ATMIS) on 1 April 2022.[215] The termination of the AMISOM operation did not mark the triumph of the African Union's counter-terrorism objectives, as envisaged under its counter-terrorism normative framework. The growing frustration of the African Union, United Nations, and donors, compounded by a sense of mission fatigue, determined the fate of the African Union's longest and most costly, but also least successful, peace support operation. For both the African Union and the United Nations, the existence of Al-Shabaab and other terrorist groups elsewhere in Africa constitutes a continuing threat to peace and security on the continent and a challenge to the system of collective security generally.

---

[214] *Ibid.*, para. 3.
[215] SC Res. 2628 of 31 March 2022, UN Doc. S/RES/2628(2022), endorsed the AU Peace and Security Council's decision to reconfigure AMISOM and replace it with ATMIS. The Security Council authorised, for an initial period of 12 months, the member states of the African Union, inter alia, to carry out its mandate to reduce the threat posed by Al-Shabaab.

In concluding this section, I turn briefly to the issue of violent extremism, to which both Cai and Van den Herik have also briefly turned. Both reiterate the widely accepted view that terrorism and violent extremism have emerged as related phenomena – indeed, as twin notions. Cai notes that this interrelatedness has not resulted in the incorporation of counter-extremism measures into the UN Counter-Terrorism Strategy and concludes that neither the General Assembly nor the Security Council has developed any meaningful rules on counter-extremism.[216] Van den Herik underscores the point that the most prominent failure of the UN Plan of Action for Preventing Violent Extremism is the absence of a definition of 'violent extremism'.[217] I generally agree with these observations. The lack of a definition of the phenomenon has implications for the principle of legal certainty. This also leads to lack of transparency and accountability, as was noted by the Special Rapporteur on the Promotion and Protection of Human Rights and Fundamental Freedoms while Countering Terrorism.[218]

The African Union has also engaged with the issue of violent extremism, but in a more limited manner than it has with terrorism. There is recognition among African states that the two issues are separate and thus require separate counter-strategies. The PSC has discussed the threat of violent extremism in Africa at various levels.[219] Some proposals have been floated, but none have been adopted yet. These include developing a new peace support operations doctrine that would empower the African Union to deploy counter-terrorism and counter-violent extremism measures as part of its peacekeeping missions, and which would obviate the need to carry out such operations on an ad hoc basis, as is currently the case. The other is for the African Union to reach an understanding with the UN Security Council that will enable AU counter-terrorism operations to access UN assessed contributions.[220] Both of these scenarios present considerable challenges for

---

[216]   Cai, 'Maintaining Peace during a Global Power Shift', Chapter 1 in this volume, section IV. B (p. 65–6).

[217]   Van den Herik, 'A Reflection on Institutional Strength', Chapter 2 in this volume, section VI (p. 174).

[218]   Office of the High Commissioner for Human Rights, *Report on the Human Rights Policies and Practices Aimed at Preventing and Countering Violent Extremism*, UN Doc. A/HRC/43/46, 21 February 2020.

[219]   See, e.g., AU Peace and Security Council, Communiqué of 812th Meeting (on the fight against terrorism and violent extremism in Africa), AU Doc. PSC/PR/COMM. (DCCCXII), 6 December 2018; AU Peace and Security Council, Communiqué of 749th Meeting, AU Doc. PSC/AHG/COM.(DCCXLIX), 27 January 2018 (held at the level of Heads of State and Government); AU Peace and Security Council, Communiqué of 687th Meeting, AU Doc. PSC/PR/COMM. (DCLXXXVII), 23 May 2017.

[220]   See Institute for Security Studies, 'Will Africa Adapt its Counter-Terrorism Operations to Changing Realities?', *Peace and Security Council Report* 129 (2020), 1–4.

the African Union. While the Security Council has increasingly depended on the AU deployments to collaborate with it in response to terrorism in Africa, such as in AMISOM, the United Nations continues to insist that UN-mandated peace support operations cannot take part in military responses to terrorism.

I would thus suggest that, as far as the issue of combating violent extremism is concerned, as a regional organisation the African Union faces a challenge. The first aspect of this challenge is doctrinal, with implications for the principle of legal certainty raised by Van den Herik: neither the African Union nor the United Nations has agreed on a common definition of violent extremism. The second is operational: the African Union cannot undertake its own counter-violent extremism operations as part of UN-mandated peace operations. In the final analysis, the issue is not about the tension between the Security Council's author-ity and the principle of non-intervention, as Cai suggests; rather, it is the failure within the United Nations to find common ground and to anchor the Security Council's standard-setting in core principles of law, thereby achieving legal certainty, as Van den Herik has argued.

IV. CONTINUING CHALLENGES, FUTURE TRAJECTORIES, AND THE NEED FOR REFORM

A. *The African Quest for Permanent Seats on the Security Council*

As an organisation whose members comprise the largest regional bloc of the UN membership, with 54 of the 193 members, the African Union has pushed for greater visibility, influence, and recognition of its interests within the world body. Apart from efforts by the A3 to assert their voices on issues of direct concern to Africa in Security Council decision-making and calls for strength-ening the AU–UN relationship, the African Union has also demanded per-manent seats for the African region on the Security Council. The African Union regards this as a necessary step to make the Security Council more representative and legitimate, and to give Africa its rightful place in the balance of power in a reformed United Nations.

Reform of the Security Council has been back on the agenda since 2005, following the collapse of the Razali Plan in 1997.[221] UN Secretary-General

---

[221] Report of the Open-Ended Working Group on the Question of Equitable Representation on and Increase in Membership of the Security Council and Other Matters Related to the Security Council, UN Doc. A/51/47(SUPP), 8 August 1997, 6–9. The Razali Plan called for

Kofi Annan presented his report, *In Larger Freedom*, in March 2005 to set the agenda for the September 2005 World Summit. The report proposed an agenda involving a broad package of institutional reforms, including two models for the Security Council.[222] Under either model, all UN geographical regions except Africa would have at least one member with veto power.

The 'Ezulwini Consensus', to which I referred earlier in connection with Article 4(h) AU Constitutive Act, is premised on the argument that the current configuration of the Security Council is undemocratic and unable to protect weaker states against the major powers. This characterisation of the Security Council is, of course, not limited to the African states; other UN member states have expressed similar sentiments in the debates that have ensued over the years and have also responded with their own counter-proposals. I sketch the core demands of these respective groups only briefly.[223]

- The G4 plan (of Brazil, India, Germany, and Japan) seeks to add to the Security Council six permanent members, who would forgo the veto for the first 15 years of their membership or possibly longer, and four-non-permanent members.
- The Uniting for Consensus (UfC) group (comprising 12 members, including Argentina, Canada, Italy, Mexico, Pakistan, South Korea, Spain, and Turkey) opposes the G4 proposal to add any new permanent seats and advocates instead for the addition of only ten non-permanent seats, bringing the total membership of the Security Council to 25, and for the abolition of the veto or at least restricting its use.
- The L69 group (consisting of 25 developing countries from various regions of the world, and including Brazil and India) proposes six new permanent seats and six new non-permanent seats, distributed across the regions. Like the African group, the L69 would prefer to abolish the veto or extend it to all permanent members.
- A group of 22 Arab states demands a permanent seat for the Arab region but offers no suggestions about the veto, although it is highly critical of it.

expanding membership of the Security Council by adding five permanent and four non-permanent seats. It did not extend the veto to the new permanent members, regarding it as anachronistic; instead, it urged current permanent members to refrain from using their veto.

[222] *In Larger Freedom: Towards Development, Security and Human Rights for All*, Report of the Secretary-General, UN Doc. A/59/2005, 21 March 2005, paras 167–70.

[223] Each of these groups introduced their proposals as draft resolutions to the General Assembly, which were not voted on: G4 Group, Draft GA Res. A/59/L.64 of 6 July 2005; African Group, Draft GA Res. A/59/L.67 of 18 July 2005; Uniting for Consensus Group, Draft GA Res. A/59/L.68 of 21 July 2005; S5 Group, Draft GA Res. A/60/L.49 of 17 March 2006.

In 2013, a group of states emerged as an informal caucus to advocate for improved Security Council working methods. The group replaced an earlier group of five small states (S5) – namely, Jordan, Liechtenstein, Costa Rica, Singapore, and Switzerland. The Accountability, Coherence and Transparency (ACT) Group, as the larger group is known, was launched on 2 May 2013, comprising small and medium-sized countries from all continents. It aims at enhancing the effectiveness of the Security Council by means of improvement of its working methods, including limiting the use of the veto. Coordinated by Switzerland, the ACT Group builds on the S5's many years of effort and addresses both the Security Council's internal functioning, as well as its relations to the broader UN membership. The ACT Group's core objective is to ensure that the Security Council really 'acts on their behalf', as stated in Article 24(1) UN Charter, and is a well-functioning organ that keeps all UN members involved in the decision-making process. The Group has also proposed a code of conduct on the use of the veto by the P5 that I discuss below.[224]

The African Union has rejected the models presented in Secretary-General Annan's proposals – especially the lack of a veto power for an African member. Instead, it demands the allocation of two permanent seats to Africa, with all of the prerogatives and privileges of permanent membership, including the right of veto. It also demands five non-permanent seats, in what would become a 26-member Security Council. Notably, the 'Ezulwini Consensus' spells out that '[even] though Africa is opposed in principle to the veto, it is of the view that so long as it exists, and as a matter of common justice, it should be made available to all permanent members of the Security Council'.[225] Furthermore, overlooking the selection criteria proposed in the report, *In Larger Freedom*, the African Union has demanded the right to establish its own criteria for African members and to select its representatives to the Security Council. The African Union, however, has not yet defined these criteria nor has it clarified if it expects other regions too to establish their own criteria. The 'Ezulwini Consensus' provides only that it shall take into consideration 'the representative nature and capacity of those chosen'.[226] The AU Assembly reaffirmed this position at its summit on 9–10 February 2020.[227]

The General Assembly has debated Security Council reform annually since 2009, based on Decision 62/557, adopted by the General Assembly in 2008 'to

---

[224] Van den Herik, 'A Reflection on Institutional Strength', Chapter 2 in this volume, section III.
[225] Ezulwini Consensus (n. 43), sect. C(e), para. 3.
[226] *Ibid.*, para. 5.
[227] Decision on the Reform of the United Nations Security Council, AU Doc. Assembly/AU/Dec.766 (XXXIII), 9–10 February 2020, para. 8.

commence intergovernmental negotiations (IGN) in informal plenary of the General Assembly'.[228] The Decision stipulates that the negotiations should seek 'a solution that can garner the widest possible political acceptance by Member States'.[229] The most recent debate, which took place on 16–17 November 2020 during the 75th Session of the General Assembly, once again heard many delegates call for limits on the veto power and improved geographical representation in the Security Council, particularly for Africa. As in previous debates, African delegates, to a person, echoed the long-standing position of the African Group, as expressed in the 'Ezulwini Consensus'. Significantly, support for the common African position during this debate did not come only from countries of the Global South but also from Global North members, including Denmark, Germany, Ireland, Japan, and the United Kingdom.[230]

Formally, almost all UN member states continue to profess their support for reform. Yet, because of obvious self-interest, there does not appear to be any prospect of imminent consensus on what that reform should look like. Clearly, the P5 members, which have a stake in maintaining the status quo, will prefer to guard jealously their coveted positions and the veto power in the Security Council, effectively resisting any change that threatens their hegemony. Their critics accuse them of engaging in double-speak: they speak publicly of their support for reform in official diplomacy, while pursuing their real agenda behind the scenes in unofficial diplomacy.[231] I argue that regional rivalries and the multiplicity of alliance groups with seemingly irreconcilable proposals have been just as culpable in stalling reform.

[228] GA Res. 62/557 of 15 September 2008, UN Doc. A/RES/62/557 (on the question of equitable representation on, and increase in the membership of, the Security Council and related matters).

[229] *Ibid.*, para. (d).

[230] 'Security Council Must Reflect Twenty-First Century Realities, Delegates Tell General Assembly, with Many Calling for Urgent Expansion of Permanent Seats', UN Doc. GA/12288, 16 November 2020, available at https://press.un.org/en/2020/ga12288.doc.htm; 'Delegates Call for Veto Power Limits, More Permanent Seats for Africa, as General Assembly Concludes Debate on Security Council Reform', UN Doc. GA/12289, 17 November 2020, available at https://press.un.org/en/2020/ga12289.doc.htm.

[231] In September 2022, President Joe Biden told the UN General Assembly that '[the] United States supports increasing the number of both permanent and non-permanent members in the Council. This includes permanent seats for those nations we've long supported and permanent seats for countries in Africa, Latin America, and the Caribbean.' See 'Remarks by President Biden before the 77th Session of the United Nations General Assembly', 21 September 2022, available at www.whitehouse.gov/briefing-room/speeches-remarks/2022/09/21/remarks-by-president-biden-before-the-77th-session-of-the-united-nations-general-assembly/.

For the African Union, Security Council reform appears to have become a debate without end, but the African states cannot escape blame. I see the maximalist positions that many member states have adopted on this question – and this includes the common African position – as an added problem. The paradox here is that the 'Ezulwini Consensus' demands a share in the veto power while reiterating the African Union's opposition to the veto as a matter of principle. At the same time, anecdotal evidence suggests that '[it] seems many African countries are more interested in having increased influence when it comes to peacekeeping missions on the African continent, than they are in obtaining the veto right'.[232] Assuming this to be the case, I would agree with Bjarke Winther's observation that the addition of veto rights to more countries would be more a symbolic act than a measure equalising the current zenith of global power.[233] Even in an expanded Security Council with more veto-possessing members, none of the other members would match the global power and influence that goes with the military might of China, Russia, and the United States. They also would be hard-pressed to justify using their veto on the pretext of protecting their national interests to prevent the global community from taking action to deal with situations threatening international peace and security – which is quite possibly part of the explanation why France and the United Kingdom effectively do not use their veto power.

In my view, the maximalist demand that the African Union should set its own criteria for selection of its representative and that the African Union select them is problematic. The Security Council is empowered to take decisions that bind all UN members in terms of Article 25 UN Charter. Allowing one region alone to select its representatives to the Security Council and denying all other UN members a vote in their selection would ironically negate the democracy and legitimacy that the African Union claims to be the motivation for its demand for Security Council reform.

B. *The Russian Invasion of Ukraine: Ramifications for African Perceptions of the Security Council*

For the African Union and African states, nothing exemplifies the unfairness of the current Security Council structure and the potential of the P5 members to abuse the veto power better than the failure of the Council to adopt a decision condemning the Russian invasion of Ukraine. On 25 February 2022, the day

---

[232] Bjarke Zinck Winther, 'A Review of the Academic Debate about United Nations Security Council Reform', *The Chinese Journal of Global Governance* 6 (2020), 71–101 (100).
[233] *Ibid.*, 101.

following the invasion, the Security Council held a debate.[234] Russia vetoed a draft resolution that would have demanded Moscow immediately stop its attack on Ukraine and unconditionally withdraw all of its troops. While 11 of the Council's 15 members voted in favour of the draft text,[235] China, India, and the United Arab Emirates abstained. Russia vetoed it, even though the word 'condemns' was replaced by 'deplores' and a reference to Chapter VII UN Charter was deleted to water it down to gain more support.

In the context of the foregoing discussion, I would make two observations. The first is that the A3 – namely, Gabon,[236] Ghana,[237] and Kenya[238] – all spoke unequivocally in their condemnation of the invasion as a violation of Ukraine's territorial integrity and sovereignty, and as a violation of both the UN Charter and international law. They were, of course, neither speaking for the African Union nor conveying a collective African common position. The second observation is that China abstained rather than use its veto in support of its P2 ally. Notably, however, in his statement to the Council, China's representative reaffirmed its respect for the sovereignty and territorial integrity of all states and the need to uphold the purposes and principles of the Charter. China also called upon all parties to resolve their problems peacefully and encouraged efforts for a diplomatic solution through negotiations between Russia and Ukraine.[239]

On its part, on the day of the invasion, the African Union issued a joint statement by AU chair, President Macky Sall of Senegal, and the chairperson of the AU Commission expressing 'their extreme concern at the very serious and dangerous situation created in Ukraine', calling upon 'the Russian Federation and any other regional or international actor to imperatively respect international law, the territorial integrity and national sovereignty of Ukraine', and urging 'the two Parties to establish an immediate ceasefire and to open political negotiations without [delay]'.[240] It is plausible to argue that the joint statement outlined a possible common stance. The reality is that the African Union did not adopt an African common position on the Ukraine war.

---

[234] UN Doc. S/PV.8979, 25 February 2022.
[235] Albania, Brazil, France, Gabon, Ghana, Ireland, Kenya, Mexico, Norway, United Kingdom, and United States.
[236] UN Doc. S/PV.8979, 25 February 2022, 4–5.
[237] *Ibid.*, 9–10.
[238] *Ibid.*, 11.
[239] *Ibid.*
[240] Statement from Chair of the African Union, H.E. President Macky Sall, and Chairperson of the AU Commission, H.E. Moussa Faki Mahamat, on the situation in Ukraine, 24 February 2022, available at https://au.int/en/pressreleases/20220224/african-union-state ment-situation-ukraine.

After the failure of the Security Council to adopt the draft resolution, some members called for an emergency session of the General Assembly to discuss the matter. On 27 February 2022, the Council members voted in favour of the General Assembly convening to discuss the crisis.[241] By an overwhelming majority of 141 in favour, 5 against, and 35 abstentions, on 2 March 2022, the 11th Emergency Session of the General Assembly adopted a resolution deploring the Russian invasion of Ukraine and demanding that Russia immediately end its military operations there.[242] In doing so, the General Assembly utilised the 'Uniting for Peace' procedure to address a situation representing a grave breach of international peace and security after the Security Council's failure to take a decision, consistent with Article 11(2) UN Charter, which empowers it to discuss any questions relating to the maintenance of international peace and security.[243]

The voting positions of African states revealed an equal split between those who supported the Resolution and those who did not. Of the 54 African members, 27 voted in favour, 1 voted against, 17 abstained, and 9 were absent. Four possible explanations may be offered for the countries that did not support the Resolution by voting negatively, abstaining, or being absent. First, several of the opposing or abstaining countries – especially the southern African states (i.e., Angola, Mozambique, Namibia, South Africa, and Zimbabwe) – remain grateful for the former Soviet Union's support for their national liberation struggles. Thus, on the one hand, South Africa was unequivocal in its demand for Russia's withdrawal from Ukraine.[244] On the other hand, however, it also expressed sympathy for the argument, probably shared by many abstainers, that if NATO had taken greater account of Russia's security interests and given it the assurances that had been promised since the dissolution of the Warsaw Pact, the crisis might never have arisen.[245]

---

[241] SC Res. 2623 of 27 February 2022, UN Doc. S/RES/2623(2022).

[242] GA Res. ES-11/1 of 2 March 2022, UN Doc. A/RES/ES-11/1.

[243] The 'Uniting for Peace Resolution' was adopted to circumvent further Security Council vetoes by the Soviet Union during the Korean War (1950–53): GA Res. 377(V) of 3 November 1950, UN Doc. A/RES/377(V).

[244] South African Department of International Relations and Cooperation, 'South African Government Calls for a Peaceful Resolution of the Escalating Conflict between the Russian Federation and Ukraine', 24 February 2022, available at www.dirco.gov.za/south-afr ican-government-calls-for-a-peaceful-resolution-of-the-escalating-conflict-between-the-rus sian-federation-and-ukraine/.

[245] See op-ed article by Clayson Monyela, 'Ukraine Needs an Inclusive and Lasting Roadmap to Peace', *Daily Maverick*, 11 March 2022, available at www.dailymaverick.co.za/opinionista/2 022-03-11-ukraine-needs-an-inclusive-and-lasting-roadmap-to-peace/. Clayson Monyela is head of public diplomacy at the South African Department of International Relations and Cooperation.

Secondly, there seemed to be a reluctance among many African states to be drawn into any resurrection of the Cold War in which some of them were used as proxies. This reluctance stems from the desire of African states to stick to the principles of non-alignment between East and West. Ironically, however, the differences in the positions adopted in the General Assembly may have exposed emerging 'new Cold War' divisions within the African continent.

The third factor is Russia's growing influence in Africa, which I discussed earlier. On this point, one may wonder whether the African states that did not support the Resolution were motivated solely by their wish to please Russia or, more probably, the desire not to offend China – the more significant partner for most of these states, given the latter's position on the invasion, which Cai has discussed in admirable detail.[246] Here, it is notable that China uses Russia's characterisation of its invasion of Ukraine as 'a special military operation', as does Cai, instead of describing it as 'a war', the term used by most UN member states and legal commentators. If the ramifications of the war in Ukraine escalate globally and a 'new Cold War' including China settles in, African countries will likely split into antagonistic blocs defined by their support for or opposition to Russia – an outcome that would negate the non-alignment that they traditionally proclaim.

A final factor that may have played a part in the motivations behind the voting was the perception of double standards on the part of some members of the Security Council – in particular, the P3. This can be viewed through two lenses: one, the perception that, even as one acknowledged the gravity of the situation caused by the unprovoked aggression of a nuclear-powered P5 member against a less powerful neighbour, one might recall that some past aggressions by other P5 members in other parts of the world were never seriously challenged or condemned by the Security Council; the other, the view that the attention given to the plight of victims of these past aggressions by Western powers was nowhere near that accorded to Ukrainians affected by the war.

This latter sentiment had been expressed by the representative of Kenya in his address to the Security Council during the 25 February 2022 session. In remarks that did not attract any comment at the time, he recalled the Council's 2011 authorisation of intervention in Libya and its consequences:

> Even as deserved condemnations ring out today about the breach of Ukraine's sovereignty, history's condemnations are allowed silence in this room. We cannot help but recall that Africa's Sahel region is in terrible

---

[246] Cai, 'Maintaining Peace during a Global Power Shift', Chapter 1 in this volume, section III.B.

turmoil due to the hasty and ill-considered intervention in Libya a decade ago.

On that occasion, the African Union sought more time for diplomacy. Its Peace and Security Council was ignored and what resulted was not peace or the safety and security of the Libyan people. Instead, terror was unleashed on African peoples in the countries to the south of Libya. There have been yet other actions of similar magnitude that have brought us to this unfortunate pass.[247]

I agree with this sentiment up to a point, because it accords with some of the observations and criticism that I have advanced regarding the NATO intervention in Libya. I do not agree, however, with the implied suggestion of a moral equivalence between the Russian invasion of Ukraine, which undoubtedly violated the Charter and international law (a point accepted even by those who support or sympathise with Russia's rationalisation of its action), and the intervention in Libya. The latter, as I have argued, was justifiably authorised by the Security Council within its Chapter VII powers, even if the manner of its execution by NATO tainted its legality and legitimacy.

Despite the absence of an AU or African common position, there was subsequent engagement between both parties to the conflict and representatives of the African Union. On 3 June 2022, the AU chair and the chair of the AU Commission met with Russian President Vladimir Putin. President Sall of Senegal was reported to have pleaded Africa's cause, telling the Russian president that the continent was threatened by an unprecedented food crisis resulting from the blockading of Ukrainian ports and the Western sanctions on Russia, and to have asked Putin 'to be aware that [African] countries, even if they are far from the theatre [of action], are victims of the crisis at the economic level'.[248] Subsequently, on 20 June 2022, Ukrainian President Volodymyr Zelensky addressed the Bureau of the AU Assembly in a closed-door virtual meeting in which he reiterated that Ukraine was a victim of 'a brutal war – a war of invasion' by Russian troops – and acknowledged that Ukraine was aware of the economic difficulties and food crisis that some African countries were facing as a result.[249]

---

[247] UN Doc. S/PV.8979, 25 February 2022, 11.

[248] Christophe Châtelot, 'Vladimir Putin Promises to Facilitate Ukrainian Wheat Export to Africa', *Le Monde*, 5 June 2022, available at www.lemonde.fr/en/international/article/2022/06/05/vladimir-putin-promises-to-facilitate-ukrainian-wheat-export-to-africa_5985719_4.html.

[249] See Noé Hochet-Bodin, 'Volodymyr Zelensky Seeks Support from the African Union', *Le Monde*, 21 June 2022, available at www.lemonde.fr/en/le-monde-africa/article/2022/06/22/volodymyr-zelensky-seeks-african-union-support_5987621_124.html.

The impact of the war for many developing countries, especially in Africa, as measured in terms of rising food and fuel prices and the knock-on effects of the sanctions imposed on Russia, may be long-lasting. Consistent with their traditional opposition to unilateral sanctions, African countries did not support these sanctions. The AU chair underscored this when he addressed an EU summit on 31 May 2022, warning that Western sanctions had made it difficult for African countries to buy grain from Russia, and that this only compounded the difficulties and slowdown in economic growth that African countries already faced from the effects of the climate crisis and the COVID-19 pandemic.[250]

As regards the sanctions, it may also be noted that neither the African Union nor any individual African state publicly supported Russia's argument, echoed by China, that the sanctions were illegal and a breach of international law. This argument reprised the position that Russia took when the European Union and the United States imposed sanctions against it following its annexation of Crimea in 2014. The Russian position was premised on the argument that only the Security Council can decide on sanctions and that, if it has not done so, any sanctions adopted are, by definition, unilateral and illegal.[251] I do not share this view. The argument implies that sanctions could never be legally adopted against a permanent member of the Security Council, since it is inconceivable that any P5 state would forgo its veto and allow the Council to adopt a decision that would harm that state. To my mind, the non-UN sanctions imposed by the European Union and other Western countries were legal and legitimate countermeasures to the Russian invasion, which represented a violation of a peremptory norm of international law prohibiting the use of force.

One of the lessons from the Security Council's handling of the war in Ukraine is that it is unable to deal with threats to international peace and security in which the principal or sole offender is its permanent member. For Africa, the most immediate ramification of the war was the understandable decision by Ukraine to withdraw its 250-strong contingent and eight helicopters that made up a third of the UN fleet from the UN peacekeeping mission in

---

[250] Victoria Mallet and Andy Bounds, 'African Union Warns of "Collateral Impact" as EU's Russia Sanctions Hit Food Supplies', *Financial Times*, 31 May 2022, available at www.ft.com/content/e558de33-6064-4b10-a784-eb344cb17915.

[251] Russian Foreign Minister Sergey Lavrov reiterated this point on 1 April 2022 in relation to the new Western sanctions during a visit to India. See Patrick Wintour, 'Russia and India Will Find Ways to Trade Despite Sanctions, Says Lavrov', *The Guardian*, 1 April 2022, available at www.theguardian.com/world/2022/apr/01/russia-and-india-will-find-ways-to-trade-despite-sanctions-says-lavrov.

the Democratic Republic of Congo (MONUSCO).[252] Although MONUSCO was already expected to end its operations in 2024, Ukraine's withdrawal did not augur well for the DRC's deteriorating security situation. Ukraine also pulled out of the UN missions in Mali and South Sudan.

C. *The Problem of Security Council Inaction and Failure to Decide*

The failure of the Security Council to act to prevent or stop the Rwanda genocide was a painful reminder that, while the founders established it as the organ with the primary responsibility for the maintenance of international peace and security, when faced with a crisis within the scope of its mandate, it has no obligation to decide whether to act or not. Although it was a domestic genocide perpetrated by domestic actors, few would argue that the Rwanda crisis did not fall within the scope of Article 39 UN Charter. The Charter gives the Security Council legal authority to authorise binding measures necessary to restore peace and security, but it does not establish any obligation requiring it to decide on any measures in any situation. Yet failure by the Security Council to decide is itself a form of decision. Put differently, the Security Council 'speaks' both when it takes a decision and when it does not. 'Inaction' is a perverse form of 'action' – and it is a legally relevant omission.[253]

Most of the discussion on Security Council reform by UN member states and scholars has focused on substantive issues, such as its outdated membership structure and the use of the veto power; not as much attention has been given to exploring the possibility of procedural reforms. Such reforms could take the form of amendments to the Security Council's Rules of Procedure and Working Methods, without necessitating the more complex process of amending the Charter provided for under Articles 108 and 109. Anna Spain and Anne Peters are among the few scholars who have written on the issue of procedural reforms to improve the Security Council's decision-making.[254] Specifically, Spain proposes that the Security Council adopt three new procedural duties: the duty to decide; the duty to disclose; and the duty to consult to improve its decision-making processes. Peters proposes the duty to give reasons.[255]

---

[252] See Samba Cyuzuzo, 'Ukraine Troops Leave DR Congo Peacekeeping Mission Monusco', *BBC News*, 18 September 2022, available at www.bbc.com/news/world-africa-62945971.

[253] See generally Jennifer Trahan, *Existing Legal Limits to Security Council Veto Power in the Face of Atrocity Crimes* (Cambridge: Cambridge University Press, 2020).

[254] Anna Spain, 'The U.N. Security Council's Duty to Decide', *Harvard National Security Journal* 4 (2013), 320–84.

[255] Anne Peters, 'The Security Council's Responsibility to Protect', *International Organizations Law Review* 8 (2011), 1–40.

According to Spain, the duty to decide would require the Security Council to decide affirmatively whether it will take action to deal with crises falling within the scope of its authority. The duty to disclose would require it to explain publicly its reasons should it not do so. Finally, the duty to consult would obligate it to engage in broader dialogue with affected parties before taking serious action, aiming to understand the will of the people whom the Security Council's decisions may affect, so as to integrate their preferences into its decision-making.[256] Spain argues that: '[These] duties would serve as a commitment mechanism that would encourage the UNSC to make decisions or explain to the public its justifications for not doing so.'[257]

The proposal is cogent and viable. I think, however, that the third duty proposed, the duty to consult, may prove the most problematic, because it requires the Security Council to go beyond governments of the states concerned as interlocutors and engage directly with the people in those states 'to understand their will'. The politics and practicalities of achieving this engagement may prove to be a difficult – perhaps even an insurmountable – challenge. Leaving aside this quibble, in my reading, the idea of the Security Council adopting internal procedural reforms establishing procedural duties is consistent with some of the proposals advanced by member states, such as the S5 and ACT Group. The ACT Group's position is particularly apposite in this respect. As noted in the previous section, the core objective of the ACT Group initiative is to improve the working methods of the Security Council. An important aspect of this is to encourage more Arria formula meetings and improve the relationship between the Security Council and the broader UN membership. As Van den Herik has rightly argued, these meetings provide opportunities for other states to participate and to mobilise.[258]

African states and many others rightly faulted the United Nations generally for its inaction in Rwanda and the Security Council specifically for failing to adopt any decision as the genocide was unfolding. But the inaction was not the result of a P5 member using the veto to block a draft resolution on the issue; the Council did not even deliberate the need for such a resolution.

Regarding more recent situations involving allegations of genocide, for example in Syria and Myanmar, the use of the veto on multiple occasions by the P2 members has prevented the Security Council from authorising any

---

[256] Spain, 'Security Council's Duty to Decide' (n. 253), 326.
[257] *Ibid.*
[258] Accountability, Coherence and Transparency (ACT) Group, *Better Working Methods for Today's UN Security Council* [Factsheet], May 2019, available at https://centerforunreform .org/wp-content/uploads/2015/06/FACT-SHEET-ACT-June-2015.pdf, 1. See Van den Herik, 'A Reflection on Institutional Strength', Chapter 2 in this volume, section III (p. 122).

action. Since 2011, when the P5 united to adopt Resolution 1973 on Libya, Russia and China have used their veto power 13 and 7 times, respectively, to block resolutions addressing war crimes and crimes against humanity committed in Syria. These instances have increased the calls among UN member states for there to be a restraint on the use of the veto by the P5 in situations of mass atrocity. For example, at the 70th Session of the General Assembly in 2015, France and Mexico presented a proposal entitled 'Political Statement on the Suspension of the Veto in Case of Mass Atrocities' and invited UN member states to sign it.[259] At the same time, the ACT Group launched a draft code of conduct regarding Security Council action against genocide, crimes against humanity, or war crimes. The Code of Conduct, launched officially on 23 October 2015, calls upon *all* members of the Security Council, both permanent and non-permanent, not to vote against any credible draft resolution intended to prevent or stop mass atrocities.[260] Prior to the ACT Group's campaign, Anne Peters had argued for the Security Council's '*duty* to intervene', as a moral or even legal obligation, to protect populations against genocide or crimes against humanity. The existence of such a duty would preclude the use of the veto by the P5 in relevant situations.[261]

The ACT Code of Conduct is a legally non-binding instrument to which UN member states voluntarily commit themselves. On the one hand, until all of the P5 members make that pledge and abide by it, the veto power will remain a potential tool for some members of the Security Council to use against resolutions aimed at addressing future situations of genocides, crimes against humanity, and war crimes. On the other hand, if all of the P5 members were to embrace it (which is most unlikely), the Code of Conduct would in effect be a procedural reform of the working methods of the Security Council without formal Charter amendment. Such a development would have enormous political significance but little normative consequence for the law of peace and war and for the system of collective security. Statements made by states at the General Assembly pledging their support for the Code of Conduct, or signing it, are not resolutions of the General Assembly, still less

---

[259] See generally Jean-Baptiste Jeangène Vilmer, 'The Responsibility not to Veto: A Genealogy', *Global Governance* 24 (2018), 331–49. See also Ariela Blätter and Paul D. Williams, 'The Responsibility not to Veto', *Global Responsibility to Protect* 3 (2011), 301–22.

[260] Annex I to the letter dated 14 December 2015 from the Permanent Representative of Liechtenstein to the United Nations addressed to the Secretary-General, UN Doc. A/70/621– S/2015/978 ('Code of Conduct Regarding Security Council Action against Genocide, Crimes against Humanity or War Crimes').

[261] Anne Peters, 'Humanity as the A and Ω of Sovereignty', *European Journal of International Law* 20 (2009), 513–44 (538–40).

of the Security Council.[262] To date, only France and the United Kingdom, among the P5 members, have signed the ACT Code of Conduct.

From the perspective of the African states, the voluntary pledge requested of permanent and non-permanent members of the Security Council is of huge symbolic significance, even if it yields no immediate normative outcomes. Article 4(h) was incorporated into the AU Constitutive Act to address the crimes of genocide, crimes against humanity, and war crimes, which are widely regarded as violations of peremptory norms of general international law (i.e., ius cogens).[263] Given this fact, it is surprising that there are only 22 AU member states among the current 122 signatories to the Code of Conduct.[264] That list does not include Rwanda – the country whose painful experience in 1994 was arguably a critical factor behind the adoption of Article 4(h). This illustrates the double bind of voluntary pledges: some states sign such pledges precisely because of their non-binding nature and hence lack of normative consequences; others choose not to sign them because they see no point in committing to a pledge that has no binding legal effect and carries no enforceable obligations. Yet, in my view, the ACT Code of Conduct remains a valuable vehicle for garnering the necessary international consensus that may help, over time, to push both the General Assembly and Security Council in the right direction towards a norm-creating trajectory. To this extent, the Code will remain a relevant negotiating point in future deliberations on UN reform.

In an unrelated move, in April 2022, the General Assembly adopted by consensus a resolution co-sponsored by 83 countries mandating an automatic meeting in the event of any Security Council veto.[265] Under Resolution 76/262, the General Assembly decided to meet automatically within ten days if the veto is used in the Security Council by one or more of the P5, inviting the concerned P5 members to account to the meeting for the circumstances behind its use of the veto, so that all UN members might have an opportunity to scrutinise and comment on it. The General Assembly also decided to include in the provisional agenda of its 77th Session an item entitled 'Use of

---

[262] As of 8 June 2022, 122 UN member states and 2 observers had signed the Code of Conduct: see Global Centre for the Responsibility to Protect, 'List of Signatories to the ACT Code of Conduct', 8 June 2022, available at www.globalr2p.org/resources/list-of-signatories-to-the-act-code-of-conduct/.

[263] See *Draft Conclusions on Peremptory Norms of General International Law* (Jus Cogens), Report of the International Law Commission, UN Doc. A/74/10, Pt V, Annex. The Commission included these crimes in an illustrative list of norms that it considered 'candidates' for ius cogens.

[264] Global Centre for the Responsibility to Protect, 'List of Signatories' (n. 262).

[265] GA Res. 76/262 of 26 April 2022, UN Doc. A/RES/76/262.

the veto'.[266] Liechtenstein led this initiative, which it had embarked upon with a core group of states more than two years earlier out of growing concern that the Security Council had found it increasingly difficult to carry out its work in accordance with its mandate under the Charter.[267]

Two brief observations may be made about this Resolution. First, although not formally directed at Russia, its adoption came in the wake of Russia's use of the veto of the draft Security Council resolution on Ukraine. Since General Assembly Resolution 76/262 is non-binding, it is unlikely that any concerned P5 member will feel compelled to explain themselves in the General Assembly other than, perhaps, to reiterate their earlier justifications given in the Security Council. Yet by deciding to maintain, on the agenda of its future sessions, an item on the use of the veto, the General Assembly will ensure that the debate about the veto power of the P5 remains alive. This will be symbolically significant.

Secondly, Resolution 76/262 followed the General Assembly's adoption of Resolution ES-11/1 on 2 March 2022, in which it demanded that Russia cease its invasion of Ukraine and withdraw its troops immediately. There is thus an implied link between the two resolutions. Both highlight two critical issues that Van den Herik and I have raised and on which we agree: broadening the inclusion of other voices beyond the Security Council, and the Council's inevitable dysfunction when a permanent member is involved in the crisis.

D. *Unconventional Global Threats: The Climate Crisis and Climate Security*

The notion of unconventional threats to security is elastic and their identification depends on whether one adopts a narrow or expansive conception of security. A few candidates emerge in most accounts of such threats, including health pandemics, cyber tools, artificial intelligence, biotechnology, transnational organised crime, the climate crisis, and autonomous or unmanned systems, to mention only a few. By their nature, most of these new threats are transnational and potentially impact all regions of the world.

Climate – or the climate crisis – is one of the most transnational of these threats and is currently of particular concern to the African region. I regard this as a new threat that deserves serious attention from both the African Union and the United Nations going forward. This is not to suggest that the other

---

[266] *Ibid.*, para. 4.
[267] Security Council Report, 'Monthly Forecast (May 2022)', available at www.securitycouncilre port.org/atf/cf/%7B65BFCF9B-6D27-4E9C-8CD3-CF6E4FF96FF9%7D/2022_05_forecast. pdf, 2.

unconventional threats are of no consequence or matter less to Africa. Global pandemics and epidemics, such as malaria, tuberculosis, and HIV-AIDS, or more recently Ebola and COVID-19, are of equal concern to African states as threats to their security. However, there appears to be a consensus, which African countries share, that global health issues are for the World Health Organization (WHO) to deal with. The impacts of the climate crisis – desertification, land degradation, droughts, and so on – have affected communities across most of the African continent for decades and continue to do so. These impacts are more visible and observable, and more enduring, and thus make the climate–security nexus obvious and urgent. It is for this reason that I propose to devote the remainder of this section to this issue.

Van den Herik has given a succinct account of the first open debate in the Security Council, convened by the United Kingdom, on the relationship between energy, security, and climate in 2007, at which many delegations expressed concern and resistance against any suggestion of the Security Council expanding its remit to deal with these matters. She rightly points out that the concerns expressed by some members were twofold: fear of Security Council mission creep; and the potential weakening of the UN system that would result from letting the Security Council deal with matters falling under the mandates of other UN agencies.[268] Van den Herik quotes the representative of Sudan, who, speaking on behalf of the African Group, expressed the fear that the 'increasing and alarming encroachment by the Security Council on the mandates of other United Nations bodies [compromises] the principles and purposes of the United Nations Charter and is also undermining the relevant bodies'.[269] A decade later, subsequent open session debates and discussions on climate and security in the Security Council suggest a growing acceptance among states that this is a legitimate issue for the Security Council to take on.[270]

There is widespread agreement that, although it contributes least to global warming in comparison to other regions, Africa is disproportionately vulnerable to the impact of climate change. Moreover, some of the countries most

---

[268] Van den Herik, 'A Reflection on Institutional Strength', Chapter 2 in this volume, section VII (p. 176).

[269] UN Doc. S/PV.5663, 17 April 2007, 12.

[270] For recent Security Council discussions on climate and security, see Ministerial-Level Open Video Teleconference on Maintenance of International Peace and Security: Climate and Security, 24 July 2020, available at https://media.un.org/en/asset/k1z/k1z5jgco4h; High-Level Open Video Teleconference Debate on Climate and Security, 23 February 2021, available at www.youtube.com/watch?v=ToZV7vV6Mdc; 'Climate Change "Biggest Threat Modern Humans Have Ever Faced", World Renowned Naturalist Tells Security Council, Calls for Greater Global Cooperation', UN Doc. SC/14445, 23 February 2021.

affected by the climate crisis are also among the most politically fragile and prone to conflicts.[271] The African Union recognises that climate and ecological crises have led to forced displacement and migration, food and water insecurity, inter-communal conflicts between herders and farmers, and the scourge of violent extremism and terrorism.[272] The war in Darfur was an early example of a climate-related conflict. In a resolution on Darfur adopted some 15 years after the start of the conflict, the Security Council still recognised the 'adverse effects of climate change, ecological changes and natural disasters, among other factors, on the situation in Darfur, including through drought, desertification, land degradation and food insecurity'.[273]

Since 2015, the African Union has officially included the climate crisis as a security threat on its agenda. The APSA Roadmap 2016–20, adopted by the PSC, identifies the climate crisis as one of the cross-cutting issues in peace and security, and addresses 'the issues of continental coordination, collaboration and research to mitigate the impact of climate change as a threat to peace and security in Africa'.[274] Furthermore, the APSA Roadmap characterises the climate crisis as a 'threat multiplier that exacerbates security trends, tension and stability'.[275] Since 2016, the PSC has held open sessions on climate change. At these meetings, AU members have acknowledged, among other things, 'the inextricable link between climate change, peace and security in Africa', and 'stressed the importance of the AU Commission to mainstream climate change in all its activities, particularly in early warning and conflict prevention efforts'.[276] Members have also essentially described the climate crisis as an existential threat to all countries and regions in Africa, and to continental peace, security, and

---

[271] Hannah Ritchie, 'Global Inequities in CO_2 Emissions', *Our Word in Data*, 16 October 2016, available at https://ourworldindata.org/co2-by-income-region. It is estimated that 57 per cent of the countries facing the highest double burden of climate exposure and political instability are in sub-Saharan Africa. See generally United States Agency for International Development (USAID), *The Intersection of Global Fragility and Climate Risks* (Washington, DC: USAID, 2018).

[272] African Union, Declaration of the 9th African Union High-Level Retreat on 'Promotion of Peace, Security and Stability: "Strengthening African Union's Conflict Prevention and Peacemaking Efforts"', Accra, 25–26 October 2018.

[273] SC Res. 2429 of 13 July 2018, UN Doc. S/RES/2429(2018).

[274] African Union, *African Peace and Security Architecture: APSA Roadmap 2016–2020*, December 2015, available at https://au.int/sites/default/files/documents/38310-doc-9_2015-e n-apsa-roadmap-final.pdf, 60.

[275] *Ibid.*, 20.

[276] African Union, 585th Meeting of the AU Peace and Security Council: An Open Session on the Theme: 'Climate Change: State Fragility, Peace and Security in Africa', 30 March 2016.

stability.[277] In 2018, the PSC proposed the appointment of an AU Special Envoy for Climate and Security to work with the Committee of African Heads of State and Government on Climate Change.[278]

The debates in the PSC compare with the open session debates on climate convened by the Security Council since the first meeting in 2007. It is notable that the 2019 Security Council debate introduced the notion of 'threat multiplier' to describe the impacts of the climate crisis on global security – a notion already incorporated into the APSA Roadmap in 2015. Apart from two other open session debates held in 2011 and 2018, the Security Council has convened special events on climate-related security risks.[279] The president of the Security Council has also issued statements addressing the climate–security nexus following meetings on country- or region-specific situations in Africa. An early example was the statement on West Africa and the Sahel, issued on 30 January 2018, in which the Security Council recognised the link between the climate crisis and violence in the regions.[280] This was reiterated most recently in another presidential statement issued on 3 February 2021, in which the Security Council recognised 'the adverse effects of climate change, ecological changes and natural hazards on the stability of West Africa and the Sahel region'.[281] More importantly, despite refraining from officially addressing the climate crisis, several Security Council resolutions and missions since 2017 have operated on the premise of the adverse effects and implications of climate change, natural disasters, and other ecological changes on stability and security in relation to specific countries or regions. In addition to the resolution on Darfur mentioned earlier,[282] these include resolutions on some of the conflict situations discussed in this chapter – namely, Mali[283] and Somalia[284] – and others, such as in the Lake Chad Basin Region,[285] the CAR,[286] and the DRC.[287]

[277] African Union, 774th Meeting of the AU Peace and Security Council: An Open Session on the Theme: 'The Link between Climate Change and Conflicts in Africa and Addressing the Security Implications', 21 May 2018.
[278] *Ibid.*
[279] See above, n. 269.
[280] Presidential Statement on West Africa and the Sahel, UN Doc. S/PRST/13189, 30 January 2018.
[281] Presidential Statement on West Africa and the Sahel, UN Doc. S/PRST/14428, 3 February 2021.
[282] SC Res. 2429 of 13 July 2018, UN Doc. S/RES/2429(2018).
[283] SC Res. 2423 of 28 June 2018, UN Doc. S/RES/2423(2018); SC Res. 2480 of 28 June 2019, UN Doc. S/RES/2480(2019).
[284] SC Res. 2408 of 27 March 2018, UN Doc. S/RES/2408(2018).
[285] SC Res. 2349 of 31 March 2017, UN Doc. S/RES/2349(2017).
[286] SC Res. 2499 of 15 November 2019, UN Doc. S/RES/2499(2019).
[287] SC Res. 2502 of 19 December 2019, UN Doc. S/RES/2502(2019).

Some African states have also taken the initiative both individually and as African members of the Security Council to advocate for the climate crisis as an issue of importance to not only their own national security but also that of all other countries. Thus, in April 2020, two recently elected African members of the Security Council, Niger and Tunisia, participated in a Security Council Arria formula meeting that they co-hosted with other Council members on climate security risks.[288] Building on the fact that the Security Council's Resolution 2349 on the Lake Chad Basin Region had already, in 2017, acknowledged the link between the climate crisis and violence,[289] the representative of Niger underlined the need to consider the climate crisis as a threat to peace and security, pointing towards the situation of 'climate driven conflicts' in the Sahel region.[290] Although Tunisia did not mention the climate crisis as one of its priority issues at its election as a member of the Security Council, focusing instead on conflict prevention and settlement, and terrorism, it advocated during the meeting for the inclusion of the topic within the Security Council's remit. It also acknowledged that the impacts of the climate crisis can 'exacerbate existing conflicts' and supported the appointment of a special envoy for climate security to improve coordination with the UN system,[291] separate from the current UN envoy on climate action and finance.[292]

South Africa rejoined the Security Council for its third term in 2019–20, during which it set out to position Africa as a strong, resilient, and influential global player by bolstering the African Union's relationship with the United

---

[288] On 22 April 2020, Belgium, the Dominican Republic, Estonia, France, Germany, Niger, Saint Vincent and the Grenadines, Tunisia, the United Kingdom, and Viet Nam hosted a virtual meeting of the Security Council in Arria formula to assess climate-related security risks and to exchange ideas on what the United Nations can do to prevent climate-related conflicts: see Permanent Mission of France to the United Nations in New York, 'Event on Climate and Security Risks', 29 December 2020, available at www.onu.delegfrance.org/Eve nt-on-Climate-and-Security-risks. Because of their informal character, no record and no outcomes are usually made available for Arria formula meetings. The key points made in statements by participants at the meeting of 22 April 2020 are summarised in Judith Nora Hardt and Alina Viehoff, *A Climate for Change in the Security Council: Member States' Approaches to the Climate–Security Nexus*, Research Report No. 5, Institute for Peace Research and Security Policy, University of Hamburg, July 2020.

[289] SC Res. 2349 of 31 March 2017, UN Doc. S/RES/2349(2017), para. 26.

[290] Statement by Abdou Abarry, representative of Niger, during the Security Council virtual meeting on climate and security risks, 22 April 2020: see Hardt and Viehoff, *A Climate for Change* (n. 288), 61.

[291] Statement by Tarek Laded, representative of Tunisia, during the Security Council virtual meeting on climate and security risks, 22 April 2020: see Hardt and Viehoff, *A Climate for Change* (n. 288), 83.

[292] The Secretary-General appointed Mark Joseph Carney of Canada to serve in this capacity on 1 December 2019.

Nations.[293] During its previous tenures in the Security Council in 2007 and 2011, South Africa had questioned whether it was appropriate that the Council should deal with the climate crisis, arguing that such an issue went beyond its mandate and that other UN forums were better placed to address it. South Africa repeated these concerns in 2019, but it shifted its position in the April 2020 Arria formula meeting. The South African representative stated there that, 'while it is still important to question the exact role of the Security Council, it has become clear that climate change is a matter of security that acts as a "conflict multiplier" and is contributing to conflicts, for example in the Sahel, Lake Chad, and the Horn of Africa'.[294]

The African Union has declared its determination to factor this threat into its conflict prevention and management, and post-conflict peacebuilding strategies. The PSC has made clear recommendations on how to mainstream the climate crisis and address these impacts. Alongside its request for the appointment of an AU special envoy for climate and security, the PSC requested – in the context of the implementation of the APSA Roadmap – the AU Commission to undertake a study on the nexus between the climate crisis and peace and security in the continent.[295] Yet, to date, these recommendations have not been translated into actionable commitments. On its face, one could attribute this to lack of political commitment on the part of the political leaders at the levels of both the institution and member states. Another obstacle is the lack of dedicated funding within the AU Peace Fund, established under Article 22 Peace and Security Protocol, for climate-related security issues.[296] In addition, I would also argue that the delay in implementing the recommendations is partly because of the limited understanding of the full nature of climate-related risks and how they impact policy processes. Lack of funding and limited institutional capacity clearly impact the ability of the African Union and other regional organisations in the Global

[293] Acceptance Statement by President Cyril Ramaphosa on assuming the Chair of the African Union for 2020, 9 February 2020, available at www.thepresidency.gov.za/speeches/accept ance-statement-president-cyril-ramaphosa-assuming-chair-african-union-2020.

[294] Statement by Kgaugelo Mogashoa, representative of South Africa, during the Security Council virtual meeting on climate and security risks, 22 April 2020; see Hardt and Viehoff, *A Climate for Change* (n. 288), 78.

[295] See above, n. 277.

[296] The AU Peace Fund has struggled to secure the required contributions and, at its 33rd Ordinary Session on 9–10 February 2020, the AU Assembly decided to postpone its launch to 2023 to make up for the shortfall in funding: AU Doc. Assembly/AU/Dec.752 (XXXIII), para. 6. As of 28 February 2021, the AU Peace Fund had mobilised only US$208 million, which is just over 50 per cent of the target set by the organisation: Personal interview between the author and a senior official of AU Department of Political Affairs, Peace and Security, 28 February 2021.

South to operate effectively, especially with regards to managing threats to regional peace and security. Cai is right to note that I do not discuss whether and how the African Union might strengthen its institutional capability. I allude to it, but I believe a discussion of this question falls outside the scope of this chapter.[297]

In my view, the African Union's delay in implementing its own recommendations is an opportunity for it to engage more effectively with the Security Council to find common cause on an issue that both bodies have embraced more clearly in recent years than they did barely a decade ago. I echo Van den Herik's observation, made in connection with the Security Council's resolution on the Lake Chad Basin Region – namely, that the Security Council has shown that 'there is a willingness to consider the security implications of the climate crisis in concrete situations'.[298] This willingness should provide a basis for the African Union and the United Nations to address climate security issues concretely in peace operations in Africa in situations in which the impacts of the climate crisis are a factor. This would be another aspect of the realisation of the partnership between the centre and the periphery for the maintenance of international peace and security.

V. CONCLUSION

The cooperation between the United Nations and the African Union in various peacekeeping missions in Africa is predicated on the reconfiguration of regionalism and reaffirmation of the primacy of the Security Council. This reconfiguration allows space for the regional organisation that is better placed to understand the root causes of the conflicts that create the need for the peacekeeping operations to play a part in the management of those conflicts and peacebuilding processes. The relationship between the United Nations and the African Union in these partnership operations also focuses attention on the role of the A3 members of the Security Council, which alone has the power to authorise them. The question that arises, and which underlies the foregoing discussion, is: to what extent, if at all, do they bring the voices from the periphery to the centre of global decision-making that is the Security Council? A related question, addressed to some degree or another in all of the chapters in this volume, is whether, in the post-Cold-War era, the Security

---

[297] Cai, 'Maintaining Peace during a Global Power Shift', Chapter 1 in this volume, section VI.B (p. 105). But see *ibid.*
[298] Van den Herik, 'A Reflection on Institutional Strength', Chapter 2 in this volume, section VII (p. 178).

Council remains the unrivalled centre of global decision-making. As Cai and Van den Herik also ask, have the new landscape of power politics, changing dynamics among the members, and its failure to stop the war in Ukraine significantly reduced the Security Council's relevance – perhaps even exposed its obsolescence?

The changes that led to the collapse of the ideological divisions symbolised by the Cold War and the Berlin Wall affected the global power structure and the political dynamics in the Security Council in various ways. The end of the Cold War and the fall of the Wall signalled in changes in the strategic interests of the United States and the Soviet Union that had a significant impact on international relations. One of the outcomes of these changes was the growing pressure on the United Nations to engage in relatively new situations of conflict prevention, management, and resolution, and in post-conflict peace-building. The United Nations was expected to fill the void resulting from the withdrawal of military or humanitarian assistance by the two superpowers in their spheres of influence, and to deal with the fissures and conflicts that began to emerge in these spaces, driven by new forms of ethno-political nationalism, from the Balkans to the Horn of Africa and elsewhere.

These post-Cold-War challenges for the United Nations motivated UN Secretary-General Boutros-Ghali's *Agenda for Peace*, one of the key aspects of which was the invitation to UN member states to rethink the traditional approach to peacekeeping and the relationship between the global body and regional organisations in the maintenance of international peace and security. In a sense, this was an invitation to the UN members to reaffirm the primacy of the Security Council, which still symbolised the centre of power politics in the post-Cold-War order, while reimagining the role of the periphery, represented by the regional organisations, in this new order.

In this chapter, I selected the African Union as an illustrative case study to test the consequences of the changes in the international political landscape over the past two decades for Security Council decision-making and their impact on its relationships with regional organisations. Regional organisations differ from each other in many ways and there is no suggestion that conclusions drawn from an analysis of the AU–UN partnership hold true for other regional bodies. The European Union, for example, is completely different from the African Union and its relationship with the United Nations has operated differently, even in the limited cases of collaborative peace missions. But in the realm of the mainten-ance of international peace and security, no regional organisation other than the African Union has collaborated more with the United Nations. The regional perspective that the African Union brings to the United Nations – through the participation of African non-permanent members of the Security Council and the engagement by AU member states with the broader UN membership – is as critical to understanding the dynamics of the post-Cold-War political universe as are the perspectives of other rising powers and influential states that periodically get elected to sit on the Security Council. These rising powers include states that have also enhanced their engagements and cooperation with the African Union and African states individually within the Security Council, in the United Nations broadly, and in other global forums. Pre-eminent among these is China, which is itself widely acknowledged as a 'resurgent' global power whose behaviour is changing the inter-relationships and power dynamics within the Security Council. The discussion of China's relationship and interactions with the African Union, especially in the context of peacekeeping, was aimed at illustrating this.

The African Union's peacekeeping partnerships with the United Nations are only one aspect of the interactions between the global body and the regional body. Other issues that are intimately connected to the Security Council's primary role as custodian of the system of collective security include current threats to security, such as the fight against terrorism, and future threats, such as the climate crisis. The African Union is as deeply invested in confronting these challenges as is the rest of the UN membership. The Security Council's stewardship on these issues is critical to future institutional and normative developments in the United Nations, and to how its decisions and actions may contribute to the development of international law as it relates to collective security.

The Security Council is not a legislative organ and does not create general international law. Yet when members of the Security Council deliberate on issues and adopt decisions, they often claim to base their positions on the provisions of the UN Charter and principles of international law, thereby invoking international legal norms to justify their political choices. In their turn, the decisions and actions of the Security Council can shape normative developments in various ways. As a site for political discourse, the Security Council can also be the crucible for legal diplomacy and a vehicle for shaping future trajectories in the law of peace and war. Aside from the issue of peace operations, the African Union's engagement with the United Nations also plays out in the larger context of the Security Council's contribution to other developments. Some of the issues addressed in this chapter relate to normative questions, such as the R2P principle (in the context of the much-contested intervention in Libya by UN-authorised NATO forces), international terrorism (in relation to the peacekeeping missions in Mali and Somalia), and the climate crisis as an unconventional threat to security. Other questions relate to

Security Council reform, such as contestation over permanent seats, and the problem of Security Council inaction and failure to decide.

By participating in the decision-making processes of the Security Council through its A3 representatives and in other formal and informal debates, African states bring to bear their multilateralist perspectives on the international rule of law – sometimes forged as a common AU regional perspective – on a whole range of issues. But, in the final analysis, as I have argued, the relationship between the African Union and the United Nations, and the assertion by the African Union of its regional perspectives, do not challenge but rather complement and reaffirm the primacy of the Security Council in the maintenance of peace and security. The Security Council remains relevant and continues to hold the centre of the widening gyre of the somewhat decentralised collective security system in the post-Cold-War era – or, as some have suggested, the 'new Cold War' period that the world is already entering.

Conclusion

Power, Procedures, and Periphery: The UN Security Council in the Ukraine War

Anne Peters

I. INTRODUCTION

The war launched in February 2022 by Russia against Ukraine has become a stress test for the role of the UN Security Council: 'new geopolitical challenges have led to unprecedented levels of fragmentation within the Council', as the most recent concept note by Albania on Security Council working methods put it.[1] The ongoing war confirms some of the findings of the three authors gathered in this Trialogue.

Congyan Cai, Larissa van den Herik, and Tiyanjana Maluwa have examined the manifestations of law and power in the Council, substance and procedure in its workings, and the relationship between the Council at the centre and its periphery in the form of regional organisations. This concluding chapter revisits these three dichotomies in the light of the Russian invasion, asking: has power eclipsed law (section II)? Are empty ritualistic procedures unable to deliver substantive outcomes (section III)? And has the centre been disabled so that peripheral actors dominate the scene (section IV)?

The chapter concludes (section V) that the Security Council remains important not only as a centre of power but also as a creature of law and as a law-producer – challenging Congyan Cai. The Council's action and inaction is highly dependent on legal procedures (as opposed to mere 'politics'), as Larissa van den Herik has shown. Moreover, the Council – in its response to the Ukrainian war – is firmly embedded in a network of other international bodies and actors, following Tiyanjana Maluwa.

---

[1] Concept Note for the Security Council open debate on the theme 'Security Council Working Methods', 28 June 2022, annexed to Letter dated 21 June 2022 from the Permanent Representative of Albania to the United Nations addressed to the Secretary-General, UN Doc. S/2022/499, 2.

II. LAW AND POWER

Congyan Cai writes that 'the Security Council was, and continues to be, deeply embedded in power politics' and that its functioning 'largely depends on the relations between the great powers'.[2] Others, especially Ian Hurd, have observed, more specifically, that the Security Council's working seems completely 'dependen[t] on great power unanimity'.[3] If indeed 'great power unanimity' is the key to the body's working, it does not seem true that the Council is 'dominated by Western hegemony', as Cai writes.[4] Rather, the Security Council is entirely reliant on the consent of the non-Western permanent members, too. It can become active only when all five permanent members (the P5) agree, and it lies 'dormant', as Hurd writes, when this is not the case.[5]

That logic has again manifested in the Ukrainian crisis. Obviously, the Security Council could not condemn the Russian aggression in Ukraine, because Russia exercised its veto.[6] As Tiyanjana Maluwa points out, the Council's partial paralysis is by legal design: it is 'unable to deal with threats to international peace and security in which the principal or sole offender is a permanent member of the Council'.[7] Given that Russia is the offender in the Ukraine war, it seems that the member states gave up trying to involve the Council, as Congyan Cai found.[8] Indeed, fewer attempts have been made to reach a Security Council resolution in this case than in that of the Syrian war, which has been waging since 2012.

The Council has been far from inactive, however, as the next sections will show. The example of the Russian aggression in Ukraine illustrates that the

---

[2] Congyan Cai, 'The UN Security Council: Maintaining Peace during a Global Power Shift', Chapter 1 in this volume, section VII (p. 107).

[3] Ian Hurd, 'The UN Security Council', in Alexandra Gheciu and William Wohlforth (eds), *The Oxford Handbook of International Security* (Oxford: Oxford University Press, 2018), 668–82 (673–4). See also Niels Blokker, *Saving Succeeding Generations from the Scourge of War: The United Nations Security Council at 75* (Leiden: Brill, 2021), 72, who suggests that any reform should strengthen unity among the P5, not make it weaker.

[4] Cai, 'Maintaining Peace during a Global Power Shift', Chapter 1 in this volume, section V.B (p. 81).

[5] Hurd, 'UN Security Council' (n. 3), 668, 673.

[6] In 2014: SC Draft Res. 189 of 15 March 2014 – vetoed by Russia (meeting of 15 March 2014, UN Doc. S/PV.7138, 3). In 2022: SC Draft Res. 155 of 25 February 2022 – vetoed by Russia (meeting of 25 February 2022, UN Doc. S/PV.8979, 6); SC Draft Res. 720 of 30 September 2022 – vetoed by Russia (meeting of 30 September 2022, UN Doc. S/PV.9143, 4).

[7] Tiyanjana Maluwa, 'The UN Security Council: Between Centralism and Regionalism', Chapter 3 in this volume, section IV.B (p. 263).

[8] Cai, 'Maintaining Peace during a Global Power Shift', Chapter 1 in this volume, section III.C.

'dysfunction' of the Council is perhaps not as 'inevitable' as Maluwa has suggested.[9]

This is not to deny that, in the workings of the Security Council, the co-constitutiveness and the mutual interdependence of (political) power on law and of law on (political) power is more apparent than in other institutions. In all settings, the law's content reflects the power constellation in the arena within which this law is made or emerges. However, this content is also shaped by the procedural rules that govern the law's creation, such as by majority voting in a parliament, by the principle of consent and unanimity for the adoption of an international treaty, or by the voting rules in the Security Council. Moreover, the law needs the backing of political or economic power to inspire compliance. Compliance with the law (and thus the law's power to shape reality and influence human behaviour) does not flow mainly from the threat of sanctions; it depends on many factors, one being social acceptance of the prescriptions' substance and of the procedures in which they have been made. Applied to the Security Council, the problem is less about compliance with its decisions but rather about its selective action, resulting from what Larissa van den Herik would perceive as flawed decision-making procedures and what Tiyanjana Maluwa sees as inevitably national (self-)interests.[10]

Our Trialogue authors, like other observers before them, have foregrounded in their studies one or the other dimension of law (law as rules or law as an outgrowth of power politics), in line with their own intellectual predispositions and worldviews. Congyan Cai's chapter tends to align with the work of Ian Hurd, who has insisted that the Security Council framework serves not to displace power politics but to institutionalise it.[11] This is, according to Hurd, an 'imperial model' or a 'legalized hegemony'.[12]

In contrast, Larissa van den Herik foregrounds the legal dimension that is able – within limits – to structure and contain 'raw power'. The Council – from this perspective – appears to be (also) a creature of the law: a legal institution. Van den Herik's paradigm matches the recent argument by Devika Hovell – namely, that the Security Council is the fiduciary of the international community and therefore bound by

---

[9]   Maluwa, 'Between Centralism and Regionalism', Chapter 3 in this volume, section IV.C (p. 268).

[10] *Ibid.*, section IV.B.1 (pp. 204–5).

[11] Ian Hurd, *After Anarchy: Legitimacy and Power in the UN Security Council* (New Jersey: Princeton University Press, 2007), 133.

[12] Hurd, 'UN Security Council' (n. 3), 669, 671.

fiduciary duties such as the duties to inform, to consult, to give reasons, and to account. This reconceptualisation of the legal status of the Council posits that a permanent member violates its fiduciary duties – notably, the 'duty of non-exploitation' – when it exercises the veto out of self-interest and not for the purpose of maintaining peace.[13] But this reconstruction of the UN Charter, persuasive and convincing as it is, confronts the chaotic and inconsistent practice of the Council and its members. Self-interested vetoes have been a constant feature of voting in the Security Council. Against the idea of public trust and concomitant duties, the more conservative reading of the Charter is that it allows the P5 (as it does any other member) to pursue their own interests by all legal means at their disposal. This is perfectly fine: 'It is impossible and not necessarily always desirable to eliminate the politicking that goes on at the Council, nor to eliminate the use of the Council as a foreign policy tool in pursuit of national interests.'[14]

Taking a closer look at power and law in the Security Council, we see that the root cause of problems of effectiveness and legitimacy is not the dependency of the working of the Council on a given power constellation but the fact that the composition of the Council *freezes a historic moment*. This anachronism privileges those states that were powerful in 1945 but which are no longer equally important on the global stage – especially in comparison to the non-European states that are now economic and political giants, such as Brazil or India. In 1945, the voting scheme for the projected Security Council (including the requirement of a 'concurring vote' among the permanent members) was conceived at a conference of the four victorious powers in Yalta in 1945, without participation of the rest. The 'Yalta formula' foreshadowed the text of Article 27 UN Charter.[15] The four sponsoring states made clear that there would be no world organisation without such a prerogative: the voting

---

[13] Devika Hovell, 'On Trust: The UN Security Council as Fiduciary', *William and Mary Law Review* 62 (2021), 1229–95 (esp. 1290). See also, for the fiduciary relationship, Andreas S. Kolb, *The UN Security Council Members' Responsibility to Protect* (Berlin, Heidelberg: Springer, 2018), 176–8.

[14] Jane Boulden, 'Past Futures for the UN Security Council', *Georgetown Journal of International Affairs* 21 (2020), 80–5 (84).

[15] Protocol of Proceedings at the Yalta Conference, Yalta (Crimea), 11 February 1945, C. ('Voting'): '3. Decisions of the Security Council on all other matters should be made by an affirmative vote of seven members including the *concurring votes of the permanent members*; provided that, in decisions under Chapter VIII, Section A and under the second sentence of paragraph 1 of Chapter VIII. Section C, *a party to a dispute should abstain from voting*' (emphasis added).

scheme was 'essential' to the new organisation.[16] The veto was 'a price to be paid for the creation of the UN'.[17]

At the same time, certain procedures were at work in 1945 – an observation that underscores the message of Van den Herik's chapter. The draft Charter text was not, in formal terms, an *octroi* of the victors; rather, a negotiation process took place in which the rules of diplomatic conferences were applied and formal voting was organised. Thus '[t]he Yalta formula was approved by a vote of 30 to 2, with fifteen delegations abstaining'.[18] A cynical view on procedural rules is that these only embellished the fact that the other states had to swallow the privileges of the great powers if they wanted to get what all sides wanted: a new world organisation through which peace and security could be maintained. However, the veto was accepted not only because of the over-whelming military, political, and even economic power of (some of) the P5 but also because the other states had the normative expectation that this would be a guarantee of peace and security. The four sponsoring powers of the Yalta formula (later joined by France) pledged, at least implicitly, to continue to safeguard world peace, as they had just proven capable of doing in World War II. They proclaimed: 'It is not to be assumed, however, that the perman-ent members, any more than the non-permanent members, would use their "veto" power wilfully to obstruct the operation of the Council.'[19]

That historic promise has been broken several times in the history of the United Nations – most recently by Russia, in the context of Ukraine.[20] This fact seems to confirm Cai's statement that 'political considerations regularly prevail over law in the workings of the Security Council'.[21] One of the

---

[16] Statement at San Francisco by the delegations of the four Sponsoring Governments (China, the UK, the USA, and the USSR) on 'The Yalta Formula' on Voting in the Security Council, 8 June 1945, INCIO, XI (1945), 710–14, sec. I.9: '9. In view of the primary responsibilities of the permanent members, they could not be expected, in the present condition of the world, to assume the obligation to act in so serious a matter as the maintenance of international peace and security in consequence of a decision in which they had not concurred.' *Ibid.*, sec. I.10: 'For all these reasons, the four sponsoring Governments agreed on the Yalta formula and have presented it to this Conference *as essential* if an international organization is to be created through which all peace-loving nations can effectively discharge their common responsibil-ities for the maintenance of international peace and security' (emphasis added).

[17] Blokker, *Saving Succeeding Generations* (n. 3), 73.

[18] Francis Orlando Wilcox, 'The Yalta Voting Formula', *The American Political Science Review* 39 (1945), 943–56, at 950; also quoted in Andreas Zimmermann, 'Article 27', in Bruno Simma, Daniel-Erasmus Khan, Georg Nolte, and Andreas Paulus (eds), *The Charter of the United Nations: A Commentary* (Oxford: Oxford University Press, 4th edn, 2024 forthcoming), MN 20, fn. 21.

[19] Statement on Yalta (n. 16), sec. I.8.

[20] See n. 6.

[21] Cai, 'Maintaining Peace during a Global Power Shift', Chapter 1 in this volume, section II.D (p. 33).

cynicisms of the Russian aggression was that the state's Article 51 letter to the Council paid respect to its formal authority. In this way, Russia attempted to furnish its attack on Ukraine with a veneer of legitimacy by abusing the legal formalities of notifying self-defence (which is obviously absent).[22] Moreover, the Russian letter refers to prior cases before the Security Council. It denounces 'the distortion of all United Nations Security Council decisions on the Libyan question' (of 2011).[23] It also deplores that 'combat operations conducted by the Western coalition' on the territory of Syria (since 2012) 'without ... authorization from the United Nations Security Council are nothing more than aggression and intervention'.[24] Such respect to the Security Council is unsurprising because, as a veto-holding permanent member, Russia basically benefits from the Security Council. The Security Council is a body that, by legal design, amplifies the power of the P5 and is never able to take measures running against their interests[25] – which brings us back to the power constellation of 1945.

What to make, then, of Russia's Article 51 letter? It has been – rightly – pointed out that states which try to justify particular military operations in the Security Council 'at least reinforce the sense that use of force decisions are matters of collective concern and for the Council's deliberation, not within the exclusive purview of individual states'.[26] Such explanations in the language of the law – especially those that rely on self-defence and include an Article 51 letter to the Security Council – have been famously treated as a confirmation of the rule on the prohibition of the use of force established by the International Court of Justice (ICJ) in its *Nicaragua* judgment:

> If a State acts in a way prima facie incompatible with a recognized rule, but defends its conduct by appealing to exceptions or justifications contained within the rule itself, then whether or not the State's conduct is in fact justifiable on that basis, the significance of that attitude is to confirm rather than to weaken the rule.[27]

---

[22]   Letter dated 24 February 2022 from the Permanent Representative of the Russian Federation to the United Nations addressed to the Secretary-General, UN Doc. S/2022/154, annexing the text of the address of Russian President Vladimir Putin to the citizens of Russia, informing them of the measures taken in accordance with Art. 51 of the Charter of the United Nations in exercise of the right of self-defence.

[23]   *Ibid.*, 3.

[24]   *Ibid.*

[25]   Hurd, 'UN Security Council' (n. 3), abstract.

[26]   Monika Hakimi, 'The Jus ad Bellum's Regulatory Form', *American Journal of International Law* 112 (2018), 151–90 (185).

[27]   ICJ, *Military and Paramilitary Activities in and against Nicaragua* (Nicaragua v. United States), merits, judgment of 27 June 1986, ICJ Reports 1986, 14, para. 186.

However, not all legal cheap talk really manifests a commitment to the law that strengthens the law's normative force. There is a boundary beyond which the language of the law is simply being abused and the 'justification' is a sham. I submit that this line has been crossed with the Russian Article 51 letter to the Security Council. The reason is that no armed attack (ongoing or imminent), neither by Ukraine nor by the North Atlantic Treaty Organization (NATO) nor by any other actor – the minimum requirement for the lawful exercise of self-defence, as all participants in the legal discourse agree – could be shown. While, according to Congyan Cai, 'China considers the Ukrainian crisis, including the SMO [special military operation], largely attributable to NATO's expansion',[28] this is no legal assessment of the situation, because China too does not consider 'expansion' to amount to an armed attack.

With regard to the relationship between law and power, Cai sees a 'fundamental distinction between international and domestic society'.[29] Larissa van den Herik and Tiyanjana Maluwa do not dwell explicitly on this point. From their perspectives, those two different levels of law and governance (domestic and international) rather seem to resemble each other in structural terms. Procedures matter everywhere, and the division of competences and labour between centre and periphery is a standard problem for all polities. The Ukraine war has actually brought to the fore that the specific feature of international society – namely, the absence of a central law-maker and centralised enforcement mechanisms – does not inevitably make a crucial difference to the domestic scenario. In this war – in the face of brute violence – even well-functioning legislation and implementation would have no chance of resolving the problem. No legal or institutional barriers prevent law enforcement against the Russian aggression in form of collective self-defence; rather, it is geostrategic considerations, domestic politics, and the fear of nuclear escalation that prevent Western states from entering the war against Russia. Compare this situation to a police officer facing someone fully armed and holding hostages. The police officer could lawfully try to overpower them but will refrain from doing so for fear that the action might result in casualties. The difference between the domestic and the international level of law and politics here seems thus to be a matter of degree not of kind.

[28] Cai, 'Maintaining Peace during a Global Power Shift', Chapter 1 in this volume, section III (p. 58).B, citing Ministry of Foreign Affairs of the People's Republic of China, 'Wang Yi Expounds China's Five-Point Position on the Current Ukraine Issue', 26 February 2022, available at www.fmprc.gov.cn/eng/zxxx_662805/202202/t20220226_10645855.html.
[29] Cai, 'Maintaining Peace during a Global Power Shift', Chapter 1 in this volume, section II.A (p. 27).

To conclude, while Congyan Cai's main message is that political power often stymies the functioning of the law in the working of the Security Council, Larissa van den Herik offers examples of where and how legal procedures in fact *do* check 'P5 raw power'.[30] Tiyanjana Maluwa's chapter confirms, rather than negates, the shaping power of law by means of an analysis of quite impressive legal developments in the relationship between the UN Security Council and African actors – Article 4(h) being a particularly 'substantial legal innovation'.[31] The Ukraine war, however, ultimately confirms Cai's overall stance – namely, that the Security Council is 'fundamentally disabled' by struggles among the great powers.[32]

<h3 style="text-align:center">III. PROCEDURE AND SUBSTANCE</h3>

A. *The Power and Powerlessness of Procedures*

Process also matters in the Security Council. All of the authors in this Trialogue have examined procedures – particularly Larissa van den Herik. Her findings are in line with those of a recent empirical investigation, comprising both a large-N data analysis and case studies, aiming to trace the decision-making processes in the Security Council: 'The powerful hold the veto, but they do not hold sway over the entire process. ... The rules of the institution have an impact.'[33] The Security Council is not a simple 'pass-through for powerful states'.[34]

Why and how do institutional rules matter? Generally speaking, legal procedures for decision-making convey a modicum of legitimacy to the resulting decision. When it is created by means of the proper procedures, an outcome will be acceptable to all affected, independently of its actual substance and content. This 'legitimation through procedures' is highly relevant for the Security Council. The Council's procedures are notoriously under-regulated, as illustrated by the fact that the Council still works under only 'provisional' Rules of Procedure that have not been updated since 1982.[35] In

---

[30] Larissa van den Herik, 'The UN Security Council: A Reflection on Institutional Strength', Chapter 2 in this volume, section I (p. 112).

[31] Maluwa, 'Between Centralism and Regionalism', Chapter 3 in this volume, section III.A (p. 198).

[32] Cai, 'Maintaining Peace during a Global Power Shift', Chapter 1 in this volume, section III.A (p. 44).

[33] Susan Allen and Amy Yuen, *Bargaining in the Security Council: Setting the Global Agenda* (Oxford: Oxford University Press, 2022), 165.

[34] *Ibid.*, 169.

[35] Security Council, Provisional Rules of Procedure, UN Doc. S/96/Rev.7, 21 December 1982.

the face of persistent criticism of the Security Council's secrecy and exclusion, and the resulting lack of accountability, the procedures and working methods have very slowly evolved.[36]

Larissa van den Herik suggests applying several procedural principles, distilled from the practice of various international organisations, more stringently to the working of the Security Council. She asks for more transparency,[37] inclusion,[38] and deliberation.[39] A related procedural mechanism are hearings, accompanied by the decision-maker's obligation to take into account the statements of participants in such hearings.[40] The 'veto initiative procedure', as established by the General Assembly, can be considered an ex post hearing. It assigns the duty of explanation not to the Security Council as a whole but to the permanent member(s) who used the veto to block the Council: that permanent member is now asked to respond to the General Assembly.[41]

Legal limits imposed on power are 'stronger' when the law is more precise. For example, an authorisation by the Security Council to use 'all necessary means' to respond to a threat of the peace leaves such ample leeway to the implementing actors that it can be difficult to draw a line between activities that are faithful to such a mandate and those that overstep it. The controversial intervention in Libya in 2011 brought this problem to the fore. Van den Herik therefore asks for more precision: 'The lesson to be learnt from Libya [is] ... that the limits to an authorised use of force need to be spelled out in much more detail in the authorising resolution.'[42]

---

[36] See, e.g., Note by the President of the Security Council on working methods, UN Doc. S/2017/507, 30 August 2017; Security Council, *Working Methods Handbook*, January 2021, available at www.un.org/securitycouncil/content/working-methods-handbook. In scholarship, see Joanna Harrington, 'The Working Methods of the United Nations Security Council', *International & Comparative Law Quarterly* 66 (2017), 39–77.

[37] Van den Herik, 'A Reflection on Institutional Strength', Chapter 2 in this volume, section IV.B.2 (p. 134).

[38] *Ibid.* See, along these lines, Note by the President of the Security Council, UN Doc. S/2017/507, 30 August 2017, para. 38: 'It is the understanding of the members of the Security Council that open debates can benefit from the contributions of both Council members and the wider membership.'

[39] Van den Herik, 'A Reflection on Institutional Strength', Chapter 2 in this volume, section VIII (p. 184).

[40] *Ibid.*

[41] GA Res. 76/262 of 26 April 2022 on a standing mandate for a General Assembly debate when a veto is cast in the Security Council, UN Doc. A/RES/76/262.

[42] Van den Herik, 'A Reflection on Institutional Strength', Chapter 2 in this volume, section IV.A (p. 128).

B. *Checks and Balances, and Accountability*

Larissa van den Herik has called also for checks and balances.[43] Importantly, in the multilevel legal system constituted by international and domestic law, such checks can arise at the national level. National commissions of inquiry into the resort to war powers by a government represented in the Council indirectly check the powers exercised by the Council too.[44] Van den Herik cites as an example the British select committee inquiry into the military intervention in Libya that many observers argued had overstretched the Security Council mandate.[45]

Michael Wood and Eran Sthoeger have pointed out that '*the* principal check' on the Security Council's powers are its decision-making procedures – namely, the majority requirement for procedural decisions and the possibility that the elected members can block even the united P5.[46] Congyan Cai finds that this majority rule would be problematic without the counterweight of the veto; he opines that restraining the veto power might give rise to a 'tyranny of the majority' in the Council.[47] My view is that an antidote to such a phenomenon would be the acceptance of constitutional rules that even the majority – or, at least, an unqualified simple majority – cannot overturn. The UN Charter can plausibly be conceptualised as a constitutional document for the world community that embodies global values and which enjoys a higher normative status than 'ordinary' international rules (as expressed in its Art. 103).[48] Such constitutional rules – which are to be respected by the Council itself and by all of its members – are the purposes and principles of Article 1, by which the Council must abide when fulfilling its primary responsibility for maintaining peace and security.[49] After the Cold War ended in 1990, intergovernmental actors and experts sketched out in more detail the parameters that the Security Council should respect. One of the most influential documents is the 2001 report of the International Commission on State Sovereignty and Intervention (ICISS). A major objective of the ICISS was to

[43] *Ibid.*
[44] *Ibid.*
[45] House of Commons Foreign Affairs Committee, *Libya: Examination of Intervention and Collapse and the UK's Future Policy Options*, Third Report of Session 2016–17, September 2016, HC 119.
[46] Michael Wood and Eran Sthoeger, *The UN Security Council and International Law* (Cambridge: Cambridge University Press, 2022), 84–85 (quote at 84), emphasis original.
[47] Cai, 'Maintaining Peace during a Global Power Shift', Chapter 1 in this volume, section VI.A.1 (p. 100).
[48] Bardo Fassbender, *UN Security Council Reform and the Right of Veto: A Constitutional Perspective* (The Hague: Kluwer Law International, 1998), 129–30.
[49] Art. 24(2) UN Charter: 'In discharging these duties the Security Council shall act in accordance with the Purposes and Principles of the United Nations.'

formulate principles for military action to be applied by the Council itself (as the most appropriate body to authorise military measures), such as just cause, precautionary principles, and operational principles.[50] The ICISS also suggested a 'code of conduct' to be agreed upon by the P5 to that end.[51] The UN Secretary-General, too, recommended in 2005 'that the Security Council adopt a resolution setting out these principles and expressing its intention to be guided by them when deciding whether to authorize or mandate the use of force'.[52]

Additionally, Wood and Sthoeger point out that member states may simply disregard the binding obligations, and that this prospect incentivises the Council to exercise self-restraint: 'That is the most effective check on the Council's power.'[53] This 'check' is most often no legal mechanism but simply an expression of the fact that unlawful non-compliance by member states is possible. Only under very narrow conditions can a member's disobedience be framed as an admissible countermeasure against a breach of international law by the Security Council itself. However, the legal limits, including the 'constitutional' constraints of the Security Council, are notoriously controversial. Moreover, the more frequent problem is not too much Security Council action but its inaction. The threat of non-compliance does not help against the Council's undesirable passivity.

With regard to reporting requirements, Congyan Cai rightly points out that there must be a recipient of such reports who is 'immune from the control of the great powers'.[54] I agree that reporting cannot generate any accountability (however mild) if the recipient has no freedom to respond critically. The application of the veto initiative in two instances since its introduction in April 2022 has been rather sobering in this regard. After the Russian veto of the draft Security Council resolution that sought to condemn its annexation of four Ukrainian regions, especially, the mandatory General Assembly debate convened under the new procedure did not generate much criticism of the veto but concentrated instead on the violation of the territorial integrity of Ukraine.[55]

This observation is not an argument against the new procedure as such but a reminder that the political constellation inevitably influences how the procedures are used. Cai has consistently called for a close ex ante assessment of the likely practical implementation and outcomes of any suggested

---

[50]   *The Responsibility to Protect*, Report of the International Commission on State Sovereignty and Intervention (ICISS), December 2001, esp. paras 6.13–6.14 and 6.27.

[51]   *Ibid.*, para. 6.21.

[52]   *In Larger Freedom: Towards Development, Security and Human Rights for All*, Report of the Secretary-General, UN Doc. A/59/2005, 21 March 2005, para. 126.

[53]   Wood and Sthoeger, *UN Security Council* (n. 46), 89.

[54]   Cai, 'Maintaining Peace during a Global Power Shift', Chapter 1 in this volume, section VI.A.2 (p. 102).

[55]   UN Doc. A/ES-11/PV.14, 12 October 2022.

procedural reforms, to gauge whether they are feasible at all – or might even backfire.[56] This strategy of caution and pragmatism needs to be applied to various other procedural proposals at which this concluding chapter looks next.

C. *Procedural Arguments against Manifestly Obstructive Vetoes*

All three authors in this Trialogue have grappled with the (renewed) malfunction of the Security Council in the current era of a 'new Cold War'. Even now, though, the Security Council is adopting more resolutions than ever before, including on difficult topics such as the war in Syria.[57] However, the substance of these resolutions does not strike at the heart of the matter: they do not condemn serious violations of international law if committed by a permanent member or one of its clients nor do they authorise military action against such law-breakers.

This malfunction has materialised acutely in the ongoing Ukrainian crisis. Russia has repeatedly vetoed draft Security Council resolutions that have concerned its activities in the neighbouring state.[58] In this context, the US ambassador to the United Nations has stated that 'any Permanent Member that exercises the veto to defend its own acts of aggression loses moral authority'.[59] Additionally, it is arguable in law that a veto exercised to shield one's own aggression not only lacks moral authority but also is legally problematic, because it risks violating the duty to abstain under Article 27(3) UN Charter (in a plausibly broad reading), constitutes an abuse of rights, infringes the principle of good faith, and deepens the violation of the right to life committed through the aggression.[60]

Two procedural strategies to end abuses of the veto have been espoused, as Larissa van den Herik mentions.[61] First, more than 100 states, including three permanent members of the Security Council, have, in different ways,

---

[56] Cai, 'Maintaining Peace during a Global Power Shift', Chapter 1 in this volume, section VII (p. 107).

[57] See the figures given in Christian Marxsen, 'The Security Council's Four Defining Fields of Tension', Introduction in this volume, section II (p. 6).

[58] See n. 6.

[59] United States Mission to the United Nations, Remarks by Ambassador Linda Thomas-Greenfield on the Future of the United Nations, 8 September 2022, available at https://usun .usmission.gov/remarks-by-ambassador-linda-thomas-greenfield-on-the-future-of-the-united nations/.

[60] Anne Peters, 'The War in Ukraine and the Illegitimacy of the Russian Vetoes', *Journal on the Use of Force and International Law* 10 (2023) 162–72.

[61] Van den Herik, 'A Reflection on Institutional Strength', Chapter 2 in this volume, section III (pp. 118–19). See also Marxsen, 'The Security Council's Four Defining Fields of Tension', Introduction in this volume.

promised not to exercise the veto in certain situations – notably, in the face of mass atrocities – under the Code of Conduct of the Accountability, Coherence and Transparency (ACT) Group,[62] the French–Mexican initiative,[63] and the recent UN–American pledge.[64] The Ukraine war has also led to the 'veto initiative' under General Assembly Resolution 76/262 of 2022. This Resolution introduced a mandatory General Assembly meeting at which any state that casts its veto must explain itself before the entire UN membership.[65] I have analysed these strategies elsewhere.[66]

The new procedures and procedural arguments do not call into question the P5's legal right to use the veto at their discretion to further their own interests, even if doing so is in tension with their responsibility to contribute to the maintenance of world peace. However, they do call into question the legitimacy of a veto shielding the aggression of the state casting it. The new developments also show how procedures matter. The Security Council is not simply a 'purely' political body but is governed by law, albeit imperfectly. Importantly, however, this law has so far contributed only to avoiding war among the P5 themselves; it has not contained wars led by a permanent member against other states. Ultimately, the most unique procedural feature in the working of the Security Council, the veto, precisely facilitates violations of international law by a permanent member. In this Trialogue, both Van den Herik and Maluwa concur that the procedure needs to be modified if it is to uphold and safeguard the substance of the prohibition on the use of force. In contrast, Cai sees no need for a change of working methods, cautioning against 'unexpected risks'.[67]

---

[62] Accountability, Coherence and Transparency (ACT) Group, Submission to the United Nations, 'Code of Conduct regarding Security Council Action against Genocide, Crimes against Humanity or War Crimes', 23 October 2015, annexed to Letter dated 14 December 2015 from the Permanent Representative of Liechtenstein to the United Nations addressed to the Secretary-General, UN Doc. A/70/621–S/2015/978.

[63] Global Centre for the Responsibility to Protect, Political Declaration on Suspension of Veto Powers in Cases of Mass Atrocities, 1 August 2015, available at www.globalr2p.org/resources/political-declaration-on-suspension-of-veto-powers-in-cases-of-mass-atrocities/.

[64] See Remarks by Ambassador Linda Thomas-Greenfield (n. 59).

[65] GA Res. 76/262 of 26 April 2022, on a standing mandate for a General Assembly debate when a veto is cast in the Security Council, UN Doc. A/RES/76/262, adopted by consensus.

[66] See, on both procedures, Anne Peters, 'The War in Ukraine and the Curtailment of the Veto in the Security Council', *Revue Européenne du Droit* 5 (2023) 87–93, available at https://geopolitique.eu/en/articles/the-war-in-ukraine-and-the-curtailment-of-the-veto-in-the-security-council/.

[67] Cai, 'Maintaining Peace during a Global Power Shift', Chapter 1 in this volume, section I (p. 24).

IV. CENTRE AND PERIPHERY

The Ukrainian crisis shows – in line with the findings of Tiyanjana Maluwa – the importance of regional actors and alliances that do not ultimately call into question the primacy of the Security Council.

The regional alliance between China and Russia seems to remain intact. In 2021, Russia and China had expressed 'a need to hold a *summit of the permanent members* of the UN Security Council in order to establish a direct dialogue between them on ways to resolve common problems facing humanity, in the interests of maintaining global stability'.[68] In February 2022, Russia and China issued a 'joint statement on the international relations entering a new era and the global sustainable development'.[69] Less than three weeks before the Russian invasion into Ukraine, Russia and China 'reaffirm[ed] their strong mutual support for the protection of . . . territorial integrity'.[70] In that statement, the two states also promised to 'respect the rights of peoples to independently determine the development paths of their country', and to 'seek genuine multipolarity, with the United Nations and its *Security Council playing a central and coordinating role*'.[71] Besides the cynical lip service one of these two authors paid to territorial integrity and self-determination just three weeks before it broke these principles, a striking feature of these statements is the oscillation between a focus on the P5 as the actual power-holders and upholding the role of the Security Council as a whole. Both of these foci directly serve the interests of these two permanent members.

Other (regional) actors have not – and this is Tiyanjana Maluwa's main finding – challenged the Security Council's primordial role in matters of peace and security.[72] A 2017 note by the Security Council's president commits the members of the Council to 'continu[ing] to expand consultation and cooperation with regional and sub regional organizations, including by inviting relevant organizations to participate in the Council's public and

---

[68] Ministry of Foreign Affairs of the Russian Federation, Joint Statement by the Foreign Ministers of China and Russia on Certain Aspects of Global Governance in Modern Conditions, 23 March 2021, available at www.mid.ru/en/foreign_policy/news/-/asset_publisher/cKNonkJEo2Bw/content/id/4647776.

[69] President of Russia, Joint Statement of the Russian Federation and the People's Republic of China on the International Relations Entering a New Era and the Global Sustainable Development, 4 February 2022, available at www.en.kremlin.ru/supplement/5770.

[70] *Ibid.*

[71] *Ibid.* (emphasis added).

[72] Maluwa, 'Between Centralism and Regionalism', Chapter 3 in this volume, section V (p. 277).

private meetings, when appropriate'.[73] The involvement of such regional actors is 'now a standard element in the Council's response to conflict situations'.[74] These practices preserve the leading role of the Security Council even in relation to the African Union – a regional organisation that is itself equipped with military powers, yet still follows the Council's lead.[75]

The Western response against Russia's attack on Ukraine again underlines the centrality of the Security Council. Ukrainian territorial integrity against the Russian armed attack could be lawfully defended under the heading of collective self-defence, for example by NATO or any other alliance of Western states. There would be no practical military difference between a pushback under that heading and a response under the authority of the Security Council. From a formal juridical perspective, too, both legal grounds are equally good. Still, it seems as if all actors agree that the blessing of the Security Council would furnish a higher degree of legitimacy to the response – likely because the Council represents the entire UN membership and acts as the official universal authority for the upholding of peace and security.

Zooming in on the African Union, Maluwa describes the relationship between the Security Council and regional organisations as a division of labour and a 'partnership between the centre and the periphery for the maintenance of international peace and security'.[76] This 'partnership' worked on the occasion of the Russo-Ukrainian war. A wide range of regional organisations and bodies immediately condemned the Russian invasion in Ukraine as a flagrant violation of international law. Among them are the European Council (of the European Union),[77] the League of Arab States,[78]

---

[73] Note by the President of the Security Council, UN Doc. S/2017/507, 30 August 2017, para. 96.

[74] Boulden, 'Past Futures', (n. 14), 83.

[75] Interestingly, the African Union did not, as Maluwa finds upon closer examination, manifest a common AU position on the Russian invasion in Ukraine: see African Union, Statement from Chair of the African Union, H.E. President Macky Sall, and Chairperson of the AU Commission, H.E. Moussa Faki Mahamat, on the situation in Ukraine, 24 February 2022, available at https://au.int/sites/default/files/pressreleases/41529-pr-english.pdf. See also Maluwa, 'Between Centralism and Regionalism', Chapter 3 in this volume, section IV.B (p. 259).

[76] *Ibid.*, section IV.D (p. 274).

[77] European Council, Joint Statement by the Members of the European Council, 24 February 2022, available at www.consilium.europa.eu/en/press/press-releases/2022/02/24/jo int-statement-by-the-members-of-the-european-council-24-02-2022/.

[78] Communiqué on developments in the crisis in Ukraine issued by the Council of the League of Arab States at the level of permanent representatives at its Extraordinary Session, annexed to Identical letters dated 1 March 2022 from the Permanent Representative of Kuwait to the

the Association of Southeast Asian Nations (ASEAN),[79] NATO,[80] the Organization for Security and Co-operation in Europe (OSCE),[81] and the Organization of American States (OAS).[82] The various organisations adopted measures and undertook activities in their respective spheres of competence. These range from the European Union's economic and financial sanctions,[83] through the OSCE's reports on violations of international humanitarian law,[84] to the reputational sanction of expulsion from the Council of Europe (CoE).[85] In addition, all parliamentary assemblies of the regional organisations in Europe (i.e., that of the European Union,[86] the CoE,[87] and the OSCE[88]), the Parliamentary Assembly of

United Nations addressed to the Secretary-General and the President of the Security Council, UN Doc. A/76/737–S/2022/169, 3 March 2022.

[79] ASEAN, ASEAN Foreign Ministers' Statement on the Situation in Ukraine, 26 February 2022, available at https://asean.org/wp-content/uploads/2022/02/ASEAN-FM-Statement-on-Ukraine-Crisis-26-Feb-Final.pdf.

[80] NATO, Statement by NATO Heads of State and Government on Russia's Attack on Ukraine, 25 February 2022, available at www.nato.int/cps/en/natohq/official_texts_192489.htm?selectedLocale=en.

[81] OSCE, Joint Statement by OSCE Chairman-in-Office Rau and Secretary General Schmid on Russia's Launch of a Military Operation in Ukraine, 24 February 2022, available at www.osce.org/chairmanship/512890.

[82] OAS, Statement from the OAS General Secretariat on the Russian Attack on Ukraine, 24 February 2022, available at www.oas.org/en/media_center/press_release.asp?sCodigo=E-008/22.

[83] See the EU sanctions map, available at www.sanctionsmap.eu.

[84] OSCE, *Report on Violations of International Humanitarian and Human Rights Law, War Crimes and Crimes against Humanity Committed in Ukraine since 24 February 2022*, 13 April 2022, available at www.osce.org/odihr/515868; OSCE, *Report on Violations of International Humanitarian and Human Rights Law, War Crimes and Crimes against Humanity Committed in Ukraine (1 April–25 June 2022)*, 14 July 2022, available at www.osce.org/odihr/522616; OSCE, *Interim Report on Reported Violations of International Humanitarian Law and International Human Rights Law in Ukraine*, 20 July 2022, available at www.osce.org/odihr/523081; OSCE, *Second Interim Report on Reported Violations of International Humanitarian Law and International Human Rights Law in Ukraine*, 14 December 2022, available at www.osce.org/odihr/534933.

[85] CoE Committee of Ministers Res. CM/Res(2022)2 of 16 March 2022 on the cessation of the membership of the Russian Federation to the Council of Europe, adopted at the 1428th meeting of the Ministers' Deputies, available at https://rm.coe.int/0900001680a5da51.

[86] EU European Parliament Res. (2023)0015 of 19 January 2023 on the establishment of a tribunal on the crime of aggression against Ukraine, para. 5, available at www.europarl.europa.eu/doceo/document/TA-9-2023-0015_EN.html.

[87] PA Rec. 2231(2022) of 28 April 2022 on the Russian Federation's aggression against Ukraine: ensuring accountability for serious violations of international humanitarian law and other international crimes, available at https://pace.coe.int/en/files/30024#trace-4.

[88] OSCE PA, Resolution on the Russian Federation's war of aggression against Ukraine and its people and its threat to security across the OSCE region, adopted at the 29th Annual Session,

NATO,[89] and the CoE Committee of Ministers[90] have called for a special tribunal to try President Putin and other officials who might be held accountable for the crime of aggression. In addition, the UN General Assembly is most active under the 'Uniting for Peace' mechanism, under which the Security Council had convened the 11th Emergency Special Session that is ongoing at the time of writing.[91]

The regional and sectorial organisations have mainly adopted statements, and the European Union has also imposed economic sanctions on Russia. Although both NATO and the African Union are well equipped to take military action, and although collective self-defence against the Russian attack is in any case available to all, military support for Ukraine is currently taking the form of weapons supply and training. It does not amount to actual participation in combat. The contribution by all other players outside the United Nations is thus both symbolic and material.

V. CONCLUSIONS: THE EMBEDDED SECURITY COUNCIL

These analyses of the dichotomies of law and power, substance and procedure, centre and periphery, as applied to the war in Ukraine, yield sobering results.

The first dichotomy is law and political power. The dialectics between law and politics in the Security Council was well captured by the dissenters in the ICJ's 1948 Advisory Opinion on the admission to membership of the United Nations.[92] Judges Basdevant, Winiarski, Sir Arnold McNair, and Read conceded that any Security Council decision is 'pre-eminently a political act', but they argued that 'does not mean that no legal restriction is placed upon this liberty. We do not claim that a political organ and those who contribute to the formation of its decisions are emancipated from all duty to respect the law.'[93]

2–6 July 2022, available at www.oscepa.org/en/documents/annual-sessions/2022-birmingham/4409-birmingham-declaration-eng/file, para. 36.

[89] NATO PA, Declaration of 30 May 2022 on standing with Ukraine, available at www.nato-pa.int/document/2022-declaration-standing-ukraine-111-sesp-22, para. 18.

[90] CoE Committee of Ministers, Decision CM/Del/Dec(2022)1442/2.3 of 15 September 2022 on the consequences of the aggression of the Russian Federation against Ukraine: accountability for international crimes.

[91] The 11th Special Emergency Session was convened in response to the Russian invasion by SC Res. 2623(2022) of 27 February 2022 on a decision to call an emergency special session of the General Assembly, UN Doc. S/RES/2623 (2022); GA Res. ES-11/1 of 1 March 2022 on aggression against Ukraine, UN Doc. A/RES/ES-11/1.

[92] ICJ, *Conditions of Admission of a State to Membership in the United Nations (Article 4 of the Charter)*, advisory opinion of 28 May 1948, ICJ Reports 1948, 82–93, dissenting opinion of Judges Basdevant, Winiarski, Sir Arnold McNair, and Read.

[93] *Ibid.*, para. 9.

The legal principles that are normally accepted to guide the political behaviour of the Security Council as a whole and of its members are not being taken seriously in the Ukrainian crisis. The aggressive politics of a permanent member has not been contained by the Security Council. Legal options that would be available, such as tabling a draft Security Council resolution under Chapter VI and insisting on a Russian abstention under Article 27(3) UN Charter, are not espoused by Council members, for reasons of political expediency. Neither have the political actors picked up the legal argument of the abuse of Russia's veto power. Thus the current crisis rather confirms Congyan Cai's overall assessment that the Security Council is 'deeply embedded in power politics, whether we like it or not'.[94]

The second dichotomy, between substance and procedures, is mainly examined in this Trialogue by Larissa van den Herik, who finds that procedures have been strengthened and modified in response to the Ukrainian crisis. The 'Uniting for Peace' procedure has been set in motion by the Security Council[95] and lingering doubts about its lawfulness have been put to rest.[96] This procedure activates the General Assembly and does not involve the Council. But the inability of the Security Council to condemn Russia's aggression and to take robust action against it is not owed to the current power constellation, which forms the focus of Congyan Cai's chapter; rather, it is rooted in the power constellation of 1945, when the P5 secured for themselves, in the written provisions of the Charter itself, a power to block their own suspension, their own expulsion, and all formal Charter amendments that do not meet with their approval.[97]

The third dichotomy, of centre and periphery, has been analysed by all three of the Trialogue authors – but their assessment of the future relevance of the Security Council differs. Congyan Cai sees a clear risk of the Council being marginalised in the maintenance of international peace, comparable to the situation during the Cold War.[98] Larissa van den Herik is more optimistic and perceives 'a certain expectation that the Security Council will remain the

---

94   Cai, 'Maintaining Peace during a Global Power Shift', Chapter 1 in this volume, section VII (p. 107).

95   See n. 91.

96   Nico Schrijver, 'A Uniting for Peace Response to Disuniting for War: The Role of the two Political Organs of the UN', *Leiden Law Blog*, 18 March 2022, available at www.leidenlawblog .nl/articles/an-uniting-for-peace-response-to-disuniting-for-war-the-role-of-the-two-political-or gans-of-the-un.

97   Arts 108–9 UN Charter.

98   Cai, 'Maintaining Peace during a Global Power Shift', Chapter 1 in this volume, section VII (p. 108).

world's primary organ for peace for the near future'. Despite its imperfection, she argues, the Council has not (yet) 'become permanently and fully dysfunctional'.[99] In contrast, Tiyanjana Maluwa devotes much of his chapter to the question of 'whether, in the post-Cold-War era, the Security Council remains the unrivalled centre of global decision-making'.[100] He concludes that 'recent practice has reaffirmed the centrality and primacy of the Security Council'.[101]

The question of relevance leads to the issues of the Security Council's effectiveness and legitimacy. All three authors wish for a legitimate and effective Council, and these two parameters are interlinked.[102] Legitimacy depends, inter alia, on effectiveness ('output legitimacy'), while effectiveness depends, at least in part, on legitimacy, because the more the addressees of Council measures perceive the composition, procedures, and results of Council action to be 'fair', the more readily they will comply with the Council's decision.

The current problems of the effectiveness and legitimacy of the Security Council arise out of a combination of law and power. First are the *legal* rules on Charter revision that prevent the adaptation needed if the Council is to respond to changed circumstances and to changed ideals – ideals about representativeness in a postcolonial world of which Europe is no longer the centre; second is the political power of those who push for reform, which is not (yet) sufficient to overcome the staying power of the P5. Despite these de facto barriers to formal Charter amendment, the Security Council *has* changed its working methods and its overall role repeatedly and in significant ways throughout its decades of existence, 'even during times of animosity among the permanent members'.[103] Here, some promise lies in procedures: new working methods, internal rules, codes of conduct, and the like are – within limits – capable of changing the normative context and of setting new benchmarks for the behaviour of the Security Council as a body and for the conduct of each of its members.

---

[99] Van den Herik, 'A Reflection on Institutional Strength', Chapter 2 in this volume, section VIII (p. 184); cf. Beth van Schaack, *Imagining Justice for Syria* (Oxford: Oxford University Press, 2020), 53–119.

[100] Maluwa, 'Between Centralism and Regionalism', Chapter 3 in this volume, section V (pp. 274–75).

[101] *Ibid.*, section I (p. 189).

[102] As Pascal famously put it, 'La justice sans force est impuissante, et la force sans justice est tyrannique': Blaise Pascal, *Pensées sur la religion et sur quelques autres sujets* [Lafuma fragment 103/ Brunschvicg fragment 298] (posthumous 1669), quoted – with regard to the Security Council – by Blokker, *Saving Succeeding Generations* (n. 3), 72.

[103] Boulden, 'Past Futures' (n. 14), 83–4.

Problems of effectiveness typically arise when situations run counter to the interests of a permanent member: this leads to Security Council inaction. Conversely, when the P5 agree, this risks resulting in Security Council 'hyper-activism', which generates a problem of legitimacy. All three Trialogue authors note that the Security Council is very active in those areas in which the P5 share interests, such as counter-terrorism activities. The intense and far-reaching regulatory activity of the Council in the sphere of anti-terrorism and non-proliferation has generated 'innovative tools'.[104]

Especially in the field of anti-terrorism, the two key trends of recent decades have been individualisation – that is, the Council's assertion of direct or indirect authority over individuals – and domestication – that is, the inter-action (both collaborative and conflictual) between Security Council measures and domestic law.[105] These two trends are likely to continue in the current period of inter-state confrontation and war. Two of the Trialogue authors are of the opinion that constraints are needed on the anti-terror action of the Security Council – an opinion I share. Larissa van den Herik calls the Council's over-activism in this field 'most worrisome'.[106] While Congyan Cai does not criticise the Security Council on this matter, Tiyanjana Maluwa points out that, 'for China, as for Russia, participation in UN-led efforts to fight terrorism in Africa and elsewhere affords a cover of legitimacy for their own campaigns against alleged terrorist groups at home (for China) or in the so-called near-abroad (for Russia)'.[107] Maluwa also deplores the 'lack of transparency and accountability', and rightly identifies 'the failure within the United Nations to find common ground and anchor the Security Council's standard-setting in core principles of law, thereby achieving legal certainty'.[108]

Importantly, the Security Council can – in the present world – no longer act in isolation (if it ever could), but it is '[o]perating in a decentred, polycontextural environment'.[109] It is embedded in a *legal* pluriverse whose rules it must

---

[104] Leonardo Borlini, 'The Security Council and Non-State Domestic Actors: Changes in Non-Forcible Measures between International Lawmaking and Peacebuilding', *Virginia Journal of International Law* 61 (2021), 489–551.

[105] See, for the authority over individuals, Leonardo Borlini, *Il Consiglio di Sicurezza e gli Individui* (Milan: Guiffrè, 2018). See, for the interaction with domestic law, Machiko Kanetake, *The UN Security and Domestic Actors: Distance in International Law* (London: Routledge, 2018).

[106] Van den Herik, 'A Reflection on Institutional Strength', Chapter 2 in this volume, section VIII (p. 184).

[107] Maluwa, 'Between Centralism and Regionalism', Chapter 3 in this volume, section III.C (p. 236).

[108] *Ibid.*, section III.E.2 (pp. 253–54).

[109] Borlini, 'The Security Council and Non-State Domestic Actors' (n. 104), 551 (footnote omitted).

respect.[110] In this pluriverse, there is a need [for finding] 'a new balance, both between the UN Security Council and the UN General Assembly, as well as between the UN Security Council and other international organisations, including those at the regional level'.[111]

To paraphrase the ICISS, the United Nations – including its most powerful organ, the Security Council – 'exists in a world of sovereign states, and its operations must be based in political realism. But the organization is also the repository of international idealism, and that sense is fundamental to its identity.'[112] Thus '[t]he task is not to find alternatives to the Security Council as a source of authority, but to make the Security Council work much better than it has.'[113] The realisation of this task needs both good legal ideas and political will. The Trialogue authors have presented a wide gamut of good legal ideas. It is to be hoped that the political momentum to put them into practice can be built up in the current context of extreme tension, bearing in mind that catastrophes have historically been the sad prompt for evolution in international law.

---

[110] *Cf.* Pia Hesse, 'UN Security Council Resolutions as a Legal Framework for Multinational Military Operations', in Robin Geiß, Heike Krieger, and Henning Lahmann (eds), *The 'Legal Pluriverse' Surrounding Multinational Military Operations* (Oxford: Oxford University Press, 2020), 267–86.

[111] Van den Herik, 'A Reflection on Institutional Strength', Chapter 2 in this volume, section VIII (p. 185).

[112] ICISS, *The Responsibility to Protect* (n. 50), para. 6.25.

[113] *Ibid.*, para. 6.14.

Index

References such as '178–9' indicate (not necessarily continuous) discussion of a topic across a range of pages. Wherever possible, in the case of topics with many references, either these have been divided into subtopics or only the most significant discussions of the topic are listed. Because the entire work is about the UN 'Security Council', the use of this term (and certain others that occur constantly throughout the book) as an entry point has been restricted. Information will be found under the corresponding detailed topics.

BOOKS IN THE SERIES

For EU product safety concerns, contact us at Calle de José Abascal, 56–1°,
28003 Madrid, Spain or eugpsr@cambridge.org.

www.ingramcontent.com/pod-product-compliance
Ingram Content Group UK Ltd.
Pitfield, Milton Keynes, MK11 3LW, UK
UKHW020359140625
459647UK00020B/2550